Jacob P. Dunn

Indiana

A Redemption from Slavery

Jacob P. Dunn

Indiana
A Redemption from Slavery

ISBN/EAN: 9783742833532

Manufactured in Europe, USA, Canada, Australia, Japa

Cover: Foto ©Thomas Meinert / pixelio.de

Manufactured and distributed by brebook publishing software
(www.brebook.com)

Jacob P. Dunn

Indiana

American Commonwealths

INDIANA

A REDEMPTION FROM SLAVERY

BY

J. P. DUNN, Jr.

SECRETARY INDIANA HISTORICAL SOCIETY ; AUTHOR OF " MASSACRES
OF THE MOUNTAINS "

BOSTON AND NEW YORK
HOUGHTON, MIFFLIN AND COMPANY
The Riverside Press, Cambridge
1900

PREFACE.

It will be matter of information to the general reader that slavery ever existed in Indiana. Those whose attention has been directed more particularly to American history are aware of its former existence, and, to some extent, of its origin and termination. No one, I think, since it has passed into history, has had any conception of its true significance. Historians, who have alluded to its continuation under the Ordinance of 1787, appear to have regarded it merely as one of the incongruities of frontier life, — an unlawful condition which nothing but the imperfection of government permitted to exist. A like haziness has enveloped the petitions of Indiana for the further admission of slavery. Their existence has often been mentioned, and sage reflections have been builded on them, but the physical and political conditions that produced them have been totally ignored. The historical fact that the local slavery question was the paramount political influence in Indiana, up to the time of the organization of the state government, has never been hinted at.

The assertion may be ventured that it is time these matters were explained. This task has been essayed in the following pages. An endeavor has been made to bring to light the causes which produced the pro-slavery feeling, and the difficulties which anti-slavery sentiment was obliged to overcome. In this endeavor an investigation of the ancient French civilization, which existed within our borders, became a necessity ; and there appeared no stopping-point for this investigation short of the original exploration of the country. While it is besides the central purpose of the work, it is hoped that enough light has been thrown on this obscure subject to reconcile the reader to the devotement of so much space to its consideration.

I cannot offer my work to the public without acknowledging the assistance and counsel which have made its completion possible. My thanks are due to George Stewart, Jr., of Quebec ; to Douglas Brymner, Archivist of Canada ; to Lindsay Swift, of the Boston Public Library ; to C : A. Cutter, of the Boston Athenæum ; to Rev. Joseph Anderson, of Waterbury, Conn. ; to John Gilmary Shea, of Elizabeth, N. J. ; to A. R. Spofford, of the Congressional Library ; to James Mooney, of the Bureau of Ethnology ; to C. C. Baldwin, of Cleveland, O. ; to W. F. Poole, E. G. Mason, and A. D. Hager, of Chicago, Ill. ; to Peter G. Thompson, of Cincinnati, O. ; to Charles B. Lasselle, of Logansport ; to John Levering, B. Wilson Smith, and Albert Henderson, of Lafayette ; to H. S. Cauthorn, of Vincennes ; to W. P. Huckleberry, of Charlestown ; to W. W. Borden, of New Albany ; to Timothy Nicholson, of Richmond ; to W. H. English, J. R. Wilson, D. W. Howe, W. W. Woollen, Samuel

Morrison, and A. J. Hay, of Indianapolis. Special acknowledgments of numerous courtesies are due to Mrs. Lizzie Callis Scott, State Librarian of Indiana, and W. De M. Hooper, of the Public Library of Indianapolis.

In the existing written history of Indiana there has been so little citation of authorities that it has become almost impossible to distinguish those statements which are founded on authority from those whose basis is mere conjecture. On this account, and as there is no bibliography of Indiana history, and as many statements are made herein which might otherwise be disputed, it has been deemed proper to cite authorities fully. In doing this, however, reference is made to the actual source of the author's information, authentic copies being ranked as originals, — this particularly as to documents from the Canadian archives.

INDIANAPOLIS, *March* 14, 1888.

CONTENTS.

CHAPTER IX.

CHAPTER X.

CHAPTER XI.

CHAPTER XII.

INDIANA.

A REDEMPTION FROM SLAVERY.

———•———

CHAPTER I.

THE FIRST WHITE MAN.

It is difficult to realize fully that Indiana was ever subject to the dominion of kings. It seems more like a dream than the sober truth of history that the approval of Louis the Great was a prerequisite to the exploration of her lands, and commercial intercourse with her naked denizens; that the sensual monster Louis XV. held in his hands the supreme power over the welfare of her first settlers; that George III. controlled her course in the tottering advances of her infancy. These men delayed for some years the fulfillment of her destiny, but they left few marks on her laws and customs, and what they did leave have been so nearly effaced for many years that they have attracted but little attention even from the historian. In considering the history of the older states, several of which were not inhabited until after Indiana, the mind more readily grasps the status of the early period; for society crystallized in them much sooner than in our remote wilds, and they had within their boundaries their capitals where records of dealings between crown and subjects always remained, preserving to them indelibly the impress of foreign rule. Indiana had no capital within her boundaries for one hundred and thirty years after white men had been upon her soil. She was but a part of a province of a province. For ninety years her provincial seat of government vacillated between Quebec, New Orleans, and Montreal, with intermediate authority at Ft. Chartres and Detroit, and the ultimate power at Paris. Then her capital was whisked away to London, without the slightest regard to the wishes of her scattered inhabitants, by the treaty of Paris. Sixteen years later it came over the Atlantic to Richmond, on the James, by conquest; and after a tarry of five years at that point it shifted to New York city, then the national seat of government, by cession. In 1788 it reached Marietta, Ohio, on its progress towards its final location. In 1800 it came within the limits of the state.

With the seat of government so frequently changed, and the papers referring to public affairs scattered through the archives of various sovereignties, it is not surprising that the history of the early settlements has been in a confused condition; and this confusion was heightened through the destruction by fire of a part of the few records existing at Vincennes, her earliest permanent town, on January 21, 1814.[1] Almost everything that has been written concerning them is conjecture, with a slight foundation of tradition. Volney visited Vincennes in 1796, and had conversations with old settlers from which he concluded that the place had been founded in 1735.[2] Monette adopted this as the

---

[1] Cauthorn's *Vincennes*, p. 8; *Western Sun*, January 29, 1814; Thomas's *Travels*, p. 189.

[2] *View of the U. S.*, Phila. ed. p. 373.

date of our first settlement,[1] and so did Flint;[2] but Bancroft, more cautiously, says this date "is not too early:" he considered it probable that the route from the lakes to the Mississippi by way of the Maumee and Wabash came into general use in 1716, and, "in conformity to instructions from France, was secured by a military post."[3] Bishop Bruté, the first incumbent of the see of Vincennes, from what information he had obtained, made the following statement: "The first establishment of Vincennes, as the mission of St. Francis Xavier or Wabash, dates about 1700. The friendly tribes and traders called to Canada for protection, and then M. de Vincennes came with a detachment, I think, of Carignan, and was killed in 1735."[4] He also conjectured that during the later years of the 17th century traders and missionaries may have passed "down from the St. Joseph, left the Kankakee to the west, and visited the Tippecanoe, the Eel River, and the upper parts of the Wabash." In his first edition, Mr. Dillon, the historian *par excellence* of Indiana, adopted this conjecture as probable.[5] In his edition of 1859 Dillon affirms his belief that the Indian villages on the Wabash were visited by the French as early as 1702, and quotes from a memoir of the Marquis de Denonville, dated March 8, 1688, as to posts having then been established on the Ohio and Wabash, but ventures no further supposition.[6]

All of the writers who have examined the subject

[1] *Hist. Miss. Valley,* vol. i. p. 165.
[2] *Condensed Hist. and Geog.* vol. ii. p. 153.
[3] *Hist. U. S.* vol. iii. p. 346.
[4] *Butler's Hist. Ky.* Introduction, p. xviii.
[5] *Hist. Notes,* etc., 1843, p. 31.
[6] *Hist. Indiana,* p. 400.

recognize the certainty of an exploration of our territory previous to the formation of permanent settlements, but with singular unanimity they have overlooked the ancient traditions concerning this exploration, which were recorded before they could have become much corrupted by historical research. Two of these records are worthy of notice here. In 1816, David Thomas, a Quaker gentleman of New York, visited Vincennes, and in a careful search for information concerning its early history obtained two statements, both from traditional sources, as follows : —

1. "About the year 1690 the French traders first visited Vincennes, at that time a town of the Piankeshaw Indians, called Cippecaughke. Of these the former obtained wives and raised families. In the year 1734 several French families emigrated from Canada and settled at this place. The first governor, or commandant, was M. St. Vincent, after whom the town is now called."

2. "About the year 1702, a party of French from Canada descended the Wabash River, and established *posts* in several places on its banks. The party was commanded by Captain St. Vincennes, who made this his principal place of deposit, which went for a long time by no other name than the Post." [1]

A Gazetteer of Indiana, published in 1833, makes this statement: "In the year 1680, this country was first explored by some adventurers, with a view of deriving advantages from the Indian trade, chiefly in the article of furs. The ground on which the town of Vincennes now stands was then chosen as a place of trade, and

---

[1] *Travels through the Western Country,* Auburn, N. Y., 1819, p. 189.

from that time continued to be occupied by a few traders, who lived in a manner but little different from the natives. In 1735 a company of French made an addition to the Wabash settlements." [1] The writer cites no authority, but, as up to this time no history of Indiana had been attempted, it seems reasonably certain that his statement was founded on tradition. We have therefore a space of fifty-five years, 1680–1735, within which tradition has fixed the exploration and settlement of the Wabash country, and conjecture has varied even more widely, for it has been maintained that the settlement was not made before 1750.[2] .

Let us now abandon the old attempt to go backwards over a course lined out by such uncertain landmarks, and, having begun at the beginning, build up the early history of this commonwealth from reliable historical sources, trusting that the question of permanent settlement will be simplified when thus approached. We shall at least be able to brush away some of the rubbish that has accumulated in the course over which we must make our way. The year 1669 may safely be set as a limit before which no Frenchman explored to the south of the great lakes. There is no account known of any such exploration, and the maps up to that date represent the lower country as unknown.[3] The Iroquois Indians had shown such strength and such hostility that the French had not even attempted to go west by Niagara

[1] At p. 23. This is a revised and enlarged edition of John Scott's *Gazetteer* of 1826, of which I have been unable to find a copy. Hon. James Scott, one of the judges of the supreme court of Indiana, aided in the revision.

[2] *N. Am. Rev.*, vol. xlix. p. 69.

[3] Winsor's *Narrative and Critical Hist. U. S.*, vol. iv. pp. 202–205.

and Lake Erie. The trading posts which they had established on the upper lakes were reached by the Ottawa, or Grand River, and Lake Huron.[1] In 1665, the celebrated regiment of Carignan-Salieres was sent into the Iroquois country, and from this and other military operations peace had been fairly established by 1669, though affairs were somewhat unsettled for several years.[2] The Senecas, the most westerly of the Five Nations, had made a treaty in 1666, and Father Fermin had established a mission among them in 1668. It has been claimed that missionaries visited Indiana and Illinois prior to this date, but there is no foundation for the statement. The probable sources of the error are the records of certain missions to the Miamis in this earlier period; but the Miamis referred to were a detached band who lived in Wisconsin, with the Kickapoos and Mascoutins, as appears by the same records.

With these facts in view we can accept the statement concerning Robert Cavalier,[3] Sieur de la Salle, which is made in the sketch prefaced to the original edition of the journal of Henri Joutel, as follows: "Many Discoveries had been made to the Northward, before Monsieur *de la Sale's* Time; because there being Plenty of very good Furs, the traders of *Quebeck* and *Montreal*, by Means of the Adventurers call'd *Wood-Men* [*coureurs de bois*], from their traveling thro' the Woods, had penetrated very far up the Country that Way; but none

---

[1] Parkman's *Disc. of Gr. West*, p. 17, n.

[2] *N. Y. Col. Docs.*, vol. ix. pp. 63, 71, 85; Garneau's *Hist. of Canada*, vol. i. p. 220.

[3] The name René, which is sometimes added, was not given him at baptism. *Vide Chevalier de la Salle de Rouen*, par Gabriel Gravier, Paris, 1871, p. xi.

had advanced far towards the South or South-West, beyond Fort *Frontenac*, which is on the Lake *Ontario*, the nearest this Way of the five great Lakes. However, upon the Report of the Natives, it was supposed, that great and advantageous Discoveries might be made. There had been much talk of the rich Mines of St. *Barbara*, in the Kingdom of *Mexico*, and some were tempted to give them a Visit. Something was known of the famous River *Mississippi*, which it was supposed might fall into the South Sea, and open a Way to it. These Conjectures working upon Monsieur *de la Sale*, who being zealous for the Honour of his Nation, design'd to signalize the *French* Name, on Account of extraordinary Discoveries, beyond all that went before him ; he form'd the Design and resolv'd to put it in Execution. He was certainly very fit for it, and succeeded at the Expence of his Life ; for no Man has done so much in that Way as he did for the Space of twenty Years he spent in that Employment. He was a Man of a regular Behaviour, of a large Soul, well enough learned, and understanding in the Mathematicks, designing, bold, undaunted, dexterous, insinuating, not to be discourag'd at any Thing, ready at extricating himself out of any Difficulties, no Way apprehensive of the greatest Fatigues, wonderful steady in Adversity, and what was of extraordinary Use, well enough versed in several Savage Languages." [1]

The "space of twenty years" would indicate a beginning of these explorations in 1667, for La Salle was assassinated in 1687, but it is perhaps not intended to be precise. The earliest mention of his departure is in a letter of Sieur Patoulet, dated November 11, 1669, stating " that Messrs. de la Salle and Dolier, accom-

---

[1] Joutel's *Journal*, London ed. of 1714, pp. xvi, xvii.

panied by twelve men, had set out with a design to go and explore a passage they expected to discover communicating with Japan and China." [1] On October 10, 1670, M. Talon, Intendant General of Canada, writes to the king : "Since my arrival I have dispatched persons of resolution, who promise to penetrate further than has ever been done ; the one to the West and Northwest of Canada, and the others to the Southwest and South." [2] In February, 1671, the minister Colbert replied : "The resolution you have taken to send Sieur de la Salle towards the South, and Sieur de St. Luisson to the North, to discover the South Sea passage, is very good." [3] Concerning this voyage there remain two accounts, one by the Abbé Gallinée, who accompanied the explorers, and the other by a friend of his who claimed to have his information from La Salle. It is unquestioned that they left La Chine in July, 1669, and journeyed together to the western extremity of Lake Ontario. Here they were presented a Shawnee slave, who assured them that he could lead them to the Ohio in six weeks ; but here also they met Louis Joliet, who was returning from an unsuccessful search for the copper mines of Lake Superior. On his report, in spite of the protestations of La Salle, Dolier and Gallinée, who were Sulpitian priests, decided to go to the upper lakes to instruct the Pottawattamies. They separated on the last day of September ; the priests passed on through Lake Erie, making the first

---

[1] *N. Y. Col. Docs.*, vol. ix. p. 787; Margry's *Découvertes et Etablissements des Français dans L'Amerique Septentrionale*, vol. i. p. 81. For convenience this work will be cited hereafter simply as Margry.

[2] *N. Y. Col. Docs.*, vol. ix. p. 64.

[3] *Ibid.*, vol. ix. p. 789.

recorded traverse of that lake, though Joliet had probably just come over it on his return; they returned in 1670, having accomplished nothing further.

Gallinée's account follows La Salle only to this point, and the other relation, which is very obscure, has been savagely attacked on account of a claim founded upon it that La Salle discovered the Mississippi before Joliet. Margry, Shea, Parkman, Harrisse, Whittlesey, Faillon, Gravier, and others have so wrestled backwards and forwards over this ground that hardly any authority has escaped unscathed, and this one has suffered most of all. It proceeds: "Meanwhile M. de la Salle continued on his way by a river which runs from East to West; and passed to Onondaga, afterwards to six or seven leagues below Lake Erie; and having reached as far as the 280th or 283d degree of longitude, and to the 41st degree of latitude, he found a rapid which falls to the West into a low land, marshy, covered with dead trees, of which there were some that were yet standing. He was obliged to take to the land, and, following a ridge which led him a long distance, he found certain savages who told him that afar off from there the same stream, which lost itself in this vast and low country, reunited in a channel. He then continued his journey, but as the fatigue became great, twenty-three or twenty-four men who had followed him thus far quitted him in one night, regained the river, and made their way some to New Holland and some to New England. He then found himself alone, four hundred leagues from home, whither he hastened to return, reascending the river, and living by the chase, by herbs, and by what the Indians that he met on the road gave to him." [1]

[1] Margry, vol. i. pp. 377, 378.

This account is so absurd from a geographical view that it can be regarded of value only as confirmatory of other evidence and in a general way. Fortunately La Salle went over the same ground in his memorial to the king in 1677, and his account is clear and reasonable. Speaking of himself in the third person, he says: "In the year 1667, and those following, he made divers voyages with much expense, in which he for the first time explored many countries to the south of the great lakes, and among others the great river of Ohio; he followed it to a place where it empties, after a long course, into vast marshes, at the latitude of 37 degrees, after having been increased by another river, very large, which comes from the north; and all these waters discharge themselves, according to all appearances, into the Gulf of Mexico." [1] If La Salle's statement as to lati-

[1] "L'année 1667, et les suivantes, il fit divers voyages avec beaucoup de dépenses, dans lesquels il découvrit le premier beaucoup de pays au sud des grands lacs, et entre autres la grande rivière d'Ohio; il la suivit jusqu'a un endroit *ou elle tombe de fort haut dans de vastes marais*, a la hauteur de 37 degrés, après avoir été grossie par une autre rivière fort large qui vient du nord; et toutes ces eaux se déchargent selon toutes les apparances dans le Golfe du Mexique." (Margry, vol. i. p. 330.) The italicized words which I have translated "where it empties, after a long course, into vast marshes," have heretofore been rendered "where it falls from very high into vast marshes." The latter is the more natural rendering for modern French, but these words are of two centuries ago, and in the latter rendering they are incomprehensible. There are no high falls on the Ohio or any other stream that could be referred to. If we suppose the reference to be to the rapids at Louisville, which have a fall of only twenty-seven feet in two and one half miles, there can still be found nothing in their vicinity that will serve for "vast marshes." I find no place in La Salle's writings where the verb *tomber* is used in describing a cascade or rapid; but he did use it to signify the debouchure

tude be correct, — and this is not improbable, inasmuch as he was "understanding in the Mathematicks," and as the early French calculations of latitude were much more accurate than those of longitude, — he must have come nearly to the mouth of the Ohio. He may have arrived there at a time when the Mississippi was overflowing, in which case the back-water in the Ohio, the overflowed bottom-lands, and the extensive cane-brakes that then existed on both its banks below the mouth of the Tennessee, might very naturally have caused him to believe that it emptied into vast marshes.

The relation first quoted states that he made another attempt to descend the Ohio some months later, but left it and crossed to Lake Erie, whence he passed through the lakes to the southern extremity of Lake Michigan. Below this he found a stream running from east to west, and followed it to a point where it was joined by another stream flowing from northwest to southeast; he continued beyond this point to the 36th degree of latitude. The streams referred to are probably the Kankakee and Des Plaines, but the latitude is unquestionably as incorrect as that given in connection with the former voyage.[1] He could have reached parallel 36

of streams, as, for example, in reference to the discharge of the Des Plaines into the Illinois, and again of the latter into the Mississippi. Margry, vol. ii. pp. 128, 80. On the latter page he also uses *fort haut* in referring to the length of a stream. The preceding account is consistent with this reading, for, though it says he reached a rapid (*sault*), it also says "he continued his journey" beyond that point; and while the longitude and latitude of the *sault* would place it somewhere near Pittsburg, Pennsylvania, La Salle is left, at the end of his expedition, "four hundred leagues from home."

[1] La Salle erred widely in latitude estimated on the Illinois in his earliest voyages. In 1680 he put Pimetoui at 33° 45', though

only by the Mississippi, and if he had thus reached it before Joliet he would have left some mention of it. He never made that claim, and Frontenac and other friends, who certainly knew the extent of his travels, expressly concede the discovery of the Mississippi to Joliet.[1]

The maps of the period confirm the view as to the extent of these voyages which is given above. On what is called "Joliet's Larger Map," dated 1674, the Ohio is laid down, but with uncertain juncture with the Mississippi, and marked "*Route du Sieur de la Salle pour aller dans le Mexique.*" "Joliet's Smaller Map" has the Ohio also, with the inscription, "*Rivière par où descendit le Sieur de la Salle au sortir du lac Erié pour aller dans le Mexique.*" A third map, which may claim date as early as 1673, since the Mississippi does not appear upon it, shows the Ohio breaking off abruptly at a point well down towards its mouth, and marked, *Rivière Ohio, ainsy appellée par les Iroquois à cause de sa beauté, par où le Sieur de la Salle est descendu.*[2] The latter map is ascribed by Parkman, with much reason, to La Salle himself.[3] The upper part of the Illinois River is traced upon it, and in the lower part of Lake Michigan is written: "The largest vessels can come to this place from the outlet of Lake Erie, where it discharges into Lake Frontenac [Ontario]; and from this marsh, to which they can enter, there is only a distance

---

in 1682 he put the mouth of the Illinois at 38°. Shea's *Le Clercq,* pp. 119, 163.

[1] *N. Y. Col. Docs.*, vol. ix. p. 121; Margry, vol. ii. p. 285.

[2] See, for maps, Winsor's *Hist. U. S.* vol. iv. pp. 212–216; also Parkman's *Disc. Gr. West*, p. 23, n. 1.

[3] *Disc. Gr. West*, p. 406.

of a thousand paces to the River La Divine, which can lead them to the River Colbert [Mississippi] and thence to the Gulf of Mexico." It may be inferred from this that La Salle explored only a part of the upper Illinois on his second voyage, but learned of its course from the Indians. It is claimed that the tracings of the Ohio, with the accompanying legends, on the Joliet maps, are additions by another hand, and that this shows clearly on what "appears to be the original Joliet map." [1] This is probably true, for Joliet had no personal knowledge of the course of the Ohio, and it was a common practice then to alter maps by adding new discoveries, but for the purpose of identifying La Salle's exploration their value is not impaired by this.

It remains to be added that the French government always based its claim to the Ohio valley on its exploration by La Salle. The official instructions sent to M. du Quesne in 1752 recited: "The River Ohio, otherwise called the Beautiful River, and its tributaries, belong indisputably to France, by virtue of its discovery by Sieur de la Salle; of the trading posts the French have had there since; and of possession, which is so much the more unquestionable as it constitutes the most frequent communication from Canada to Louisiana." [2] Again, in 1755, M. de Vaudreuil was instructed: "It is only since the last war that the English have set up claims to the territory on the Beautiful River, the possession whereof had never been disputed to the French, who have always resorted to that river since it was discovered by Sieur de Lassalle." [3] From all this evidence

---

[1] *Mag. of Am. Hist.*, vol. ix. p. 279, note. A reprint of this map, with the suspected parts removed, is at p. 272 of the same.

[2] *N. Y. Col. Docs.*, vol. x. p. 243.   [3] *Ibid.* p. 293.

we conclude that La Salle traced the entire lower boundary of Indiana in 1669-70, for the "very large" stream which joined the Ohio from the north could have been nothing except the Wabash. That he passed through the northwest corner of the state in 1671 or 1672 seems also reasonably established.

In this connection we may advantageously dispel an error which crept into our history half a century ago. From the fact that the Ohio below the mouth of the Wabash was anciently called "Ouabache," Judge Law conjectured that the first travelers descended the Wabash to Vincennes, crossed by land to Kaskaskia for fear of hostile Indians farther south, and finding the mouth of the Ohio, as they descended to New Orleans, supposed it to be the Wabash. On this theory he asserted that "the Wabash was known and navigated by the whites long before the Ohio was known to exist." [1] It is true that the lower portion of the Ohio was called "Ouabache" until after the middle of the eighteenth century; but it is also true that it was so named before the Wabash was known, and before Vincennes, Kaskaskia, and New Orleans were dreamed of. On the map of Marquette (who died in 1675) the Ohio is marked as an unexplored stream with the name *Ouabouskiaou.* On Joliet's maps of 1673 and 1674 the same unexplored stream is marked *Ouaboustikou* or *Ouabouskigou.* These are evidently Indian names, and looking to the tribes of the country through which Joliet and Marquette passed, we find their words for *white* as follows: in Menominee *waubish-keewa;* in Knisteneaux *wapish-kawo;* in Chippewa *wawbishkaw;* in Sac *wapes-kaya,* —all of which are from the old Algonquin stem *waba*

[1] *Hist. of Vincennes,* p. 10.

or *wapi*, which has the same meaning.[1] The same
name *Waba-shikkah* is still given to the Wabash by
some of the Indians resident in Indiana.[2] The dialects
of the tribes nearer the Wabash, all of Algonquin stock,
varied but slightly from these, and those tribes were
commonly called Ouapous, Ouabans, or Ouabachi, by
the Frenchmen of the period. From the Indian name,
first applied by whites to the lower Ohio, came the
Gallicism "Ouabache," which was afterwards Anglicized
to "Wabash."[3]

Different tribes of Indians have different names for
the same stream, and it is the common custom for a
tribe to continue the name of a stream near them to the
stream into which it flows, except the main stream above
the junction be also contiguous to them. Ohio is an
Iroquois name, and naturally would not be heard among
the Algonquin tribes ; but the Iroquois applied it first to
the Alleghany, then to the Ohio proper, and finally to
the Mississippi below the mouth of the Ohio.[4] So the
Algonquin tribes continued the name Mississippi below

---

[1] *Archeologica Americana*, vol. ii. p. 346.

[2] Hough's map, in *Ind. Geol. Rep.* for 1882, p. 42.

[3] In Webster's *Dictionary*, p. 1632, Wabash is defined as "a
cloud blown forward by an equinoctial wind." I have been unable to fix the source of this remarkable misstatement, but sus-
pect that it results from mistaking an illustration for a definition.
I once applied by letter to an Indian agent for the meaning of a
word, and he replied that it signified "a mushroom or toadstool."
On further inquiry he said that it meant "anything white," and
that the Indian to whom he had first spoken had answered by
pointing to a toadstool. So, as to Wabash, the Indian of whom
inquiry was made may have answered by pointing to a white
cloud. The Miami words for a swiftly moving cloud are *kintche
seway*. Wabash means *white* and nothing more.

[4] *N. Y. Col. Docs.*, vol. ix. p. 80.

the junction of the Missouri, and the name, adopted
from them, is still retained, though in geographical propriety the Mississippi is a tributary of the Missouri and
the main stream should take the latter name.   So the
Miamis, Illinois, and other western tribes considered the
Wabash and lower Ohio as one stream, and the French
adopted their nomenclature because it was more easily
adopted than changed.   The principal streams were re-
christened in France, the Wabash receiving the name
" St. Jerome," but these high-sounding titles were soon
forgotten.   In old French documents the Wabash is
often spoken of as emptying into the Mississippi, and
on ancient maps it and the Ohio are wonderfully confounded.   On many of them but one stream appears,
sometimes marked " Ohio " or " Hohio," and sometimes
" Ouabache," sometimes with its head at the western
end of Lake Erie, and sometimes rising in the Iroquois
country.

It is noteworthy that La Salle never makes this error.
He always calls the Wabash " Agouassake," and even
in his *prises de possession,* in which all synonymous
names are supposed to be set forth, the name "Ouabache " is never given to the Ohio.[1]   With others the
name was continued until 1757, when Le Page du Pratz
wrote of it: " It is called Wabache, though, according
to the usual method, it ought to be called the Ohio, or
Beautiful River; seeing the Ohio was known under that
name in Canada before its confluence was known; and
as the Ohio takes its rise at a greater distance off than
the three others, which mix together before they empty
themselves into the Mississippi, this should make the

---

[1] *Mag. of Am. Hist.,* vol. ii. p. 619; Sparks's *Am. Biog.,* vol. xi.
p. 200.

others lose their names; but custom has prevailed on this occasion." [1] At this time both French and English were claiming the country by virtue of discoveries in the eastern part of the Ohio valley, the French on La Salle's discovery, and the English on an exploration of the Kanawha in 1671.[2] Hence the fact that the Ohio was the main stream became of importance to both parties, and when the English gained possession a few years later the geographical misnomer of the lower Ohio was laid aside.

From these early voyages of La Salle up to his expedition of 1679 there was no exploration of Indiana of which records have been found, and yet it is almost unquestionable that fur-traders passed through this region. La Salle had been rewarded and honored for his services, and had busied himself with his Indian trade at Fort Frontenac, but he was not without competition. The Ottawa River, falling into the St. Lawrence just above Montreal, afforded as good communication with the upper lakes as did Ontario and Erie; and by it much of that trade, and all of the trade ↄ. northern Canada, went to Montreal. In the Northwest were trading posts at Green Bay and Mackinaw Straits. Across Ontario were the Iroquois, but they carried a large portion of their furs to New York and Albany, and, besides, game had become so scarce in their country that already they were pushing far beyond its confines. Where, then, did La Salle trade? Who were the Indians to whom his fragile argosies carried blankets and trinkets, and from whom they returned laden with

---

[1] *Hist. of Louisiana*, London ed. of 1774, p. 180. The original is somewhat abridged at several points in this edition.

[2] *N. Y. Col. Docs.*, vol. iii. p. 194.

furs? Naturally we should expect to find among them the inhabitants of the best neighboring fur country which was not already occupied by other traders, and this was northern Indiana and southern Michigan. It is a peculiar country, — a succession of sheltered prairies, rounded sand-hills, and reedy marshes, interspersed with quiet lakes, and traversed by a network of sluggish streams; and at that time much of its surface, which has since been reclaimed by drainage, could be passed over in canoes. All game abounded in it, but chiefly the velvet-coated beaver. This was the hunter's paradise for the possession of which the Iroquois schemed so cunningly and fought so bitterly.[1] South and southeast of it lay the Ohio Valley, also well worthy the attention of the trader, though at that time very thinly populated. Is it possible that La Salle neglected these fields? Certainly his trade was carried very far, for, besides having four vessels of from twenty-five to forty tons burden on Lake Ontario, his canoe trade was so extensive that his men became known as the most skillful canoemen in the country. His trade must have been extensive, or he could not have prospered as he did. He replaced the log fort at Cadaracqui with one of hewn stone, and surrounded it with enough well-built houses for all the purposes of a thriving settlement. He stored up means for subsequent explorations, and established a credit which years of dire misfortune were unable to break down.

The most important record evidence is the memoir of the Marquis de Denonville, then governor and lieutenant-general of Canada, which was prepared for the information of the court as to the French titles in America, and was received at Versailles prior to March 8, 1688.[2]

---

[1] *N. Y. Col. Docs.,* vol. iv. p. 650; *Ibid.* vol. ix. p. 891.
[2] *Ibid.* vol. ix. p. 377.

Speaking of La Salle's Illinois establishment, Denonville says : " He caused a fort and buildings to be erected, and a bark to be begun, at a place called Crèvecœur, in order to proceed as far as the said South Sea, two thirds of which bark only were built, the said Sieur de la Salle having afterwards employed canoes for his trade in said countries, as he had already done for several years in the rivers Oyo, Ouabache, and others in the surrounding neighborhood which flow into the said river Mississippi, whereof possession was taken by him, as appears by the Relations made thereof. The countries and rivers of Oyo or Abache and the circumjacent territory were inhabited by our Indians, the Chaouanons [Shawnees], Miamis, and Illinois. . . . All the foregoing demonstrates sufficiently . . . their [the French] possession of the great River Mississippi which they have discovered as far as the South Sea, on which river also they have divers establishments, as well as on that of Oyo, Ouabache, etc., which flow into the said river Mississippi, and of the countries and lands in the vicinity of said rivers where they actually carry on trade."

Fort Crèvecœur, as is well known, was built in 1680, and if La Salle had then maintained a canoe trade on the Ohio and Wabash for several years, as here stated, it must have continued through nearly all of his stay at Frontenac. Beyond this official declaration, the chief known evidence of this early trade is La Salle's apparent familiarity with the country before he began his great exploration in 1681, which appears in his correspondence.[1] In a letter to a business associate in 1680, he states that he will use the vessel he is then building at Crèvecœur to carry furs by the Mississippi to the

[1] *Hist. Mag.* (Dawson's), vol. v. p. 196; Margry, vol. ii. p. 98.

Gulf of Mexico, or, in case the Mississippi should not
empty there, as he believes it to, he will use the vessel
to bring furs to Canada by a river which he has discovered and named Baudrane, but "the Iroquois call it
Ohio and the Ottawas Olighin-cipou." He says : "This
River Baudrane rises back of Oneiout, and after running
four hundred and fifty leagues to the West, always as
large and larger than the Seine at Rouen, and always
deeper, it discharges into the River Colbert [Mississippi]
twenty to twenty-five leagues South by Southwest of the
mouth by which the Illinois River empties into the same
stream. A barque can ascend this river very far, —
opposite Tsonnontouan — and at this place one is distant not more than twenty to twenty-five leagues from
the southern shore of Lake Ontario or Frontenac, by
which one is able to go to Fort Frontenac in fifteen
hours of good breeze, so that from this view it will be
necessary only to make an establishment at the mouth
of the river of the Tsonnontouans [the Genessee], on
the shore of Lake Ontario, and another on the river
which I call Baudrane, where horses may be kept for
the portage, which will be easy, the road being made.
. . . All the country along this river and between it
and the Illinois, and for ten or twelve days' journey to
the North, and to the South, and to the West of the
River Colbert, is full of wild cattle [buffalo] more than
one can tell." [1]

This letter also furnishes evidence of another fact.
La Salle's expeditions of 1679 and following years were
not for exploration merely. His project from the first
was colonization and exclusive trade in the Mississippi
valley, and he would probably have accomplished it

[1] Margry, vol. ii. p. 79.

with ease but for the Iroquois. At that time Indiana and much of the adjacent territory was the seat of a savage warfare which seriously impeded trade. The Iroquois could not secure the abundance of furs which the region should have furnished, because, as La Salle wrote to Frontenac in 1682, " before the destruction of the Illinois, and of the Kentaientonga, and Ganeiensaga, whom the Iroquois defeated a year since, of the Chaouanons, Ouabachi, Tistontaraetonga, Gandostogega, Mosopolea, Sounikaeronons and Ochitagonga, with whom they have also been contesting for several years, they dared not hunt in these parts infested by so many enemies ; " and the resident tribes were also of little use in the trade, because they, he continues, " have the same apprehension of the Iroquois, and little habit of profiting by the skins of these animals [beaver], having trade with the English but rarely because they are unable to go to them without great hardship, time, and risk." [1] La Salle's effort to stop this war, while at Frontenac, availed only to make the Iroquois unfriendly to him, and furnished his Canadian enemies with material for the charge that " after he had obtained permission to discover the Great River of Mississippi, and had, as he alleged, the grant of the Illinois,[2] he no longer observed any terms with the Iroquois. He ill-treated them, and avowed that he would convey arms and ammunition to the Illinois, and would die assisting them." [3] The complaints of the Iroquois were made the grounds of his removal from Fort St. Louis in 1684.[4]

[1] Margry, vol. ii. p. 237.
[2] The grant is dated May 12, 1678. *N. Y. Col. Docs.*, vol. ix. p. 127.
[3] *N. Y. Col. Docs.*, vol. ix. p. 163.
[4] *Ibid.* vol. iii. pp. 451, 452.

Of the tribes named by La Salle and Denonville in
the quotations above, the Miamis and Ouabachi are the
only ones who appear to have lived within the bounds
of Indiana. The Illinois were all to the west of the
Wabash. The Shawnees who figured in our history at
this period lived on the south bank of the Ohio below
the Cumberland, which was always called the Chaoua-
non by the French.[1] The location of the Miamis is not
certain. One band of them, afterwards known as the
Miamis of Maramech, had been living for a number of
years near the Wisconsin River, in close alliance with
the Kickapoos and Mascoutins. Some years later, at the
request of the French, they removed to the Kalamazoo
River in Michigan, after they had been joined by the
Pepikokia band (Pepicoquis), and early in the eighteenth century both moved into Indiana.[2] About the
time of their first removal the Kickapoos and Mascoutins came east also, and settled, the former on the Maumee River and the latter at Detroit.[3] The main body
of the Miamis proper, whom the English called
Twightwees,[4] were located in 1680 on the St. Joseph's
of Lake Michigan, a little above the site of South Bend.
Father Membré says that they had formerly lived west
of the Illinois, and came there a short time before at
the desire of the Iroquois.[5] The Ouiatanons appear to

---

[1] This location of the Chaouanons is given on all the early
maps. One of the most definite is that in Thevenot's *Recueil de
Voyages*, which is reproduced in Andreas's *History of Chicago.*

[2] *N. Y. Col. Docs.*, vol. ix. pp. 570, 621.

[3] Journal of the siege of Detroit, in Smith's *Hist. of Wisconsin*,
vol. ii.

[4] This word is the Miami *twah twah*, representing the cry of
the crane, which was the totem and name of one of their principal
clans.

[5] Shea's *Disc. and Exp. of the Miss. Valley*, p. 154.

have lived west of the Mississippi, for they are so located on the earliest maps.[1] It is possible, however,
that they had previously lived on the Wabash, as this
stream was called "Ouia-agh-tena" by some of the
tribes.[2] The Piankeshaws and a part of the Pottawattamies appear to have resided along the Wabash.

The manners and customs of these tribes varied little
from those of others, but it is worthy of remembrance
that at this period all of the Indian tribes were more
degraded in some respects than at a later period. The
worst of their customs was that of eating human flesh.
The Miamis remained cannibals longer than any of the
other tribes, not discontinuing the practice until after
the Revolutionary war, but with them it became a religious institution and was restricted to one family.[3] In
the seventeenth and earlier part of the eighteenth centuries, cannibalism was common from Newfoundland to
the Mississippi. Not only were the slain in battle and
prisoners of war converted into viands for feasting, but
also in times of famine the members of the various
tribes devoured the bodies of their kindred.[4] The
French explorers and missionaries were frequently
obliged to witness these revolting banquets, and refer-

---

[1] Andreas's *Hist. of Chicago*, p. 48; Winsor's *U. S.*, vol. iv.
p. 208.

[2] Lewis Evans's map of 1755; Pownal's map of 1776. Judge
Beckwith pronounces this name Iroquois, but the best authorities
at the Bureau of Ethnology say it is of Algonquin origin. In
Shawnee it means *a water eddying.*

[3] Brice's *Hist. of Ft. Wayne*, notes on pp. 121–123; *Jesuits in
America*, p. xl, note; *Pioneers of France in the New World*,
p. 330, note.

[4] Kip's *Jesuit Missions*, p. 100; Garneau's *Canada*, vol. i.
p. 157; Heckewelder's *Indian Nations*, p. 55, note.

ence to the custom is made again and again in the correspondence and records of the period.[1] The savages
also indulged in this custom in the early campaigns in
the presence of European troops, and apparently with
little or no remonstrance.   After the fight with the
Senecas, on July 13, 1687, Denonville says : " We
witnessed the painful sight of the usual cruelties of the
savages, who cut the dead into quarters, as is done in
slaughter-houses, in order to put them into the kettle ;
the greater number were opened while still warm, that
their blood might be drunk."   The cannibals here were
Ottawas, Hurons or Wyandots, Maquasses or Christian
Iroquois, Miamis, and Illinois, and among them they
disposed of twenty-five bodies.[2]   For the purpose of
terrifying their Indian enemies, the French commanders
used to threaten to turn them over to the friendly Indians to be eaten, and they did not hesitate to carry out
their threats when they wished to please their anthro-
pophagous allies.[3]   The Puritans appear to have disap-
proved of cannibalism,[4] but in 1696 the English colonists invited the Indians to join them and "eat White
meat" in their contest with the French.[5]   Even so late

[1] Memoir of La Salle, in French's *Hist. Coll. of La. and Fla.*,
2d series, p. 4 ; Smith's *Hist. of Wisc.*, vol. ii. pp. 319, 326 ; *Mich.
Pion. Coll.*, vol. vi. p. 459 ; Kip's *Jesuit Missions*, pp. 41, 155–
157 ; *N. Y. Col. Docs.*, vol. ix. pp. 79, 180, 466, 604, 624 ; *Mag.
of Am. Hist.*, vol. ii. p. 120, also vol. x. p. 31 ; *Minn. Hist. Coll.*,
vol. i. pp. 181, 235 ; *Penn. Archives*, vol. i. p. 238 ; Parkman's
Disc. of the Gr. West, pp. 218, 381 ; Parkman's *Jesuits in America*,
p. 247 ; Darling's *Anthropophagy*, pp. 38–43 ; Shea's *Le Clercq*,
vol. ii. p. 261.
[2] *N. Y. Col. Docs.*, vol. ix. p. 338.
[3] *Ibid.* pp. 578, 598, 629.
[4] *Vide* Penhallow's *Indian Wars.*
[5] *N. Y. Col. Docs.*, vol. ix. p. 644.

as 1756, Sir William Johnson told the Indians that he gave them kettles to cook the flesh of their enemies, referring presumably to the French, but it is claimed in the council notes that these words were used figuratively.[1]

Although Indian captives were obliged at times to perform menial tasks, their customs of the adoption of prisoners by a conquering tribe to take the places of their own slain, of killing prisoners by torture, and of cannibalism, make it probable that protracted slavery was not known among them until introduced by Europeans. Says Carver : "I have been informed that it was the Jesuits and French missionaries that first occasioned the introduction of these unhappy captives into the settlements, and who by so doing taught the Indians that they were valuable. Their views, indeed, were laudable, as they imagined that by this method they should not only prevent much barbarity and bloodshed, but find the opportunities of spreading their religion among them increased. To this purpose they encouraged the traders to purchase such slaves as they met with. The good effects of this mode of proceeding was not, however, equal to the expectations of these pious fathers. Instead of being the means of preventing cruelty and bloodshed, it only caused the dissensions between the Indian nations to be carried on with a greater degree of violence, and with unremitted ardour." [2] This policy was beneficial, nevertheless, for the growth of slavery caused the decline and final cessation of cannibalism, the captives having a value in fire-water that was more attractive to savage taste than even human flesh.[3]

---

[1] *N. Y. Col. Docs.*, vol. vii. p. 149.
[2] Carver's *Travels*, pp. 346, 347.
[3] Garneau's *Canada*, vol. i. p. 126.

Slavery became quite common, and many Indians were held as slaves both among the whites and among the Indians.

La Salle's movements in 1679 and 1680 had little to do with Indiana, except that the St. Joseph's and Kankakee rivers were his customary route of travel to the Illinois, the portage being made at the site of South Bend.   In January, 1681, we find him at Fort Miamis, on the south bank of the St. Joseph's, at its mouth,[1] after having found his Illinois establishment destroyed and his allies scattered by the Iroquois, an event which William Henry Harrison a century and a half later declared to have been a military impossibility.[2]   There was something almost touching the supernatural in the courage and resolution of La Salle.   At that rude fort on the bank of the St. Joseph's, in the discomforts of a severe winter, hundreds of miles from the French settlements, his faithful Tonty carried captive, killed, or a fugitive, he knew not which, his remaining comrades disheartened, his colony swept from the face of the

[1] Hennepin's and La Hontan's maps.   His first fort was at the same place until destroyed by the deserters in the spring of 1680. The post called St. Joseph's was built later, near the site of Niles, Michigan.   *Mag. of Am. Hist.*, vol. xv. p. 460; Beckwith's *Hist. Notes on the N. W.*, p. 140.   An itinerary in the Haldimand Collection fixes it at twelve miles below the South Bend portage. In Knapp's *History of the Maumee Valley*, p. 10, and Goodrich & Tuttle's *Indiana*, p. 337, this fort of La Salle's is carried over to the site of Fort Wayne, an error which probably arose from the fact that the names St. Joseph's and Miamis were applied to different streams and different forts at different periods.   La Salle could not well have been at Fort Wayne in 1680, and unquestionably he did not build any fort there in that year.

[2] Discourse on the Aborigines of the Ohio Valley, in *Ohio Hist. Coll.*, p. 250 ; same in *Fergus Hist. Series*, No. 26, p. 32.

earth, his credit shattered, his means dissipated by dis-
asters of flood and field, this man calmly reconstructed
his plans, and prepared to renew his enterprise on a
more extended basis than before. He determined to
refound his colony on the Illinois, and surround it with
a confederation of the Northwestern tribes that would
be strong enough to repel any army the Iroquois could
bring against it. His first converts were the warriors
of a little band of Abnakis and Mohegans, driven from
their New England homes in the border wars of the
English colonists, who had found no resting-place till
they reached the clear waters of the St. Joseph's. These
gladly allied themselves to the white chief who promised
to interpose the strong arm of the French king for their
protection. Scarcely were they won when a Shawnee
chief, from the village on the Ohio, appeared and asked
protection from the Iroquois. La Salle with easy confidence promised what was asked : " The Chaouanons are
too distant; but let them come to me at the Illinois and
they shall be safe." The chief promised to join him in
the succeeding autumn, and kept his word.

As soon as the weather began to moderate La Salle
started west on foot, with twenty men, to seek communication with the Illinois, who were necessary factors in his
plan. The first Indians found were some Outagamies,
from whom he received the glad tidings that Tonty was
safe with the Pottawattamies near Green Bay. Soon
after they found a band of Illinois, to whom La Salle,
after making presents and lamenting their misfortunes,
submitted his plan. They heard him with satisfaction,
and departed to carry the proposal to the remainder of
the tribe. Membré says that La Salle visited other
tribes at this time, but he does not name them. His

journey was not long, for early in the spring he was at
Fort Miamis, and, taking with him ten men, went from
there up the river to the Miamis, at the village above
the portage. It was a propitious season for approaching
them. In the late conflict they had remained neutral,
but they were now beginning to realize that the intentions of the Iroquois toward them were none of the best.
They had murdered a band of Miamis the preceding
summer, and not only had refused to make reparation,
but also had stationed parties of warriors in the Miami
country, who assumed the air of conquerors and held up
to contempt the power of the French. La Salle found
one of these bands of Iroquois at the village. He at
once confronted them, threatened them with punishment
for their attack on Tonty, and challenged them to repeat
in his presence their insults to the French. The Iroquois had not forgotten the former commander of Fort
Frontenac, and in his presence their courage oozed
away. During the following night, much to the astonishment of the Miamis, they stealthily left the village.
With so much of prestige, and by the aid of a band of
refugee Indians from the East who were wintering at
the point and who at once made alliance with La Salle,
the Miamis were easily won. On the second day after
the flight of the Iroquois they declared their determination to become brothers of the Illinois and children of
the French king, and celebrated the new order of things
with feasting and dances.[1]

In May, La Salle started for Montreal, where he
appeased his creditors and secured additional advances.
In November he was at Fort Miamis again, and during
that winter and the following summer made his explora-

[1] *Disc. of Great West*, chap. 20.

tion of the Mississippi. In the fall of 1682 he had reached Michilimackinac on his proposed return to France, when he received word that the Iroquois were on their way to attack his Indian allies, and thereupon he turned back to the Illinois. His first mission was to the Miamis. For more than a year they had been kept in a state of irresolution concerning their promised alliance. The Iroquois had threatened vengeance if they abandoned neutrality, and, in order to terrify the wavering tribe, had made several attacks and committed depredations on them. At length the Miamis sent ambassadors to Montreal to talk with Onontio in person.[1] Frontenac received them, with delegations of the Ottawas and Kiskakons, on August 13, 1682, and after the others had made their complaints, " one of the Miamis, having taken up the word, stated that they likewise were daily slaughtered by the Iroquois. The count having answered that this was the first news he had of it, and having afterwards inquired how many of his men the Iroquois had killed, and at what place, the Miami replied that he came not to complain nor to demand satisfaction. The count rejoined, Were there not Frenchmen in his country — did not M. De la Salle, who had made an establishment there, exhort them to build a fort to defend themselves against those who should attack them, and even to unite themselves with the Illinois? The Miami, concurring therein, also confessed that the Iroquois had told him to retire from their warpath, as they had nothing to say against him, but against the Illinois ; nevertheless they failed not, on four occasions, to kill him, and to seize some of his people, for

---

[1] Onontio was the title given the governors of Canada among all the Indian tribes.

which he was not asking satisfaction of Onontio. But his air and tone indicated that he intended to obtain it and to avenge himself." [1]

After two days a deputation of the Hurons arrived and a general council was held, in which it was announced that all the tribes represented had formed an alliance with the Ouiatanons, and in several subsequent councils all of the tribes declared their purpose to make war on the Iroquois. Frontenac tried to dissuade them from this, and urged them to try conciliatory measures, but in vain. Alimahoué, the spokesman of the Miamis, protested that they would trust the Iroquois no longer. The Iroquois while pretending to be their friends had bitten them, and he " wished not only to bite them in his turn but also to eat them, and to go in quest of them, begging Onontio to hinder him not." Much as Frontenac was interested in forwarding the projects of La Salle, he dared not precipitate a war with the Five Nations without permission from France, and he finally dismissed the representatives with permission to build forts and defend themselves in their own country, with which privileges they expressed themselves satisfied. Three weeks later a delegation of the Iroquois arrived and held council with Frontenac. They declared that they had no quarrel with the Hurons, Kiskakons, or Miamis. They admitted that an army of twelve hundred warriors was already prepared to depart for the west, but claimed that these intended to fight only the Illinois and La Salle, whose death they had determined to compass. The other tribes would not be molested unless they first attacked the Iroquois. Frontenac used all his influence to deter them from this expedition, and

[1] *N. Y. Col. Docs.*, vol. ix. p. 177.

particularly warned them against molesting any of the French.[1]   The expedition was afterwards abandoned, but the rumor of it frightened the western Indians as well as turned back La Salle.   The Miamis fled 'from their villages, and would not return until La Salle appeared in person.   They were then easily induced to remove to the Illinois and take up their residence near Fort St. Louis.[2]

The importance of perfecting his confederation and preparing to repel any invasion of the Iroquois was now uppermost in La Salle's mind.   During the winter of 1682–3 he was all through Indiana and Illinois, urging the tribes to unite and join him at Fort St. Louis, and chastising those who failed to keep faith with him ; [3] he extended this crusade beyond the Mississippi and far to the south.   In April he wrote that " with twenty-two Frenchmen he had obliged more than forty villages to apply to him for peace, and chastised those who have violated the promise they had given him. . . . That the Chaouanons Chaskpé, and Ouabans have, at his solicitation, abandoned the Spanish trade and also nine or ten villages they occupied, for the purpose of becoming French and settling near Fort St. Louis." [4]   In June he expresses his fear that the Miamis may be terrified into fleeing from their new homes on the Illinois, " and so prevent the Missouries from coming to settle at St. Louis, as they are about to do." [5]

The establishment of this colony of confederated

---

[1] *N. Y. Col. Docs.*, vol. ix. p. 191.
[2] *Disc. of Great West*, p. 294.
[3] Shea's *Le Clercq*, vol. ii. p. 201.
[4] *N. Y. Col. Docs.*, vol. ix. p. 799.
[5] *Disc. of Great West*, p. 295.

tribes depopulated Indiana entirely, for all of our Indians joined it. Fort St. Louis was located on what was then called Le Rocher, now Starved Rock, on the south side of the Illinois River, opposite the town of Utica.[1] Perched on this lofty and almost inaccessible sandstone cliff, the little stockade fort of the French seemed a protection to the neighboring villages which in fact constituted its best defense.[2] South of it, at a distance of about half a mile, was the village of the Shawnees, flanked by two ravines and further protected by an earthwork, containing two hundred warriors. On the north side of the river, opposite the fort, were the Illinois, numbering twelve hundred warriors. West of these, apparently away from the river, was the village of Oiatenon (Ouiatanon), afterwards so familiar in Indiana history as one of the principal villages on the Wabash. It then contained five hundred warriors. Still to the west, near the great bend of the Illinois to the south, was the village of Ouabona, with seventy warriors — probably of the Ouabans or Ouapous of whom mention has been made. East of the Illinois village, on the north side of the river, was Pepikokia, another Indiana town of later date, which was rated at one hundred and sixty warriors. Still to the east was Peanghichia, which is simply the French orthography of Piankeshaw. The Piankeshaws afterwards lived in Indiana, and this village of one hundred and fifty warriors probably included all of them. Across to the south

---

[1] For descriptions see *Disc. of Great West*, p. 221; *Mag. of Western Hist.*, vol. i. p. 213; *The Last of the Illinois*, in Fergus Hist. Series, No. 3.

[2] In his memorial of 1684, La Salle estimates the population of his colony at over 18,000 souls. French's *Hist. Coll. of La. and Fla.*, second series, p. 4.

of the river, on a small tributary, was the great Miami village, with thirteen hundred warriors. These villages, with the village of three hundred warriors opposite Ouabona, called Kilatica, constituted the colony proper. To the north, however, were the Mascoutins and their allies, who were members of the confederacy. The nearest of these was Maramech, the village of the Miami band which had for many years been separated from the remainder of the tribe. It had one hundred and fifty warriors. The most westerly village was called Kikapou, and it was probably the source of the several Kickapoo towns of this State. The aggregate of such of these Indians as were subsequently included under the name Miamis, that is, the villages of Oiatenon, Ouabona, Pepikokia, Peanghichia, Miamy, and Maramech, is over twenty-three hundred warriors, and there could not have been more than that number in the entire tribe at that time. There is no evidence of unusual decrease among them for many years afterwards, except that Lamothe Cadillac states that a short time before 1695 the Sioux made a treacherous attack on the Miamis, and killed about three thousand of them.[1] In 1718 M. de Vaudreuil reported the Miamis, Ouiatanons, Piankeshaws, and Pepikokias, into which these villages appear to have then been united, at from fourteen to sixteen hundred warriors.[2] In 1764 Captain Hutchins and Colonel Bouquet estimated the same tribes as numbering one thousand warriors.[3]

In consequence of the extensive tours through the country in gathering these Indians together, the maps

---

[1] Margry, vol. v. p. 323.

[2] *N. Y. Col. Docs.*, vol. ix. pp. 885, 892.

[3] Schoolcraft's *Hist. and Stat. Inf.* etc., vol. iii. pp. 555, 559.

of the next few years present more correctly the country between the great lakes and the Ohio than any of preceding years, and, what is somewhat singular, more correctly than any of the maps of the century following. The villages forming La Salle's colony, as given above, appear fully on Franquelin's map of 1684, which received official commendation for its correctness while in process of construction.[1] The villages also appear on a map of La Salle's explorations from 1679 to 1683, by D'Anville, which M. Margry discovered in the archives at Paris.[2] Though rude in construction, this latter map gives a more correct representation of the Indiana streams than any other ancient map. The Wabash is given its true course, and is marked *Agoussaké*, which is good evidence that La Salle furnished the information on which the map was prepared. White River is laid down and marked *Ouapikaminou*. Eel River and the Tippecanoe are also traced, but no names are given them. The Franquelin map is equally accurate except as to the courses of the streams. On it White River is marked *Oiapigaminou*, and the Wabash *Ouabach*. On both the Ohio is distinguished as the main stream to its mouth. On neither map is there any mark of an Indian village or French post within the limits of Indiana, although all other known villages and posts are marked. The reason was that there were no Indians residing in Indiana. They had all removed to the Illinois. So far as has yet been discovered, none of them returned before the opening of the eighteenth century.

[1] *N. Y. Col. Docs.*, vol. ix. p. 205. A part of the map, covering the colony, is prefixed to Parkman's *Disc. of the Great West*.

[2] A reproduction of Margry's print of this map is in Andreas's *Hist. of Chicago*, at pp. 58–9.

Time brought changes. La Salle was murdered, but his colony remained. The country of the Senecas was invaded by the French, and the Iroquois, turning on them, shifted the seat of war to the St. Lawrence, where it raged fiercely. The only recorded Iroquois invasion of the West after this time was an unsuccessful attack on Ft. Miamis, in 1695. In that year the Ouiatanons were located at Chicagou; a part of the Miamis were at the River St. Joseph's; and the Pepikokias had joined the Miamis of Maramech who were still in Wisconsin.[1] In August, 1695, Frontenac held councils with the western Indians, and insisted that the Miamis of Maramech should move eastward to the remainder of the tribe, and "make one and the same fire, either at the River St. Joseph, or some other place adjoining it."[2] Later came a fear that the English might get a foothold in the West, and Callieres and De Vaudreuil, governors after Frontenac, used all their powers to induce the Indians to come towards the east and settle about Detroit, but the tribes could not be persuaded to change their locations during the seventeenth century.[3]

At the beginning of the eighteenth century there was a general relocation of the tribes, from French influence. After the arrival of Lemoine d'Iberville as governor, in 1698, Louisiana began to receive greater favors from the French court and to exercise control over a large portion of the Mississippi Valley. In his memorial of 1702, D'Iberville asked possession of the lower Ohio, and that the Illinois Indians might be colonized there.

[1] *N. Y. Col. Docs.*, vol. ix. pp. 619, 621; Margry, vol. v. p. 123.

[2] *N. Y. Col. Docs.*, vol. ix. p. 625.

[3] *Ibid.*, vol. ix. pp. 752, 753.

He said : " The Illinois having removed, we could cause
it to be occupied by the Mascoutens and Kickapous.
This would bring four hundred and fifty men upon the
rivers which empty into the Illinois and Mississippi.
They now only hunt the beaver which they sell at the
Bay of the Puans [Green Bay] and in the country of
the Illinois.   The Miamis who have left the banks of
the Mississippi, and gone to Chicago on account of the
beaver, and those who are at Ortithipicatony, and at the
St. Joseph, could readily remove to the Illinois, where
they would join one hundred of their nation who are
still at Ouisconsin on the Mississippi.   The Miamis,
Mascoutens, and Kikapous, who were formerly on the
Mississippi, placed upon the Illinois or lower down will
withdraw from Canada yearly a commerce of 15,000
livres." [1]   Very little of these removals occurred as
planned, but one band of Mascoutins came to the mouth
of the Ohio and settled near the fort which had just
been built there by Juchereau.   These Mascoutins and
this post have been persistently transferred to Vincennes
by all our local historians except Dillon, and even he
gives the mislocation credit as a possibility.[2]

The error began with Judge Law, who in 1839
undertook to fix the settlement of Vincennes at about
1710, by the following extract from a letter of Father
Marest, dated at Kaskaskia, November 9, 1712 : " The
French had established a fort on the River Ouabache ;
they demanded a missionary ; and Father Mermet was
sent to them.   This father thought he ought to labor
for the conversion of the Mascoutins, who had made a
village on the banks of the same stream — this is an

[1] *Minn. Hist. Coll.*, vol. i. p. 341.
[2] Ed. of 1859, p. 31.

Indian nation using the Illinois language." [1] The fort referred to, he claimed, was at Vincennes, apparently not knowing of the Juchereau post. At the same time a correct exposition of the whole matter appeared in a review of Sparks's " Life of Marquette." [2] This was brought to the attention of Judge Law, but he still contended for his view on two grounds : 1. That the Mascoutins lived on the Wabash. 2. That there was not, prior to 1712, any fort on the Ohio. [3] Neither proposition is tenable. Beyond question the Mascoutins lived in Wisconsin up to 1702. In 1712 they were all at Detroit. [4] It has been maintained that there is no record of their residing on the Wabash prior to 1765, [5] and certainly there is none indicating that they were there prior to 1712. There was a fort established at or near the site of Cairo, Illinois, by Juchereau, in the winter of 1702–3, which was abandoned some three years later. It appears on nearly all the maps of the eighteenth century, marked " Ancien Fort," " An. F. F.," " Old Fort," " Antient Fort Destroy'd," and by similar titles. [6] Local writers of later date have sought

[1] Law's *History of Vincennes*, ed. of 1858, p. 12, — quoting *Lettres Edifiantes et Curieuses*, Tome 6, p. 333. A translation of the entire letter is in Kip's *Early Jesuit Missions*, p. 191.

[2] *N. Am. Rev.* for January, 1839.

[3] Law's *Vincennes*, ed. of 1858, p. 46.

[4] Dubuisson's *Journal*, in Smith's *Hist. of Wisc.*, vol. ii. p. 315.

[5] Schoolcraft's *Hist. Cond. and Prosp. of Indian Tribes*, vol. iv. p. 244.

[6] See Popple's maps ; Bellin's map of 1757, in De La Harpe's *Abrégé de L'Histoire Générale des Voyages*, prefix ; Lt. Ross's map of 1772 ; D'Anville's map of 1772 ; Harris's *Voyages* (1740–50), vol. ii. p. 1, etc. The oldest map on which I have found it marked is the curious and ancient one in Breese's *Early History of Illinois*. This is entitled, " Marquette's & Hennepin's map. Drawn

to reconstruct the exploded theory by asserting that the settlement of Vincennes was made by Juchereau in 1702. and a tablet giving this date ornaments the front of the Knox County court-house.[1]

This last absurdity appears to have originated with Mr. O. F. Baker, who claims to have found documents to support his statement, but who has never seen fit to produce them. There is no evidence whatever to support it, and there is an abundance of evidence totally disproving it. One of the objects of the founding of the post was to keep the English from the Mississippi, and it was recognized that the mouth of the Ohio was the only point where this could be done effectively. In a letter of November 10, 1701, the directors of the Canadian Company, pointing out the danger and proposing remedies, say: "These remedies are, Monseigneur, to establish certain posts on the routes, as at the Miamis, and at the River Ouabache, at the place where it discharges into the Mississippi; this river will serve as a boundary between this colony and that which is established on the Mississippi, for it is by it that one goes to Carolina and that the English come also to our lands."[2] In his memorial of 1702, quoted above, D'Iberville says that his plans "make it necessary to establish three posts on the Mississippi. One at the Arkansas, another at the Ouabache, and the third at the Missouri."[3] The loca-

A. D. 1687," but it has been revised to as late a date as 1720, as appears by such legends as "*Route de Mr. Denis en* 1716," "*Natchitoches, atablissement Français, fait en* 1717 *par Mr. Quachois,*" and half a dozen similar instances of post-dating.

[1] *Hist. Atlas of Ind.*, p. 248 ; Potter's *Am. Mo.* vol. xii. p. 165 ; *Hist. Knox Co.* p. 15.

[2] *Margry*, vol. v. pp. 178, 361.

[3] *Minn. Hist. Coll.*, vol. i. p. 343.

tion of the post is recorded, contemporaneously with its founding, in the Journal of La Harpe for 1703, as follows: "On the 8th February, a pirogue arrived from the Ouabache, and brought the news that M. de Juchereau, lieutenant-general of Montreal, had arrived there with thirty-five Canadians to form a settlement at its mouth, and to collect buffalo skins." [1] Juchereau died a few months later.[2] In 1704, war having broken out among the Indians, M. de Lambert, who commanded after Juchereau's death, abandoned the post and went to New Orleans. It was never reoccupied, and never mentioned afterwards except as a matter of history.[3]

The story of the controversy between Father Mermet and the Mascoutin medicine-men is also recorded by Father Charlevoix, who made his voyage down the Mississippi in 1721. He says: "The labors among the Mascoutins met with less success. The Sieur Juchereau, a Canadian gentleman, had begun a post at the mouth of the Ohio, which empties into the Micissipi, constituting the shortest and most convenient communication between Canada and Louisiana, and a great many of the Indians had settled there. To retain them he had persuaded Father Mermet, one of the Illinois missionaries, to endeavor to gain them to Christ; but that missionary found an indocile tribe, excessively superstitious, despotically ruled by medicine-men." [4] It has also been stated

[1] French's *Hist. Coll. of La.*, pt. 3, p. 29; *N. Y. Col. Docs.*, vol. ix. p. 487.

[2] Margry, vol. v. p. 368.

[3] French's *Hist. Coll. of La.*, pt. 3, pp 32, 33, 116 note.

[4] Shea's *Charlevoix*, vol. v. p. 133. The original words as to the location are: "Le Sieur JUCHEREAU, Gentilhome Canadien, avoit commencé un Etablissement a l'entrée de la Rivière *Ouabache*, qui se décharge dans le Micisipi, & fait la communication la

that Juchereau left a garrison at Vincennes as he went
down the Wabash, and afterwards located his principal
post at the mouth of the Ohio. This, too, is bald assertion. Juchereau did not come down the Wabash. He
went by Lake Michigan and the Wisconsin River to the
Mississippi. He was met at the mouth of the Wisconsin
by Le Sueur, who had been exploring the upper country,
and the two journeyed together down the Mississippi.[1]
Although the Indian tribes were returning to the Wabash about the year 1702, and though white traders may
have accompanied them, Sieur Juchereau had nothing to
do with our territory or our settlements. He belongs to
Illinois. Our posts were founded after he was buried
and probably after he was forgotten.

plus courte et la plus commode du Canada avec la Louisiane."
Paris ed. of 1744, Tome 2, p. 266. The anecdote follows, as related by Father Marest.

[1] Margry, vol. v. p. 426.

CHAPTER II.

THE history of the eastern portion of the Mississippi valley during the eighteenth century is in the main a history of a series of Indian wars, and yet these were wars in which the Indians had little real interest. Those of the first two-thirds of the century were caused by the giant struggles of England and France over the political questions of Europe. Those of the latter part of the century grew out of the American determination to be independent, and to control the lands south of the great lakes. In the earlier period some minister would pen a few lines in his luxurious chambers beyond the Atlantic ; a few weeks later some commandant in the depths of the American wilderness would assemble the neighboring tribes, give them some powder, some blankets, and some rum, and inform them that the Great French Father, or the Great English Father, had dug up the tomahawk, and now directed them to strike it in the heads of his enemies ; after another interval the night would be lightened by burning wigwams or frontier cabins, and the forests would resound with the shrieks of dying women and children. This would be but a beginning. Weeks might pass, or months, or years, but the day of retaliation would come, and the conquering tribe would see its villages destroyed, its fields laid waste, its warriors burned at the stake or boiled and

eaten, its women and children slain or carried captive.
And what cared the great people of Europe? Basta!
A few Indians more or less amounted to nothing. There
were plenty more of them.

The intervals between wars were the seasons of advance on the frontiers of America. Then settlements
were formed, governments were established, trade and
production flourished. Such an epoch came with the
treaty of Ryswick in 1697. Louis XIV. renewed his
exertions to carry into effect the great plan of opening
the Mississippi valley which La Salle had begun so
bravely. D'Iberville was sent to form a settlement at
the mouth of the Mississippi, and founded Biloxi. His
plan for concentrating the northwestern tribes on the
Ohio was not successful, but it had a permanent effect
on the population of the region. The Mascoutins who
came to Juchereau's post went away in a few years, but
the Kaskaskias, who left their old home on the Illinois
in 1700 and went to the site of the present town of Kaskaskia, held to their new location.[1] At the same time
the Hurons, Miamis, Ouiatanons, and other tribes, partly
because they had become involved in war with the great
Illinois nation, but chiefly in compliance with the urging
of French officers, began straggling eastward through
southern Michigan and northern Indiana. The colony
and the great confederation of La Salle were no more.
During this period also the French posts along the line
of communication between Louisiana and Canada were
repaired and strengthened. In 1700 the British Lords
of Trade declared that France had fifteen hundred men
constantly employed in this work.[2]

[1] *Kaskaskia and its Parish Records*, p. 5.
[2] *N. Y. Col. Docs.*, vol. iv. p. 701.

The English watched the movements of the French with jealousy, both because they claimed that their colonies included all of the territory south of the great lakes indefinitely to the westward, and because their merchants were desirous of obtaining the Indian trade of this region for themselves. In 1700 Robert Livingston, Colonial Secretary of Indian Affairs, urged "that all endeavors be used to obtain a peace between the 5 Nations and the Dowaganhaas [Outagamies or Foxes], Twichtwicks [Miamis], and other far Nations of Indians, whom the Governour of Canada stirs up to destroy them, not only because the 5 Nations have been mortall enemies to the French & true to the English, but because they hinder his trade with the said far Nations, trucking with them themselves and bringing the bevers hither. The best way to effect this is to build a fort at Wawyachtenoke,[1] cal'd by the French De Troett. . . . Hither all the far Nations will come and trade, to wit, the Twichtwicks, Kichtages [Illinois], Wawyachtenokes, and Showonoes, and a multitude of other Nations, some whereof live behind Carolina, Roanoke, Caratuck, &c., leaving the Ottawawes, Dionondadoes [a tribe of Hurons] and those other Nations that live to the North side of the Ottowawa Lake to the French."[2]   On January 16, 1701, the Earl of Bellomont, commanding in Massachusetts, New York, and New Hampshire, to whom this report was addressed, wrote to the Lords of Trade, declaring his intention " to ingage the Dowaganhaas, Twichtwicks, Dienondades and all those numerous nations in a

---

[1] Ouiatanon.   This name may indicate a former location of the Ouiatanons in the neighborhood of Detroit.   On Franquelin's map of 1688, Lake St. Clair is named *Oiatinon-chikebo.*

[2] *N. Y. Col. Docs.,* vol. iv. p. 650.

trade with us, which the French by their missionaries have at present monopoliz'd." [1]   The French, however, anticipated this projected settlement. Sieur de Lamothe Cadillac had been in command of the Mackinaw post for several years, and had become thoroughly acquainted with the northwestern country.   In his relation of 1695 he says, after describing the Indian locations to the west of Lake Michigan : "The post of Chicagou comes next. The word signifies the River of Garlic, because a very great quantity of it is produced naturally there without any cultivation.   There is here a village of the Miamis, who are well-made men ; they are good warriors and extremely active. . . . We find next the river of St. Joseph.   There was here a fort with a French garrison, and there is a village of this same nation of Miamis. This post is the key to all the nations which border the north of Lake Michigan, for to the south there is not any village on account of the incursions of the Iroquois, but in the depths of the north coast country and looking towards the west there are many, as the Mascoutins, Piankeshaws, Peorias, Kickapoos, Iowas, Sioux and Tintons." [2]   Seeing this vacant country to the southeast of Lake Michigan, Lamothe Cadillac conceived the idea of securing it by a post at Detroit, and, after obtaining approval of his plan, carried it into effect in 1701.

With this protection guaranteed, the expatriated tribes began moving still farther to the east.   In a council at Albany, on July 10, 1702, a Huron chief said : "The greater part of ye Dionondes and many of ye Twictwighs are removed and come to live at Tjughsaghrondie, hard

----

[1] *N. Y. Col. Docs.*, vol. iv. p. 834.

[2] Margry, vol. v. pp. 123, 124.

by the Fort which ye French built last summer." [1] On
La Hontan's map of 1703, a village of Ouiatanons is
marked near Detroit; one of Saukies on Saginaw Bay;
two of Hurons on the lower eastern shore of Lake
Huron; one each of Miamis, Mascoutins, and Ouiatanons on the St. Joseph's of Lake Michigan.[2] The
movement towards the east continued for ten or fifteen
years. In 1712 the Miamis were on the Wabash and
the Maumee, and the other tribes were grouped about
Detroit. In that year the Mascoutins, under British
influence, tried to capture the fort at that point, but
Dubuisson, reinforced by M. de Vincennes with eight
men, held them at bay until the friendly Indians arrived,
and after twenty-three days of fighting and massacre the
living Mascoutins were in hot flight, leaving a thousand
dead behind them.[3] The little remnant united with the
Kickapoos, and in the course of years became wholly
lost in that tribe. By 1718 the Miamis, Pepikokias,
Piankeshaws, and Ouiatanons had taken substantially
the locations they afterwards held in Indiana.[4]

With the founding of Detroit came the war of the
Spanish succession, which diverted the attention of the
European powers from their American possessions and
stopped the advance of colonization for a season. The

---

[1] *N. Y. Col. Docs.*, vol. iv. p. 979. Tjughsaghrondie was the
Iroquois name of Detroit. Ibid. p. 982; Beckwith's *Notes on the
N. W.* p. 120.

[2] These of course are locations of 1701, 1702, as the map appeared in the *Nouveaux Voyages* published in Europe in 1703.

[3] Dubuisson's "Journal of the Siege of Detroit," in Smith's
Wisconsin, vol. ii. p. 315.

[4] *N. Y. Col. Docs.*, vol. ix. pp. 885–892. This is partially
quoted in Dillon, p. 401, in Beckwith's *Hist. Notes*, pp. 103, 104,
and in other local histories.

war closed with the treaty of Utrecht, on April 11, 1713, but France and England had entered into secret negotiations in the spring of 1712 which practically insured peace,[1] and therefore resumed operations in America before the war formally closed. In September, 1712, the king of France gave to Anthony Crozat the control of the Mississippi valley " from the edge of the sea as far as the Illinois ; together with the river of St. Phillip, heretofore called the Missouri, and of St. Jerome, heretofore called Ouabache," and the country adjacent. The territory north of the Illinois was made part of New France, or Canada, and the government of Louisiana was made dependent on that of New France. Crozat's management of his province was energetic, but it was so wholly directed to the lower Mississippi that our territory was left unnoticed, with one slight exception. Coincident with the insurrection of the Chevalier St. George in England, there was a marked activity of the English on the American frontiers which caused alarming reports from the French officers and missionaries.[2] On this account Bienville was sent up the Mississippi in 1716 with instructions to establish one post at the Natchez and another at the Ohio. Becoming involved in difficulty with the Natchez Indians, he accomplished nothing but the establishment of Fort Rosalie in their vicinity.[3] In 1717 Crozat surrendered his charter, and in August of that year the commerce of the Mississippi valley was granted to the Company of the Occident. In September all of the Illinois country was added to Louisiana for

---

[1] Guizot's *England*, vol. iv. p. 120.

[2] *N. Y. Col. Docs.*, vol. ix. p. 931 ; French's *Hist. Coll. of La.*, pt. 3, p. 43 ; Margry, vol. v. p. 509.

[3] French's *Hist. Coll. of La.*, pt. 3, pp. 45, 46, 241–252.

governmental purposes,[1] and Bienville was put in control of the province. In 1718 he sent his cousin Pierre Dugué de Boisbriant, who had just returned from France with the appointment of Governor of Illinois, with one hundred men, to establish a post in the neighborhood of Kaskaskia, for the protection of the upper colony.[2] De Boisbriant selected a point about sixteen miles above Kaskaskia and began the erection of the fort. It was completed in 1720 and named Fort Chartres, in honor of the Duc de Chartres.[3]

During these same years a peculiar change was in progress on the Wabash on the Canada side, or rather in the portion claimed by Canada, for, although the grants to Crozat and the Company of the Occident included the entire Wabash, the governors of Canada claimed jurisdiction over the upper half of the river, because the tribes located there were dependent on Detroit; and though their claim was contested by the Louisiana officials, they exercised exclusive jurisdiction there from the earliest period. Having but a short time before induced the tribes to locate there, they were now equally anxious to induce their return to the west, because venturesome English traders were already coming to them, and English officials were soliciting their friendship through the eastern Indians. No one fort could prevent access to them by the English so long as they remained on the Maumee and the Wabash, for they could be reached from the Ohio by the well-known routes of the Muskingum, Scioto, Big Miami,[4] and Wa-

[1] Margry, vol. v. p. 589.
[2] *Ibid.* vol. v. pp. 553, 554.
[3] *Old Fort Chartres*, in Fergus Hist. Ser., No. 12.
[4] The Indian name of this stream was Assereniet, which the

bash; and the Ohio could be reached by any of its
southern tributaries.   The simplest solution of the matter, therefore, was to move the Indians.   The chief band
of the Miamis, or Twightwees, was located at the head
of the Maumee.   The Ouiatanons, who were on the Wabash, declined to remove because they were still at war
with the Illinois, and for this reason it was determined
to frustrate the schemes of the English by establishing a
post in their country.   The task of inducing the Miamis
to remove had been given to Sieur de Vincennes, who
had more influence with them than any other Frenchman.   He had almost succeeded in obtaining their consent when he was taken sick and died in their village of
Kekionga, and thereupon the Miamis refused to leave
that place.[1]   This necessitated a change of plans.   On
October 28, 1719, De Vaudreuil wrote to the Council of

French merely translated, calling it Rivière Pierreuse, or sometimes Rivière à la Roche.

[1] Kekionga is the commonly adopted form of the name.   It is
usually said to mean " blackberry patch," or " blackberry bush,"
this plant being considered an emblem of antiquity because it
sprang up on the sites of old villages.   This theory rests on the
statement of Barron, an old French trader on the Wabash.   It is
more probable that Kekionga is a corruption or dialect form of
Kiskakon, or Kikakon, which was the original name of the place.
Thus, in 1749, M. de Céleron urged the fugitive Miamis to return
to *Kiskakon*, "the place where repose the bones of your ancestors,
and those of M. de Vincennes whom you loved so well."   Margry,
vol. vi. p. 718.   The Kiskakons were the principal tribe of the
Ottawas or Pierced Noses, — the Nez Percés of the early French
chroniclers, — who lived on the Maumee at a very ancient time,
for which reason this stream was sometimes called Ottawa River.
(*Archeologica Americana*, vol. i. p. 278.)   The probability is, therefore, that the Kiskakons or Clipped Scalp-locks (Queues Coupées)
had a village at this point, and that their name attached to the
locality.   As to the Kiskakons, see Margry, vol. v. p. 80.

Marine : " I learn from the last letters that have arrived from the Miamis, that Sieur de Vincennes having died in their village, these Indians had resolved not to move to the river St. Joseph, and to remain where they are. As this resolution is very dangerous, on account of the facility they will have of communicating with the English who are incessantly distributing belts in secret among all the nations, to attract them to themselves, by means of certain Iroquois runners and others in their pay, I had designed Sieur Dubuisson for the command of the post of the Ouyatanons, and that he should, on going thither, employ his credit among the Miamis so as to determine that nation to proceed to the river St. Joseph, or, if not willing to leave, that he should remain at its place of residence in order to counteract the effect of all those belts it was but too frequently receiving, and which, as they caused eight or ten Miami canoes to go this year to trade at Orange [Albany], might finally induce all that nation to follow their example." [1]

This service of Dubuisson lasted but a short time, for François Morgan, a nephew of the late Sieur de Vincennes, who had succeeded to his title, was sent to fill his place with the Miamis, with whom he soon became as influential as his uncle had been.[2] The post of Oui-

[1] *N. Y. Col. Docs.*, vol. ix. p. 894.

[2] The fief of Vincennes was established in 1672. The Sieur de Vincennes who died in 1719 was Jean Baptiste Bissot, the son of the first holder of the fief. Clara Frances Bissot, one of his sisters, was the wife of Louis Joliet. Louise Bissot, another sister, married Seraphin Morgane, and her son François Morgane (he dropped the *e* final in writing his name) was the founder of Post Vincennes. The proper orthography of the name is Vincennes, though our founder usually wrote it Vinsenne, and others in divers ways. The fief passed to Joseph Roy in 1749 by judicial decree. *Actes*

atanon was then founded, as had been contemplated,
probably in the year 1720. It was the first military
post established on the Wabash, and probably the first
within the bounds of Indiana. Its location has been
universally misstated by historical writers, it being usually confounded with the Indian town of Ouiatanon,
which was on the opposite side of the Wabash and two
or three miles lower down. Post Ouiatanon was located
on the north bank of the Wabash, eighteen miles, by the
river, below the mouth of the Tippecanoe, and a short
distance above Indian Creek, which the French called
Rivière de Boisrouge. It was always a trading-post of
considerable consequence, but it attained its greatest
importance several years after its foundation, when the
Wabash became the principal line of communication
between Canada and Louisiana. On account of the
rapids near it, just below the city of Lafayette, it was
the head of navigation for pirogues and large canoes,
and consequently there was a transfer at this place of
all the merchandise that passed over the Wabash, from
the small canoes that were used between Ouiatanon and
Kekionga to the larger vessels used below Ouiatanon.
The fort stood about seventy yards from the river, and
consisted of a dozen cabins surrounded by a stockade.[1]

de Foy et Homage, vol. iv. p. 348 (Ottawa copy); Tanguay's
Dict. Geneal. The Sieurs de Vincennes must not be confounded
with the members of the St. Vincents family, of whom there were
two or three in the French service in the Northwest. *N. Y. Col.
Docs.*, vol. ix. p. 1010; vol. x. pp. 107, 109, 183.

[1] Hutchins's *Top. Desc.*, p. 30; Croghan's Journal, in Butler's
Ky., App., pp. 371–373; Itinerary of road from Detroit to the
Illinois, in Haldimand Coll., Canadian Archives; Letter of Governor Hamilton to General Haldimand, dated Ouiatanon, December 4, 1778, Canadian Archives; also maps of Thos. Hutchins

Jealous of this advance of the Canadians, and apprehensive of the approach of the English, the directors of the Mississippi Company (into which the Company of the Occident had merged), on September 15, 1720, called on the government to establish a post on the Ouabache, and place a company of troops there " to occupy first the entire country, and prevent the English from penetrating it." [1] The government did not act, but the desirability of such a post was continually urged by persons acquainted with the region. In November, 1721, Charlevoix explained its importance in a letter to the Duchess de Lesdiguieres.[2] In 1724, La Harpe warned the company 'of the danger of the English securing a foothold there.[3] On February 9, 1725, Dugué de Boisbriant wrote to the company : " It would have been very advantageous to establish a post on the Ouabache, but as until now they [*i. e.* the government] have not maintained that of the Illinois, there is little probability that they will undertake to establish this post. Meanwhile it is much to be feared that the English will take possession of it, and this would entirely ruin the Upper Colony, because it would be easy for them, with the prodigious quantities of merchandise which they ordinarily

(1778), John Carey (1783), Brion de la Tour (1784), D'Anville (1772), A. Arrowsmith (1804), Joseph Bouchette (1815), and John Melish (1812). An extended discussion of the location of Ouiatanon, in which nearly all the authorities are quoted, will be found in the *Lafayette Call*, February 24, March 3, March 7, March 11, March 24, 1887 ; *Crawfordsville Journal*, March 9, March 16, March 23, 1887 ; *Indianapolis Journal*, March 12, March 25, March 26, 1887.

[1] Margry, vol. v. p. 624.
[2] French's *Hist. Coll. of La.*, pt. 3, p. 123.
[3] *Ibid.*, pt. 3, p. 114, note.

carry, to win all of the Indians of this region. The
company will have the goodness to consider this." [1]
On receiving this, the company concluded that it could
not with safety to its trade wait longer on the government, and therefore directed De Boisbriant to establish
the post at the company's expense. On December 22,
1725, they wrote to him : "It would be well for you to
write to M. de Vincennes, who is at the Miamis, to ask
him to come to an understanding with the commandant
of the Ouabache [*i. e.* the post to be established] in regard to the Indian nation where he commands, and to
advise him of the enterprises which the English may
undertake in that quarter. The company will entreat
Monseigneur the Count de Maurepas to be pleased to
give orders in Canada by the first vessels that leave for
Quebec, in order that the Sieur de Vincennes may be
directed to act in conformity, and that all the other
officers located with the Indian nations of the government of Canada, who are within reach of the Ouabache,
shall protect in every way they can the post which the
company will establish there, and concert with him who
shall command there to expel the English who may be
able to penetrate towards this river." [2]

Soon after this letter was dispatched more alarming
information of English encroachments was received
from Louisiana, and through the Canadian authorities
came the report of Sieur de Longueil, under date of
October 31, 1725, that "the English of Carolina had
built two houses and some stores on a little river which
flows into the Ouabache, where they trade with the
Miamis, the Ouyatanons, and other Indians of the Up-

---

[1] Margry, vol. vi. p. 657.
[2] *Ibid.*, vol. vi. p. 658.

per Country." [1] In the summer of 1726 the directors learned that their post was not yet established, and on September 30, 1726, wrote to M. Périer, who had just succeeded Bienville as Governor of Louisiana, as follows : " The Company has ordered the establishment of a post on the river Ouabache, and has requested M. the Governor of Canada, on his part, to direct Sieur de Vincennes, who commands at the home of the Ouyatanons-Miamis, established towards the head of the Ouabache, to come to an understanding with the commandant of the new post to bring this nation nearer, as much to protect the post as to watch the actions of the English and to expel them in case they approach.

" M. Périer will see by the copies, annexed, of the letter written to M. de Boisbriant and of the memoir delivered to M. the Count de Beauharnois, what the Company has thought proper to be done in this matter. M. de Boisbriant writes in reply that the lack of goods has prevented him from proceeding to the establishment of the said post, and that he thinks it necessary to give command of it to M. de Vincennes, who is already a half-pay lieutenant of the Louisiana infantry, and who can do more with the Miamis than any one else.

"On the other hand, the Company learns from M. Desliettes, commandant at the Illinois,[2] that M. de Vincennes had come to find him to tell him that he had information that the English had already formed an establishment on the upper part of the river Ohio ; and that he had sent Sieur de Vincennes back with presents

---

[1] *N. Y. Col. Docs.*, vol. ix. p. 953.

[2] Desliettes succeeded De Boisbriant when Bienville was displaced. In 1733 he was succeeded by Jean St. Ange de Belle Rive, who gave place the next year to Pierre d'Artaguiette.

for the Indians, ordering him to ascertain the truth of
this report. If it should be confirmed, there will not be
a moment to lose in causing the lower part of the river
Ohio [*i. e.* the Ohio above the mouth of the Wabash] to
be occupied by the Ouyatanons; and he should then
establish the fort about the mouth of the Casquinam-
boux [Tennessee], placing there as commander an
officer who will get along with M. de Vincennes, whom
it will not be well to remove from the home of the
Ouyatanons if you are to get the usefulness from them
that is hoped for. M. Périer will reflect well on this
subject, and consider if, by giving eight or ten soldiers to
the said Sieur de Vincennes, with the missionary des-
tined for the Ouabache, he will not find himself in condition to assure, by the Indians, the communication
between Louisiana and Canada, and to prevent the
English from penetrating into our colony, without obliging the Company to construct a fort on the lower Ouabache, of which the expense of the establishment and
the support of the garrison make an object of consequence.

" To induce Sieur de Vincennes to attach himself to
the colony of Louisiana, M. Périer will advise him that
he has obtained for him from the Company an annuity
of three hundred livres, which will be paid to him with
his salary as half-pay lieutenant." [1]

No direct record of the founding of the post has yet
been discovered, but it was unquestionably as outlined
in the latter part of these instructions. The report that
the English had founded a post on the Ohio was erroneous; and Périer had had sufficient experience in Louisiana to avoid any unnecessary expense to the company.

[1] Margry, vol. vi. pp. 659, 660.

Vincennes was won over from Canada to Louisiana, and with a few soldiers proceeded to build a little palisade fort at the Indian village lowest on the river and nearest the English, which was the Piankeshaw town of Chippecoke or Chipkawkay. The exact date of the establishment is not known, but it was probably in 1727, for in October of that year the names of "Vinsenne" and "St. Ange *fils*," his lieutenant, were inscribed on the parish records of Kaskaskia in witness of the marriage of Joseph Lorrin and Marie Phillipe.[1] The next known documentary trace of M. de Vincennes is in a deed by him and his wife, dated January 5, 1735, and recorded at Kaskaskia.[2] In this he is styled *commandant au poste du Ouabache.* His wife, who was at the post at the time, was the daughter of Philip Longprie, then the wealthiest trader at Kaskaskia. The date of their marriage cannot be given, as there is a gap in the Kaskaskia marriage record from June 7, 1729, to January 3, 1741, but it was probably in 1733, as in that year is dated the acknowledgment by Vincennes of the receipt of 100 pistoles given by his father-in-law as dowry.[3] Possibly it was due to the influence of Madame Morgan that the loneliness of the little post was relieved by the settlement of a number of families about it, for this occurred in 1734-5, and so the first permanent European village was established within our borders.[4]

In presenting the evidences that Post Ouiatanon was founded about the year 1720, and Post Vincennes in

[1] *Kaskaskia and its Parish Records*, p. 15; *Mich. Pion. Coll.*, vol. v. p. 104.

[2] Law's *Vincennes*, p. 19.

[3] *Ibid.*, pp. 19, 20.

[4] *Vincennes Sun*, March 16, 1822.

1727, we have used only the affirmative testimony of
French official documents. There is, however, a mass
of negative testimony in these documents which clearly
limits the foundation of Vincennes to the period from
1724 to 1731. Considering how great collections of
documentary history of the Mississippi valley have been
made of recent years, the total failure to find any mention of a post before a certain date, or any indication of
it on any map, is very strong evidence that there was no
such post until that date. Of especial weight are a
number of documents which purport to give exhaustive
accounts of all posts and settlements and yet make no
mention of our posts. On the Louisiana side we have
the Journal of La Harpe and the Relation of Penicaut
giving very full accounts of all occurrences in Louisiana, including the Illinois and Ouabache countries, from
1698 to 1722, but in neither of them is there any mention of a post or settlement that could possibly be Vincennes. In the Canadian documents there is no mention
of the Ouiatanon post before the one of 1719 quoted
above; nor is there any intimation of the existence of
any other post on the Ouabache until 1731-2, when
Beauharnois went beyond his territorial jurisdiction in
giving directions to guard against the approach of the
English.[1] In the Canadian papers and in the British
papers, which show an almost equal knowledge of the
country, although there are lengthy descriptions of the
Wabash country in 1718 and 1719, there is no mention
of any post or settlement on the Wabash.[2]

Recurring to the testimony of tradition, it will be
remembered that four years — 1680, 1702, 1716, and

---

[1] *N. Y. Col. Docs.*, vol. ix. pp. 1027, 1035.
[2] *Ibid.*, vol. ix. pp. 885, 892; *Ibid.* vol. v. pp. 620–621.

1735 — have been given by various authors as the date
of the founding of Vincennes. The first, which so
eminent an authority as Thomas H. Benton asserted
positively in the Senate of the United States to be the
correct date,[1] evidently had its origin in the exploration
of the region by La Salle. The second has been adopted
chiefly on account of confounding Vincennes with Juchereau's post at the mouth of the Ohio. The third would
not, perhaps, have been suggested by Mr. Bancroft if he
had reflected that at that time the French were trying to
induce the Indians to leave the Wabash; and that the
line of communication which they were then commonly
using, and which in fact they then strengthened, was the
Mississippi and Illinois rivers route. The date 1735,
which Volney and others following him adopted, had its
source in the first arrival of families in that year. Although this variegation of error shows that tradition is
a very unreliable guide, there is still a satisfaction in
knowing that the conclusions which we have reached are
confirmed by the oldest known traditions, for there were
records of traditions before Volney visited Vincennes.
General Harmar was sent there in 1787 by the United
States authorities, and in his letter to the Secretary of
War, dated August 7, 1787, he says of the post:
"Monsieur Vincennes, the French officer from whom it
derives its name, I am informed, was here and commenced the settlement sixty years ago."[2] This places
the foundation of the post exactly in 1727. Major
Ebenezer Denny, who accompanied Harmar, is not so
exact, but is sufficiently so to bar all the earlier dates.
He says: "It was first settled by a Monsieur Vincennes

---

[1] *Cong. Globe*, 2d Sess. 28th Cong. p. 80.
[2] *St. Clair Papers*, vol. ii. p. 27.

near 70 years ago, from whom it takes its name." [1]   Colonel Croghan, who was carried prisoner up the Wabash
in 1765, does not give the date of the settlements, but he
says that Post Ouiatanon "was the first on the Ouabache." [2]   This statement is of more weight than ordinary tradition, for Croghan had then been engaged for
at least fifteen years in trade with the Miamis, and during much of this time he was acting as an agent of the
British officials, in which service he would naturally
make careful inquiries as to French establishments in
territory claimed by the English.

Post Vincennes, from its foundation to the close of
the French occupation, was included in the District of
Illinois, in the Province or Colony of Louisiana.   Fort
Chartres was the seat of government of the District,
and New Orleans of the Province.   Post Ouiatanon and
Fort Miamis belonged to Canada, and were under control of the commandant at Detroit.   The dividing line
between Louisiana and Canada was not very well ascertained, and, as Du Pratz says, " It is of little importance
to dispute here about the limits of these two neighboring colonies, as they both appertain to France." [3]   The
boundary limit on the Wabash, however, was fixed at an
early day, probably soon after the Mississippi Company
surrendered its charter, in 1732, at the site of the city
of Terre Haute.   This locality was always called *Terre
Haute* by the French, and the English, by an enlarged
translation, called it " the Highlands of the Wabash." [4]

[1] Denny's Journal in *Penn. Hist. Soc. Publications,* p. 311.

[2] Butler's *Ky.,* App. p. 373.

[3] *Hist. of La.,* Lond. ed. of 1774, p. 181.

[4] *Western Sun,* November 9, 1811; Itinerary from Detroit to
the Illinois, in Haldimand Coll., *Can. Archives.*

In 1736 came a call to arms on the Louisiana side. A part of the Natchez Indians, after their defeat and dispersion by the French, had taken refuge with the Chickasaws, who, urged on by English traders, also committed some acts of hostility. Bienville, who had been reappointed Governor of Louisiana in 1733, determined to crush them. He repelled all proposals for peace, and ordered the forces of Illinois to unite with him in the Chickasaw country. D'Artaguiette departed from Fort Chartres in February, 1736, with the greater part of his garrison, a company of volunteers from the villages, and a large band of Illinois Indians. Vincennes met him at the mouth of the Ohio with his little garrison, forty Iroquois, and a number of the Wabash Indians. They reached the rendezvous, but the New Orleans troops had not arrived, and the Army of the Illinois was almost out of provisions. A council of war was held, and it was determined to attack an isolated village of about thirty cabins, which it was supposed could be easily taken. The cabins of the Chickasaws were made with mud walls, a foot or more in thickness, and had thick roofs of mud plastered over a framework of sticks. They were usually surrounded by palisades. In such a village the forces of D'Artaguiette could have defended themselves against the Chickasaws, and there, probably, they would have found enough provisions to supply them until the arrival of Bienville. The attack was made with spirit, but scarcely was it begun when a force of five hundred Indians and thirty Englishmen swept down on the flank of the attacking party from behind a little hill. The Indian allies of the French fled, except the Iroquois and twenty-eight Arkansas, who had joined them on the Mississippi, and the French were overwhelmed with terrible slaughter. Lieutenant St. Ange was the first to fall, and Vincennes soon followed him. D'Artaguiette and fifteen others were captured and burned at the stake.[1] Charlevoix tells us that, "Vincennes ceased not until his last breath to exhort the men to behave worthy of their religion and their country." Be that his epitaph ; and be it a matter of pride to Indiana that her first ruler was so brave a man and so true.

His successor also was a man of merit. Soon after the Chickasaw campaign, Jean St. Ange de Belle Rive, the former commandant of Fort Chartres, made a petition to Bienville reciting his service to the king of more than fifty years, the death of his son Pierre Grosson St. Ange in the late disastrous battle, and the vacancy of a half-pay lieutenancy by the death of Sieur de Vincennes ; he asked "this advancement for the son who remains to him, now commanding a post on the Missouri."[2] Bienville favored the request, and the king granted the promotion. This second son, Louis St. Ange, had already been appointed to the command of Post Vincennes.[3] His occupancy lasted through the French possession of the country. In a certificate made by him on August 30, 1773, he says that he "commanded at Poste Vincesnes in the name of His Most Christian Majesty, with a garrison of regular troops, from the year 1736 until the year 1764, and that my first commission as commandant of the said post was from His

[1] Gayarré's *La.*, vol. i. pp. 485–489; *Old Fort Chartres*, pp. 29, 30.

[2] Margry, vol. vi. p. 448, note.

[3] His order to take command of the post was dated July 1, 1736; his commission as *lieutenant réformé* was dated October 16, 1736. *Mag. of West. Hist.*, vol. ii. p. 64.

Most Christian Majesty under the government of M. de Bienville, Governor General of 'Louisiana in the said year 1736 ; that thereafter I was continued under the government of Messieurs de Vaudreuille, de Kerlerec, and D'Abadie, successors one to another in the said government, until the said year 1764 ; . . . that further, the said post was established a number of years before my command, under that of M. de Vincesne, officer of the troops, whom I succeeded by order of the king." [1]

It should be noted here that the name of Vincennes does not appear to have attached to the post for a long time after its establishment. The oldest known reference to it by that name was in 1752.[2] The first mention of the post, in the deed of Vincennes above referred to, is in the indefinite term "*poste du Ouabache.*" This, or simply the "*poste,*" was the most common name for it, and from the French phrase *au poste* the early American settlers commonly wrote the name Opost. There were, however, other names for the place in early times. In the order to St. Ange to take command, it is designated as "the post of Pianguichats," referring of course to its location among the Piankeshaws.[3] On many of the English maps of the last century the only indications of any posts or settlements on the Wabash are at two points, the upper one marked " G. Wiaut," and the lower one " L. Wiaut." An explanation of this is found in a report of Lieutenant Fraser, who visited the country during Pontiac's war. He says the French had " two forts on the Ouabach ; the one called the great Ouiachtonon was dependant on Canada, and the other

[1] Haldimand Coll., *Can. Archives.*

[2] *N. Y. Col. Docs.*, vol. x. pp. 248, 249.

[3] *Mag. of West. Hist.*, vol. ii. p. 64.

at little Ouiachtonon or St. Vincent dependant on Orleans."[1]   Post Vincennes also occasionally took name
from M. St. Ange, but in these cases it was generally corrupted to Ft. St. Anne or Ft. Anne.   These are found
chiefly on French maps.   Some map-makers, misled by
the various names, have placed on their maps as many
posts as there were names.

The greater portion of St. Ange's rule was a quiet,
hum-drum period for the little post of Vincennes, as
also for Ouiatanon and Fort Miamis.   The great conflicts in other portions of the Mississippi valley seldom
reached the Wabash, and when they did they touched
it but lightly.   The inhabitants devoted their attention
to agriculture and the fur trade, and lived in quiet and
happiness.   Much of their peaceful prosperity was due
to St. Ange.   He was not an educated man, for the
unsettled life of his father in the frontier service had
given him no opportunities for instruction.   Pierre Chouteau, the elder, who knew him well, deposed that " he
could not write well, but that he could sign his name."[2]
He was, however, a discreet officer and a wise ruler.
That he always possessed the affection and confidence
of the people of the Wabash, the Illinois, and the Mississippi is unquestionable.   Tradition describes him as
prudent, pacific, generous, and philanthropic.   All of
the existing documentary evidence confirms this estimate, while his promotion to a half-pay captaincy in
1738,[3] and his long continuance in office at Vincennes,
show that his administration was satisfactory to his
superiors as well as to the people.   In marked contrast

[1] Report dated Pensacola, May 4, 1766, in *Can. Archives.*
[2] Admrs. of Wright *v.* Thomas, 4 Mo. 577.
[3] *Mag. of West. Hist.*, vol. ii. p. 64.

with his term at Vincennes was the frequent changing
of his superiors, the commandants at Fort Chartres.
D'Artaguiette, the victim of the Chickasaws, was succeeded by Alphonse de la Buissonière, who remained in
command for four years ; and he by Captain Benoist St.
Claire, who two years later gave place to the Chevalier
de Bertel. This officer held through the period of the
War of the Austrian Succession ; and at the close of the
forties Benoist St. Claire again took command and held
until the arrival of the Chevalier de Makarty, the re-
builder of Fort Chartres, in 1751. After the battle of
Fort Du Quesne, Makarty was succeeded by Neyon de
Villiers, who was the last appointed French governor of
the District of Illinois.[1]

During this period the only Indians in Indiana lived
along the Wabash and to the north of it. There were
no villages and no resident tribes to the south of the
Wabash valley. The Shawnees moved to the east —
nearly all of them to within the present bounds of Pennsylvania — in 1697, and did not begin the movement to
the west for more than thirty years. None of them
relocated in Indiana until 1745, and the greater number
of them at a much later period. The Delawares were
eastern Indians. Our tribes called them *Elanabah*, or
People from the Sunrise. Portions of their tribes were
straggling westward all through the French occupation,
but their great migration from Pennsylvania was between the years 1763 and 1768. The Wabash Indians
and the Miamis of the Maumee lived in most amicable
relations with the French until 1747, the only trouble
before that time being a drunken affray between some

[1] *Old Ft. Chartres*, pp. 30-37.

Ouiatanon youths and two or three voyageurs.[1] Belts
were sent to them occasionally by the English, and they
had not a little clandestine trade through the Ohio valley with the enterprising traders of Pennsylvania and
Virginia.   The French were unable to prevent this, for
the English paid twice as much for skins as they did,
and were also liberal in presents, hoping thereby to secure the trade.   About the year 1745 a band of Hurons,
under a war chief named Nicholas, settled at Sandusky
Bay, where they were visited by English traders and won
to the English side.   With much finesse Nicholas stirred
up feeling against the French, and arranged a conspiracy
of portions of nearly all the tribes except the Illinois,
under which, on one of the holidays of Pentecost, 1747,
each tribe was to strike the French nearest it, and so
exterminate all who were in the country.   The plot was
discovered and largely thwarted by Chevalier de Lon-
gueuil, then commanding at Detroit, though numerous
depredations were committed.[2]   The most effective blow
was struck at Fort Miamis.   Ensign Douville, who commanded there, had gone on a visit to Montreal with
Coldfoot and the Hedgehog, two of the most reliable
Miami chiefs, when the plot ripened.   The hostile Miamis took the fort by surprise and burned it to the ground.
The eight men who formed the garrison were captured,
but afterwards released.[3]   Governor de la Galissonière,
of Canada, sent troops to the relief of the western posts,
but before they arrived the hostile tribes were all begging for peace or fleeing to the wilderness.   Kekionga
was abandoned.   Part of the Miamis, under a chief

---

[1] *N. Y. Col. Docs.*, vol. ix. pp. 1050, 1051.
[2] *Ibid.*, vol. x. pp. 114, 115, 119.
[3] *Ibid.*, vol. x. p. 140.

called La Demoiselle, located on the Big Miami, and
the remainder established a village on a small tributary
of the Ohio called White River.[1] In December Nicholas
and others were at Detroit, suing for peace, and La
Demoiselle promised to return to Kekionga, but he did
not do so.

The fort was rebuilt by Sieur Dubuisson soon after
its destruction, and through the influence of Coldfoot a
part of the Miamis on White River were induced to return. The others did nothing but promise and break
their promises. In 1748 the fugitive Miamis sent deputies to Lancaster, Penn., and entered into a treaty of
alliance with the English.[2] They traded with the English continuously thereafter, and from them the English
influence soon spread to the Ouiatanons and Piankeshaws. In 1749 M. de Celoron made his famous expedition down the Allegheny and Ohio, holding councils
with the tribes and depositing, at important points, lead
plates on which were inscribed the reëntry of the French
to possession of the Ohio valley.[3] He returned by way
of the Big Miami, reaching La Demoiselle's village on
September 13, 1749. Here he held councils for two
days, urging the Miamis to return to " Kiskakon, which
is the name of their old village." La Demoiselle and

---

[1] Rivière Blanche. It was probably what is now called White
Oak Creek, in Brown County, Ohio. Map in *Mag. of West. Hist.*,
vol. ii. p. 130; Margry, vol. vi. p. 714.

[2] *Penn. Archives*, vol. ii. pp. 9, 11.

[3] One of these plates was brought to Sir William Johnson by
the Senecas in 1750. *N. Y. Col. Docs.*, vol. vi. pp. 608, 611.
Another was found at the mouth of the Muskingum in 1798.
Archeologica Americana, vol. ii. p. 537; Hildreth's *Pion. Hist. of
the Ohio Valley*, p. 20. A third was found at the mouth of the
Kanawha in 1846. *Mag. of Am. Hist.*, vol. ii. p. 145.

his people promised surely to return in the following spring, and De Celoron proceeded on his way to Fort Miamis in high spirits. At this point he met Coldfoot and informed him of what had passed. That sagacious chief replied: " I would that I were deceived, but I am sufficiently attached to the French to tell them that La Demoiselle lies. My sole regret is to be the only one who loves you, and to see all the tribes to the south drawn away from the French." [1] He was right. La Demoiselle had no intention of returning. In the fall of 1750 he gave the English traders permission to build a fort at his town of Pickawillany, at the mouth of Loramie's Creek, and they erected one at once. This fort thenceforward served as a refuge for deserters from the French posts, as well as for a trading-place.

The disaffection of the Wabash Indians increased rapidly, and within a year they began open warfare. Early in the autumn of 1751 La Demoiselle's Indians killed two Frenchmen belonging to the Kekionga post, and sold their scalps to the English. On October 19, the Piankeshaws killed two Frenchmen below Vincennes; and two days later they killed two slaves in sight of the post. St. Ange at once put the place in condition for defense, and notified De Ligneris, who commanded at Ouiatanon, "to use all means to protect himself from the storm which is ready to burst on the French." At Christmas five more Frenchmen were killed by the Piankeshaws at the Vermillion.[2] Early in 1752 the French influence was more seriously weakened. Coldfoot and a part of his Indians had gone to White River to endeavor to induce Baril's band to return, and

[1] Margry, vol. vi. pp. 716-723.
[2] *N. Y. Col. Docs.*, vol. x. pp. 247-249.

had them in preparation for doing so, when small-pox broke out among them with disastrous effect. Coldfoot and his son died of it, as did also Le Gris, the chief of the Tepicon band, who had always been a good friend to the French.[1] The French now concluded that per-

---

[1] *N. Y. Col. Docs.*, vol. x. p. 246. The existence of a band cf Miamis called Tepicons suggests a meaning for Tippecanoe whose import is as yet very uncertain. The full name of the town at the mouth of the Tippecanoe River was *Keth-tip-pe-can-nunk*. This is rendered by some "the place of the great clearing," from *Keth* or *Kehti*, meaning "great," *tippena*, "open," "clear," and *nunk*, the terminal locative. I should think a more reasonable translation would be "the great place of the Tepicons," or "the great place on the Tepicon River," as old translations indicate that the stream took name from the tribe; thus "River de Thopicanos" on Hutchins's map, and "River Trippecans" in the Haldimand itinerary. Usually the name is said to refer to some fish found in the stream. Barron, the old trader, gave the meaning to Hon. C. B. Lasselle as "Catfish River." Flint says it is "from a kind of pike called *Pic-ca-nau* by the savages." *Geog. and Hist. of West. States*, vol. ii. p. 125. Judge Beckwith insists on having it from "*Ke-non-ge* or *Ke-no-zha*, meaning the longbilled or wall-eyed pike." (*Hist. Notes on the N. W.*, p. 218, *n.*; *Ind. Geol. Rept.* 1882, p. 39.) The following very plausible conjecture is furnished to me by Rev. Joseph Anderson, of Waterbury, Conn.: "I think the name is substantially identical with Tuppeek-hanna, one of the sources of the Little Lehigh in Pennsylvania. *Hanna*, in composition, occurs in most of the Algonquin languages as meaning a rapidly flowing stream. *Thupeek* (tuppik) is given in Zeisberger as meaning a well or spring; and Heckewelder, in his essay on Indian names, translates *Tuppeek-hanna* as meaning 'the stream that flows from a large spring,' — Big Spring River." The Tippecanoe might very appropriately bear this name, for it is peculiarly a river of springs; and the possibility of the name coming from the Delawares is heightened by the fact that there is no known reference to the stream by that name prior to the British occupation. The *Topicanich* of Dubuisson's *Journal of the Siege of Detroit* was a locality on the upper

suasion was useless, and an expedition against the Pickawillany town was ordered, with instructions that "two
of the chiefs are to have no mercy," but that the others
would be pardoned if they submitted.[1] On the morning
of June 21, 1752, a party of two hundred and forty
French and Indians attacked La Demoiselle's town by
surprise, but most of the people escaped to the fort, which
they defended resolutely. In the afternoon, having done
all the damage they could outside the fort, and realizing
that its capture would be difficult, the besiegers offered
to withdraw if the Pickawillanies would surrender the
Englishmen who were with them. After consultation,
there being no water in the fort, the Englishmen agreed
to this, and were surrendered, with the exception of two
who were kept concealed. One of the prisoners, who
was wounded, was at once killed before the fort, and
the others were held captive. Among the Indians who
had been captured was the principal chief of the Piankeshaws, called " Old Britain " on account of his friendship for the English. He was killed, cut in pieces,
boiled, and eaten, in full view of the fort; after which the
French and their allies moved away.[2]

In the following year M. Du Quesne established a
post at the site of Erie, Penn., and another on French
Creek. George Washington, then Adjutant-General of
the Virginia militia, was sent to him to notify him to
withdraw, but the French commander gave no heed to
the notice. In 1754 a party of English who were build-

lakes. Other forms of the name are *Quitepiconnae*, Gamelin's
journal; *Tepeconnae*, Hough's map; *Kithtipaconnou*, letter of
John Conner and Wm. Wells, in *Liberty Hall*, July 23, 1808;
Rippacanoe, *Imlay's Top. Desc.*, p. 403.

[1] *N. Y. Col. Docs.*, vol. vi. p. 730.
[2] *Journal of Captain Trent*, Cincinnati, 1871.

ing a fort at the site of Pittsburg were driven away by
the French, and Fort Du Quesne was built at that point.
It is not our intention to trace the events of the French
and Indian War. Suffice it to say, that, by these active
measures at its inception, the whole Ohio country was
brought under French control, and, from the time of
Braddock's defeat at least, the tribes continued loyal.
The friends of the English were either awed into submission or driven from the country, and the Indians
generally were engaged in active assistance of the
French. The seat of war was transferred to the frontiers of Pennsylvania and Virginia, and the Wabash
country was left quiet, save for the beat of the war-drum
as the warriors marshalled for the conflict of the white
kings, and the voice of lamentation for the dead, and the
shriek of the tortured captive, when they returned.

When Canada was surrendered at the capitulation of
Montreal, Major Robert Rogers was sent west to take
possession of the posts. The great chieftain Pontiac
stopped him for a few hours, but apparently only to impress the new-comers with a proper respect for himself,
for he acted favorably towards the English for many
months afterward. On November 29, 1760, Rogers
took possession of Detroit, and soon after officers were
sent to take possession of posts Ouiatanon and Miamis.
Post Vincennes, not being within Canada, and therefore
not included in the capitulation, was still held by St.
Ange for His Most Christian Majesty. The three years
that passed before the final treaty, by which all the territory east of the Mississippi was surrendered to England,
formed an era of disquietude in the West, though there
were no outbreaks. The English, feeling sure of their
conquest, took little trouble to retain the favor of the

Indians. The presents which had formerly been so
plentiful now became rarities, and a corruption in the
management of Indian affairs caused the savages to pay
for much that had been sent as gifts for them. Still
more exasperating was the total lack of that ceremonious
respect which is so soothing to the Indian mind, and
which the French had observed with all their national
courtliness. The irritation was inflamed by many of the
French traders, who still hoped that their king would
arouse and win back his American empire. That he
would relinquish more of it was not dreamed. Plots for
the destruction of the English garrisons were formed by
the Indians in 1761 and 1762, but they were discovered
and frustrated. In the spring of 1763 another conspiracy was formed, with Pontiac at its head; and the news
of the cession by France, which the Indians understood
to be a sale and delivery of their lands to the English,
inspired the tribes to a desperate attempt to throw off
the European yoke entirely. Evidences of this were discovered, but the English had become over-confident and
did not heed them. On March 28, 1763, Lieutenant
Edward Jenkins, commandant at Ouiatanon, wrote that
the Canadians were continually lying to the Indians;
that one La Pointe had recently said that the English
would all be prisoners in a short time; that an army
was coming from the Mississippi to retake Detroit, Montreal, Quebec, and all the small posts.[1] Ensign Holmes,
commanding at Fort Miamis, had already reported the
arrival of "a Bloody Belt" at the Kekionga village.
On March 30 he wrote that he had obtained the belt
and accompanying message from the Indians "after a
long and troublesome spell with them," and that "This

[1] *Consp. of Pontiac*, vol. i. p. 178, n.

Affair is very timely Stopt." [1] Special warning saved Detroit from surprise on May 7, the day appointed for its capture, and two days later Pontiac threw off all pretense of friendship and began the siege of the fort, which he maintained with extraordinary ability.

The storm broke on the Indiana posts a little later. On May 27, Holmes, who appears to have been more on his guard than any other commandant, was decoyed from Fort Miamis by his Indian mistress, under pretense of visiting a sick woman, and shot from ambush. The garrison was then summoned to surrender by Godefroy, a Canadian who had left Detroit just before the discovery of the conspiracy, and who probably was concerned in it. He told them their lives would be spared if they surrendered, but that they would all be killed if they resisted. They threw open the gates and yielded as prisoners of war without striking a blow. [2] The soldiers at Ouiatanon were to have been surprised and killed on the night of May 31, but Maisonville and Lorraine, two of the French traders there, induced the Indians to proceed with more moderation. On the next morning Lieutenant Jenkins was requested to come to one of the Indian cabins, and on arriving there was seized and bound. He found several of his soldiers in the same condition, and was induced to command the few remaining in the fort to surrender. The Ouiatanons told him that they would not have molested him if they had not been compelled to do so by the other tribes. They treated the captive soldiers kindly, but held them as prisoners for some time. [3]

[1] *Consp. of Pontiac*, vol. i. p. 189, and note.

[2] *Ibid.*, vol. i. p. 278.

[3] *Ibid.*, vol. i. pp. 276, 277, and note.

For the next two years the whole Ohio valley and much of the adjoining territory was under the control of Pontiac and his allies. The English government had no more authority in Indiana and Illinois than it had in China. The French king had agreed to surrender his posts in the District of Illinois, but the English were unable to reach them to take possession. The Shawnees and Delawares barred the eastern entrance to the Ohio. After he had abandoned the siege of Detroit, at the beginning of November, King Pontiac took his stand by the Maumee, and closed "the glorious gate" of the Miamis. The Indians of the upper lakes and the Mississippi were equally vigilant on their side. Consequently the French officers were obliged to remain at their posts, awaiting the arrival of the new owners to whom they had been ordered to surrender them. In the spring of 1764 Neyon de Villiers grew weary of this thankless task, and ordered St. Ange to relieve him of the command of Fort Chartres, which our faithful commandant at once prepared to do. His last proclamation on our soil, "*donné au poste Vincene le* 18 *de May* 1764," gave the command of the post jointly to M. Deroite de Richardville, "acting as captain of militia," and Sieur le Caindre, "a soldier of the troops." He charged them that "their first care ought to be to maintain a good understanding with the Indians. To prevent disorder during the time it rests with them, whenever complaint shall be made against any one they will take care to call an assembly of the most notable inhabitants of the place, where the matter will be decided by the plurality of votes."[1]

[1] The original of this proclamation was loaned to the Indiana Historical Society, in 1859, by Hon. C. B. Lasselle. It has dis-

St. Ange made his way across the uninhabited prairies of Illinois, and was placed in command at Chartres.
Neyon, accompanied by a goodly number of the Illinois
people, descended the Mississippi to New Orleans, which
was still supposed by them to belong to France, the cession to Spain being yet kept secret. It was a weary
business for St. Ange, waiting through the weeks in that
grand old fortress — "the most convenient and best
built fort in North America" — until the enemy of his
country should come to possess and to rule. Surely he
could not sit in the cool of the evening on the stone
porch above the northern gate, for that looked towards
the old settlements that he had known from childhood, —
half of their people now gone with La Clede to St. Louis,[1]
or with Neyon to New Orleans; the other half, sullen
and petulant, waiting for the coming of the hated red-
coats. Nor was the eastern view pleasing, for in that
direction was the old post that he had commanded so long
and loved so well. The porch of the south gate looked
towards Kaskaskia and the lower settlements, but better
thoughts came there, for on that side was the great river
that crushed all obstacles and bore its burden to the sea
without heed to changing dynasties; and so must he, as
a true soldier, follow his path of duty to the end. Best
of all, I think, he loved to stand on the western battle-
ments, for when his release should come, there, beyond
the stream, was yet French territory where he could
begin life anew. There was the land of the Missouri,

appeared. It is not known whether some gentleman stole it or
some thrifty janitor sold it for old paper. Fortunately Mr. Lasselle kept a copy, which he has kindly furnished me.

[1] At its foundation in 1763. *Mag. of West. Hist.*, vol. ii. pp.
301-321.

where he had served in the flush of his early manhood, and where many of his old friends now awaited him. Aye, even after the painful news of the cession to Spain came up the river, the happiest prospect was to the west, for the Spaniards were Latins and Catholics at least, and if France must go it were best that Spain should come.

But St. Ange had more substantial trials than the endurance of his own sorrow. The uneasy settlers were to be quieted and consoled, and the Indians were to be kept in as good-humor as possible. This was no light task, for they wished to resist the English and insisted that the French should help them. Neyon de Villiers had notified Pontiac that he could hope for no aid from the French, in the fall of 1763, and thereby induced the abandonment of the siege of Detroit; but notwithstanding this, the persistent chief had come to Fort Chartres and demanded the coöperation of Neyon in fighting the English, until that officer, exasperated by his importunities, kicked away the proffered wampum belt and told him to be gone. He now sent embassies to St. Ange, and when these were sent away without encouragement, and the necessity of immediate action had been made imperative by Bouquet's subjugation of the Delawares and Shawnees, he came himself. Still resolute and defiant, he infused courage into the wavering tribes along his route, and brought the Illinois into his alliance by threatening their destruction if they failed him. At Fort Chartres he recounted his friendship to the French, and asked assistance in men and arms. St. Ange firmly refused both, but sought to soothe him by presents and kind words. The chieftain would not be put off so easily. He prepared a great belt and sent it down the

Mississippi by a delegation of his ablest chiefs. They were received at New Orleans by Governor D'Abadie, who was then so ill that he could scarcely leave his bed, and who died on the night following the first day's council. On the next morning M. Aubry acted for the French, and dismissed the indignant warriors with the assurance that the French Father could do no more, — that the French and English were now one people.

Meanwhile the attempts of Major Loftus and Captain Pittman to reach Fort Chartres from New Orleans, and of Captain Morris to gain the same point by the Maumee, had been baffled. In the spring of 1765 Lieutenant Fraser was permitted to reach the fort by the Ohio, on a mission of conciliation, but after a very brief stay he was glad to escape down the Mississippi in disguise. Croghan followed Fraser down the Ohio in May, but he had barely passed the mouth of the Wabash when he was seized by a party of Kickapoos, who carried him to the Ouiatanon towns. The Weas were found to be quite friendly, and Croghan was quickly placed in a state of comparative freedom. A few days later Maisonville arrived with a message from St. Ange, asking Croghan to come to Fort Chartres; and this message, backed by Maisonville's counsel, caused the Indians to withdraw all restraint and treat their former captive as a guest. On the next day Croghan started down the Wabash, but was soon met by Pontiac, who was coming to Ouiatanon with a large following. He had become convinced by the reports of his ambassadors to New Orleans that the French would fight no longer, and on being assured that the cession was not a sale of the Indian lands he became reconciled to the exchange of Great Fathers. He and Croghan went up the Wabash together to Post Ouiatanon, and there, in council, he announced that the French had deceived him and his people, and that he would war against the English no longer. This pledge, given at our little Wabash post and ratified at Detroit, was kept in good faith. Pontiac threw aside his rank and supported himself by hunting, while the Englishman was left free to come and go as he liked.[1]

On October 10, 1765, St. Ange made formal delivery of Fort Chartres to Captain Sterling of the 42d Highlanders, — the famous " Black Watch," — and our territory passed under English rule. The yoke of England was not heavy. Captain Sterling at once issued a proclamation of General Gage, dated December 30, 1764, granting the inhabitants liberty of conscience and guaranteeing them fully their personal and property rights. He gave them complete freedom of emigration, but required them if they remained to take the oath of allegiance to England. Sterling lived but three months after he took command, and after him Major Farmer, Colonel Edward Cole, and Colonel Reed held command for short terms. On September 5, 1768, Lieutenant-Colonel John Wilkins, of the Royal Irish regiment, took command; and two months later he issued a proclamation for the government of the country, and established a court of common law, the first that existed west of the Alleghanies. It consisted of seven judges, and dealt out English justice at monthly terms until the British Parliament restored the civil law to its French-Canadian subjects in 1774. It was during his command, on a gloomy spring night in 1772, that the Mississippi made its last

[1] *Conspiracy of Pontiac ; Old Ft. Chartres ; Kaskaskia and its Parish Records ; N Y. Col. Docs.*, Index, " Pondiac."

wild leap at the old fort, and swept away the southern curtain and bastions. The troops vacated the place as speedily as possible, and soon afterwards built Fort Gage, on the bluffs near Kaskaskia, which was head-quarters during the remainder of the British occupation. Fort Chartres was never reoccupied. Its walls formed a convenient quarry for the people of the neighborhood, who carried them off stone by stone until now there remain only broken mound lines to show its extent. The old magazine alone remains intact, and solitary lifts its bramble-covered arch amid the modern features of the farmyard into which the place has been converted; but its solid masonry aids one to imagine something of the structure of the ancient capitol of Illinois and Indiana.

There was no fort of any importance besides Chartres to be taken possession of by the English. Says Lieutenant Fraser: "The French have had Besides Fort Charters a small Fort at Cascaskias and another at Coake [Cahokia]; there was a third called Assomption on the Bank of the Ohio opposite to the mouth of the Cherakee River,[1] besides two Forts on the Ouabach, the one called the great Ouiachtonon was dependent on Canada, & the other at little Ouiachtonon or St. Vincent dependent on Orleans. All those excepting fort Charters are intirely in ruins, some of them that you can scarce see any appearance of. They did not seem to me of any great consequence were they even on a better footing as they were situated."[2] Many months passed before the English came to take possession of Post Vincennes. On November 15, 1768, Lieutenant Thomas Hutchins wrote

---

[1] The Tennessee. This is evidently a reference to that mysterious establishment commonly called Old Fort Massac.

[2] Report of May 4, 1766, Haldimand Coll., *Can. Archives.*

from Fort Chartres: "The Fever and Augue since our
arrival has raged with such uncommon violence as to put
it out of our power to do scarce anything more than bury
some of our Officers and Men who were carried off by
those disorders.   We expect next spring if the Health
of the Garrison permit to take possession of Post St.
Vincent on the Ouabache." [1]   This intention was not
accomplished, though in the next year a census of the
Wabash posts and Fort Miamis was taken.   The only
indication in this census of any government at any of
them is the following note concerning M. Nicholas of
Vincennes: " Nicholas is the most substantial Inhabitant
and has been employed as justice of the Peace there, by
some authority from the commanding officer at the
Illinois." [2]   There seems also to have been some change
in the authorities at the post, whatever they may have
been, at about this time.   From 1770 to 1773 all concessions of land were made by Ste. Marie, whose proper
name was Jean Baptiste Racine.   There were but two
concessions between the departure of St. Ange and
1770; one is signed "Chaparlee," and the other "Cha-
pard,"—apparently the same person,—and both were
made in 1768.   As to what became of the authority of
Deroite de Richardville and Sieur le Caindre, conferred
by St. Ange, we have no intimation except so much as
may be found in the fact that in the census of 1769
" Mrs. Richardville" is listed as the head of a family.

In 1772, while in this neglected condition, the French
at Vincennes received peremptory orders from General
Gage to quit the Indian country at once.   In September
they forwarded a remonstrance to him asserting the

---

[1] Hutchins to Haldimand, *Can. Archives.*
[2] Haldimand Coll., *Can. Archives.*

ancient establishment of their village and the legal character of their titles. In the spring of 1773 he replied
requiring them to furnish "convincing proofs" of their
statements.[1] On receipt of this second demand there
was a great ransacking of closets and chests at the old
post, and doubtless much cursing of this English general
who put them to so much trouble to prove something
that every one in the settlement knew. Perdition take
such an ignoramus! Did he expect a man to keep a
little scrap of paper forever? After all their search, so
many deeds were lacking that Ste. Marie had to go to
St. Louis with "M. Perthuit" (probably Perthwaite),
who had been sent by Gage to investigate the matter,
for the purpose of getting the testimony of St. Ange.
The old commandant certified his rule from 1736 to
1764, as above given, "and that during the said time I
have conceded to many inhabitants divers lands and
pieces of ground, by order of my said Srs. the Governors,
in the name of His Most Christian Majesty," and further
"that faith should be given to the concessions which I
have signed and delivered to the said inhabitants; that
in addition to this I have permitted verbally a number
of individuals to establish themselves and cultivate the
lands of which they have been in possession for many
years."[2] Etienne Phillibert, the village notary, certi-

---

[1] Dillon, pp. 86–88. The remonstrance of the French settlers
has not been found. Mr. Dillon makes his abstract of its contents
from Gage's reply. The words which General Gage refers to as
"insinuating that your settlement is of seventy years' standing,"
were perhaps misunderstood. The writing and spelling of the
French settlers were execrable, and they furnished no proof of
the time of settlement except the certificate of St. Ange above
mentioned.

[2] Certificate in Haldimand Coll., *Can. Archives.*

fied, " that many inhabitants of Poste Vincenne, while
I performed the duties of notary at said post before the
flight of the late Baumer, notary after me, gave to him
many contracts of concession belonging to the inhabitants, and that the flight of the said Sr. Baumer, as well
as the transfer of the record-office of this post to that of
the Illinois, have caused to be lost a quantity of concession papers, as well as contracts of sale, in the year one
thousand seven hundred and sixty-one, when was this
removal of the said papers as also the flight of the said
notary." [1]   In addition to these, Ste. Marie wrote a letter explaining that part of the title papers had been
carried away and " others eaten by rats &c. ; " and all
these papers were bundled together and forwarded to
" M. de Gage."

While all this worriment was in progress on the Wabash, Gage had gone over to England and found that
his policy as to these settlers would not be enforced.
Lord North and Lord Dartmouth wanted the Indian
country left clear of whites, but they would not oblige
the settlers to leave their homes, and in consequence
they were in embarrassment concerning the matter.[2]
The rapidly increasing difficulties of the ministry with
the original colonies had begotten a desire to assure the
loyalty of the settlers in the territory acquired from
France, as well as of the Indians, and when the subject
was brought before Parliament, in the spring of 1774, a
complete change of procedure was determined on.   The
whole territory northwest of the Ohio was put within

[1] Haldimand Coll., *Can. Archives.*

[2] Gage to Haldimand, London, September 14, 1773, *Can. Archives.*   The papers from Vincennes did not arrive until the next
year.   Haldimand to Gage, January 5, 1774. *Ib.*

the boundaries of the Province of Quebec; the civil and religious rights of the inhabitants were secured; and their ancient laws and customs were restored and guaranteed. Notwithstanding these enactments, no actual provision for the government of Vincennes was made for about three years, the attention of the administration being occupied by the proceedings of the original colonies. It was then arranged that the Lieutenant-Governor of Detroit should be "Superintendent of St. Vincennes," and take charge of the post in person.

In April, 1777, Lieutenant-Governor Abbott departed for the post, accompanied by an escort of Canadians.[1] He arrived at Vincennes on May 19th. On the 26th he reported: "Since the conquest of Canada, no person bearing His Majesty's Commission has been to take possession; from this your Excellency may easily imagine what anarchy reigns. I must do the inhabitants justice for the respectfull reception I met with, and for their readiness in obeying the orders I thought necessary to issue. The Wabache is perhaps one of the finest rivers in the world, on its banks are several Indian Towns, the most considerable is the Ouija [Wea, Ouiatanon], where it is said there are 1000 men capable to bear arms. I found them so numerous, and needy, I could not pass without great expense; The presents though very large, were in a manner despised, saying their antient Father (the french) never spoke to them without a barnfull of goods; having no Troops and only a handfull of french obliged me to esquiese [acquiesce] in part of their exorbitand demands, which has occationed a much greater expense than I could have imagined, but I believe it not thrown away, as I left them seemingly well disposed for

[1] Abbott to Carleton, April 15, 1777: *Can. Archives.*

His Majesty's Service. I have drawn . . . for 6428
Livres in favour of Jean Baptiste Racine dit Ste. Marie,
who has acted as commandant of this place since it was
conceded to His Majesty. The fair character he bears
with the certificate annexed to his account makes me
think it just." [1]

Abbott remained through the year, in active performance of his new duties, but at the opening of the next
year he received orders of recall. On January 30, 1778,
the inhabitants made him a formal address, certifying
their gratitude for his care for their interests, and he
departed full of regret " for the poor people " with whom
he had soon learned to sympathize.[2] With his departure
began a new epoch in the history of the Wabash country ;
but while we are still in the period of royal government
let us turn for a farewell glance at our old friend St.
Ange. After the surrender of Fort Chartres he had
gone to the infant village of St. Louis; and he appears
to have continued his government of that place, as a
remnant of the District of Illinois. No other source of
his authority there is known; in fact it was made the
subject of judicial inquiry many years since, and the
decision then reached was that he had no authority at
all, so far at least as the granting of lands was concerned.[3] It is said, however, that he took service under
Spain in 1766, and was in command as a Spanish officer
at St. Louis until 1770, when he was succeeded by Don
Pedro Piernas.[4] He certified in 1773 that he was a half-
pay captain in the Spanish service ; and in certifying his

---

[1] Abbott to Carleton: *Can. Archives.*

[2] Abbott to Germaine, April 3, 1778 : *Can. Archives.*

[3] Admrs. of Wright *v.* Thomas, 4 Mo. 577.

[4] *Mag. of West. Hist.*, vol. ii p. 60.

will, in 1774, Piernas calls him a "captain of infantry in the service of His Catholic Majesty." Whatever may have been the legal power appurtenant to his station, he was in actual authority at St. Louis until the arrival of Piernas, and in command of troops thereafter.

At St. Louis, as at Vincennes and Fort Chartres, his nobility of soul was evident. In 1769 he had a kindly word and friendly counsel for Pontiac, then assuming only the place of a warrior; and when the great barbarian fell a victim to his Kaskaskian assassin, St. Ange sent across the river for his body and buried it with honors of war near the fort at St. Louis.[1] In 1773 we have found him coming to the relief of the people of Vincennes with the strongest confirmations he could give for the protection of their homes. A few months later he passed to his rest. On December 26, 1774, Lieutenant-Governor Piernas was called to the house of Madame Chouteau, "where the said Mr. de St. Ange is abed," to draw and attest his will. In this, "First, As a good Roman Catholic and a true member of the Roman Catholic and Apostolic church, he commends his soul to God, to the Blessed Virgin and all the saints of heaven, praying them to intercede for him before the Almighty that it may please Him to admit his soul on its separation from his body into the kingdom of the blessed." He then recites his debits and credits, and after providing for certain masses, and appropriating the sum of 500 livres "towards the erection of the church projected in this parish," he bequeaths his little property to his nieces and nephews. And here his worthy disposition is manifest in special provision for a blind nephew, and in a provision that the two children of his Indian slave

[1] *Consp. of Pontiac*, vol. ii. p. 311.

Angelique, who are left to his niece, Madame Belestre, are to be freed on arriving at the age of twenty-one; the commandant is requested to look specially to this. Pierre Laclede is made sole executor; and finally, whether with cause of apprehension we know not, he solemnly declares that he has never entered into the married state.

His preparation was timely. On the following morning, at 9 o'clock, Piernas was summoned to view his dead body and seal his effects in accordance with the formalities of the civil law. So he set his house in order and was gathered to his fathers, at the ripe age of seventy-three years.[1] He was buried in the little churchyard at St. Louis, in conformity with his dying request, and there, like Pontiac, he sleeps beneath the bustle and din of the great city. Peace to thy ashes, faithful soldier of France, and may thy honest life be an example to all who shall follow thee as rulers of Indiana!

[1] *Mag. of West. Hist.*, vol. ii. pp. 60–65.

CHAPTER III.

THE first white residents of Indiana were *coureurs de bois*, under which title were included all those whites whose place of residence was not some French village or post. The signification of this term varied widely at different periods ; ranging from a criminal sense, in the earlier days, to the simple import of fur-traders, into which it finally settled. The original *coureur de bois* was the child of monopoly and intolerance, and, like all who are so indiscreet as to offend the powers that be, he has been painted in darker colors than he deserved. In 1685 Denonville wrote : "The youth of Canada are so badly trained that from the moment they are able to shoulder a gun, their fathers dare not say a word to them. As they are not trained to labor, and are poor, they have no other means of gaining a livelihood than to range the forest [*courir le bois*], where they are guilty of an infinitude of disorders. . . . . This savage life has great attractions for these young men, who imitate all the movements of the Indians. . . The noblesse of Canada is of the most rascally description, and to increase their body is to multiply the number of loafers."[1]

At the same time Bishop St. Valliere, of Quebec, wrote : "That the Canadian Youth are for the most part wholly demoralized ; that there are married men who,

[1] *N. Y. Col. Docs.*, vol. ix. pp. 276, 277.

in addition to their own wives, keep Squaws whom they publicly deceive; and that the most frightful crimes are perpetrated by the Young men and the French who resort to the woods." [1]

In these statements, some force is the product of the exaggeration of piety, and this with Denonville as well as with the bishop; for Denonville was pious even under the Romanism of Canada, which at that time was as severe and exacting as Puritanism ever was. At Montreal and Quebec, attending a ball, wearing lace, and playing cards, were offenses that received denunciation from the pulpit, while dramatic performances and masquerading were held by the clergy to be crimes that ought to be prevented by the civil authorities. The young gallants from France found these restraints very irksome; so much so that La Hontan preferred hunting with the Indians to society life in the settlements, and Lamothe Cadillac declared that no one could live in the provincial cities except " simpletons and slaves of the ecclesiastical domination." [2] To the reduced members of the nobility, who were quite numerous in Canada, and even to the commonalty, these bonds were as irritating as they were to those more newly arrived, so that all through the social system of the country the youth of spirit and enterprise found the most pleasant life in the freedom of the forests. To maintain this life they became of necessity fur-traders, for there was no other means of support.

Before the year 1670 there appears to have been no restraint of law on their habit of trade or the adoption of the savage life, but in that year Talon, the Intendant,

[1] *N. Y. Col. Docs.*, vol. ix. p. 279.
[2] *Old Régime in Canada*, pp. 348, 349.

who was thoroughly in harmony with the economic theories of Louis XIV., and was also of a religious turn of mind, commenced taking measures to crush these libertines.   On November 10, 1670, he reported: "The edict enacted relative to marriages has been enregistered, and, proclaiming the intention of the King, I caused orders to be issued that the volunteers (whom, on my return, I found in very great numbers, living, in reality, like banditti) should be excluded from the [Indian] trade and hunting; they are excluded by the law also from the honors of the Church, and from the Communities if they do not marry fifteen days after the arrival of the ships from France.   I shall consider some other expedient to stop these vagabonds; they ruin, partially, the Christianity of the Indians and the commerce of the French who labor in the settlements to extend the Colony. It were well did his Majesty order me, by *lettre de cachet*, to fix them in some place where they would participate in the labors of the community." [1]

Driven by these edicts from lawful trade, the *coureurs de bois* showed their independence by defiant proposals to turn the fur-trade to the English settlements.   For the common security, they organized leagues among themselves, under the leadership of Du Lhut and others, and gave "notices of rendezvous, threatening to build forts and to repair towards Manatte (New York) and Orange (Albany), boasting that they will be received and have every protection there." [2]   Their boasts were not without foundation, for the English exerted themselves to induce them to come,[3] and there was always thereafter more or less of this illicit trade.   The require-

[1] *N. Y. Col. Docs.*, vol. ix. p. 65.
[2] *Ibid.*, vol. ix. p. 91.   [3] *Ibid.*, vol. iv. pp. 715, 740.

ment to marry they held in derision.   Says Denonville :
" They despise the peasantry, and consider it beneath
them to espouse their daughters, though they are themselves peasants like them.   In addition to this, they will
condescend no more to cultivate the soil, nor listen any
longer to anything except returning to the woods for the
purpose of continuing the same avocations.   This gives
rise to innumerable excesses that many of them are
guilty of with the squaws, which cause a great deal of
mischief in consequence of the displeasure of the Indians
at the seduction of their wives and daughters, and of
the injury thereby inflicted on religion, when the Indians behold the French practicing nothing of what the
Missionaries represent as the law of the Gospel." [1]   In
truth, it would have been more appropriate to have
made some law to restrain marriage than to make a
requirement of it, for these bushlopers made matrimony
an avocation.   Many of them took new wives from
among the Indian maidens every eight days, according
to the Indian custom ; and La Salle's enemies averred
that some of his Illinois colonists took " a new squaw
every day in the week." [2]

Wild, reckless, and licentious as the *coureurs de bois*
were, they were no worse than their contemporaries, or
many who followed them.   They sold brandy to the
Indians, but so did the licensed traders, the English,
and the soldiers ; and so have people of many nationali-
ties and classes since then.   They debauched Indian
women, but so did every one else, except the clergy and
a few officers of the sterner stripe ; and this evil is very
far from being unknown at the present day.   They

[1] *N. Y. Col. Docs.*, vol. ix. pp. 442, 443.
[2] *Discovery of the Great West*, p. 291.

carried on unlawful trade, but there was scarcely an officer or merchant in Canada, from Frontenac and La Salle down, who escaped the same charge; and it is sometimes whispered that this offense has been committed in the nineteenth century. There was one misdemeanor, of which they were guilty in the early days, that was peculiar to them: they discarded clothing entirely, and not only roamed the forests and went among the Indians in this airy mode, but also appeared in the settlements without addition to their raiment.[1] They were veritable lilies of France, with no aspirations to rival the artificial magnificence of Solomon. In this matter they merely adopted the Indian custom, but both the Indians and their white allies adopted the semblance of clothing before many years had passed.

The laws against the *coureurs de bois* were of no avail. In 1672 Frontenac reported that their numbers increased daily, "despite of all the ordinances that have been made, and which I have, since coming here, renewed with more severity than before." Their numbers continued to increase, and the impossibility of managing them became so manifest that Frontenac recommended a general amnesty, and the employment of the *coureurs* in the regular trade. The amnesty was granted,[2] and thereafter matters progressed more favorably until the arrival of Denonville. Although Denonville did not approve of the bushlopers, he found that he could not throw away their assistance. By his permission Du Lhut fortified and held Detroit, and his "vagabonds," to the number of one hundred and eighty, aided in the campaign against the Senecas in 1687. For their loyal conduct

---

[1] *N. Y. Col. Docs.*, vol. ix. p. 277; *Old Régime in Canada*, p. 312.

[2] *N. Y. Col. Docs.*, vol. ix. p. 145.

Denonville reported that they "would richly deserve some reward."[1] As the intrigues of the English with the Indians became more formidable, the value of the *coureurs de bois* became more apparent. They were the links that bound the Indians to France, and except they remained loyal the beaver-trade must go to England. They found a champion in Lamothe Cadillac, who reported, in 1694, that, "Those who would insinuate to the Court that it is only licentiousness that creates those *coureurs de bois*, whom people represent as vagabonds, are for the most part of the time influenced by other motives than those of conscience and religion."[2] In 1701 the king pardoned all *coureurs de bois* then under arrest, and gave them permission to join the colony at the mouth of the Mississippi, but for the future he restricted their trade to buffalo skins only. A few of those who accepted this permission went with Juchereau, and remained at his establishment at the mouth of the Ohio during its brief continuance.

From this time there was no complaint of these rovers from the Canadian authorities ; and though there was an occasional growl from Louisiana on account of their insubordination, there was also frequent commendation of their usefulness. As the fur-trade became controlled by monopolists, with whom independent traders could not contend, the *coureurs de bois* dropped into the channels of lawful trade, and their title became practically synonymous with the word *voyageur.* These were the *coureurs de bois* of Indiana in the eighteenth century, and in this phase they were the most romantic and poetic characters ever known in American frontier life. Their every

---

[1] *N. Y. Col. Docs.*, vol. ix. p. 351.
[2] *Ibid.*, vol. ix. p. 586.

movement attracts the rosiest coloring of imagination.
We see them gliding along the streams in their long
canoes, shapely and serviceable as any water-craft that
man has ever designed, and yet buoyant and fragile as
the wind-whirled autumn leaf. We catch afar off the
thrilling cadence of their choruses, floating over prairie
and marsh, echoing from forest and hill, startling the
buffalo from his haunt in the reeds, telling the drowsy
denizens of the posts of the approach of revelry, and
whispering to the Indian village of gaudy fabrics, of
trinkets, and of fire-water. We feel the genial warmth
of the camp-fire that breaks the chill of the night-wind,
and dissipates the fog which rises from stream, bayou,
and marsh, as the men gather about it and whiff the
narcotic incense from their stumpy pipes; or later on,
when they bring forth the inevitable greasy pillows, roll
in their grimy blankets, and speed away to dreamland.
Another night they have reached the little post, and we
are overwhelmed by the confusion of chattering, laugh-
ing, singing, and bargaining; we almost taste the fiery
brandy that is rapidly preparing them for the wild whirl
of the dance and the delirium of the debauch beyond.

What a rollicking life was this! And yet it takes but
little experience in wild life to satisfy one that there is
far more romance in imagining all this in an easy-chair
than there is in living it. True, the melody of

> "Je suis jeune et belle,
>   Je veux m'engage
>   Un amant fidèle,"

and their similar ballads (for they all had more of wine
and women than the English words that are usually set
to the airs), were charming to one "who idly heard the
magical strain;" but it was true also that paddles must

keep time with the song, in ceaseless stroke, from dawn
to dark. True, the repose of camp was pleasant, at least
as compared with the fatigues of the day ; but the supper that preceded it offered no attraction to an epicure.
A quart of hulled corn [1] and a pint of bear's grease constituted a day's rations, though at a .later period, when
settlements were more numerous, the *voyageurs* sometimes revelled in bean or pea soup, flavored with a piece
of boiled pork, and reinforced by sea-biscuit.[2] Here is
the account of their fare given by a traveller, in 1776:
" A bushel of hulled corn with two pounds of fat is reckoned to be a month's subsistence. No other allowance
is made, of any kind, not even salt ; and bread is never
thought of. The difficulty which would belong to an
attempt to reconcile any other men than Canadians to
this fare seems to secure to them and their employés the
monopoly of the fur trade." [3] For every real or imag-
inary joy they knew, there was an offset of hardship and
privation, so that the contentment and jollity for which
they were noted should be ascribed to the French temperament, not to the happiness of their lot.

The *coureur de bois*, as a resident of Indiana, established no French village ; he lived with the Indians and
in the Indian mode. The priest was evidently only a
bird of passage until after the establishment of military
posts. The first inhabitants who made the landmarks
of a permanent civilization were the soldiers. Just who
these soldiers were is not known, but the conjecture

---

[1] This corn was prepared something like what is called "home-
made hominy." The skin or hull of the grain was removed by
soaking it in lye, after which it was washed, mashed, and dried.

[2] *Wis. Hist. Coll.*, vol. ii. p. 110.

[3] *Henry's Travels*, p. 52.

heretofore mentioned, that they were of the Regiment
Carignan-Salières, is a mistaken one. All of that regiment that remained permanently in America had been
disbanded, and the soldiers were married and colonized
before they were even fur-traders in Indiana. The
regiment was reorganized from the remnant that returned to France, but it remained beyond the Atlantic
thereafter.[1] That the soldiers were "King's troops"
appears from the record concerning M. Vincennes which
has heretofore been quoted, as also from the certificate
of Louis St. Ange, preserved in the Canadian archives,
that he "commanded Post Vincesnes in the name of
His Most Christian Majesty with a garrison of regular
troops from the year 1736 to the year 1764."[2] The
soldiers ordinarily were from the worst classes of France.
According to the priests, their piety was about on a par
with that of the *coureurs*.[3] La Harpe, after thirty years
experience in the Louisiana colony, said : "The soldiers
which the company has sent over have been deserters
and persons collected promiscuously from the streets of
Paris."[4] In this respect they differed from the troops
sent to Canada at an earlier day, and possibly for this
reason the early Canadian custom of establishing seign-
iories, in which the disbanded soldiers became dependants
and the officers seigniors, did not prevail in the West.
La Salle introduced the system in his Illinois colony, but
it was short-lived. Indeed, the feudal system left very
slight traces of any kind in the West, the most important ones being the provisions, in ancient patents of land,

---

[1] *Old Régime in Canada*, pp. 218, 182 note.
[2] *Ante*, chap. 2.
[3] *Old Régime in Canada*, p. 319.
[4] Memoir in *La. Hist. Coll.*, p. 117 note.

for a recognition of the royal prerogatives by assisting in planting a maypole every year.[1]

Although there were three posts in Indiana during the greater part of the French occupation in the eighteenth century, Vincennes was the only one that could be considered a town. In 1769 there were sixty-six heads of families at this settlement, with fifty women and one hundred and fifty children; while at Fort Ouiatanon, near Lafayette, there were only twelve heads of families, and at Fort Miamis, now Fort Wayne, there were but nine.[2] At Vincennes a majority of the settlers were supported by agriculture; at the other two posts the only employment was trading in furs. In 1778 the annual fur trade of Vincennes was estimated at £5,000, while that of Fort Ouiatanon, at the same period, was estimated at £8,000.[3]

As to its agriculture, Vincennes had somewhat the nature of a commune. This resulted partly from a general saving of labor and expense that could be effected by a community of interest in some things, and partly from the necessity of grouping the houses about the fort to prevent exposure to attack from hostiles. Like all other French settlements in the West, Vincennes had its large commons for the pasturage of stock, and, in a certain sense, also its common fields, in which each individual's tract was marked but not separated from the others by fencing. At Kaskaskia the inhabitants were at the first accustomed to cultivate land in their commons, as well as in their individual concessions, keeping watchers stationed to drive the cattle away from the

[1] *Mich. Pion. Coll.*, vol. i. p. 352.
[2] Census in Haldimand Coll., *Can. Archives.*
[3] Hutchins's *Top. Desc.*, pp. 28–30.

grain, but as their cattle increased it became impossible
to protect the crops, notwithstanding all their precau-
tions. In February, 1727, on the arrival of Desliettes,
they presented to him and M. Chaffin, the judge of the
district, a memorial setting forth all their trials and
tribulations, among others this of their fields and their
cattle. They recite therein that they have agreed to put
a fence around the fields, and have already cut more
than eighteen thousand pickets for the purpose, their
mode of fencing being to set the pickets upright in the
ground close enough together to prevent the passage of
animals. This fence was soon afterwards completed and
the fields were safe.[1] In this great field, each villager
tended and reaped the crop on his own allotment; but
after the harvesting, which was all done at one time, the
field was thrown open to the cattle of all the settlers.[2]
No person was allowed to pasture his cattle within the
field, even on his own land, except he had them "dili-
gently watched." The commons belonged to the village;
no individual had separate property in it. It is so held
by the town of Kaskaskia to this day, and the rent paid
by those who now cultivate it furnishes a large revenue
to the municipality.[3]

At Vincennes the titles were similar, but the management of the property was different. In an official report,
in 1790, Winthrop Sargent, Secretary of the Territory
Northwest of the Ohio River, said: "A petition has
also been presented by the inhabitants of Vincennes,

[1] Breese's *Early Illinois*, pp. 173-176, 286-293.

[2] Brown's *Early Illinois*: Ferg. Hist. Ser. No. 14, p. 83; Breese's *Early Illinois*, pp. 294-296.

[3] Breese's *Early Illinois*, pp. 294-296; *Kaskaskia and its Parish Records*: Ferg. Hist. Ser. No. 12, p. 22.

praying a confirmation of their commons, comprehending about two thousand four hundred acres of good, and three thousand acres of sunken lands. They have been, it appears, thirty years under a fence, which is intended to confine their cattle within its boundaries, and keep them out of their wheat fields; for, contrary to the usage of farmers generally, the cattle are enclosed, and the cultivated lands are left at large, except ·those parts which immediately approach the commons. But this fence, and quiet possession under the French and British governments, they seem to think entitles them to a good prescriptive right." [1] It was very natural and proper that they should imagine that they had a prescriptive right to this land, and Congress thought so too, for it gave the commons to them. Until 1790 the commandants at the post exercised a supervising control over the commons and the fields, as well as over other interests of the people. In his last proclamation, of May 18, 1764, St. Ange said to his deputies: "Messieurs Deroite de Richardville and de Caindre cannot watch too carefully that the inhabitants keep up their fences, it being to the interest of the public that the animals should not pass from the commons to the grain." Authority over these lands was also exercised by Major Hamtramck, as we shall see hereafter. This authority was a part of the right of eminent domain under the French system, and was based on the necessity of securing supplies for the use of the government. Lieutenant Fraser reported as to this: "The Commandants of the French Troops in the Illinois were always impowered to prohibit the Exportation of any provisions from the Illinois till the King's Magazines shou'd be first supplyd. This how-

[1] Am. State Papers: *Public Lands*, vol. i. p. 10.

ever the Com^{dts} often permitted in consequence of pecuniary considerations from those who exported them." [1] Some of this reflection on the thrift of the commandants may properly be attributed to Fraser's bad humor, for he was evidently sore over his rough usage at the Illinois.

With the actual inception of the government of the Northwest Territory in Indiana and Illinois, in 1790, the control of the lands devolved on the owners; and as American settlers came thronging in, with other customs, and with cattle that were not always fenced in, a change became necessary. In 1799 it was provided by law that the owners of any common field might assemble, elect officers, and decide on such regulations as they deemed proper for the management of their property, including the right to levy assessments for necessary expenses. All questions were to be decided by the vote of the majority in interest. The immediate supervision of the field was to be by three persons selected as a "field committee." Any proprietor who so desired might fence in his allotment and hold it in severalty at any time. The common field was required to be enclosed by a "good and sufficient fence" on or before the first day of May of each year, and no stock of any kind was to be admitted to it between the first day of May and the fifteenth of November of each year, unless the assembly of owners should determine otherwise. [2] This law remained in force until 1807, when a special law was made for the common fields of Vincennes, whose owners appear to have still neglected the fencing. By this law the fields were required to be fenced, on or before the last day of

---

[1] Report, May 4, 1766, *Can. Archives.*
[2] *Laws of N. W. Ter.*, p. 280, Act approved Dec. 19, 1799.

March, 1808, with a rail fence five feet high surmounted by stakes and riders. The control and apportionment of the work were put in the hands of a syndic, who was to be elected by the people owning the lands.[1] Through subsequent legislation, both the commons and the common fields were converted into holdings in severalty.

In imitation of the French inhabitants, a number of Piankeshaw Indians adopted an agricultural life at Vincennes prior to 1764, as appears from this same report of Mr. Sargent. He says: "In addition, sir, to the ancient possessions of the people of Vincennes, under French and British concessions here, is about one hundred and fifty acres of land, constituting a part of the village, and extending a mile up the Wabash River, in front of their improved claims, which was granted by M. St. Ange to some of the Piankeshaw Indians, allotted into small divisions for their wigwams, and by them occupied and improved until the year 1786, when the last of them moved off, selling individually, as they took themselves away, their several parts and proportions. The inhabitants now hold this land, parcelled out amongst them in small lots, some of which are highly improved, and have been built upon before and since 1783." This Piankeshaw tract extended north from what is now Busseron Street; the commons and fields lay south and southwest of the village. It seems odd that any grant of land should have been made to these Indians, who were the original owners of the country, at so early a period of its history, but a satisfactory explanation of it is found in the fact that at a very early date the Indians had made a large cession of land to the colony.

[1] Laws of 1807, p. 502.

This is set out in a petition of Pierre Gamelin and others, dated November 20, 1793, in these words: "In 1742, some time after the foundation of this post, the natives of this country made the French and their heirs an absolute gift of the lands lying between the point above (*pointe coupée en haut*) and the river Blanche below the village, with as much land on both sides of the Wabash as might be comprised within the said limits.[1] At first the ignorance of the value of those lands was the reason why there have been no authentic writings concerning this donation; but such as were in existence an unfortunate register[2] carried off, with several consequential papers; afterwards the war of 1759 prevented the obtaining of them. However, the donors ratified the gift in all the councils which have since been held both with the officers of France and with those of His Britannic Majesty; and when the English agents, in 1774, came to purchase lands of the Indians, the donors, at that time, also ratified anew the said donation. We observe that at the time the English, as they wished to deceive the unfortunate Indians, by inserting in the contract both sides of the river instead of one, which the latter consented to dispose of, they would not subscribe to it. The last year in councils, the first which have been held between the United States and these Indians, they unanimously spoke of the donation in these terms: 'Americans, this is the first time I have come to see you

[1] Pointe Coupée is the abrupt bend of the Wabash five miles below Merom. It was reckoned to be twelve leagues above Vincennes, and the mouth of White River was estimated to be an equal distance below. The grant was intended to be twenty-four leagues square.

[2] Baumer, a royal notary during St. Ange's rule.

and to hearken to you. I shall, however, tell you the truth. Our fathers gave to the French and their heirs all the lands between *la pointe coupée* and the River Blanche, on both sides of the Wabash river, to enable them to live, and for the pasturage of their animals. The French and us are but one people; our bones are mingled in this earth; we are not now come to take it from them; on the contrary we say that all those who are here [shall] dwell here; these lands are theirs. We have never sold lands. I do not think that there is a son capable of selling the grave of his mother. Were we to sell our lands, the Grand Source of Life would be displeased, for we should also sell the bones of our fathers and the roebucks [*i. e.* deer, game], and we should die with hunger. I do not come to jest with you, or to ridicule our brethren the French. I refer to the writings for what our fathers have given to the French; writings properly drawn never deceive. Tell the great chief what I have just said; they are our unanimous sentiments.'" [1]

Although this ancient writing was never found, there is little room to doubt that this grant was actually made. Aside from the evidence recited by the petitioners above, and the grant to the Piankeshaws by St. Ange, this tract is expressly reserved to "the inhabitants of Post St. Vincent" in a deed made in 1775,[2] though in council with Putnam, in 1792, the Indians denied the validity of this deed, except as to the recital of the original grant to the

---

[1] Am. State Papers: *Pub. Lands*, vol. i. p. 32. That this speech is authentic, see certificate of General Rufus Putnam, *ibid.*, p. 340. The records of the proceedings at this council appear to have been removed from the government archives at an early day.

[2] *Ibid.*, vol. i. pp. 338–340; Dillon, ed. of 1859, p. 107.

people of Vincennes. Furthermore, the various sovereignties which held the post always treated the Indian
title to this tract as being extinguished, and it was never
pretended to have been extinguished otherwise than by
this grant. The French and British commandants made
grants of parts of the tract to individuals, as did also
the official representatives of Virginia; and the United
States surveyed and sold what was left of it.[1] The oldest
of these individual grants, for which the deed is preserved at Vincennes, dates June 15, 1759, but in 1773
there were ten deeds of earlier date existing. In 1772
the people of Vincennes were required by General
Thomas Gage to verify their titles by submitting to him
the names of the claimants, the date and quality of the
title, the names of the commandant who made the concession and the governor-general who confirmed it. In
their certificate, a copy of which is before me, there appeared eighty-eight claimants, only one of whom professed to have acquired title previous to 1742. This was
M. Delorier, who claimed to have had a deed from Vincennes, which must of course have been made as early
as 1736, but which had been lost. Of the remaining
claimants, seventy-four claimed grants from St. Ange,
and thirty-four of these produced deeds, which ranged
in date from 1749 to 1764. Those who could not produce deeds fortified their claims by a certificate from
St. Ange that he had made concessions; and one from
Etienne Phillibert, the village notary, that numerous
deeds had been carried off by Baumer, the former
notary, when he left the country. There were thirteen
who claimed under the British commandants, all of

---

[1] Am. State Papers: *Pub. Lands*, vol. i. p. 10; Law's *Vincennes*, pp. 106-121.

whom produced their deeds. These individual claims were allowed, or other provision made for the claimants, by the United States, but the claim for the twenty-four leagues square was rejected by the commissioners for want of evidence.[1] The decision is justifiable only on the ground that the title passed from the Indians to the French throne, and not to the inhabitants of the village.[2]

Within this little state of twenty-four leagues square our French colonists of Vincennes held their residences, and passed the greater part of their contented, careless lives. Their agriculture was of a very primitive style. Fertilization was never thought of. In winter they ordinarily carted the accumulations of manure out on the ice of the streams, on which their settlements were invariably made, to be washed away in the spring; and it was asserted by their early American neighbors that in some cases, barns were removed when the piles of manure had been allowed to accumulate until it had become more difficult to remove them than to move the building. "The plow was of wood, except the share. Its long beam and handles extended ten or twelve feet, and it had a wooden mould-board. In front were two wheels, also of wood, of different sizes; a small one to run on the unplowed side, and a larger one in the furrow. There were neither chains nor whiffle-tree; oxen were fastened by a pole which had a hinged attachment to the beam, and very good though shallow plowing was performed by this rude but ingenious implement. Both oxen and horses were used in the various operations. The harness was very simple, and constructed of withes

---

[1] Am. State Papers: *Pub. Lands*, vol. i. p. 301.

[2] This was the position taken by Governor St. Clair. *St. Clair Papers*, vol. ii. p. 400.

or twisted raw-hide.   No yoke was used, but a rope of
the kind mentioned was passed around the oxen's horns
and they pushed with their heads." [1] Other descriptions
of the plow and the plowing varied slightly from this.
Governor Reynolds says: "They had no coulter and
had a large wooden mould-board. The handles were
short and almost perpendicular; the beam was nearly
straight, and rested on an axle supported by two small
wheels; the wheels were low, and the beam was so fixed
on the axle, with a chain or rope of raw-hide, that the
plow could be placed deep or shallow in the ground.
The wheels made the plow unsteady.   The French
settlers seldom plowed with horses, but used oxen.   It
is the custom of the French everywhere to yoke oxen
by the horns, and not by the neck.   Oxen can draw as
much by the horns as by the neck, but it looks more
savage. . . . The ox-yoke was almost a straight stick of
wood, cut at the ends to fit the horns of the ox, and was
tied to the horns with a strap of raw-hide." [2]   When
horses were used they were driven tandem.   The only
agricultural implement besides the plow was a heavy
iron hoe with a long shank, such as was in use among
the Indians long after the French had adopted lighter
tools of American make.

The cultivation was rude, but the rich soil, then in its
virgin strength, produced crops that supplied all the
needs of the settlers, and left an abundance for export
when prices justified exportation.   Nearly every year
barges loaded with flour, pork, tallow, hides and leather,
passed down the Mississippi to New Orleans, from which

---

[1] *Mich. Pion. Coll.*, vol. i. p. 353.

[2] *Pioneer Hist. of Ill.*, pp. 49, 50.   Breese's account is similar
to this.   *Early Hist. Ill.*, p. 196.

point the cargoes were reshipped to France and the
West Indies; in return came sugar, metal-goods, and
European fabrics.[1] " About the year 1746 there was a
great scarcity of provisions at New Orleans, and the
French settlements at the Illinois, small as they then
were, sent thither, in one winter, upwards of eight hundred thousand weight of Flour." [2] It is recorded that
one farmer in the Illinois furnished the king's magazine
eighty-six thousand pounds of flour, and this was but
part of his crop. Indian corn was not so much cultivated as wheat, and what was raised was used for feed-
ing cattle and hogs. Some was consumed in the shape
of hominy, but corn-bread was an unknown article of
diet.[3] Mills of various kinds were in use among the
French settlers from the earliest times, as also among
the Indians who adopted agriculture. In 1711, Penicaut writes of the Kaskaskias: " They have near their
village three mills for grinding their grain, to wit; a
wind-mill, belonging to the Reverend Jesuit Fathers,
which is much used by the settlers, and two others, horse-
mills, which belong to the Illinois themselves." [4] In
1727 the people of Kaskaskia were objecting to the
grant of half a league of land to three *habitants* who
were erecting a water-mill there.[5] Flour was transported
almost altogether in bags made of tanned elk skins.[6]
That the French had convenient mills was due to their
flocking together in settlements. The scattered Ameri-

[1] Davidson & Stuvé's *Ill.*, p. 127.

[2] Hutchins's *Top. Desc.*, p. 18, note; Du Pratz's *Hist. of La.*,
Lond. ed. of 1774, p. 182.

[3] Breese's *Ill.*, p. 195.

[4] Margry, vol. v. p. 490.

[5] Breese's *Early Ill.*, p. 289; Reynolds's *Ill.*, p. 92.

[6] Breese's *Ill.*, p. 206.

can farmers, who came later, subsisted largely on corn-meal, and made it in hand-mills, or with rude crushers or scrapers.[1]

The one vehicle of the French settlements was the *calèche*, or cart, a light, two-wheeled affair without tires or iron-work of any kind.[2] The same is in use in Normandy and other French provinces now; and it is still used, in the wilder parts of Canada and the Northwest, by the fur-traders and Indians. In some of them the bed resembled a dry-goods box; in others it was a platform surrounded by a low railing; in others the railing was along the sides only. It was used for all kinds of farm-work, hauling, and transportation. It had no seat. When used as a carriage, a buffalo robe spread on the floor served for a cushion, or, if the owner made pretensions to aristocracy, chairs were placed in it. For traveling through the wilderness, it was and is superior to a four-wheeled vehicle, but for farm use it could not compete with the wagon; and so it disappeared, with many others things once common to the Mississippi valley, so long ago that scarcely the memory of it remains where once it creaked and groaned over the rough trails.[3]

The houses varied in construction with the age of the settlements. In 1727, the missionary Du Poisson wrote: " A man, with his wife, or his associate, clears a small section, builds him a house with four forked sticks, which he covers with bark, plants some corn and rice for his

---

[1] Reynolds's *Pion. Hist. Ill.*, p. 144; *Hist. Knox Co.*, p. 88.

[2] These were also known by the more indefinite name of *voiture*. The Americans sometimes called them " barefooted wagons " One of them, as now used by the traders of the Northwest, is in the National Museum at Washington.

[3] *Mich. Pion. Coll.*, vol. i. p. 354; Law's *Vincennes*, p. 18; Cauthorn's *Vincennes*, p. 21.

food ; another year he raises more provisions, and begins a plantation of tobacco ; and if he finally attains to the possession of three or four negroes, behold the extent to which he can reach. This is what they call a plantation and a planter." [1] The next advance in architecture, which was as far as the poorer classes ever went, was the construction of log-houses in the mode called *poteaux au terre.* In some of these the posts which formed the walls were set on end in trenches, close one to another, and the interstices chinked with a mud mortar mixed with sticks, straw, or moss. In others the posts were grooved on the sides and set three or four feet apart, the intervening spaces being filled with puncheons, laid cross-wise, and fitting in the grooves. The mud was then applied and the surface was whitewashed inside and out. The roofs were sometimes thatched, sometimes covered with strips of bark, or, at a more recent day, covered with oak clapboards fastened by wooden pegs. The best class of houses, which began to appear in the later days of the French régime, were also built in this manner, or occasionally of stone. These were generally one story in height, with a loft above, lighted by dormer-windows, though occasionally they boasted two full stories. Ladders were always placed on the roofs for use in case of fires. The piazzas extended around the building. In this class of residences the doors were usually in the centres of the sides, opening into a hall which crossed from front to rear. On each side of the hall were two rooms ; on one side the *grande chambre* or parlor, and the *salle à manger* or dining-room ; on the other the *cabinet* or bed-room, and the *cuisine* or kitchen. No fire was used in the sleeping apartment.

[1] Kip's *Early Jesuit Missions,* p. 233.

The other rooms were usually heated by open fireplaces, though sometimes luxury reached the height of a stove set in the wall between the parlor and dining-room, with the doors opening into the latter.[1]

Adjoining the kitchen was the *boulangerie*, or bake-house, furnished with a brick oven and a trough for kneading bread. Butter was very seldom seen in one of the old French houses, probably on account of the difficulty of making it; they had no churns, and the little butter they used was made by shaking the cream in a bottle, or placing it in a bowl and beating it with a spoon. The washing was done at the nearest stream, whither the clothing was conveyed, and there cleansed by beating it with a mallet, as in parts of France at present. The furniture of the houses was ordinarily rude, though in some houses might be seen wardrobes, dressing-tables, and rush-bottomed chairs. Sometimes an odd bit of silverware, an heir-loom in the family, was conspicuously displayed; and not infrequently a Madonna or a print of the Passion appeared on the walls. The bed was the object of more attention than anything else in the line of furniture, for our French settlers loved comfort. Feather pillows were universal, and all who could possibly afford them had great feather beds spread on the rope network of their stilted bedsteads, and covered with quilts of bright patchwork. Carpets were unknown, but parlor floors were often covered with mats of Indian workmanship. About the house was always a garden, in which was to be seen a profusion of both vegetables and flowers. This was enclosed by a

---

[1] *Mich. Pion. Col.*, vol. i. p. 357; *Hist. Knox Co.*, pp. 241, 242; Breese's *Early Ill.*, p. 197; Reynolds's *Ill.*, p. 50; "Vincennes a Century Ago," in Potter's *Am. Mo.*, vol. xii. pp. 165, 166.

fence of sharpened pickets, set close together in the ground.[1]

The mechanical industries of the French settlements were in quite a primitive state. Says Governor Reynolds: "Mason-work of that day was good; but of the rest I can say nothing in praise of them. The cooperage of the country amounted to very little more than making well-buckets. The carpenters were unskillful in their profession. They framed houses and covered them with peg shingles; made batton doors, &c., in a rough fashion. No shoemakers or tanners; but all dressed deer skins, and made mawkawsins. Almost every inhabitant manufactured his own cart and plough, and made his harness, traces, and all, out of raw hides. Blacksmith shops were like iron — scarce. . . . In fact, neither male or female worked much; but the females assumed their prerogative, of doing less than the males. There was neither spinning-wheels or looms in the land. It must be awarded to the French, and particularly to the ladies, that they expended much labor, and showed much taste, in making nice gardens."[2] In the way of pure luxuries the settlers had tobacco and various liquors. The men smoked their pipes much of the time, and both men and women used snuff; elderly ladies were very seldom seen without their snuff-boxes. The Jesuits had breweries, in which a medium article of beer was made, from very early times; but the principal beverage of the French period was a native wine. Says Fraser: "They make, however a very bad Wine, from the natural vine of the Country which grows spontanious in every part of that

[1] Breese's *Ill.*, pp. 197, 198, 204; Reynolds's *Ill.*, pp. 51, 87, 88; *Mich. Pion. Coll.*, vol. iv. p. 73.
[2] *Pioneer Hist. Ill.*, pp. 87, 88.

Colony, this Wine tho' seemingly very unhealthy is sold at a most exorbitant price, when they have none else to drink." Others give a more favorable opinion of this wine than the disgruntled lieutenant, but it was probably nothing extra. About the beginning of the British period it rapidly gave way to "tafia," a rum made from molasses and the refuse of sugar-cane, which was imported from New Orleans. Clark's men were furnished with rations of this; but after American immigration had become rapid, tafia disappeared and Monongahela whiskey became the popular stimulant. At the same time very good native wines and liquors began to be manufactured by the Swiss colonists on the Ohio. The French had always their public houses, where the villagers could pass their time in conviviality, and where they often became boisterous and disorderly. St. Ange, in 1764, instructed his successors to "do away, as far as possible, with the disorder which arises from drinking." When Hamilton came and took possession of Vincennes, in 1778, he wrote that he had seized all the spirits in the place, and would destroy the billiard tables.[1] Think of it! Billiard tables on the Wabash in 1778! What a time they must have had getting them there; and what rare games they must have had on those vast expanses of green cloth, with dead cushions, uneven balls, and crooked cues!

The costumes of the people were, of course, of French mode, tinged somewhat with Indian characteristics. In summer the men wore shirts and pantaloons or leggings, the latter supported by a leathern girdle; the feet were

---

[1] Hamilton to Haldimand, December 28, 1778, *Can. Archives.* For preceding matters see Reynolds's *Ill.*, pp. 87, 229; Breese's *Ill.*, p. 195; Hutchins's *Top. Desc.*, pp. 29, 43.

bare ; the head was covered with a straw hat of domestic manufacture, or a knotted handkerchief of gaudy color. In winter moccasins or list shoes were worn ; also a long vest and a *capote* or cloak, with a hood for the head. For dress occasions, a broad sash, tied behind and dangling to the knees, replaced the leathern belt. It was usually of Indian make, adorned profusely with beads. The voyageurs affected leathern shirts, worn outside the pantaloons, and covered their heads with gay-colored, tasseled, cloth caps. The exterior garment of the women was the *habit*, a skirt reaching to the knees, below which the gaudy petticoat continued to the ankles. They wore large straw hats in summer, and fur hats or bonnets in winter.[1]

The religion of the French settlers was exclusively Roman Catholic, and with it were associated numerous customs which have since fallen out of remembrance in this state. Marriage was the great event of a lifetime. The banns were published on three successive Sundays. The ceremony was preceded by the contract of betrothal, drawn with the consummation of notarial skill, and witnessed by relatives and friends of the contracting parties ; it was followed by feasting, dancing, and pledging the health of the happy pair through the chief part of the succeeding night, and sometimes for several days. When a widow or widower married for the third time, the youth of the neighborhood indulged in a *chari-vari*, and the recipients of the discordant serenade could obtain peace only by payment to their tormentors of a sum of money, which professedly went to the poor in olden times, but in later years was used in purchasing

[1] *Mich. Pion. Coll.*, vol. i. p. 359; vol. iv. p. 74 ; Law's *Vincennes*, p. 18; Potter's *Am. Mo.*, vol. xii. p. 108.

refreshments for the serenaders. The American settlers
entered into this sport with so great zest that it came to
be common at any marriage, and, what was worse, it
became a method of insult and the cause of serious
affrays.[1] One instance, of modern years, in Michigan,
resulted in the killing of one of the serenaders by the
bridegroom, who was roused to desperation by the fact
that his mother was sick in the house at the time, and
her illness was dangerously aggravated by the noise.
He was convicted for the act in the lower court, but the
supreme court of the state reversed the decision because
the instructions did not concede to the prisoner the full
measure of his right to defend his home and family.[2]

Mardi Gras was always an occasion of celebration,
though, of course, not in the elaborate style that obtained
in cities. The evening was passed in entertainment at
the house of some one of the wealthier citizens. Cook-
ing pancakes, such as we call flap-jacks, was made an
amusement in which all the guests took part, the sport
consisting in the rivalry of tossing and turning them.
The one who tossed them highest and landed them
safely again in the long-handled skillet received the
compliments of all, while laughter and ridicule were the
lot of the unskillful. When cooked, the cakes were
piled up on plates, with maple-sugar, to form the chief
dish of the supper. After the feast came dancing until
midnight, when the guests bade farewell to wordly gay-
eties till Lent was over. On New Year's Day presents
were given, and calls were made by the gentlemen. Instead of saluting a caller with, " We have had fifty-seven

---

[1] Reynolds's *Pion. Hist. Ill.*, pp. 145, 146; Potter's *Am. Mo.*,
vol. xii. p. 167.

[2] Patten *v.* The People, 18 Mich. 313.

calls. How many have you made?" the hostess presented her cheek for a kiss, which was gallantly given.
After the English took possession of the country the
officers' wives attempted to break up this custom, but
they soon adopted it, substituting, however, the lips for
the cheek: the prudery of American settlers was proof
against any such familiarity, and so the charming old
fashion had to go. With it have also gone the christen-
ing of bells, the distribution of blessed bread and small
cakes on fête days, the taking of a collection by a lady
of the congregation on days of solemn feasts, and many
other of the manners of mother France. One that has
been revived a few times of recent years, at Detroit and
Grosse Pointe, is that of young men masking on New
Year's Eve and singing a peculiar carol from house to
house. In the olden time they took with them a cart,
in which the people placed clothing and provisions that
were afterwards distributed among the poor.[1]

Those who visited the settlements on the Wabash during the French and British occupations regarded them
as prosperous and promising. Captain Thomas Hutchins,
of His Majesty's 60th Regiment of Foot, afterwards
Geographer to the United States, who saw the country
in his occasional service there from 1764 to 1775, described them as follows: "Two *French* settlements are
established on the *Wabash*, called *Post Vincient* and
Ouiatanon; the first is 150 miles, and the other 262
miles from its mouth.[2] The former is on the eastern

[1] Potter's *Am. Mo.*, vol. xii. p. 167; *Mich. Pion. Coll.*, vol. iv.
pp. 70–78.

[2] He means 262 miles above Vincennes, as appears by his statements elsewhere. The estimate is too great, — an error that is
very common with Hutchins. See Volney's *Climate and Soil of
U. S.*, p. 4.

side of the river, and consists of 60 settlers and their families. They raise Indian Corn, — Wheat; and Tobacco of an extraordinary good quality; — superior, it is said, to that produced in Virginia. They have a fine breed of horses (brought originally by the *Indians* from the *Spanish* settlements on the western side of the River *Mississippi*) and large stocks of Swine and Black Cattle. The settlers deal with the natives for Furrs and Deer skins, to the amount of about 5000 l. annually. Hemp of a good texture grows spontaneously in the low lands of the *Wabash,* as do grapes in the greatest abundance, having a black, *thin* skin, and of which the inhabitants in the Autumn, make a sufficient quantity (for their own consumption) of *well-tasted Red-wine.* Hops, large and good, are found in many places, and the lands are particularly adapted to the culture of Rice. All European fruits: — Apples, Peaches, Pears, Cherrys, Currants, Gooseberrys, Melons, &c. thrive well, both here, and in the country bordering on the River Ohio.

"Ouiatanon is a small stockaded fort on the western side of the *Wabash,* in which about a dozen families reside. The neighboring Indians are the *Kickapoos, Musquitons, Pyankeshaws, and a principle part of the Ouiatanons.* The whole of these tribes consists, it is supposed, of about one thousand warriors. The fertility of the soil, and diversity of the timber in this country, are the same as in the vicinity of *Post Vincient.* The annual amount of Skins and Furrs obtained at Ouiatanon is about 8000 l. By the River *Wabash* the inhabitants of *Detroit* move to the southern parts of *Ohio* and the *Illinois* country. Their rout is by the *Miami River* to a carrying-place, which, as before stated, is nine miles to the Wabash, when this river is raised with Freshes;

but at other seasons, the distance is from 18 to 30 miles
including the portage. The whole of the latter is through
a level country. Carts are usually employed in trans-
porting boats and merchandise, from the *Miami* to the
Wabash river." [1] In connection with this portage a
curious fact is recorded in an itinerary made about
1773, and preserved in the Canadian archives, in these
words: "Between the Miami and the Ouabache there
are Beaver Dams which when water is low Passengers
break down to raise it, and by that means pass easier
than they otherwise would. When they are gone the
Beaver come and mend the Breach; for this reason
they have been hitherto sacred, as neither Indians or
White people hunt them." Here, then, was the first Wabash canal, in full operation, with beavers for keepers
of the locks, serving the traveling public without money
and without price. When Hamilton was camped at the
eastern terminus of the portage, on his way to attack
Vincennes, in 1778, he wrote: "By damming up the
water of this petite riviere 4 miles below the landing,
the water is backed and raised an inch here. At the Dam
it rose an inch the first hour. The Beavers had worked
hard for us, but we were obliged to break down their
dam to let the Boats pass, that were sent forward to
clear the river & a place called the chemin couvert." [2]

The journal of Captain Croghan, who was carried up
the Wabash by the Indians, in 1765, tells us how the
same places appeared to a Yankee and a prisoner. He
says: "On my arrival there [Vincennes] I found a village of about eighty or ninety French families settled on

---

[1] Hutchins's *Top. Desc.*, pp. 28–30.

[2] Hamilton to Haldimand, November 1, 1778, Haldimand Coll.,
Can. Archives.

the east side of this river, being one of the finest situations that can be found. The country is level and clear, and the soil very rich, producing wheat and tobacco. I think the latter preferable to that of Maryland or Virginia. The French inhabitants hereabouts, are an idle, lazy people, a parcel of renegadoes from Canada, and are much worse than the Indians. They took a secret pleasure at our misfortunes, and the moment we arrived, they came to the Indians, exchanging trifles for their valuable plunder. As the savages took from me a considerable quantity of gold and silver in specie, the French traders extorted ten half johannes [about $40] from them for one pound of vermilion. Here is likewise an Indian village of the Pyankishaws, who were much displeased with the party that took me. . . . Port Vincent is a place of great consequence for trade, being a fine hunting country all along the Ouabache, and too far for the Indians, which reside hereabouts, to go either to the Illinois, or elsewhere, to fetch their necessaries.

"The distance from Port Vincent to Ouicatanon is two hundred and ten miles. This place is situated on the Ouabache. About fourteen French families are living in the fort, which stands on the north side of the river. The Kickapoos and Musquattimes, whose warriors had taken us, live nigh the fort, on the same side of the river, where they have two villages ; and the Ouicatanons have a village on the south side of the river. The country hereabouts is exceedingly pleasant, being open and clear for many miles ; the soil is very rich and well watered ; all plants have a quick vegetation, and the climate is very temperate through the winter. This post has always been a very considerable trading place. The great plenty of furs taken in this country induced

the French to establish this post, which was the first on
the Ouabache, and by a very advantageous trade they
have been richly recompensed for their labor. On the
south side of the Ouabache runs a big bank, in which
are several fine coal mines, and behind this bank, is a
very large meadow, clear for several miles." [1]

The only additional French settlement within Indiana
at this time was at Kekionga [Fort Wayne], which
Croghan describes thus: " The Twightwee [Miami] village is situated on both sides of a river called St. Joseph.
This river, where it falls into the Miame river, about a
quarter of a mile from this place, is one hundred yards
wide, the east side of which stands a stockade fort,
somewhat ruinous. The Indian village consists of about
forty or fifty cabins, besides nine or ten French houses,
a runaway colony from Detroit, during the late Indian
war; they were concerned in it, and being afraid of
punishment, came to this post, where ever since they
have spirited up the Indians against the English. All
the French residing here are a lazy, indolent people,

---

[1] Butler's *Kentucky*, App., pp. 371–373. The nearest coal
mines now known are fifty miles or more below the site of Fort
Ouiatanon, though it is said by old settlers that there were formerly coal beds even above the Tippecanoe. Fort Ouiatanon had
no garrison, as far as known, after the surprise of the fort during
Pontiac's war. The place continued to be occupied by traders,
some of whom were in quasi-official relations, for many years.
It is even mentioned as in existence in the current century.
Brown's *Western Gazetteer*, p. 72. The greater part of the Indians
and traders removed to the mouth of the Tippecanoe, about the
beginning of the American occupation, and established the town
of Kethtippecanunk, which, with its "120 houses, eighty of which
were shingle-roofed," has often been confused with Ouiatanon.
Kethtippecanunk was the town destroyed by General James
Wilkinson in 1791. Imlay's *Top. Desc.*, p. 404.

fond of breeding mischief, and spiriting up the Indians against the English, and should by no means be suffered to remain here." There was no material change in the relative size and importance of these three settlements until the abandonment of Fort Ouiatanon.

The mention of European fruits, by Hutchins, brings to view a characteristic of the French colonists which is worthy of notice — their practice of planting orchards. Wherever was made a settlement that was expected to be permanent, fruit trees were planted, and long before the English occupation the inhabitants reveled in the annual burden of lusciousness that came to them almost without labor or care. Tradition puts the establishment of orchards about Detroit in the year 1720, and from these stocks, whose origin is now unknown, have sprung many of the most esteemed varieties of American fruit, especially those which have made Michigan famous. Hutchins's statement shows that nearly all species of large and small fruit had been planted on the Wabash and had proven thrifty before his time; and while this appears to be the earliest explicit mention of Indiana horticulture, there is a strong probability that the fruit trees came soon after the first influx of families, in 1735. The Jesuit fathers had introduced vegetables and fruits to the Illinois country at an early day. Penicaut, who was at Kaskaskia in 1711, says : "Grain grows here as well as in France, and every kind of vegetables, roots, and herbs ; there are also all sorts of fruits of an excellent taste."[1] They were therefore easily accessible from the Wabash. Le Page du Pratz, writing of the District of Illinois in 1758, says : "All the plants transported thither from France succeed well, as do also the fruits."[2] A large proportion of the apple

[1] Margry, vol. v. p. 489.   [2] *Hist. of Louisiana*, p. 182.

crop was made into cider, in mills of rude construction, but effective operation. " The crusher was a large stone or wood cylinder six to eight feet in diameter, and from six to ten inches in thickness. It turned on a wooden axis, fastened to a centre-post, and was carried around by horse-power. It ran in a trough, dug out of a large tree and put together by sections. The press consisted of a long wooden lever acting upon a platform and held down by tackling." [1]

In their personal characteristics, on account of their isolation from the world, the French of the Wabash country remained much as in the early years of the settlement. When Volney visited them, in 1796, his philosophic mind was impressed with this fact. He wrote : " In studying the manners of the settlers at Gallipolis and Fort Vincents I have found remarkable differences in many respects ; and I have clearly perceived that the French subjects of Lewis XIV. and XV., with their feudal and chivalrous sentiments, were far inferiour in industry and ideas of police to that generation, which since the year 1771 has received the impression of so many liberal ideas respecting the organization of society." [2]   Even their language retained very much of its original purity.   Volney says : " The language of these people is not a vulgar provincial dialect [*patois*], as I had been told, but tolerable French, intermixed with many military terms and phrases." [3]   The sneer which one of our recent historical writers gives at " that mixture of bad Spanish and bad English which did duty as a language at Vincennes " [4] is only a specimen of bad

[1] *Mich. Pion. Coll.*, vol. i. p. 355.

[2] *View of the Climate and Soil of the U. S.*, p. 391.

[3] *Ibid.* p. 373.

[4] McMasters' *Hist. People of U. S.*, vol. i. p. 380.

guess-work. Their written language was much worse than their speech. All that they knew was handed down from father to son. They had no other education. There was never a school in the state until during the American occupation. In the petitions that were sent to Congress from Indiana Territory, the number of French citizens who made their marks was only equaled by the number of those who might better have made their marks than the remarkable autographs they did make.

It is not surprising that these people were somewhat superstitious, though as to that they do not appear to have been worse than their American neighbors. In the record book of Colonel John Todd, who was sent out as civil governor by Virginia after the conquest by George Rogers Clark, there appear orders for the execution of two persons for witchcraft. One of these victims, a negro named Manuel, was chained to a post at the brink of the river, at Kaskaskia, and burned alive, after which his ashes were scattered. The other, a negro named Moreau, was hanged near Cahokia; he acknowledged his guilt of destroying his master by magic spells, but said "his mistress had proved too powerful for his necromancy." Both of these executions occurred in 1779.[1] As the American governor approved these executions, it would be unjust to hold them caused by a superstition that was peculiarly French. The fact is that Voudouism was very generally believed in and feared at that time, and even at this day the number of those who hold to its verity is astonishing. There have

[1] *Colonel Todd's Record Book.* in Fergus Hist. Ser., No. 12, pp. 58, 59; Reynolds's *Pioneer Hist.*, pp. 142, 143; Davidson & Stuvé's *Ill.*, p. 230.

always been, and probably will always be, blacks who claim the power of casting spells over others, causing them to be inhabited by snakes and toads, and relieving them of these disagreeable tenants when possessed of them by the influence of others.　The color and usually the appearance of these quacks adds to the power of their pretensions, so that when they resolutely undergo the severest punishments for their asserted powers the timid spectator can scarcely avoid some belief in them. There are many traditions of these people, who have flourished at various periods in the Mississippi valley. One of the best authenticated, of the olden time, is of an old negress named Janette, living in the Illinois country, who was considered so formidable in the exercise of her " evil eye " that even adults used to flee at her approach.　It may be mentioned in this connection that, although the laws of England no longer permitted the punishment of witchcraft by death, those who *pretended* to its use were subject to a year's imprisonment and to stand four times in the pillory.[1]　Sir William Blackstone, whose Commentaries appeared only fourteen years before these executions, was apparently in some doubt on the subject.　He says: " To deny the possibility, nay, actual existence, of witchcraft and sorcery, is at once flatly to contradict the revealed word of God, in various passages both of the Old and New Testament ; and the thing itself is a truth to which every nation in the world hath in turn borne testimony, either by examples seemingly well attested or by prohibitory laws, which at least suppose the possibility of commerce with evil spirits."　After some reflections on the numerous impostures and delusions that had occurred in connection with

---

[1] 9 Geo. II. c. 5.

the offense, he concludes with Addison, "that in general there has been such a thing as witchcraft; though one cannot give credit to any particular modern instance of it." [1]

Powers similar to those of the negro Voudous were often claimed by the medicine-men of the Indian tribes, and the account is preserved of the execution of three Indians in Indiana on charges of witchcraft. This was in the year 1806, just after the Shawnee prophet Law-lewasikaw [The Loud Voice], brother of Tecumthe, had assumed the name Pemsquatawah [The Open Door], and begun his career as a spiritual leader. He claimed the power of detecting those who practiced witchcraft, and told the Indians that the Great Spirit commanded them to put such persons to death. He soon preferred charges of witchcraft against Tatebockoshe,[2] an old Delaware chief, who had been instrumental in securing the assent of the Delawares to the treaty of 1804, by which lands north of the Ohio were ceded, contrary to the wishes of the other tribes. Tatebockoshe was tried, condemned, and tomahawked; his body was burned. Accusations were then made against his wife, a nephew called Billy Patterson, and an old Indian called Joshua, all of whom were condemned. The two men were burned at the stake, but the woman was saved by her brother, who boldly led her out of the council-house and checked the growing superstition by solemnly exclaiming: "The evil spirit has come among us, and we are killing each other." This protest, and some strong re

---

[1] *Blackstone's Commentaries*, book iv. p. 60; *Spectator*, No. 117.

[2] Teteboxke, Tatebuxica, Tatabaugsuy — The Twisting Vine. *Ind. Gazette*, April 12, 1806; *Penn. Archives*, vol. i. p. 100.

monstrances from Governor Harrison, put an end to this
feature of the Prophet's work.[1]

It does not appear that the French civilization had
any material effect on the manners and customs of the
the Indians in general. Some of them were converted
to Catholicism; a few undertook something like an
agricultural life. As a general rule, these advances
were merely grafted on the savagery which still remained, yet those who were best acquainted with them
thought they saw proofs of improvement. In 1796,
William Wells [2] said to Count Volney: "The Indians
of the Wabash, the Miamis, Putewoatimies, &c., are
better than they were three or four score years ago.
The peace they have enjoyed in consequence of the decline of the Six Nations has enabled them to cultivate
with the hoe Indian corn, potatoes, and even our cab-
bages and turnips: our prisoners have planted peach
and apple trees, and taught them to breed poultry, pigs,
and lately cows; in short, the Choctaws and Creeks of
Florida are not farther advanced." [3] All of their advancement is substantially summed up in this statement.
On the other hand, in one respect at least they were
infinitely worse off than they were before the white
man came. They had acquired the appetite for rum,
to satisfy which they were ready and willing to sacri-

[1] Dillon, p. 425; *Ind. Gazette*, Apr'l 12, 1806. The Indian
village at which these executions occurred was at the site of York-
town, Delaware County.

[2] Wells was a noted interpreter, guide, and Indian agent in
early times. He was captured by the Indians in Kentucky when
thirteen years old and adopted by them. Heckewelder, p. 256;
Volney's *Climate and Soil*, p. 398; McBride's *Pion. Biog.*,
vol. ii. pp. 99–102.

[3] Volney's *Climate and Soil*, p. 429.

fice anything they possessed. No tribe escaped this curse, but those who were most friendly suffered most. The early French missionaries bewailed the damage done by rum; the English and Americans who took an interest in the natives, other than for profit, shuddered at its work; the Indians themselves, in their sober moments, lamented their weakness; but there was no cessation of debauchery.

Behold this picture drawn by Governor Denonville in 1690: "I have witnessed the evils caused by liquor among the Indians. It is the horror of horrors. There is no crime nor infamy that they do not perpetrate in their excesses. A mother throws her child into the fire; noses are bitten off; this is a frequent occurrence. It is another Hell among them during these orgies, which must be seen to be credited. They get drunk very often to have the privilege of satisfying their old grudges. Punishment cannot be inflicted on them as on Frenchmen who may commit a fault. Remedies are impossible as long as every one is permitted to sell and traffic in ardent spirits. However little at a time each may give, the Indians will always get drunk. There is no artifice that they will not have recourse to, to obtain the means of intoxication. Besides every house is a groggery. Those who allege that the Indians will remove to the English, if Brandy be not furnished to them, do not state the truth; for it is a fact that they do not care about drinking as long as they do not see Brandy; and the most reasonable would there had never been any such thing, for they set their entrails on fire and beggar themselves by giving their peltries and clothes for drink." [1]

[1] *N. Y. Col. Docs.*, vol. ix. p. 441.

Did the English do as badly as the French? Yes, quite as badly. Even in Pennsylvania, rum accomplished its perfect work. Can you imagine the sadness with which the Shawnee chiefs came to Governor Gordon, in 1732, with this speech: "The Delaware Indians some time agoe bid us Departt for they was Dry, and wanted to Drink ye land away, whereupon wee told them Since Some of you are Gone to Ohioh, wee will go there also; wee hope you will not Drink that away too." [1] But they did drink much of Ohio away too, and much of other lands. The habit seems to be a mania with them which they cannot control, and no tribes were more addicted to it than those of the Wabash. There have been many shocking recitals of Indian debauches, from which I select one worthy of the pen of Emile Zola, a description of the gathering of the Wabash tribes at Vincennes, in 1796, by Volney: "From early in the morning both men and women roam about the streets, for no other purpose but to procure themselves rum; and for this they first dispose of the produce of their chase, then of their toys, next of their clothes, and at last they go begging for it, never ceasing to drink till they are absolutely senseless. Sometimes this gives occasion to ridiculous scenes; they will hold the cup to drink with both hands like apes, then raise up their heads with bursts of laughter, and gargle themselves with their beloved but fatal liquor, to enjoy the pleasure of tasting it the longer; hand the cup from one to another with noisy invitations; call to one only three steps off as loud as they can bawl; take hold of one of their wives by the head and pour the rum down her throat with coarse caresses, and all the ridiculous gestures of

[1] *Penn. Archives*, vol. i. p. 330.

our vulgar ale-house sots. Sometimes distressing scenes ensue, as the loss of all sense and reason, becoming mad or stupid, or falling down dead drunk in the dust or mud, there to sleep till the next day. I could not go out in a morning without finding them by dozens in the streets or paths about the village, literally wallowing in the dirt with the pigs. It was a very fortunate cir-cumstance if a day passed without a quarrel, or a battle with knives or tomahawks, by which ten men on an average lose their lives yearly. On the 9th of August, at four o'clock in the afternoon, a savage stabbed his wife in four places with a knife within twenty steps of me. A fortnight before a similar circumstance took place, and five such the year preceding. For this vengeance is immediately taken, or dissembled till a proper opportunity offers, by the relatives, which pro-duces fresh causes for waylaying and assassination." [1] In fairness it must be said that the condition of affairs in Vincennes at this time was not wholly due to the French, for in 1796 they did not much outnumber the Americans there. It is also a striking fact that the occurrences which Count Volney witnessed happened just one year after the repeal of the first statutory liquor law of Indiana, — an absolute prohibitory law as to In-dians, — which had been in force for five years ; and this law was repealed by the American governor and judges.

There remains one other feature of the old French civilization to be noticed, — the institution of slavery. So far back as the records of the settlements take us, slavery existed on the Wabash, as in all the other French colonies. Of the legal aspects of this we shall

[1] *View of Climate and Soil of U. S.*, pp. 395, 396.

treat hereafter ; for the present it suffices to say that
the slavery which existed at Vincennes, and in the country below the present site of Terre Haute, was regulated
by the laws of the Province of Louisiana, of which this
country was a part; while that which existed at Fort
Ouiatanon, Fort Miamis, and other points above Terre
Haute, was regulated by the customs of Canada. In
Canada the greater portion of the slaves were Indians,
commonly called panis, who had been taken in war and
sold. In Louisiana the greater portion of the slaves
were negroes, brought from Africa or from the French
islands. Indian slaves also were held in Louisiana, but
not in so great numbers. At the destruction of the
Natchez nation, all the prisoners were reduced to slavery
and scattered among the French colonies. Both negro
and Indian slaves were commonly carried between
Canada and Louisiana and sold in either. In early
times nearly all the slaves at Vincennes were Indians,
it being remote from the centre of agricultural pursuits,
and its inhabitants being largely engaged in the Indian
trade. The old church records [1] contain frequent mentions of the births, baptisms, and deaths of panis down
to the time of the British occupation, but from that time
they decline in frequency, as Indian slavery gradually
gave way to negro slavery. The causes of this were
the importation of negroes, the amalgamation of Indian
and negro slaves, and the stoppage of the source of supply of panis by the Indian tribes becoming gradually
united among themselves and turning on their white
foes.

[1] The Parish Records of Vincennes are at present being prepared for publication by John Gilmary Shea, D. D., who is perhaps better fitted for this work than any other person.

In Canada the provisions of law governing slavery were confined to a few brief and unimportant edicts of colonial governors and intendants. In Louisiana quite an elaborate code was in effect. It is said by Montesquieu that Louis XIII. was reluctant to admit negro slavery to his colonies, but consented to it because it was urged that the conversion of the negroes to Christianity would thereby be furthered.[1] Louis XV. was also much concerned for the eternal welfare of the slaves, and, in March, 1724, published an ordinance which made minute provision for the management of slaves, and particularly for their education in the Catholic religion. This ordinance continued in effect during the French régime.[2] Under its provisions slaves were required to be baptized and educated in the Catholic religion ; they were not allowed to work on Sundays or holy days ; their masters were required to furnish them a regular amount of food and clothing fixed by public officers, and to support them in sickness and old age. For criminal offenses, and running away, slaves were punished by the courts ; masters were forbidden to torture, mutilate, or otherwise punish a slave, except by whipping with rods or cords. Slaves might be levied on by a creditor, but families were not allowed to be separated on sale. When freed, slaves at once became enfranchised with all the rights and privileges of white citizens, including the right to hold slaves. Masters were prohibited from living in concubinage with slaves under penalty of a heavy fine, and the forfeiture of the slave and any children she may have borne ; except that when the master

---

[1] *Spirit of the Laws*, vol. i. ch. iv.

[2] *Code Noir*, p. 281. The ordinance is given in full in Dillon, pp. 31–43.

was a negro he was required to marry the slave, and
thereupon she and her children became free. The public
officers were required to see that these laws were properly enforced; and, in case a slave was not properly
provided for by his master, the officers provided for him
and obliged the master to repay the expense.

The lot of the slaves of the Northwest has aptly been
compared to that of children. The laws gave them
broad protection; the temperament of the colonists was
not productive of brutality; there was no market for
surplus crops which gave any great incentive to extensive
or careful agriculture. The peculiarity of temperament
which made the French masters lenient to their slaves
was a lack of what we call thrift. They were a careless,
happy-go-lucky people, who took little thought for the
morrow. They worked as little as possible themselves,
and took no pleasure in making others work. A man
that we would call prudent, or saving, or thrifty, would
have been to them a miser. The great majority of them
were satisfied if they had comparative ease and comfort,
and their ideas of comfort were not so high as to call
for much effort in satisfying them.[1] In addition to this,
the French settlers had none of those theories of independence and natural rights which make English-speaking
peoples look down on those who are contented in servile
positions. They did not participate in their own government and did not desire to do so. Their slaves had
much nearer as great rights as the masters than they
did under any other American system of slavery. The
same officers who governed the masters were required to
see that the slaves received their lawful rights at the
hands of the masters. It is to be remembered also that

[1] Reynolds's *Ill.*, p. 37.

the slaves of the southern parts of Louisiana were
worked harder than those of the upper part, chiefly
because exportation was more ready and the products
of labor therefore of more value. This, with the difference of climate, made the lot of slaves in the lower
country more unenviable than that of those to the north.
On the whole, the slavery that existed north of the Ohio
was as endurable as any slavery could be, and the
slavery in all Louisiana was much less objectionable
than that which existed in the English colonies. English
writers conceded this, and attributed the difference to
the slave codes then in force, the contrast between which
was well summed up by Edmund Burke in the statement that the French slaves "are not left, as they are
with us, wholly, body and soul, to the discretion of the
planter." [1]

Such were the French settlers of Indiana — yet not
such; for we have scanned too closely what we might
esteem their faults, and given little heed to what we
must admit to be their virtues. In many respects they
were admirable. They were simple, honest, and patriotic. In personal courage and resolution they often
rose to the heights of heroism. In their social life they
were kindly, sympathetic, and generous. Above all, they
were unselfish and public-spirited. The numerous instances of their self-sacrifice which have come down to
us, and of which we shall note several later on, will
ever rank among the brightest pages of our local history.
Notwithstanding the prejudices of race, the American
settlers who lived among them, and quarreled with them,

[1] *Account of the European Settlements in America*, London, 1757,
vol. ii. p. 45. This book was published anonymously, but is commonly accorded to Burke.

and at odd times hated them, as human beings are prone
to do with their neighbors, still had for them feelings of
hearty respect and esteem. When the older generations
were gone, and the younger stock had adopted American
ways, the older Americans looked back with wistful
memory to their former associates. We see this in the
brief retrospects they have left for us, and as we read
their words we pass, by some subtle sympathy of soul,
into their fancies. The ancient *habitant* rises before us
lithe and erect as in his prime. The old capote is there,
the beaded moccasins, the little earrings, and the black
queue. His dark eyes glisten beneath his turban handkerchief as of yore. There stands his old calèche. He
mounts upon it and moves away — away — away —
until its creaking sounds no longer, and we realize that
he is gone forever.

CHAPTER IV.

THE opening of the Revolution brought evil times to the American frontiers. The Indians, supplied with English arms, and led by men in English pay, carried devastation everywhere. I am aware that bills authorizing the employment of Indians were repeatedly defeated in Parliament, and that British officers claimed that the natives were driven to war by the cruel wrongs inflicted on them by Americans; but these were the orders: "It is the King's command that you should direct Lieutenant-Governor Hamilton to assemble as many of the Indians of his district as he conveniently can, and placing a proper person at their head, to conduct their parties, and restrain them from committing violence on the *well-affected, inoffensive inhabitants,* employ them in making a diversion and exciting an alarm on the frontiers of Virginia and Pennsylvania." [1] Such proper persons as Simon Girty, William Lamothe, Joseph Brant, and others, were employed by Hamilton as leaders of these parties, and, in order to restrain them still further, he offered a premium for the scalps of Americans. [2] The frontiersmen made the matter worse by their own suicidal policy in imprisoning and murder-

[1] Lord George Germaine to Sir Guy Carleton, March 26, 1776: Haldimand Coll.

[2] Jefferson's *Works*, vol. i. p. 456.

ing Cornstalk, Red Hawk, and Ellinipsco, Shawnee
chiefs, at the mouth of the Great Kanawha, whereby
many Indians who were inclined to be friendly were
driven over to the enemy.[1]   A great leader was needed
on the frontier, and one was at hand.   George Rogers
Clark, a young Virginian of extraordinary character,
had settled in Kentucky in 1776.   He had secured the
organization of Kentucky as a county of Virginia; he
had persuaded the Executive Council to contribute 500
pounds of powder to the defense of the frontier; and
now his fertile brain was developing a great project.

For adequate relief from the depredations of the savages young Clark could see but one method.   Kaskaskia,
Vincennes, and Detroit were the points from which the
Indians received their arms and ammunition, and to
which they carried their booty.   If these posts could be
taken and held, the Indians would be deprived of their
bases of action, and would be compelled either to make
peace or to continue the war on their own lands.   This
course he decided must be adopted, but he knew that
there were many difficulties in the way, one of the most
serious being the task of convincing the authorities of
the wisdom of the attempt.   In the summer of 1777, to
obtain definite information, he sent out two spies, who
brought back intelligence that the British garrisons were
actively promoting Indian depredations, and that, notwithstanding the misrepresentations of the English, there
were still many of the French settlers who felt kindly
towards the Americans.   Clark went to Virginia and
laid before Governor Patrick Henry and the Executive
Council his plan for the conquest of the Northwest.
Governor Henry was pleased with the boldness of the

[1] *Annals of the West*, p. 176.

project, and the Executive Council was speedily persuaded of its feasibility. There were some objections
made, but Clark was ready to answer them. The men
in authority were disposed to act. The recent victory
at Saratoga had inspired them with confidence in their
cause, and Congress had already considered the necessity of taking possession of the Northwest, and had
taken action looking towards it. On January 2, 1778,
the Governor issued two sets of instructions to Clark:
one, for public use, authorizing him to raise seven companies of fifty men each, for militia service in Kentucky;
the other, private, directing him to raise the same force
and attack the British post at Kaskaskia. The instructions were specially explicit that the French settlers
should be treated with humanity, and that, if any would
accept the sovereignty of Virginia, they should be
"treated as fellow-citizens and their persons and property duly secured." He was to receive ammunition at
Pittsburg; and, to defray expenses, he was furnished
£1200 in the depreciated colonial currency. He had
also the promise of Thomas Jefferson, George Mason,
and George Wythe, that they would use their influence
to secure a bounty of 300 acres of land for each man
engaged in the expedition, if it were successful. With
this shadowy provision for his army, Clark's next business was to get the army. He tried to raise recruits at
Fort Pitt with but little success, but while here he received information that his subordinate officers were
progressing more rapidly; that Major W. B. Smith,
who had gone to the settlements on the Holston, had
raised four companies; and that Captains Leonard Helm
and Joseph Bowman had collected two companies on the
Monongahela. Meanwhile, however, Clark's enemies

had been at work, hindering men from enlisting, encouraging those who had enlisted to desert, and stirring up prejudice against the youthful commander, until, says Clark, "they set the whole Fronteers in an uproar." The longer he remained the worse it became. Uniting his recruits with those of Bowman and Helms, he started down the river with 150 men. At the mouth of the Kentucky he was joined by Captain Dillard with less than one company; the rest of Smith's men had dispersed. On went Clark to the Falls of the Ohio, where he landed on what is now called Corn Island and built a block-house for the protection of his supplies. At this time there was no settlement at the Falls, though 2,000 acres now included in Louisville had been patented in 1773 to Connolly, the notorious commander of Fort Pitt at that time. Here Clark first informed his men of the real design of the expedition, and naturally enough it put a damper on the ardor of many of them. A number of the Tennessee men asked leave to return home, but were refused; guards were placed over the boats to prevent desertion. In the night a part of the Tennesseeans evaded the sentinels, waded to the Kentucky shore, and started for the settlements. A force was sent after them in the morning with instructions to shoot any one who would not return, but only eight of them were captured. Strict discipline was now enforced, and though there still remained many who would gladly have abandoned the hazardous task set before them, they found no opportunity to escape. Says the dare-devil commander: "I knew that my case was desperate, but the more I reflected on my weakness the more I was pleased with the Enterprize."

On June 24th, leaving his block-house in possession of

several pioneer families which had followed him down
the river, Clark embarked with his army of 153 men.
They rowed up-stream far enough to gain the main
channel, and then plunged down through the Indiana
chute "at the very moment of the sun being in a great
eclipse, which caused various conjectures among the
superstitious." Clark abandoned his original design of
attacking Vincennes first, as he had erroneous information that there was a large garrison there, besides Indians. The oars were double-manned and plied night
and day until, on June 28th, the party landed on an
island at the mouth of the Tennessee River. We must
pass the details of their march across southern Illinois,
the surprise of Kaskaskia on the night of July 4th, the
terror of the French settlers on finding themselves in
the hands of the Americans, and their transports of joy
on learning that they were not only to be unmolested, but
also to be received and protected as fellow-citizens, — a
joy which Clark tells us they manifested by "addorning
the streets with flowers & Pavilians of different colours,
compleating their happiness by singing &c." On receipt
of information of the actions and intentions of the Americans from their Kaskaskian brethren, the Cahokians also
came over to the American cause, with manifestations
of great pleasure. Vincennes remained to be secured,
but Clark supposed that for want of men and supplies
he was unable to march against it with hope of success,
on account of the strength of its garrison. He was
desirous that some of the Kaskaskians should go there,
and seek to win the inhabitants to the American cause,
but he was also desirous that none of the French should
know his actual feeling on the subject. He attributed
his success thus far to his policy of intimidation, and this

was probably correct, to some extent. He had entered
Fort Gage at night, and by misrepresenting his actual
force, and excluding the villagers from the fort, he had
made them believe his command much larger than it
was.   He had also pretended that he had a strong garrison at the Falls, and could obtain any number of men
he wanted from Kentucky by calling for them. This
policy was still necessary to be pursued, because the Indians were yet to be dealt with, and there was no possible way of bringing them to subjection except overaw-
ing them.   After reflection, he announced that he was
about to march against Vincennes, and should send a
messenger to the Falls ordering a body of troops from
there to join him at a certain point, to aid in destroying
the post.   The Kaskaskians at once interposed to save
their friends at Vincennes.   Father Gibault and Dr.
Lafonte volunteered to go to the post and win over the
inhabitants. The proposition was accepted, and on July
14, 1778, the two emissaries departed with a little ret-
inue, in which, for additional security, the wary Clark
had placed a spy.   In two days after their arrival Vincennes was an American post.   Abbott was at Detroit,
and there was no garrison.   The people went to the village church in a body and took the oath of allegiance;
an officer was elected, the fort garrisoned, and the
American flag was raised for the first time on Indiana
soil.

The Indians were astonished at the transformation.
When they were informed by their French friends that
the French king had come to life and joined with the
Americans, — that he was angry with them for fighting
for the British, — they began to experience a change of
heart.   Father Gibault returned to Kaskaskia about the

first of August and brought the cheering news to Clark, but Clark now had a new trouble. The time for which his men had enlisted had expired, and he had no authority to extend it. Very little time was needed for arriving at a decision that he must hold the acquired territory, even without authority. He reënlisted for eight months all his men who could be induced by liberal promises to longer service. About one hundred of them decided to remain with him, and the vacancies were quickly filled by French settlers. Those who did not reënlist were sent home, and at the same time orders were sent to the Falls to move the stores to the Kentucky shore and build a fort there.[1] Captain Leonard Helm was put in command of Vincennes, and appointed Superintendent of Indian affairs on the Wabash by Clark. The principal business entrusted to him was securing the friendship of the Indians of the Wabash, particularly of the Piankeshaws, as they were located at and near Vincennes. Their head chief was Tabac,[2] who, inasmuch as his tribe lived lower down the Wabash than any other, and therefore commanded its navigation, was called the Grand Door of the Wabash. Clark sent a message to him by Helm, telling him to espouse the cause of the British, or the Big Knives, as he pleased, — to select peace or war, — but to stand firmly by his choice when it was made. After several days of ceremonious negotiation,

---

[1] An unsuccessful attempt to recover compensation for building this fort was made in 1841 by the heirs of Richard Chenowith. *House Reports*, No. 183, 2d Sess. 26th Cong. The families left by Clark had removed to the Kentucky shore and built cabins soon after his departure. They were joined by others in the spring of 1779. Louisville was laid off in 1780 by William Pope.

[2] Tobacco ; his father had the same name, hence this chief was sometimes called Young Tabac, or Tobacco's Son.

during which the causes of the war were explained to the Indians in a figurative way, Tabac declared himself satisfied that the British were wrong, and that, if they succeeded in conquering the Americans, they would treat the Indians with similar oppression; from which considerations he announced himself a Big Knife. His example was followed by some of the other Wabash tribes; and as the news of the doings of the French and their neighboring Indians passed from village to village through the wilderness, the tribes of the Northwest began flocking to Cabokia to treat with the Big Knife captain, some of them coming a distance of 500 miles. Clark treated them with a characteristic assumption of coolness and indifference, until they were in fear that they were in danger of immediate destruction, and then granted their humble prayers for a treaty of peace, which was what he wanted above all things. Soon afterwards Helm went up the Wabash with a small force to attack Celeron, the British agent at the Wea towns, who was interfering seriously with the pacification of the Indians. Celeron fled, but his red adherents were surprised and captured. Helm made a treaty with them and released them.

Clark continued to use every art of diplomacy to attach the French and Indians to the American cause, and his efforts were completely successful; but the English had a very clear knowledge of his strength, and rightly attributed his successes to his extraordinary spirit and tact.[1] They were not ready to relinquish the West without a struggle. In the fall of 1778, General Henry Hamilton, Lieutenant-Governor of Detroit, raised a force of thirty regulars, fifty Canadian volunteers, and four

---

[1] *Annual Register* for 1779, p. 16.

hundred Indians, and proceeded by the Wabash to Vincennes. His expedition was successful. He captured the spies that Clark had put out, and on December 15th appeared at Vincennes. Helm was in the fort with only one man, but he stood by a loaded cannon with a lighted match in his hand, and declared that no one should enter until he knew the terms that would be given, whereupon Hamilton conceded the honors of war to the garrison, and Vincennes was again an English post. Hamilton sent his Indians out to harass the frontier, and also sent a party of forty to attempt the capture of Clark, but the plans of the latter party were frustrated and they returned empty-handed.

Clark remained at Kaskaskia without any exact information of the situation at Vincennes, knowing only that it was in the hands of the British, until January 29, 1779, when his state of uncertainty was relieved by the appearance of Colonel Francis Vigo. Vigo was a Sardinian, born at Mondovi in 1740: he left his home in his youth and enlisted in a Spanish regiment, with which he went to Havana, and afterwards to New Orleans. After brief service there, he left the army and engaged in the Indian trade, the capital being supplied by persons of importance in the colony. His headquarters were at St. Louis. Governor de Leyba, who resided there, was interested in business with him. He became acquainted with Clark and tendered him his services. Clark requested him to go to Vincennes and report from time to time the exact condition of affairs there, for which purpose Vigo at once departed, accompanied by one servant. At the Embarrass River he was captured by hostile Indians, who carried him before Hamilton, then lately arrived at the post. For several weeks he was held on a parole requirement to report every day at the fort, then called Fort Sackville, he having refused to accept liberty which was offered him if he would agree "not to do any act during the war injurious to the British interests." Father Gibault, who was at Vincennes, interested himself actively in Vigo's behalf, and finally, after services one Sunday morning in January, went to the fort, at the head of his parishioners, and notified Hamilton that they would furnish no more supplies to the garrison until Vigo was released. Hamilton, having no evidence against Vigo, and being desirous of retaining the friendship of the villagers, released his prisoner on condition that he should "not do anything injurious to the British interests on his way to St. Louis." Vigo embarked in a pirogue with two voyageurs and sped away, down the Wabash, down the Ohio, up the Mississippi, until the Illinois settlements were left behind and the village of St. Louis was reached. He spent a few minutes changing his clothes and obtaining a few supplies, and was in the boat again; the flying paddles stir the chill waters; he is at Kaskaskia, and Clark has minute and exact intelligence concerning all matters at Vincennes.

The situation was desperate. Hamilton had eighty men behind the stockades of Fort Sackville, with artillery and an abundance of ammunition. He might receive reinforcements at any time. If unmolested until spring opened, he would certainly have a large force of soldiers and a thousand or more of Indians. Clark flung his gauntlet in the face of Fate and assumed the offensive. On February 4th he dispatched a large boat, mounting two four-pounders and four large swivel guns, commanded by Lieutenant Rogers, with orders to go within ten leagues of Vincennes and there await orders. Says Clark: " This Vessel when compleat was much admired by the Inhabitants, as no such thing had been seen in the country before." She was called The Willing. On the next day Clark began his march overland with one hundred and seventy men. It is probably impossible that any one at this time could conceive the hardships of that march of one hundred and sixty miles. The weather was not severe, though it was the depth of winter, but rain fell during the greater part of the time. The prairies were very wet, and that meant more in those days than it does in this era of drainage and elevated roadways, although no experienced person would select a pilgrimage through Illinois in wet weather for a pleasure trip even now. They were twelve days in reaching the Embarrass River. Three of those days were consumed in passing the Little Wabash and one of its affluents, which had united their floods, overflowing the bottom lands to a breadth of five miles. The channels of the two streams were passed by means of a large canoe; the remainder of the distance the men waded through water three and at times four feet deep. On the evening of the 17th, when they reached the Embarrass, they found it impassable and marched down it till eight o'clock, seeking for a dry camping-place, but as they could find none they remained over night at a place where they " found the water falling from a small spot . of ground." In the morning they marched on to the banks of the Wabash.

They were now ten miles from Vincennes, separated from it by two rivers and by more than seven miles of land that was overflowed to a depth of three feet or more, over which they must pass. They were entirely out of provisions. The Willing was not expected for two or three days. Four men were sent out to steal boats from opposite Vincennes, but returned unsuccessful and reported it impossible to cross the Embarrass. Rafts were made and four others were sent to look for boats, but they too returned unsuccessful, having "spent the day and night in the water to no purpose; for there was not one foot of dry land to be found." By the time they returned (three o'clock on the afternoon of the 19th) a canoe had been made, in which Clark sent two men to search for The Willing, with orders for it to come on day and night, but their search was fruitless. On the 20th signs of despair began to appear in the famishing party; many of the French volunteers talked of going back. To employ them, Clark set them all to work making canoes. At noon a boat containing five Frenchmen from Vincennes was hailed on the river and brought to shore. The men gave information that the party was not discovered; that the villagers were favorable to them; and that there were two canoes adrift on the river above. One of these canoes was secured by a party sent to look for them. This day one of the men killed a deer and brought it in. It furnished a mouthful of food for each of the one hundred and seventy hungry men, and saved the expedition.

On the 21st the men were all ferried across the Wabash channel, after which they marched for three miles, through water that was at places deep as to their necks, and camped on a little hill. It rained all day and they were without provisions. On the 22d they succeeded in getting three miles farther, wading all the way, with not a morsel to eat. That night the weather turned cold, and the wet clothing of the men froze upon them.

Morning found the little army almost exhausted. Before them stretched for four miles the Horseshoe Plain, covered with water breast deep, through which they must march if they reached Vincennes. Clark addressed them briefly, telling them that at the woods which they saw beyond the plain their fatigues would be over. He turned without waiting for any reply and entered the water, crushing the thin ice that covered its surface. The men gave a shout and followed him. He turned, after a few had entered the water, and directed Captain Bowman to fall back with twenty-five men and shoot any one who refused to march. Another shout of approbation went up at this order, and the men pressed forward to the task, which they soon found to be a heavy one. The woods were reached, but the dry land was beyond them, and the strength of the men was well-nigh spent. Swiftly as possible the canoes plied along the line, picking up the weak and carrying them on to the shore. Here a failing soldier was aided by a stronger comrade ; there one clung to a tree or lay helpless on a log. Nature was taxed to her utmost. Says Clark : " Many would reach the shore, and fall with their bodies half in the water, not being able to support themselves without it."

Recuperation was rapid. The day was bright, and the fires which had been built by the first arrivals quickly dried and warmed the band of heroes. Luckily enough, some squaws and children came along in a canoe and were captured. They had with them half a quarter of a buffalo, some corn, some tallow, and several kettles. Broth was made and carefully doled out to the exhausted men. The spirits of the party were soon raised to the highest pitch. Warmed, dried, and re-

freshed, they jested over the hardships of which they
were still feeling the effects, but those effects were doubtless felt by many of them in later years, and certainly
those hardships were never forgotten. Nine months
later, writing to his friend George Mason, of Virginia,
Clark said : " If I was sensible that you would let no
Person see this relation, I would give You a detail of
our suffering for four days in crossing those waters, and
the manner it was done, as I am sure that You wou'd
Credit it, but it is too incredible for any Person to believe except those that are as well acquainted with me
as you are, or had experienced something similar to it."

The Rubicon was now passed. The Americans were
in a position from which there was no escape except by
victory. They were in good spirits, and did not for a
moment doubt that they would succeed ; but Clark knew
that there was little hope of taking Fort Sackville by
mere force of arms, unless the village was secured and
its inhabitants deterred from aiding the garrison. He
determined to resort to braggadocio. In the afternoon
his men captured a Frenchman who was out shooting
ducks, and Clark made his first move by sending the
prisoner to the villagers with a message, in which he announced that his "army" was about to storm the place,
and that all who were friendly to him must remain
within doors, while all hostile must, on pain of severe
punishment, repair to the fort and aid Hamilton, whom
he designated as the Hair-Buyer General, in allusion to
his having offered premiums for scalps. As evening
fell he marched to the town, keeping carefully on low
ground where his men were not visible from the post,
but giving a view of the numerous standards that he had
brought with him, thus causing the villagers to believe

that his force was several times stronger than it really was. The village was occupied, without resistance, just after dark. The French were all favorably disposed and had given no warning to the garrison. Some of them offered to join Clark, but their services were declined. Tabac also was on hand, tendering a hundred warriors to aid in taking the fort, but was informed that no assistance was needed.

The garrison had no knowledge of the approach of the Americans until the firing began, which was immediately after they reached the town, fifteen men having been detached for that purpose. Hamilton was at Captain Helm's quarters, playing piquet with his prisoner, when he was startled by the cracking of the rifles and the rattling of the bullets on the sticks and mud of the chimney, which the riflemen, from a spirit of mischief, had taken for a target on learning where Helm was located. There was a fine apple toddy brewing on the hearth, into which part of the débris tumbled, and the jovial captain sprang to his feet, exclaiming that Clark was there and would take the place, but at the same time cursing the assailants for spoiling his beverage. All night a heavy fire was kept up on both sides, but with no material damage, though several were wounded. The Americans under cover of the darkness made a strong entrenchment across the road one hundred and twenty yards in front of the main gate. At nine o'clock in the morning Clark sent a flag of truce to Hamilton, and during the cessation of firing his men had their breakfast, which Major Bowman feelingly refers to as " the only meal of victuals since the 18th inst." The message sent under this flag was so characteristic of the man and his project that no part of it can be omitted : —

"Sir, — In order to save yourself from the impending storm that now threatens you, I order you immediately to surrender yourself, with all your garrison, stores, &c., &c., &c. For if I am obliged to storm, you may depend on such treatment as is justly due to a murderer. Beware of destroying stores of any kind, or any papers, or letters that are in your possession ; for, by Heavens, if you do, there shall be no mercy shown you.

"G. R. Clark."

To this fierce missive Hamilton replied that he and his garrison were "not disposed to be awed into an action unworthy of British subjects." The firing was at once renewed with great vigor. The advantage of the Americans was quickly manifest. They surrounded the fort on all sides, stationed nowhere more than a hundred and twenty yards from the stockade and in many places within sixty yards of it, sheltered by buildings, earth-works, and logs. These frontiersmen were at that time the best marksmen known to the world, and at these distances a silver dollar was as large a target as they cared for. Whenever a port-hole was opened dozens of bullets flew through it, playing such havoc with the gunners that the cannon could not be fired with any effect, and causing them soon to be abandoned. Every crack at which a sign of life appeared was made a target. Several of the British soldiers fell with bullets through their eyes. The garrison became disheartened ; the attacking party were confident and enthusiastic : they wished to storm the fort at once. As the afternoon wore away, Hamilton sent a flag of truce, asking a cessation of hostilities for three days and a conference with Clark at the gate of the fort. Clark replied that he

would accept no terms but surrender at discretion, and
would confer with him at the village church if he so
desired. The conference was held at once, in the presence of Major Hay of the garrison, Major Bowman of
Clark's party, and Captain Helm. Hamilton offered to
surrender if he and his men would be permitted to go to
Pensacola on parole. Clark refused anything but unconditional surrender, and warned the British commander that he might not be able to restrain his men if they
were obliged to storm the fort. Captain Helm inter-
ceded in favor of milder terms, but was sternly reminded
that he was a prisoner and could not speak with propriety. Hamilton at once said that Captain Helm was
from that moment at liberty and might do as he liked.
Clark answered that he would permit nothing of the
kind; that Helm must return to the fort and take his
chances as a prisoner.

As Hamilton turned to leave, he stopped and asked
Clark for his reasons for insisting on the terms he mentioned. Clark replied that it was because there were
several noted Indian partisans (*i. e.* white men who
had been employed in inciting the Indians to war and
leading their war-parties) in the fort, whom he desired
to be at liberty to put to death, or otherwise punish as
he might see fit. "Who is it that you call Indian partisans?" asked Major Hay, visibly disquieted by this remark. "Sir," said Clark, "I take Major Hay to be one
of the principal." At this Hay turned pale, and trem-
bled so violently that Hamilton blushed at his display of
terror. There was a silence of a few moments, and
then Clark, determining to moderate his demands, told
Hamilton that he would reconsider the matter and inform him of the result; in the mean time they would

return to their posts, and not resume offensive measures until a conclusion was reached. A consultation of officers was held, and before the sun set terms had been proposed and accepted of surrender as prisoners of war with all stores and supplies. This was carried into effect on the next morning (February 25) at ten o'clock.

In the negotiations Hamilton had risen noticeably in the estimation of the Americans, especially of Clark, who says that Hamilton never deviated " from that dignity of conduct that became an officer in his situation." His men, so he says, were unanimously in favor of accepting the terms offered, and this probably resulted from their anticipation that, if the fort were stormed, the Americans would take vengeance on them for the Indian depredations on the frontier. This apprehension was not a little heightened by an event that occurred while the conference was progressing in the church. As the men were resting from their attack on the fort, they saw approaching over the plain below Vincennes a party of nine Indians, who had been on a war expedition to the Falls of the Ohio. Captain Williams started towards them with a party of men. The Indians supposed this to be a party sent by Hamilton to conduct them to the fort, as this honor was commonly conferred on their war-parties, and advanced whooping and making demonstrations of joy which signified a successful raid. The American party encouraged their delusion by similar action until the wretches were fairly in their clutches, and then fell upon them. Six were made prisoners, two were killed, and one escaped badly wounded. The captives were brought into town and ordered to be put to death, but two of them were afterwards pardoned on discovery that they were white men,

and one of them a son of one of the French volunteers
from Cahokia. The others were tomahawked in front
of the fort and their bodies thrown into the river. This
action brought the terror of the garrison to a climax,
and also raised the enmity of the hostile Indians against
Hamilton, as they thought he should have made some
effort to save his allies.

On the 26th, Captain Helm and Major Legare were
sent up the Wabash to meet a convoy of boats which
were coming from Fort Miamis with provisions and
stores. They returned on March 5, having captured
M. Dejean, the Grand Judge of Detroit, M. Adimar,
the Commissary, and thirty-eight private soldiers, with
seven boat-loads of goods. During their absence, on the
27th, The Willing had arrived in safety, but the crew
were much disgusted at finding the work finished. On
March 7, Hamilton, Major Hay, Captain Lamoth, and
Judge Dejean, with twenty-two subordinate officers and
privates, were sent to the Falls of the Ohio, whence
they were taken East. The subordinates were soon released on parole, but the four named were kept in prison,
notwithstanding the protests of British officials, until,
after some months, they were released on recommendation of General Washington.[1] On March 16, the
remaining prisoners at Vincennes took the oath of neutrality and were released. So closed this most memorable campaign, by which the Northwest was brought into
the possession of Americans and secured to the Union, in
the conduct of which General Clark had fairly earned
the title which heads this chapter, and which was after-

[1] *Va. Calendar*, vol. i. p. 321; Washington's *Writings*, vol. vi.
pp. 317, 407, 240, 291.

wards bestowed upon him by that eccentric genius, John
Randolph of Roanoke.[1]

The immediate benefit of the success was the check
to Indian hostilities, and this was due not more to their
being driven farther back for bases of supplies than to
the capture of Hamilton, whom they had regarded as
the head and front of the British cause. Clark, on the
other hand, was magnified in their estimation to the
chiefest of the Big Knife warriors. The loyal Piankeshaws were much rejoiced at the American success, as
it insured them immunity from molestation by their hostile brethren, but their joy was still greater when Clark
called them to council and assured them that the repre-
sentations of the English that the Americans wanted
their lands were false; that whoever tried to take their
lands "must first strike the tomahawk in his head."
They held a council on the following day and insisted
on presenting Clark a tract of land, which he at first refused, but, on finding that this made them fear that he
would not remain among them, he accepted a deed for
it. It was two and one half leagues square, on the west
side of the Falls of the Ohio, the location of Clark's
subsequent grant from Virginia. On August 5, 1779,
Clark issued general orders for the management of the
Northwest, by which the garrison at Vincennes was
put under command of Captain Shelby. The name of
the post had been changed from Fort Sackville to Fort
Patrick Henry immediately after its capture, and it was

---

[1] Howison's *Virginia,* vol. ii. p. 237. The sources from which
the preceding narrative is drawn are chiefly Clark's memoir,
prepared at the request of Jefferson and Madison; Clark's letter
to George Mason; Clark's letter to Jefferson; and Major Bowman's journal.

so known for about ten years. Captain Helm was also stationed at the post as Superintendent of Indian Affairs for the Wabash. No garrison was stationed at the Ouiatanon villages, or the old post, but " M. Gamilian " [Gamelin], who resided there, was made agent under Helm.[1]

We must now turn for a moment from the proud contemplation of the success of American arms to a sorry record of American ingratitude. It required money and supplies for Clark to carry on his operations, and these had been furnished him very sparingly. The French merchants came to his relief with the utmost liberality, furnishing him with everything he needed and taking in return his orders on Virginia. In 1780 Charles Gratiot, one of the leading merchants, went to Virginia to get a settlement of his own claims, and also as attorney for Godfroy Linetot, Nicholas Janis, Vital Beauvois, François Bosseron, Philip Legras, and François Charbonneau. After two years of unsuccessful effort he was about to return home, ruined and disheartened, but Colonel Monroe, Mr. Preston, and some other influential friends, advised him to remain and make one more effort. It was successful. In 1783 the Virginia legislature allowed his claims, but his report was so discouraging to his fellows that many of the remaining claims were never presented, and those that were presented were neglected for years.[2]

Faithful, patriotic Father Gibault, whose services had been so valuable to Clark, was excommunicated by the Bishop of Quebec for his action, and also suffered in a pecuniary way for his attachment to our cause.

[1] *Va. Calendar*, vol. i. p. 324.
[2] *House Report*, No. 13, 3d Sess. 25th Congress.

When Arthur St. Clair came west, as Governor of
Northwest Territory, the good old father presented a
memorial showing that he had " parted with his tithes
and his beasts " to aid Clark, and in return had received
depreciated paper currency, which he had sent to the
United States Commissioner for redemption, and thereafter had heard of it no more. Says the memorial :
" The want of seven thousand eight hundred livres [or
upwards of $1500 in our currency] of which the non-
payment of the American notes has deprived him the
use, has obliged him to sell two good slaves, who would
now be the support of his old age, and for the want of
whom he now finds himself dependent on the public."
He asked for a small tract of land that had been formerly held by the parish priests of Kaskaskia.   St.
Clair reported that his claims were just, and that no injury would be done by granting his request, " but it was
not for me to give away the lands of the United States." [1]
It appears from the records that it was not for any one
to give away the lands of the United States, so far as
Gibault was concerned, for his request was not complied
with. He received a lot of fourteen toises [about ninety
feet] front in Vincennes, on a personal claim,[2] and an
allowance of 400 acres was afterwards made to him,
as to others resident at the post prior to 1783, but his
needs had caused him to sell his claim to John Rice
Jones before the land was allotted.[3]

Perhaps the worst case was that of Francis Vigo, the
man who most deserved reward. His services were
widely known long before his name became famous, he

---

[1] Am. State Papers: *Pub. Lands*, vol. i. pp. 14, 15.

[2] *Ibid.* p. 9.

[3] State Papers: *Pub. Lands*, vol. ii. p. 190.

being referred to as "the Spanish merchant" in the
early writings concerning Clark's campaign.[1] Besides
his contribution of time and labor, Vigo had advanced
nearly $12,000 in specie value, receiving drafts from
Clark to Oliver Pollock, agent for Virginia at New
Orleans, which were presented and payment refused
"for want of funds." The principal one was for
$8,616. Being wealthy at that time, Vigo made no
special effort to push his claim. In 1788 he met Pollock in Pennsylvania and again presented the draft, but
Pollock still had no funds. He advised Vigo to keep
his drafts, as they would be paid "some time or other."
Vigo sold the smaller drafts at a discount of eighty per
cent., but held the large one until 1799, when, being
pressed for money, he handed it for collection to Judge
Burnet and Arthur St. Clair, Jr. In some way the
draft was lost, and nothing was done towards the payment of the claim for more than a third of a century.
In this same year of 1799 Vigo contracted a sickness
which confined him to his house during nearly five
years, and in the course of it his business affairs became
so deranged that he was reduced to poverty. The
years rolled away. Indiana and Illinois passed their
territorial probations and became states. Their population increased with marvelous rapidity. Farms, villages,
cities, covered the wilderness through which Vigo journeyed at the risk of his life in aid of the struggling
colonies, and he, more than a score of years past the
allotted time of man's life, tottered about the streets of
Vincennes still unrecompensed. The year 1833 had
come, and in the attic of the capitol at Richmond, cov-

[1] Marshall's *Life of Washington*, vol. iii. p. 566; Jefferson's
Works, vol. iii. p. 217.

ered with the dust of half a century, was found a mass
of papers relating to Clark's campaign. They proved
that many claims which had been disallowed ought to
have been allowed, and they added valuable evidence to
Vigo's claim. Judge John Law (the historian of Vincennes), now took charge of the case, but in 1836, before
it was fairly presented to Congress, Vigo died, at the
advanced age of ninety-six years. By his will he had
provided that, when his claim was allowed, $500 should
be appropriated to purchase a bell for the court-house
at Terre Haute: he felt grateful to the citizens of that
place on account of a flattering public reception they
had given him in 1832, and because Vigo County had
been named in his honor. His heirs pushed the claim.
Seven times House committees reported favorably on it;
twice Senate committees did the same. Lawyers died,
but new ones took their places and fought on. In 1872,
worn out by importunities, Congress referred the case
to the Court of Claims with full authority to decide
it. The heirs recovered judgment. The United States
appealed to the Supreme Court because the Court of
Claims had allowed interest at five per cent. on the
claim. It is a dogma of United States law that the
government is always ready to pay its just debts, when
properly presented, and consequently no interest can be
allowed against it except on loans and contracts in which
interest is expressly stipulated. Carelessness, political
animosity, neglect, or a desire to become reputed
"watch-dogs of the treasury," on the part of its agents,
make no difference, no matter how long they may delay
justice. If a man have not sufficient political influence,
or some equivalent, to induce action by Congress, he
must wait until it is pleased to be just. The readiness

of the government to pay its just debts has ruined many
unfortunate men who had permitted their patriotism to
get the better of their business judgment.   The Supreme Court strained a point in favor of equity, and
affirmed the judgment of the lower court in 1875, allowing the claim and interest, amounting in all to more than
fifty thousand dollars.[1]   It was but tardy justice.   There
lacked but five years of a century since the claim was
due ; and the noble man, whose praises had been sung
by every one who knew him, or had read of Clark's expedition, had been buried for thirty-nine years.   When
the fever of gratitude sets in, republics can be very
grateful, but such fevers are intermittent, and very slow
of attack.

In October, 1778, on receipt of information of Clark's
success at Kaskaskia, the Virginia Assembly had passed
a law organizing all the territory northwest of the Ohio
as the county of Illinois.   By its provisions, the religion
and civil institutions, with the personal and property
rights of the people, were preserved to them.   The
governor was authorized to appoint a " county lieutenant
or commandant in chief," who was to be at the head of
the civil government, with power to appoint deputy
commandants, militia officers, and commissaries.   He
had also the privilege of pardoning offenders, except in
cases of murder and treason, in which he had only power
of respite until the case could be brought before the
governor or assembly.   It has been stated that the laws
of Virginia were extended over the Northwest by this
act, but this is erroneous.   The French laws and cus-

---

[1] U. S. v. McKee, 91 U. S. p. 442.   See *House Report*, No. 13,
3d Sess. 25th Congress ; *House Report*, No. 117, 1st Sess. 33d Congress ; *Mag. of West. Hist.*, vol. i. p. 230 ; *Hist. Vigo County*,
pp. 14–22.

toms were carefully preserved, by provision that " all
civil officers to which the said inhabitants have been accustomed, necessary for the preservation of peace and
the administration of justice, shall be chosen by a majority of the citizens in their respective districts, . . .
which said civil officers, after taking the oaths as above
prescribed, shall exercise their several jurisdictions, and
conduct themselves agreeable to the laws which the present settlers are now accustomed to." [1]   This law was to
remain in force " twelve months, and from thence to the
end of the next session of assembly."   It was continued
for an equal period by act of May, 1780,[2] and thereafter no farther provision was made, presumably because this carried the act into the period when Virginia
had agreed to release her claim to the general government.

    Under this statute, Colonel John Todd was appointed
county lieutenant of Illinois, by Governor Patrick Henry,
on December 12, 1778.   He was instructed to use every
effort to win the friendship of the French ; to conciliate
the Indians as far as possible and punish all violations
of their property, especially of their lands ; and to give
every possible assistance to General Clark in his proposed operations against Detroit.[3]   Todd arrived at
Kaskaskia early in May, 1779, and at once assumed the
reins of civil government, leaving Clark, to his great
satisfaction, free to attend to his military affairs.   In
accordance with the Virginian statute, he called an election of civil officers.   This was the first election ever
held in Indiana, and as the officers chosen then appear

[1] 9 Hening's *Statutes*, p. 552.
[2] 10 Hening, p. 303.
[3] *Virginia Calendar*, vol. i. p. 312

to have retained their positions until General Harmar established a military government in 1787, their names are worthy of record: " The Court of St. Vincennes: 1, P. Legras; 2, Francois Bosseron; 3, Perrot; 4, Cardinal (refused to serve); 5, Guery La Tulippe; 6, P. Gamelin; 7, Edeline; 8, Dejenest; 9, Barron; Legrand, Clerke; —— Sheriff. Militia Officers of St. Vincennes: P. Legras, L. Col.; F. Bosseron, Major; Latulippe, 1 Capt.; Edeline, 2; W. Brouilet, 3; P. Gamelin, 4 —— rank [of last two] not settled. Goden, 2 Lieut.; Goden, 3 Lieut. Joseph Rougas, 2 ——; Richerville, 3 ——; Richerville 4 ——." The blank ranks of the last three were probably lieutenancies.[1]

Todd appears to have left the Illinois country in the following winter. He was elected a delegate to the legislature of Virginia from Kentucky in the spring of 1780, and in November of the same year was appointed colonel (commandant) of Fayette, one of the three counties into which Kentucky was divided in that year. He was killed at the battle of Blue Licks, August 18, 1782. The statutory organization of Illinois expired by its own limitation in the year 1781, but the civil officers, who had been elected and commissioned, continued to exercise the functions of their offices as before. Their authority was not questioned by the people, and probably would not have been by the United States had they restricted themselves to their proper original powers; but they assumed power to make grants of land, and having used it freely for the benefit of others, they generously divided all that remained of the old Indian

---

[1] Todd's Record, from which these details are taken, is in possession of the Chicago Hist. Soc. An interesting account of the Record, by E. G. Mason, is in No. 12 of the Fergus Hist. Series.

grant, of twenty·four leagues square, among themselves, each judge, in turn, absenting himself for a day while his associates voted him his portion.[1] The United States of course repudiated this action ; and yet the French judges had arrived at the conclusion that they possessed this power, in a very natural way.   Todd, whom they labelled " *Colonel et Grand Juge civil pour Les Etats Unis*," had been sent to govern them.   He had commissioned Le Gras Lieutenant-Colonel of the militia of Vincennes, and consequently Le Gras was commandant of the post.   The commandants had always made concessions of land ; hence Le Gras had the same power, and Le Gras had given the court permission to make grants.   Such was the source of their authority, as they explained it to Secretary Sargent.[2]

The situation of the French settlers of Indiana during the Virginia occupation, and the years intervening before the arrival of General Harmar, was very unfortunate.   All commerce with Detroit was cut off at once by the capture of Vincennes.   The trade down the Mississippi was greatly impeded by the Chickasaws, Cherokees, and other southern Indians, whose friendly relations with the British developed into active hostilities against the Americans on account of the erection of Fort Jefferson, on the east side of the Mississippi, five miles below the mouth of the Ohio, in territory claimed by them.   The fort was besieged by the Indians for five days, but they were driven off by Captain George and his garrison of thirty men with great carnage.   It was abandoned in 1781, because it was found to be of no protection to the frontier.[3]   In consequence of these

---

[1] Law's *Vincennes*, pp. 110-116.   [2] *Ibid*. pp. 111, 112.
[3] Collins's *Kentucky*, vol. ii. p. 19.

impediments to trade, provisions advanced four to five hundred per cent. at Vincennes, and Clark charged that " Lagrass, Boison, Lanitot and others," merchants of the place, took advantage of the situation to advance their fortunes at expense of the public welfare. The settlements on the Mississippi also suffered at this time, but not so much as Vincennes. In the winter of 1780– 1781 the garrison at Vincennes was withdrawn, and con- solidated with other troops at Fort Jefferson, its place being supplied by the militia. At the same time a number of inhabitants abandoned the post, on account of the high price of provisions. From this time the re- spect of the Indians for American arms, which had been created by General Clark, began to diminish, and in a short time many of them became hostile.[1]

There were almost continual hostilities with those of the tribes which had not come under Clark's personal influence, but these had little effect on the French settle- ments. Colonel Bowman and Captain Logan, with a party of frontiersmen, destroyed the Indian towns on the Little Miami in 1779. Colonel Byrd, of the British service, led a successful Indian raid on the settlements in the Ohio valley in 1780. General Clark retaliated by destroying the Indian towns on the Big and Little Miami rivers in the fall of the same year. At the same time a Frenchman named La Balme, in the em- ploy of Virginia, marched from Kaskaskia with thirty men against Detroit. He received a reinforcement from the citizens of Vincennes, and proceeded up the Wabash, expecting the French of Detroit to join their countrymen and throw off the British control. Ke- kionga was secured, and the British traders there plun-

[1] *Va. Cal.*, vol. iii. p. 501 ; also vol. i. p. 338.

dered, but when the bold band reached the river Aboité they were attacked by a party of Miami Indians and disastrously routed. La Balme and a number of his men were killed. In 1781 Clark prepared for an expedition against Detroit from the Falls of the Ohio, but the project was frustrated by the destruction of a part of his forces under Colonel Archibald Lochry. These were surprised by a party of Indians under Joseph Brant, at the mouth of Loughery Creek.[1] More than a third of the party were killed, and the remainder carried captive.[2] In this year also Captain Eugenio Pourré led a Spanish force from St. Louis across Illinois and northwestern Indiana, and captured Fort St. Josephs from the British, war having been declared between Spain and England two years earlier. Spain afterwards claimed a large portion of the Northwest, as against the United States, on the ground of this conquest, but our commissioners declined to concede it.[3]

The year 1782 was the most terrible ever known on the Western frontier. It opened with the villainous massacre of the Moravian Indians on the Muskingum, which was followed two weeks later by the fight at Estill's Station. In May, Colonel Crawford started on his expedition to the Sandusky, with 480 men, resolved "not to spare the lives of any Indians that might fall into their hands, whether friends or foes," which resulted in the overwhelming defeat of the party, with a loss of one hundred men, and the death of the unfortu-

[1] The dividing line between Dearborn and Ohio counties, Indiana. It was named for Colonel Lochry, but is commonly misspelled.

[2] Ind. Hist. Soc. Pamph. No. 4.

[3] A full account, by E. G. Mason, is in *Mag. Am. Hist.*, vol. xv. p. 457.

nate commander at the stake after blood-curdling torture. In August came Girty's attack on Bryant's Station, and the battle at Lower Blue Licks, where the Indians were again victorious. During the summer Clark was making every effort to organize an expedition against Detroit, but by a combination of adverse circumstances he was obliged to abandon this attempt, and in November he marched against the Indian towns on the Miami at the head of 1,050 men. They succeeded in destroying all the Indian villages and stores of supplies from the Ohio to the head of the Miami; very few Indians were killed, as they fled before the troops could come up with them. During the winter of 1782 Great Britain and the United States made their provisional treaty of peace and agreed on a cessation of hostilities, in consequence of which there was a season of quiet on the frontier during the years 1783, 1784, and 1785. During this period attempts were made to secure treaties with the tribes northwest of the Ohio, and a portion of them accepted the peace and friendship proffered by the government, at Fort Stanwix, Fort McIntosh, and Fort Finney. The great majority, however, were determined to hold to their lands north of the Ohio, and, realizing that the Americans were equally determined to enter there, their ablest chiefs united them in that great northwestern confederacy which stopped the march of emigration for the next ten years. All the tribes were joined in this movement, and all fought bravely but vainly for their homes. In the lull between the storms Clark was dismissed from the service of Virginia. Governor Harrison, of Virginia, on July 2, 1783, announced to him that the distressed condition of the state as to finances made this step necessary, and also

returned the thanks of himself and the council " for the
very great and singular services you have rendered
your country in wresting so great and valuable a territory out of the hands of the British enemy repelling
the attacks of their savage allies, and carrying on a
successful war in the heart of their country." [1]   If
George Rogers Clark had been furnished with supplies
from 1778 to 1781, — if Virginia had sustained his
credit, — he would have made Vincennes a stepping-
stone to Detroit, Detroit to Niagara, and Niagara to
Montreal and Quebec.   He felt this neglect keenly.
He saw a great opportunity slowly and certainly slip-
ping from his grasp.   It is said that when he received,
on the banks of the Wabash, the sword presented him
by Virginia in testimony of his services, he thrust it in
the ground, snapped it off, and flung away the hilt, exclaiming bitterly : " I asked Virginia for bread, and
she sent me a sword." [2]

In August, 1785, the non-treaty Indians held a grand
council at Ouiatanon, and determined to put a stop to
the advance of the white settlers north of the Ohio.
An envoy was sent to Vincennes who notified the inhabitants that they must leave ; that war was to be made on
the Americans ; and that the French who remained at
Vincennes would be treated as Americans.   During
the winter several isolated settlers were killed, and in
the spring a party of Indians attacked some traders at
the mouth of the Embarrass River.   A party from the
town went out and attacked them, the fight resulting in
the death of several on each side.   The homes of
American farmers who had located in the neighborhood
of Vincennes were broken up ; some settlers were killed ;

[1] Dillon, p. 179.   [2] Denny's *Journal*, p. 218.

some went to Kentucky; some took refuge at the post.[1]
As the spring advanced, the advices from the frontier
became more alarming. In May, Clark wrote to Governor Henry that the Wabash Indians, encouraged by
British traders from Detroit, had begun war. Letter
after letter brought confirmation of the statement. In
June it was reported that "the whole of the Americans
settled at Post Vincennes, on the Wabash, are massa-
cred." In July numerous depredations were reported,
and it was represented as the general desire in Kentucky that Clark should be commissioned to lead a force
to the Wabash. It was stated that the Americans at
Vincennes had been attacked by Indians; that the
French had not only refused them assistance, but also
refused to allow them to use the cannon left them for
the defense of the post; that Colonel Le Gras, after the
Indians were repulsed, had ordered the Americans to
leave Vincennes; that the Americans had called on
Kentucky for assistance, and a party had gone to their
succor.[2] The Executive Board of Virginia had convened in May, and on the 15th of that month it was
determined that Governor Henry should direct the field
officers of the Kentucky militia to assemble and take the
necessary measures for the protection of the settlements.
The field officers assembled, resolved to invade the Indian country, and appointed Clark commander of the
forces.

In September, Clark marched from the Falls of the
Ohio with 1,000 men, taking the road to Vincennes. At
Silver Creek he sent back Captain Benjamin Logan to
raise four or five hundred men and attack the Shawnee

[1] Dillon, p. 184.
[2] *Va. Cal.*, vol. iv. pp. 122, 149, 155-157.

towns on the Miami. Clark's troops were not in good
humor, and their dissatisfaction kept growing worse.
The provisions sent by boats to Vincennes were delayed
by low water, and half of them were spoiled. The men
began to desert. Clark was drinking hard all the time.
His party was reinforced by the inhabitants of Vincennes
and marched on to the Vermillion River, but found that
the Indians had deserted their town there. At this
point a rumor was put in circulation that Clark had sent
a flag to the Indians, offering them peace or war. It
was not true, but the men knew that Clark was constantly intoxicated, and their confidence in him was so
shaken that mutiny pervaded the entire force. Prayers,
tears, and curses availed nothing. Three hundred of
the men left in a body and returned home, whereupon
the expedition was given up. Logan succeeded better.
He penetrated the country to the head-waters of Mad
River, burned eight towns, destroyed a large amount of
corn, took about eighty prisoners, killed twenty, and lost
but ten men.

As Clark's expedition returned down the Wabash, a
council of the field officers was held at Vincennes on
October 8th, and it was determined that for the safety
of Kentucky they would establish a garrison at Vincennes, supplies for whose support should be raised " by
impressment or otherwise, under the direction of a commissary to be appointed for that purpose, pursuant to
the authority vested in the field officers of the district
by the Executive of Virginia." They appointed John
Craig, Jr., commissary, but he did not act, and John
Rice Jones was given the position. Colonel John Holder
was put in command of the garrison, which was to consist of 250 infantry, and a company of artillery under

Captain Valentine Thomas Dalton. Clark took control of the entire proceeding. He sent word to the Indians to meet him at Clarksville (Falls of the Ohio) on November 20, 1786, and hold a council; and afterwards, as they refused to come to that point, he told them to meet him at Vincennes on April 30, 1787. For the support of the garrison, the goods of certain Spanish merchants, lately established at Vincennes, were appropriated.

These acts were certainly of an extraordinary nature, so much so that the Executive Board of Virginia disavowed giving any authority for them, and ordered the prosecution of those responsible for them, and yet it is not clear how far they were legal and how far illegal. The right to make an expedition into the Indian country should reasonably have carried the right to establish a garrison there, if considered necessary by the officers of the expedition. It is doubtful if any serious objection would have been made to it had not the seizure of the Spanish goods been considered as straining our already delicate relations with Spain. John Jay was at this time negotiating a treaty with M. Gardoqui, the representative of that power, and they had come to a disagreement as to the navigation of the Mississippi. Jay's instructions required that free navigation of the river should be guaranteed to citizens of the United States; Gardoqui refused to concede the right of navigation, even if an agreement were made not to exercise it during the term of the treaty. On August 3, 1786, Jay suggested to Congress an amendment of his powers, permitting a temporary relinquishment of the use of the right of navigation, but making no concession as to the right itself. This the New England and Middle States favored, and the South opposed. Congress struggled with the question all through August and September, — seven states favoring, five opposing, and Delaware absent, — and finally resolved that the relinquishment might be made, the majority refusing even to instruct Jay that only seven states had consented, and that he had no constitutional power to make the relinquishment without the agreement of nine states, under the Articles of Confederation. All of this was done in secret session, the last move being the defeat, on September 28th, of Mr. Pinckney's motion to remove the injunction of secrecy and permit the delegates to communicate the details of the matter to the respective state authorities. It is not possible that Clark or any of his command could have had knowledge of it previous to the expedition, or previous to their action of October 8th.[1]

Clark and his associates did know that the Spanish authorities would not permit Americans to pass down the river with their merchandise, and they were indignant at this interference with what they considered their rights. They also believed, or at least professed to believe, that Spanish emissaries were seeking to stir up the Indians against the Americans, and there was evidence that this was true.[2] A letter preserved in the Virginia archives, written from North Carolina, in November, 1786, gives the following statement of the motives of the Kentucky officers, as coming from two men who had just arrived from Kentucky and brought the news of the

---

[1] McMasters's statement, that the meeting of officers at Vincennes "indulged in harangues against Spain, Congress, and Mr. Jay" (*Hist. Am. People*, vol. i. p. 379), has no foundation in evidence or in reasonable surmise.

[2] *Va. Cal.*, vol. iv. p. 297.

departure of the expedition: "Clarke is much exasperated against some Spaniards and others, settlers at Opost [i. e., *au Poste Vincennes*]. He charges them with furnishing the Indians with military stores, and declares his intention of using them with a heavy hand as well as retaliating on the Spaniards for some of the Seizures and Confiscations of the property of our Citizens at the Natches. They add that Clark is constantly drunk."[1] The seizure at Natchez, which was the chief cause of their warmth, was that of the goods of Thomas Amis, who was on his way down the river with a load of hardware and flour, when, on June 6th, he was stopped by Lieutenant-Colonel Grandpri, the Spanish commandant at Fort Natchez, and deprived of his property. He was released on August 29th, and made his way to Kentucky, whence he returned to his home in North Carolina. The property taken at Vincennes was seized by Captain Dalton and turned over to the commissary, John Rice Jones, who gave receipts for it to the merchants from whom it was taken. So much of it as was needed for the troops was retained, and the remainder was sold at auction. At about the same time, Major Busseron was sent to the Illinois settlements to notify the inhabitants of the Spanish seizures at Natchez, and recommend them to "be prepared to retaliate any outrage the Spaniards might commit on their property, but by no means to commence hostilities."

Clark's enemies did not neglect to represent all these proceedings in their most unfavorable light. One of the most remarkable communications on the subject is a private letter, which came into the hands of the Virginia authorities, but was not sent by them to the

[1] *Va. Cal.*, vol. iv. p. 189.

national authorities. It is in these words: " Clarke is playing Hell. He is raising a regiment of his own and has 140 men stationed at Opost, already now under the command of Dalton. Seized on a Spanish Boat with 20,000 Dollars, or rather seized three stores at Opost worth this sum, and the Boat which brought them up. J. R. Jones, Comissary General, gets a large share of the plunder, and has his family at Opost. Platt comes in for snacks. He brought the baggage and a thousand pounds of small furs to the Falls the day I left it. Plunder all. ——— means to go to Congress to get the Regiment put upon the establishment. He is the 3d Captain. The Furs, he tells his associates, are necessary to bear his expences; but he don't return. I laid a plan to get the whole seized and secured for the owners, and Bullett and Anderson will execute it. Clarke is eternally drunk, and yet full of design. I told him he would be hanged. He laughed and said he could take refuge among the Indians. A stroke is meditated against St. Louis and the Natchez." [1]

On its face, much of what is here stated as fact appears to be really only the opinion of the writer, and in the light of future developments this letter must fairly be considered as largely untrue. Although there was strong party feeling in Kentucky over the question of its relation to Virginia, and although Clark had many bitter personal enemies, no material disapprobation of his doings was manifested until in December, and then principally in connection with the movements of Thomas Green, who was either resident or had been detained at Natchez. His family was there at the time, and he had come to Kentucky apparently for the purpose of solving

---

[1] *Va. Cal.*, vol. iv. p. 202.

the Mississippi question by raising an armed force and taking possession of the country. He was in communication with Clark and other Kentuckians, and they decided to make an attempt to secure the authorization of a movement on Natchez by the State of Georgia, which claimed the territory in question. On December 4th they prepared a circular letter on the subject, which was soon afterwards distributed through Tennessee (then called the State of Franklin), and on the same day they made up a subscription to pay the expenses of a messenger to the Governor of Georgia, in case the Georgia authorities should decline to pay him. This paper had twelve signers, who, together, promised the sum of £38 10s., of which £20 was subscribed by Clark and Green. The circular letter speaks of the release of the navigation of the Mississippi for twenty-five years as having been made by "the late commercial treaty with Spain," in terms that indicate it to be a rumor of very recent date; and this is the first manifestation that Mr. Jay's proposal had come to the knowledge of the Western people, even in this incorrect and magnified form. The letter to the Governor of Georgia is dated December 23d, and is simply a proposal to raise troops and take possession of Natchez, if the Governor of Georgia in his "infinite goodness will countenance" the action and "give us the lands to settle it agreeable to the law of your state."

In all this there was no serious offense. As to the proposal to the Governor of Georgia, — of which, by the way, Clark denied knowledge, saying that he understood Green to contemplate only a settlement within the boundaries of Georgia, — it cannot be questioned that any state, under the Articles of Confederation, had the right to expel intruders from its borders; and, indeed, this same State of Georgia long afterwards exercised a very similar power, in defiance of the United States authorities, in its settlement of the Cherokee troubles. As to the proceedings on the Wabash, it should be remembered that Vincennes was in the heart of the Indian country, and was threatened by the savages there; that the authorities of Virginia were too distant to be consulted on all matters of detail; and that the expedition to quell the hostile Indians had failed. Establishing a garrison there was a less stretch of authority than Clark had often before made, and his former actions had been approved. If a garrison were established it must have supplies, and in the absence of other resources impressment was a right of war. Our relations with Spain were what made both actions objectionable. On the case presented to the Virginia Board, which was prepared by a half dozen citizens of Kentucky, who had managed to get possession of Green's letters and also the private papers of Clark, the Board disavowed any authorization of Clark's proceedings and ordered the prosecution of the offenders, but it recommended that the treaties arranged for by Clark be made by commissioners.

The most important point on the question of culpability was not before the Board at this time, and unfortunately it seems to have been overlooked by all who have written on the subject. The impressment of goods was not a mere impulse of the moment; it was the result of a carefully considered plan. The Executive Board of Virginia had convened in May, 1786, and on the 15th had ordered a convention of the field officers of the Kentucky militia, to take measures for the protection of the frontier. The field officers assembled, determined on an expedition, and chose Clark to command them; but there had been no provision for supplying the troops, and nothing could be done without supplies. The question then arose whether the Virginia authorities intended them to use their discretion on this subject, and in order to get a reliable legal opinion they laid Governor Henry's letter, the militia laws of Virginia, and the sixth Article of Confederation, before the Attorney-General and Supreme Judges of Kentucky, who, after consultation, reported as follows : —

"We are of opinion that the Executive have delegated all their power under the said Law and Article of Confederation, so far as they relate to Invasions, Insurrections, and Impressments, to the field officers of that District, and that the officers, in consequence thereof, have a right to Impress, if necessary, all supplies for the use of the militia that may be called into service by their order or orders under the said order of council.

"GEO. MUTER,
"CALEB WALLACE,
"HARRY INNIS."

It cannot be denied that the proceedings at Vincennes were within the powers of the field officers under this construction, and that ends all question of moral culpability. They obtained the best legal advice that could be had and acted under it. It is worthy of mention, in this connection, that Colonel Logan also impressed supplies for his expedition after he had been detached by Clark, and that all of the field officers maintained the propriety of their course throughout. The most astonishing feature of the affair was that, after giving this opinion, these three gentlemen were Clark's foremost accusers : in fact, Attorney-General Innis appears to have worked up the case against him.

As the winter wore away there was a visible change
of opinion in the East on the Spanish question. In
April, 1787, when the papers relating to the Amis
seizure and the action of Green and Clark were laid
before Congress, Mr. Jay's accompanying letter stated
that he was convinced "that the United States have
good right to navigate the river [Mississippi] from its
source to and through its mouth," and that, unless the
States could agree to relinquish the use for a time, as he
had suggested, they should remonstrate against Spain's
action, and in case of continued refusal "declare war
against Spain." As to the action of the people of the
West, he said: "If war is in expectation, then their
ardor should not be discouraged nor their indignation
diminished. But if a treaty is wished and contemplated,
then those people should be so advised and so restrained
that their sentiments and conduct may as much as possible be made to quadrate with the terms and articles of
it." [1] Sentiment in Congress veered continuously in that
direction until on September 16, 1788, it was "Resolved,
That the free navigation of the river Mississippi is a
clear and essential right of the United States, and that
the same ought to be considered and supported as such."
The matter of a treaty with Spain was then referred to
the new federal government, and delegates were given
leave to make public any facts necessary to remove the
"misconception" that Congress was "disposed to treat
with Spain for the surrender of their claim to the navigation of the river Mississippi." It is quite possible
that the manifestations of temper by the Western people

---

[1] *Secret Journals of Congress*, vol. iv. pp. 304, 305. The papers
relating to Clark, Green, and Amis follow. They are also in
Dillon, chap. xi.

contributed largely to make this a misconception, for it certainly was not one or two years earlier.

In the West, the people were almost a unit in supporting the action of the Kentucky officers. The French settlers felt their situation to be hard and oppressive, but they laid the fault to Congress, not to Clark. On June 12, 1787, William Grayson wrote to Governor Randolph: " We are informed [by Mr. Simms of Kentucky, late delegate from New Jersey] that the people of Kaskaskies and Post Vincent are in the most unsettled situation. They complain, and in my opinion with great justice, that Congress, notwithstanding their frequent applications, has, ever since the cession of Virginia, suffered them to remain in a state of nature, with't law, government, or protection, and talk very strongly of becoming Spanish subjects." [1]   In Kentucky, public sentiment was so clear and strong that Clark's accusers dared not follow up publicly the charges which they had secretly made. Clark, Colonel Logan, and Colonel Levi Todd, all asked for courts of inquiry, but none were granted. On July 19, 1787, the field officers of Kentucky convened and resolved that the action of the Virginia Executive had " placed us in so critical a Situation as to oblige us to decline all offensive operations at present." [2]   On July 21, Attorney-General Innis wrote to Governor Randolph refusing to institute proceedings against the officers responsible for the action at Vincennes, on the ground that he had no official power to do so, and to do so in a private capacity " would render him odious." He also objected because he had been instructed to report to the Attorney-General for the Eastern District of Kentucky, and this subordination

[1] *Va. Cal.*, vol. iv. p. 297.   [2] *Ibid.*, vol. iv. p. 344.

"the honor and dignity of this district call upon me to disavow." [1]

Not knowing the exact cause of his treatment by the Virginia authorities, but rightly attributing it to the malice of his enemies, Clark fell into a state of sullen indignation. On October 8, 1787, he concluded a letter to Governor Randolph in these words: " Contious of having done everything in the power of a person under my circumstances, not only for the defence of the country, but to save every Expense possible, I can with pleasure View Countries flourishing that I have Stained with the Blood of its Enemies, pitying mine when I deign to think of them as Citizens ; otherways with the utmost Contempt." [2] The remainder of Clark's life was passed in retirement, with the exception of one brief appearance before the public. When Genet, the French minister, undertook his reckless enterprise of raising American troops to invade the Spanish possessions, in defiance of the objections of our Executive, Clark accepted a commission as major-general of the army of invasion. He made public proposals for troops and supplies,[3] but before any more serious action was taken Genet was recalled, and the commissions he had granted were annulled. The lands given Clark by Virginia afforded him a home, but little more. Neither Virginia nor the United States paid for the property impressed at Vincennes, and in consequence the merchants sued Clark in the territorial courts and obtained judgments, under which much of his property was sold. His health became infirm. He was tortured for years by rheumatism, and this at length resulted in paralysis.

---

[1] *Va. Cal.*, vol. iv. pp. 321–323.   [2] *Ibid.*, p. 347.

[3] *St. Clair Papers*, vol. ii. p. 322, note.

In poverty, sickness, and neglect, he lived on in his little home at Clarksville — where he could look out over the Falls of the Ohio, at which so many of the great enterprises of his life had begun, and hear the constant roar of the rushing waters — until the year 1814. Then he removed to the home of his sister, Mrs. William Croghan, at Locust Grove, near Louisville, where, in February, 1818, he died and was buried.[1]

It is worthy of mention that no taint of guilt attached ', General Clark, on account of his action at Vincennes, in the minds of the great men of his day who were acquainted with the facts in connection with it. On March 7, 1791, when Indian hostilities were spreading terror through the West, and the authorities were casting about for a satisfactory commander for the frontier troops, Mr. Jefferson wrote to Mr. Innis, of Kentucky: "Will it not be possible for you to bring General Clark forward? I know the greatness of his mind, and am the more mortified at the cause which obscures it. Had not this unhappily taken place, there was nothing he might not have hoped : could it be surmounted, his lost ground might yet be recovered. No man alive rated him higher than I did, and would again, were he to become again what I knew him." [2] The defect to which Mr. Jefferson alludes was intemperance. His misfortunes confirmed him in the habit which had contributed not a little to cause those misfortunes. Says Judge Burnet, who visited him in his old age: "The cruel ingratitude to which this distinguished soldier was doomed, — for which no justifiable cause can be assigned, — and the comparative poverty which made him almost a pen-

[1] *Hist. Ohio Falls Cities*, vol. ii. p. 501.
[2] Jefferson's *Works*, vol. iii. p. 217.

sioner on the bounty of his relatives, was more than he
could bear.   It drove him to intemperance.   He sought
the inebriating bowl, as if it contained the water of
Lethe, and could obliterate from his memory the wrongs
he had endured." [1]   Thus was blighted the latter half
of the life of this great man — for he was a great man.
Of all those who preceded or followed him, La Salle is
the only one who can be compared to him in the wonderful combination of genius, activity, and courage that
lifted him above his fellows.   Ruined by drink!   In
this is another similarity to the great Carthaginian.
The only difference was that the poison which destroyed
the Hannibal of Africa acted more speedily than that
which blasted the life of the Hannibal of the West.

[1] Burnet's *Notes*, p. 81.

CHAPTER V.

In January, 1830, in the great debate on Mr. Foote's resolution of inquiry, which reached its climax in Webster's immortal reply to Hayne, there originated an historical controversy as to the authorship of the Ordinance of 1787, which has increased with the years and ramified into branches that the original debaters never dreamed of. Mr. Webster, in his argument of the motion to postpone, had said : " That instrument [the Ordinance] was drawn by Nathan Dane, then and now a citizen of Massachusetts. It was adopted, as I think I have understood, without the slightest alteration; and certainly it has happened to few men to be the authors of a political measure of more large and enduring consequence. It fixed forever the character of the population in the vast regions northwest of the Ohio by excluding from them involuntary servitude. It impressed on the soil itself, while it was yet a wilderness, an incapacity to bear up any other than free men. It laid the interdict against personal servitude in original compact, not only deeper than all local law, but deeper also than all local constitutions." In all of these statements except the first there is unquestionably much of error, and to the first Mr. Benton, with characteristic assurance, replied: " Mr. Dane was no more the author of that Ordinance, sir, than you or I, who about that

time were mewling and puking in our nurses' arms.
That Ordinance, and especially the non-slavery clause,
was not the work of Nathan Dane of Massachusetts, but
of Thomas Jefferson of Virginia." Both of these great
party leaders were recognized authorities on historical
questions; both investigated the question afterwards;
both adhered to their original statements; but neither
found proof so positive as his assertion.

Although the discussion was taken up by others, the
claims of Dane and Jefferson were the only ones considered for many years. Then it was shown that Manasseh Cutler, who all this time had been quietly ignored,
had, to say the least, an influence on the drafting of the
Ordinance.[1] Soon afterwards claims were made for
Rufus King;[2] and of later date for Arthur St. Clair,[3]
Richard Henry Lee, William Grayson, and Edward
Carrington.[4] Keeping this controversy in view, and re-
membering also the general truth that great measures
are very seldom the fruit of any one mind, let us trace
the history of this remarkable instrument, the constitution of the territories of the United States, for its provisions have been esteemed so beneficent, that, in their
general scope, they have been extended over a majority
of the states of the Union while in their territorial
stages.

The close of the War of the Revolution found the
American states deeply involved in debt, and with no
resources in prospective except such as might be derived

[1] *N. Am. Rev.*, vol. liii. p. 320; *Annals of the West*, p. 308; *N. Am. Rev.*, vol. cxxii. p. 229.

[2] *N. Y. Tribune*, February 28, 1855.

[3] *Mag. of West. Hist.*, vol. i. p. 49.

[4] Bancroft, *Hist. of Const.*, vol. ii. pp. 98–118.

from the sale of the lands west of the Alleghanies, to
which Great Britain had relinquished her claim by the
treaty of 1783. The title to this vast, unsettled domain
was claimed by some of the states to have vested in the
various colonies whose charters had extended their limits
indefinitely to the West, and there was a special claim
for Virginia on account of her conquest and retention of
possession through General Clark. These claims were
met by an equitable plea that was very forcible. All of
the colonies had united for the common defense ; all
had struggled under the burdens of the long conflict ; all
had, by engaging the common foe, aided in wresting the
western lands from the mother country ; all had been
grantees in the formal cession : why, then, should not
all participate in the advantage gained, at least to the
extent of the public indebtedness ? Maryland in particular had insisted that this must be done, and refused
to join in the Articles of Confederation until some satisfactory agreement as to western lands was reached.[1]
Other states which had no paper claims joined with her.
Congress manifested a disposition to ignore Virginia's
claims. The Old Dominion met the advance by a calm
but bold remonstrance which was an effectual notice
that she would resist any attempt to interfere with her
territory. Then came a halt and a change of base. An
appeal was made to the patriotism and liberality of the
states ; New York surrendered her claims ; Virginia re-
lented. In January, 1781, she declared her readiness to
cede her lands northwest of the Ohio to the general government when Congress should agree to the terms she

[1] For discussion of this subject see H. B. Adams's "Maryland's
Influence upon Land Cessions to the U. S." in *Johns Hopkins
Univ. Studies* in *Hist. and Pol. Science*, Third Series.

then proposed. This proposition was long considered.
Some of the states opposed any recognition of state
claims. On September 13, 1783, Congress decided on a
compromise by adopting a report which accepted some of
the terms proposed by Virginia and rejected others. On
October 20th of the same year the Virginia legislature
authorized a cession on the basis of this report, which cession was made by her delegates on March 1, 1784.

Pending these negotiations a committee, composed of
Mr. Jefferson, Mr. Chase of Maryland, and Mr. Howell
of Rhode Island, had been preparing " a plan, consistent
with the principles of the confederation, for connecting
with the union by a temporary government, the purchasers and inhabitants" of the western lands, "until
their numbers and circumstances shall entitle them to
form a permanent constitution for themselves and as
citizens of a free, sovereign and independent state, to be
admitted to a representation in the union." [1] They reported it on the day that the cession of Virginia was
formally executed, but it was recommitted to them. On
March 22 they made a second report, which differed
from the first in no material respect save in the project
for the division of the territory. The original plan provided for the formation of ten states, all in the territory
northwest of the Ohio. The region west of Lake Michigan and north of parallel 45 was to be a state under
the name of Sylvania. The lower peninsula of Michigan
north of parallel 43 was to form Chersonesus. That
part of Wisconsin between parallels 43 and 45 was to
be Michigania. Below this there were to be two states
to every two degrees of latitude, divided by a meridian
line drawn through the rapids of the Ohio, except that

---

[1] *Journals of Congress*, vol. iv. p. 294.

all the territory east of a meridian line drawn through the mouth of the Great Kanawha was to be one state named Washington. Between parallels 41 and 43, the eastern state was Metropotamia, and the western Assenisipia. Between parallels 39 and 41, the eastern state was Saratoga, and the western Illinoia. Between parallel 39 and the Ohio, the eastern state was Pelisipia, and the western Polypotamia. Indiana, therefore, would have been divided up among these six states last named.

In the second report these names were dropped, but the divisions north of parallel 39 were left as before, except that the tract which had been called Sylvania was added to the tract which had been called Michigania, and the Ohio where it runs north of parallel 39, in western Ohio and eastern Indiana, was substituted for parallel 39 as a boundary, to that extent. The real change in the report, and the one for whose making it had probably been recommitted, was in the divisions south of parallel 39. The original report provided only for the division of the lands northwest of the Ohio, and apparently was not intended to apply south of that stream, while the second report covered all territory west of the Alleghanies. The former report was in accordance with the Virginia theory, for Virginia, in her proposition to cede, had insisted that her territory south of the Ohio should be guaranteed to her by the confederacy; but this the confederacy had refused, on the ground that, if this land "is really the property of the State of Virginia, it is sufficiently secured by the confederation, and if it is not the property of that state, there is no reason or consideration for such a guarantee." This cautious stand had been taken on account of the irreconcilable conflict as to Virginia's title. So great was the bitterness of local feeling, and the danger of making a rupture which could not be healed, that Congress, by common consent, abstained from any debate on the rights of individual states.[1]

The objection to the extent of the Virginia claim had grown so strong that, even before his first report, Jefferson felt assured that his state must make further concessions or lose the support of Congress. On February 20, 1784, he had written to Madison, detailing his project for the division into states, and adding: " We hope North Carolina will cede all beyond the same meridian of Kanawha, and Virginia also. For God's sake push this at the next session of assembly. We have transmitted a copy of a petition from the people of Kentucky to Congress praying to be separated from Virginia. Congress took no notice of it. We sent the copy to the governor, desiring it to be laid before the assembly. Our view was to bring on the question. It is for the interest of Virginia to cede so far immediately, because the people beyond that will separate themselves, and they will be joined by all our settlements beyond the Alleghany, if they are the first movers. Whereas if we draw the line, those at Kentucky, having their end, will not interest themselves for the people of Indiana,[2]

---

[1] *Journals of Am. Congress*, vol. iv. p. 267.

[2] The Indiana here referred to was a tract of some 3,500,000 acres lying in what is now West Virginia. It was granted by the Indians, in 1768, to Samuel Wharton, William Trent. George Morgan, and others, Indian traders, at the treaty of Fort Stanwix, to recompense them for goods destroyed during the late war, and was under control of The Indiana Company. It was the subject of much dispute in Virginia and Pennsylvania, and of several memorials to Congress. See *Annals of the West*, p. 129 ; Hutch-

Greenbrier, etc., who will, of course, be left to our management, and I can with certainty almost say that Congress would approve of the meridian of the mouth of the Kanawha, and consider it as the ultimate point to be desired from Virginia. I form this opinion from conversation with many members. Should we not be the first movers, and the Indianians and Kentuckians take themselves off and claim to the Alleghany, I am afraid Congress would secretly wish them well."

Mr. Jefferson was not deceived. The continuance of the country west of the Alleghanies as counties of states whose public affairs must always be managed east of the mountains was already recognized as impracticable. The desire for separation in Kentucky took shape in the Danville conventions of 1784–1785, and in 1786 Virginia passed an act consenting to the independence of Kentucky, though the actual separation did not take place until 1790. The same spirit of home rule was rife in Tennessee, and culminated in 1785 in the organization of the independent state of Franklin. This Western feeling had the sympathy of Congress and of the people. It would have been strange if it had not, just after the great struggle for colonial independence, when the whole country was saturated with the doctrine of the natural right of local self-government. Jefferson saw that this was no time to stand on technicalities. He saw the coming wave of public sentiment, and turned it as much as possible to the advantage of Virginia, know-

ins's *Top. Desc.*, p. 4, note; Rees's *Cyc.*, tit. "Indiana;" *Virginia Calendar*, vol. i. pp. 276–298; *Journals of Am. Cong.*, references under "Indiana" in index. McMasters's statement, in his *History of the People of the U. S.*, vol. ii. p. 482, that it was located in what is now Indiana, is a wild error.

ing that Virginia could never obtain all she claimed
in any peaceful way.   On April 25, two days after his
ordinance had become a law, he sent a copy of it to
Madison, and wrote : " By the proposition to bound our
country to the westward, I meant no more than the passing of an act declaring that that should be our boundary
from the moment the people of the Western country and
Congress should agree to it.   The act of Congress now
enclosed to you will show you that they have agreed to
it, because it extends not only to the territory ceded, but
to be ceded, and shows how and when they shall be taken
into the union."   In brief, the resolution or ordinance of
1784, while in the words of Jefferson, was a compromise
measure dictated by the general feeling in Congress.   It
was not wholly satisfactory to the extreme Southern
States.   South Carolina voted against its passage, and
neither Georgia nor the Carolinas ceded their western
territory for several years.[1]

As a result of the extension of this ordinance south of
the Ohio, another important change was made in it before
it passed.   On April 19 Mr. Spaight, of North Carolina, moved to strike out the " article of compact " and
" fundamental principle of constitutions " for the proposed states which provided, " That after the year 1800
of the Christian æra, there shall be neither slavery nor
involuntary servitude in any of the said states, otherwise
than in punishment of crimes whereof the party shall
have been convicted to have been personally guilty."
By the rules of Congress each state had one vote, and
on motion to strike out, the question was, " Shall the
words moved to be struck out stand ? " the affirmative
votes of seven states being required to prevent striking

[1] N. Carolina in 1790 ; S. Carolina in 1787 ; Georgia in 1802.

out. The Northern States voted aye, except New Jersey,
which could not be counted under the rules, as only one
representative was present. North Carolina divided,
and lost her vote. Delaware and Georgia were absent.
The remaining Southern States voted no, Mr. Jefferson
being overruled by his two colleagues from Virginia.
The words consequently were struck out, there being
but six affirmative votes.[1] On the 20th the report
was farther amended, chiefly by striking out a clause
that provided that the new states "shall admit no person to be a citizen who holds any hereditary title."
On April 23, 1784, the ordinance, so amended, was
passed, and until July 13, 1787, remained the fundamental law for the government of the Western territory,
though not in force so as to affect the actual government
of the settlements there. It included seven articles of
compact between the new states and the thirteen original
states, which were afterwards included in the fourth
article of compact of the Ordinance of 1787. It provided that when any one of the proposed states had
20,000 inhabitants it might organize a permanent government, and when it had as many inhabitants as the
least populated original state it might be admitted to the
Union. Previous to having 20,000 inhabitants, a temporary government might be established, by the consent
of Congress and the adoption of the constitution and

---

[1] Mr. Webster erroneously stated that the votes of nine states
were requisite to sustain this clause, and this view is somewhat
supported by so skilled a parliamentarian as Mr. Cox, in his *Three
Decades of Federal Legislation* (p. 43). The error was long since
pointed out by Mr. Benton. *Thirty Years' View*, vol i. p. 135.
Other clauses of the ordinance were retained by the vote of seven
states only. *Journals of Am. Congress*, vol. iv. pp. 374, 375. See,
also, statement of Mr. Jefferson, *Works*, vol. ix. p. 276.

laws of any of the original states. In the mean time
Congress might make such legislation as was needed for
their security and peace.

The alteration of his plan which most keenly affected
Mr. Jefferson was the rejection of the slavery clause.
He confided his chagrin to Madison in his letter of
April 25, in these words: "You will observe two clauses
struck out of the report: the first, respecting hereditary
honors; the second, slavery. The first was done, not
from an approbation of such honors, but because it was
thought an improper place to encounter them. The
second was lost by an individual vote only. Ten states
were present. The four Eastern States, New York, and
Pennsylvania, were for the clause. Jersey would have
been for it, but there were but two members, one of
whom was sick in his chambers. South Carolina, Maryland, and ! Virginia ! voted against it. North Carolina
was divided, as would have been Virginia, had not Mr.
Monroe, one of its delegates, been sick in bed." It is
only necessary to read the repeated statements by Mr.
Jefferson of his views on the slavery question to comprehend the wealth of regret and state shame embodied in
those two exclamation points at Virginia's failure to
support this plan of gradual emancipation. Two years
later he said: "The voice of a single individual would
have prevented this abominable crime from spreading
itself over the new country. Thus we see the fate of
millions unborn hanging on the tongue of one man, and
Heaven was silent in that awful moment! But it is to
be hoped it will not always be silent; and the friends to
the rights of human nature will in the end prevail." [1]
The sophisms of those who defended slavery in principle

---

[1] Jefferson's *Works*, vol. ix. p. 276.

had no weight with him. He blushed that his state was not farther advanced in the principles of humanity and natural justice; he paled at the discord and danger which he saw entailed upon the Union by the spread of this institution.

On May 7, 1784, Mr. Jefferson was appointed a minister plenipotentiary to aid John Adams and Benjamin Franklin in negotiating treaties of commerce.[1] He vacated his seat in Congress, and remained abroad until 1789. There is nothing to show that he had any influence on the enactment of the Ordinance of 1787 in addition to what was naturally carried by the resolution or ordinance of 1784. The latter had been universally ascribed to him until, in 1877, Dr. Adams attributed it, in part at least, to George Washington.[2] This position is untenable. Washington's theory of settling the western lands was to create one district or state at a time, and let it become populated before another was opened for settlement.[3] This also was the original design of Congress in appointing the Jefferson committee, for the resolution directed them to prepare a plan of temporary government of "a district of the Western territory."[4] There were consultations with Washington at various times in regard to Western affairs, but the result was that they all came to Jefferson's plan, which made many districts, but put them all on equal footing. More than that, Mr. Jefferson's resolution or ordinance is not a plan for temporary government at all, and was not so considered by Congress. It provided a mode by which the people of the West might adopt a temporary govern-

---

[1] *Journals of Congress*, vol. iv. p. 400.

[2] *Johns Hopkins Univ. Studies*, Third Series, pp. 41, 42.

[3] Bancroft's *Hist. of the Const.*, vol. i. p. 177.

[4] *Journals of Congress*, vol. iv. pp. 294, 295.

ment, but no provision was made for the intervening time until an amendment, offered by Mr. Gerry, was adopted, by which Congress was authorized to take necessary action " for the preservation of peace and good order among the settlers." [1] It was purely constitutional. It fixed the limits within which the local governments must act, but left the creation of those governments wholly to the future.   In this respect it differs radically from the Ordinance of 1787, which is constitutional only as to its articles of compact, and merely statutory as to the remainder.   The entire resolution of 1784 was to be " a charter of compact," but it was not to be unal- terable until the sale of lands by the United States was begun, and that sale Congress was not yet ready for.   In the next year it caused the expulsion of all settlers north- west of the Ohio, except those protected by the Virginia deed of cession. [2]

After this action of 1784, the matter of temporary government was almost continuously in the hands of committees, and occasionally there was an attempt to amend the " charter of compact," — sometimes success- ful and sometimes unsuccessful.   Meanwhile the French settlers were left to get along as best they could under their " ancient laws and customs."   The local govern- ment of Vincennes bowled along merrily under this sys- tem.   They had their commandant and their court, their clerk and their sheriff, an overflow of Kentucky militia at odd seasons and their own militia at all times.   There was the greatest abundance of government, for the more the United States neglected them, the more authority their officials assumed.   The people of the Illinois ap-

[1] *Journals of Congress*, vol. iv. p. 378.
[2] *St. Clair Papers*, vol. ii. pp. 1-5 and notes.

pear to have been less happily situated, for they petitioned Congress to give them some sort of government,
and on August 24, 1786, Congress ordered, "That the
secretary of Congress inform the inhabitants of Kaskaskies, that Congress have under their consideration the
plan of a temporary government for the said district,
and that its adoption will be no longer protracted than
the importance of the subject and a due regard to their
interest may require."[1]

On the surface, the years from 1784 to 1787 constitute
an era of irresolution and uncertainty. Thirteen states,
absolutely independent and sovereign, were acting together for their common interest, but their harmony
was subjected to many rude jars by their conflicting individual interests. During the war, the general danger
spurred them on to agreement or compromise of their
differences, but with peace there grew an alarming laxity
in providing for the general welfare. The confederate
government was prostrate and helpless. The states were
becoming discordant. The feeling was growing that
there must be a stronger central government, or the
Union must be abandoned. The realization had come
that permanent union could be reached only through
reciprocal concessions. Yet, with all the difficulties in
view, and though they often expressed grave fears for
the future, the great statesmen of the day proceeded
much as though ultimate union were a certainty. They
made it their business to remove difficulties, and to provide for the future as though the difficulties were already
gone. There was at least as much conflict of interest
and sentiment concerning the Western territory as on
any other subject, and yet every move in regard to it

---

[1] *Journals of Congress,* vol. iv. p. 688.

was made in expressed anticipation of a continuous union and a common sentiment.

Slavery had not yet become the controlling factor in national politics. In abstract theory no man of national fame defended it, and many explicitly condemned it. No one questioned the power of even the old Congress to prohibit it in the Western territory, though no one claimed any power in Congress to interfere with it in the states. Slavery still existed in all the states except Massachusetts, but the feeling against it was very strong in the North; and in Maryland and Virginia a large minority favored emancipation. The Abolitionists of the time confined their efforts strictly to appeals to conscience and to patriotism; and although the invention of the cotton gin in 1793, and the enormous extension of the cotton and tobacco interests thereafter, turned private interest strongly against it, the abolition theory still continued to grow. In 1827 there were one hundred and thirty abolition societies in this country, and only twenty-four of them were in the free states. From 1830 the tide turned back in the Southern States and swept far into the North. The Nat Turner insurrection at Southampton, and insubordination elsewhere, determined the South to prevent any kind of interference with slavery, and soon the nation passed into that dark period of thirty years when Abolitionist and villain were synonymous, to emerge only when washed clean in her own best blood.[1]

Among the many Revolutionary soldiers who in 1784–1785 were contemplating settlement in the West,

---

[1] For collected authorities on this subject, see Poole's *Anti-Slavery Opinions Prior to* 1800, and Helper's *Impending Crisis of the South.*

was Colonel Timothy Pickering, afterwards of national fame as a senator and cabinet officer. He was in correspondence with Elbridge Gerry and Rufus King, then members of Congress, and, according to the statement of the latter, exercised much influence in the formulation of the plan for the disposition of the western lands. On March 8, 1785, writing to Mr. King concerning the ordinance of 1784, Colonel Pickering said : " There is one article in the report of the committee on which that act was made, which I am extremely sorry to see was omitted in the act. The committee proposed that after the year 1800 there should be no slavery in the new States. I hardly have patience to write on a subject in which what is right is so obvious and just, and what is wrong is so derogatory to Americans above all men, so inhuman and iniquitous in itself." Later, on the same day, he continued in a second letter to King: "In looking over the Act of Congress of the 23rd of April last, and the present report of an ordinance, relative to these lands, I observe there is no provision made for ministers of the gospel, nor even for schools and academies. The latter might have been brought into view ; though, after the admission of SLAVERY, it was right to say nothing of Christianity. . . . What pretence (argument there could be none) could be offered for its rejection ? I should, indeed, have objected to the period proposed (the year 1800) for the exclusion of slavery ; for the admission of it for a day or an hour ought to have been forbidden. It will be infinitely easier to prevent the evil at first, than to eradicate or check it in any future time. . . . To suffer the continuance of slaves till they can be gradually emancipated, in States already overrun with them, may be pardonable, because unavoidable without hazard-

ing greater evils; but to introduce them into countries
where none now exist [1] — countries which have been
talked of, which we have boasted of, as asylums to the
oppressed of the earth — can never be forgiven. For
God's sake, then, let one more effort be made to prevent
so terrible a calamity." [2]

This letter was effective with Mr. King, for on March
16, 1785, he moved the commitment to the whole house
of a resolution, "That there shall be neither slavery nor
involuntary servitude in any of the States described in
the resolve of Congress of the 23d of April, 1784, otherwise than in the punishment of crimes whereof the
party shall have been personally guilty; and that this
regulation shall be an article of compact, and remain a
fundamental principle of the constitutions between the
thirteen original states, and each of the states described
in the said resolve of the 23d of April, 1784." The
Northern States and Maryland voted for commitment.
Delaware and Georgia were absent. The other Southern
States opposed commitment, though one Virginia delegate, William Grayson, voted aye. It was referred to a
committee consisting of Mr. King, Mr. Howell, and Mr.
Ellery. This resolution, it will be observed, was exactly Mr. Jefferson's, except that it was to take effect at
once instead of being dormant until 1800. On April 6th,
the committee reported, making two important changes.
The first restored Mr. Jefferson's limit of the year 1800

---

[1] This mistaken thought was the cause of the objection of other
Northern men to Mr. Jefferson's provision. They looked at the
resolution as a provision for a new population; Jefferson was
thinking of the French settlers, with whose slave-holding he had
become familiar while governor, and member of the executive
council of Virginia.

[2] *Life of Timothy Pickering,* vol. i. pp. 504-513.

for the continuance of slavery. The second added the fugitive-slave clause: " Provided always, that upon the escape of any person into any of the states described in the said resolve of Congress of the 23d day of April, 1784, from whom labor or service is lawfully claimed in any one of the thirteen original states, such fugitive may be lawfully reclaimed and carried back to the person claiming his labor or service as aforesaid, this resolve notwithstanding." [1] This was the source of the fugitive-slave clause in the Ordinance of 1787. Who introduced it is not known, but as the only known precedent for it was a similar provision in the compact of the confederated New England Colonies in 1643, and as Mr. King afterwards moved the introduction of the clause into the Constitution of the United States, it is certain that it was not considered objectionable in the North at that time. That Mr. King did not consider it inconsistent with even the advanced views of Colonel Pickering is shown by the fact, that, on April 15, he wrote that gentleman informing him that his propositions concerning the disposal of western lands had " had weight with the committee," and added : " I likewise enclose you the report of a committee on a motion for the exclusion of slavery from the new states. Your ideas on this unjustifiable practice are so just that it would be impossible to differ from them." No farther action was taken on the resolution until it was incorporated, with a modification as to time, in the Ordinance of 1787. The reason was that Mr. King held it back until the ordinance for the sale of western lands, then pending in Congress, should have been disposed of,[2] but the resolution was

---

[1] *Papers of Am. Congress*, vol. xxxi. p. 329.
[2] Grayson to Madison, May 1, 1785.

not taken up after that ordinance had passed, probably because the cessions by the extreme Southern States were withheld, and the adoption of the clause might interfere with obtaining these cessions.

The ordinance for the disposal of lands, which passed on May 20, 1785, was unquestionably a compromise. Mr. King wrote to Colonel Pickering on May 30: "All parties who have advocated particular modes of disposing of this Western territory have relinquished some things they wished, and the ordinance is a compromise of opinions." The same might be said of the Ordinance of 1787. The matter of government was all the time in the hands of committees, and their reports were continually amended, recommitted, or postponed. The real difficulty that lay back of it was that the Southern States would not make the cessions of land south of the Ohio which the other states wished them to make. Occasionally, however, some point of agreement would be reached, and these were held to in the Ordinance. The most important of them was the change in the division of the territory for the formation of states. This subject was brought forward by a motion of Mr. Monroe, and on July 7, 1786, the committee to which his motion was referred reported in favor of recommending Virginia and Massachusetts to amend their acts of cession so that the Northwest territory might be divided into not less than two nor more than five states. This was adopted with the change that there should be "not less than three." The expressed reason for this change as to division was that the states before provided for would be too small, and that some of them would have no access to navigable waters, while others would have navigable streams entirely within their boundaries for some dis-

tance. Mr. Monroe's reason, however, as he wrote to
Jefferson on January 19, 1786, was largely political.
He says: " I am clearly of opinion that to many of the
most important objects of a federal government their
interests, if not opposed, will be but little connected with
ours; instead of weakening theirs and making it sub-
servient to our purposes, we have given it all the possible strength we could; weaken it we might also, and at
the same time (I mean by reducing the number of
states) render them substantial service." On July 16,
1786, he wrote that there was a desire on the part of
New England to hinder the new states from coming into
the Union, by enlarging the requirement as to the number of inhabitants, and possibly to relinquish the western
lands altogether to Spain. Whatever may have been
at the bottom of it, the change was made, with but one
dissenting vote, and was adopted in the Ordinance of
1787.

No action was taken that indicated an agreement as
to the whole Ordinance until the spring of 1787. On
April 23 of that year, a committee consisting of Mr.
Johnson of Connecticut, Mr. Pinckney of South Carolina, Mr. Smith of New York, Mr. Dane of Massachusetts, and Mr. Henry of Maryland, reported an " Ordinance for the government of the Western Territory,"
which was read the second time and amended on May
9. On May 10, the third reading was called for by
Massachusetts, then represented by Messrs. Gorham,
King, and Dane, but action was postponed, and this
ordinance did not come up again, except to be referred
to a new committee on July 9. The mass of it, with
some modifications, is included in the Ordinance of 1787,
forming about one third of that instrument. No provis-

ion as to slavery was included in it. It had no features
of a bill of rights, except the preservation of trial by jury
and the writ of *habeas corpus.* It was chiefly a regulation of the form of government which might thereafter
be adopted by the new states. As to the extent of its
application it is very obscure, but the title, and the absence of any restrictive provision, indicate that it was
intended to apply to the entire western country. It is
commonly understood, and is probably true, that this
was what was known as " Monroe's plan." [1]

The sudden stop in the consideration of this measure
at the point of its third reading shows that some new
motor was in action. This motor was the Ohio Company, which had been formed in New England for the
purpose of colonization in the western lands. Its effects on this ordinance, and on the entire history of the
Mississippi valley, were so great that an acquaintance
with its development is essential to an understanding of
our history. As the Revolutionary War drew to a close,
many of the soldiers and officers began to look forward
for some occupation when peace should come. On
April 7, 1783, one day before news of the Treaty of
Paris reached him, but while there was a general expectation that a treaty would be made, Colonel Pickering wrote to his friend Mr. Hodgdon : " A new plan is
in contemplation, — no less than forming a *new State*
westward of the Ohio. Some of the principal officers
of the army are heartily engaged in it. About a week
since, the matter was set on foot, and a plan is digesting
for the purpose. Enclosed is a rough draft of some
propositions respecting it, which are generally approved

[1] Monroe to Jefferson, May 11, 1786; Bancroft's *Hist. Const.,*
vol. I. p. 502.

of. They are in the hands of General Huntington and General [Rufus] Putnam for consideration, amendment, and addition." These propositions, drawn by Pickering, were for the establishment of a sort of brotherhood community of soldiers, the most important political provision being, " The total exclusion of slavery from the State to form an essential and irrevocable part of the Constitution." [1]   Possibly this project may have influenced Jefferson in drafting his ordinance, as there was certainly correspondence between the projectors and the influential men of the day.   Putnam prepared a memorial, which he sent to Washington in June, 1783, and he forwarded it to Congress.   Other similar memorials were sent to Congress, but it was urged that the title to the western lands was too unsettled for action.   On October 29, 1783, Congress formally announced that it was unable to do anything for the soldiers for the time being.   On April 5, 1784, Putnam wrote to Washington for information concerning the western lands, stating that he feared to confide in Massachusetts or New York delegates, because those states had land to sell, and their representatives would desire to impede the Ohio movement.   On June 2, Washington replied that he was persuaded that something of the sort was true.   In 1785 Putnam was elected surveyor for Massachusetts, under the land ordinance ; but as he could not then serve, General Benjamin Tupper, who had been associated with him in the Ohio project, was appointed to take his place temporarily.[2]   Tupper started for the West, but only reached Pittsburgh, the hostile attitude of the Indians preventing any surveying.

[1] The propositions in full are in the *Life of Pickering*, vol. i. p. 546.

[2] *Journals Am. Cong.*, vol. iv. pp. 527, 547.

The Indians who were objecting most strenuously to
the advance of the white man beyond the Ohio were
the Shawnees. The Iroquois had surrendered all claims
to lands northwest of the Ohio, in their treaty of
Fort Stanwix, on October 22, 1784 ; but the western
tribes were far from conceding that the Iroquois had
title there.   On January 21, 1785, a part of the Wyandots, Delawares, Chippewas, and Ottawas ceded more
than half of Ohio — lying east of the Cuyahoga and
Tuscarawas, south of a line drawn from near the mouth
of Sandy Creek to the head of the Great Miami, and
east of the last-named stream — at the treaty of Fort
McIntosh.   In the fall of 1785, General Samuel Holden
Parsons, an associate of Putnam and Tupper, came West
as commissioner to aid General George Rogers Clark
and Colonel Richard Butler in treating with the Shawnees.   The tribe was very reluctant to surrender the
country which contained their old towns, but they held
it only by sufferance of tribes that had already ceded,
and the commissioners gave them the alternative of cession or war in so plain terms that they made the same
relinquishment as the other western tribes.   They were
given, with the consent of the Wyandots and Delawares,
a tract of land running from the northern part of the
Great Miami to the Wabash. This treaty was concluded
at the mouth of the Great Miami, at Fort Finney, on
January 31, 1786. While engaged in this business, Parsons also looked for a favorable place for a settlement,
and wrote from Fort Finney, on December 20, 1785 :
" I have seen no place that pleases me so well for settlement as Muskingum." [1]

At the opening of 1786 the way appeared clear for

[1] *N. Am. Rev.*, vol. liii. p. 329.

a movement towards settlement; and on January 10, Tupper having reached Rutland, Mass., the home of General Putnam, on his return from the West, the two issued a call for those who desired to embark in the Ohio project to hold meetings in the various counties on February 15, and elect delegates, who should convene at the Bunch-of-Grapes Tavern in Boston, on March 1, and organize the Ohio Company. This plan was published in the newspapers, and was carried out at a meeting of delegates from eight counties as proposed. Subscription books were opened, and subscriptions to stock advanced so well that on March 8, 1787, Samuel H. Parsons, Rufus Putnam, and Dr. Manasseh Cutler were appointed to make application to Congress for a private purchase of land under such conditions as they might consider proper. The stock of the company was one thousand shares of $1,000 each. Each shareholder was to pay $10 in coin to defray expenses of the company, and the remainder in Continental certificates. The latter had been issued in payment to the soldiery, as well as in satisfaction of other public debts. They bore interest, but because they had been thrown on the market in large quantities, because the interest had not been met promptly, and because the general government appeared insolvent, they had fallen to a very small percentage of their face value.

The business of purchase was undertaken by General Parsons alone. He proceeded to New York, and on May 9, 1787, the same day on which the Monroe plan had its second reading, he placed before Congress a memorial asking that "a Tract of Country within the Western Territory of the United States at some convenient Place may be granted them at a reasonable Price,

upon their paying a Sum not exceeding One Million of
Dollars nor less than five Hundred Thousand Dollars, and
that Such of the Associators as by the Resolutions of
Congress are intitled to receive Lands for their military
Services, may have their Lands assigned them within
the aforesaid Grant." This memorial, in the handwriting of General Parsons, shows no objection to the ordinance then before Congress, yet the conclusion is irresist-
ible that it stopped action on the ordinance. The exact
connection between the two, however, is not clear. The
theory advanced by Mr. Bancroft, that now for the first
time there appeared a certainty of actual settlement,[1]
is not tenable, for the projectors of this company had
been trying to obtain western lands for four years, and
many others were engaged in the same effort. As far
back as November 3, 1784, George Washington wrote
to Jacob Read, a member of Congress: "Such is the
rage for speculating in and forestalling of lands on the
northwest of the Ohio that scarce a valuable spot, within
any tolerable distance of it. is left without a claimant.
Men in these times talk with as much facility of fifty,
an hundred, and even five hundred thousand acres, as a
gentleman formerly would do of one thousand. In defiance of the proclamation of Congress, they roam over
the country, on the Indian side of the Ohio, mark out
lands, survey, and even settle on them. This gives great
discontent to the Indians, and will, unless measures are
taken in time to prevent it, inevitably produce a war
with the Western tribes." In the spring of 1785 General
Harmar had caused several thousand actual settlers to
be expelled from the country northwest of the Ohio.[2]

[1] *Hist. of Const.*, vol. ii. pp. 109, 110.
[2] *St. Clair Papers*, vol. ii. pp. 3, 4, 5, note.

There was unquestionably a desire to distinguish between soldiers and other original holders of certificates and those who had bought up these securities for speculative purposes. One of Colonel Pickering's chief aims, as appears from his correspondence, was to secure the greatest possible benefit to the soldier and the actual settler, and, by the way, it was his connection with the Ohio Company that led to his correspondence with Gerry and King, for he mentions that the former had expressed a desire to purchase lands through the company. The desire to discriminate against speculators need not have interfered with the ordinance, for it could have been attained as well under the Monroe plan as under the one adopted.

The most plausible explanation is that a majority of Congress decided to abandon the old struggle over the question of the cessions by the Southern States, and to provide for an immediate opening of the territory north of the Ohio, leaving that south of the river to be provided for in the future. They were impelled to this by the financial needs of the country, the prospect of greatly reducing the public debt by one direct transaction, and the increase of value in adjoining lands by the establishment of a desirable colony. The establishment of this colony also created a necessity for the immediate enactment of some laws, especially as to the conveyance of land. Hitherto it had been easy to provide for the property rights of the French settlers by preserving to them their "laws and customs," and they were the only settlers that Congress had in actual view. On April 23, only two weeks earlier, Madison wrote to Jefferson: "The government of the settlements on the Illinois and Wabash is a subject very perplexing in itself, and ren-

dered more so by our ignorance of many circumstances
on which a right judgment depends.   The inhabitants
at those places claim protection against the savages, and
some provision for both criminal and civil justice.   It
also appears that land-jobbers are among them, who are
likely to multiply litigations among individuals, and, by
collusive purchases of spurious titles, to defraud the
United States." [1]   Now, it was not a matter of French
settlements, with a gradual growth by immigration, but
of the introduction of an organized community into the
Western territory, a community which would want nothing but American institutions, a community which would
form the nucleus for a state, a community to which the
French settlements would in a very short time become
subordinate.   To provide for this would require some
time; Congress was desirous of adjourning, but could
not agree on a place for reconvening; members began
leaving.   On May 12 no quorum remained, and none
could be obtained until July 4.

General Parsons returned to his home, and the actual
negotiation was turned over to his co-director, Dr. Manasseh Cutler.   He was a graduate of Yale, had taken
degrees in the three learned professions, and had served
as chaplain in the army.   He was a man of literary and
scientific attainments, of pleasing presence, and of great
business capacity.   He left his home at Hamilton, Massachusetts, in June; arrived at Cambridge on the 23d;
received introductory letters from President Willard, of
Harvard; and went over to Boston in company with Dr.
Williams.   At Boston he received letters from Governor
Bowdoin, Mr. Winthrop, General Putnam, and others,
and agreed with Putnam on the details of the purchase.

[1] *Madison Papers*, vol. ii. p. 640.

From here he proceeded to Middletown, Connecticut, where he had a long conference with General Parsons, and on July 2 " settled all matters with respect to his business with Congress." [1] On July 5 he arrived in New York. The following day Congress had a quorum, — the first for six weeks, except on July 4, — and Cutler presented his numerous letters of introduction and made his proposals for purchase, which went to the old committee on Parsons's memorial the same day. On the 9th the report on the Ordinance was referred to a new committee, composed of Carrington and Richard Henry Lee of Virginia, Dane, Smith of New York, and Kean of South Carolina.

On the tenth the committee on Parsons's memorial reported in favor of a grant on the terms proposed by the Ohio Company, but meanwhile Congress had determined to finish the Ordinance before taking up the sale. Cutler entered in his journal : " July 10. As Congress was now engaged in settling the form of government for the Federal Territory, for which a bill has been prepared, and a copy sent to me, with leave to make remarks and propose amendments, which I had taken the liberty to remark upon and propose several amendments, I thought this the most favorable time to go on to Philadelphia." He went that evening and remained until the 17th. On the 11th the committee on the Ordinance reported. The report was made a special order of business, and read and amended on the day following. On the 13th it came to the third reading and passed, receiv-

---

[1] Cutler's *Journal*, extracts from which were published in *N. Am. Rev.*, vol. liii. p. 520; *Annals of the West*, p. 308, etc. Since the above was written a life of Dr. Cutler, containing very full extracts from the journal, has been published.

ing the unanimous vote of the delegates, excepting Abraham Yates, Jr., of New York, who called for the yeas and nays, and put himself on record against it.

The Ordinance as adopted was an entirely different instrument from any that had before been considered by Congress, and yet it included the greater part of the preceding propositions. The identity of phraseology shows that whoever drafted it had the older reports before him at the time. The first paragraph provides that the region northwest of the Ohio, for the time, should be one district for governmental purposes. The second regulates the descent and conveyance of property, and was new. Following it comes the Ordinance as it stood on May 10, almost in entirety. Following this comes Jefferson's ordinance of 1784, modified to harmonize with the other parts, into which are injected additional magna charta principles, as " articles of compact " and the " basis of all laws, constitutions, and governments, which forever hereafter shall be formed in the said territory." Of these, the first three articles are new. The fourth includes Mr. Jefferson's articles. The fifth includes the resolution of Congress on Monroe's motion for the division of the territory into not less than three nor more than five states. The sixth is the slave clause, as reported by the committee on Mr. King's motion, except that the extension to 1800 is removed ; and this clause alone, as a whole, did not appear in the Ordinance as reported and printed. It was introduced on July 12, and appeared on the printed bill, as an amendment, in the handwriting of Mr. Dane.[1] The two features of the Ordinance which caused its harmonious and speedy pas-

[1] Dane's *Abridgment*, vol. vii. pp. 380, 390; Dane to J. H. Farnham, Secy. Ind. Hist. Soc., in *N. Y. Tribune*, June 18, 1875.

sage were withdrawals by the Northern States from the stand they had formerly maintained. The first was the restriction of the Ordinance to the region north of the Ohio, *i. e.* the lands already ceded, as in Jefferson's first report. The second was the admission of new states when they should have a population of sixty thousand free inhabitants; which quieted all fears, such as Mr. Monroe had expressed, that the North was trying to keep the new states out of the Union. Mr. Jefferson's provision was that the applicant state should have a population equal to the least of the original states at the time of application. Monroe's plan, as reported from the committee, stipulated a population equal to one thirteenth of the original states, "to be computed from the last enumeration." Either of these would have long delayed the admission of most of the Western States, but the second would have been much worse than the first. Rhode Island had only 69,000 inhabitants in 1790, and had not increased in 1800. One thirteenth of the population of the original states in 1790 was over 200,000.

As to authorship there are two declarations, contemporaneous with the passage of the Ordinance, that are of peculiar importance. On July 16, 1787, Nathan Dane wrote to Rufus King : " We have been much engaged in business for ten or twelve days past, for a part of which we have had eight states. There appears to be a disposition to do business, and the arrival of R. H. Lee is of considerable importance. I think his character serves, at least in some degree, to check the effects of the feeble habits and lax mode of thinking of some of his countrymen. We have been employed about several objects — the principal of which have been the Government inclosed [the Ordinance] and the Ohio purchase ; the former, you will see, is completed, and the latter will probably be completed to-morrow. We tried one day to patch up M——s system of W. government — started new ideas and committed the whole to Carrington, Dane, R. H. Lee, Smith and Kean. We met several times, and at last agreed on some principles — at least Lee, Smith and myself. We found ourselves rather pressed. The Ohio company appeared to purchase a large tract of federal lands — about six or seven millions of acres — and we wanted to abolish the old system and get a better one for the government of the country, and we finally found it necessary to adopt the best system we could get. All agreed finally to the enclosed plan, except A. Yates. He appeared in this case, as in most others, not to understand the subject at all. . . . When I drew the ordinance (which passed, a few words excepted, as I originally formed it) I had no idea the States would agree to the sixth article, prohibiting slavery, as only Massachusetts, of the Eastern States, was present, and therefore omitted it in the draft; but, finding the House favorably disposed on this subject, after we had completed the other parts, I moved the article which was agreed to without opposition."[1]

Three days later Cutler entered in his journal: "July 19. Called on members of Congress very early this morning; was furnished with the ordinance establishing a government in the Western Federal Territory. It is in a degree new modelled. The amendments I proposed have all been made, except one, and that is better qualified. It was, that we should not be subject to continental taxation, unless we were entitled to a full representation in Congress. This could not be fully obtained; for

[1] *N. Y. Tribune,* February 28, 1855.

it was considered in Congress as offering a premium to emigrants." The reference here is, presumably, to the territory being allowed a delegate with the right of debate but not of voting, as had been provided in Jefferson's ordinance, and as has since been continued in territorial governments.

With these facts before us, there can be little room for question as to who framed the Ordinance, or what was the source of most of its provisions. It is universally conceded that Nathan Dane was the "scribe," but to one familiar with legislative work this means more than merely writing at the dictation of others. It means that after discussing the previous propositions, after agreeing in committee with Smith and Lee on desirable changes, after receiving the suggestions of Dr. Cutler, Nathan Dane put the Ordinance together in a shape that was acceptable to all with very slight alteration, and the greatest alteration proposed by himself. He did not claim much originality. In his letter to Mr. Webster, of March 26, 1830, he says : "I have never claimed *originality*, except in regard to the clause against impairing contracts, and perhaps the Indian article, part of the third article, including, also, religion, morality, knowledge, schools, etc." [1] The ideas of the Ordinance, as we have seen, came from many sources. The great mass of it was the result of months of consideration and compromise by Congress. Of the new parts, Mr. Dane

---

[1] *Proceedings Mass. Hist. Soc.* 1867–1869, p. 479. The last twelve words are merely explanatory, showing the location of the Indian article, but not claiming authorship of the remainder of the third article. They furnish a striking example of Mr. Dane's involved style. Shosuke Sato, in his interesting and valuable study of this subject, is misled by this obscurity. *Johns Hopkins Univ. Studies*, Fourth Series, p. 264.

expressly claims that " his invention furnished the provision respecting impairing contracts and the Indian
security and some other smaller matters," [1] and there is
no reason for disputing it.

To Dr. Cutler may safely be assigned the origination
of all of the third article of compact except what refers
to the Indians.   Provisions for a university and the support of religion were his hobbies, and he stood out for
them to the extent of refusing to purchase at all unless
they were conceded, as will appear hereafter.   His ear-
marks are plain on the clause as it was originally reported, in these words : " Institutions for the promotion
of religion and morality, schools and the means of education, shall forever be encouraged, and all persons while
young shall be taught some useful occupation."   When
the bill was before Congress this was amended to read :
" Religion, morality, and knowledge, being necessary to
good government and the happiness of mankind, schools
and the means of education shall forever be encouraged."
The original looked too much like favoring a religious
establishment to be acceptable to Congress.   It is possible that Cutler may also have suggested providing temporarily for the descent and conveyance of land, as it
was of immediate importance to his company.   Possibly,
too, he may have suggested the first and the greater part
of the second articles of compact, but these might with
more plausibility be ascribed to Richard Henry Lee.
The first secures freedom of conscience, and the second personal and property rights.   Both were favorite
dogmas with Virginians of Lee's school.   According to
Dane's letter to King, above, Lee took an active interest
in the Ordinance, and according to his own statement

[1] *Abridgment*, vol. vii. pp. 389, 390.

his thought was turned in this direction. He wrote to Washington on July 15, 1787 : "I have the honor to inclose to you an ordinance, that we have just passed in Congress, for establishing a temporary Government beyond the Ohio, as a measure preparatory to the sale of lands. It seemed necessary, for the security of property among uninformed, and, perhaps, licentious people, as the greater part of those who go there are, that a strong-toned Government should exist, and the rights of property be clearly defined." [1] With such ideas prominent, his chief interest would naturally be in the articles of compact, and, indeed, it is within the range of reasonable conjecture that Jefferson's ordinance may have been included at his suggestion. There certainly must have been very material changes in the draft, after Cutler saw it on July 10, to cause him to speak of it as "in a degree remodelled" on July 19. Grayson, Carrington, and St. Clair appear to have cordially supported the Ordinance, but there is nothing to show that they had any connection with its authorship, and much to show that they had none.

On the whole we conclude, that, so far as any one man can be called the author of the Ordinance of 1787, Nathan Dane was its author. He drafted it, superintended its passage, introduced the slavery amendment, and manifested his interest by writing at once a long account of it to his friend Rufus King. In after-life it was his chief pride. He is the only man who claimed authorship over his signature, and he repeatedly made the claim, from three days after its passage to the time of his death. It has been urged against his claim that he did not realize that he was framing a great charter of

[1] Sparks's *Correspondence of the Revolution*, vol. iv. p. 174.

rights. Very probably he did not; but neither did any one else at the time. It has been urged that he appeared to consider the Ordinance a patchwork. Very true, he did; and it is a patchwork. Its joints are so plainly visible that it was considered advisable to insert in them the words, " Be it ordained by the authority aforesaid," by way of introduction, to make smooth the abrupt breaks which otherwise would have appeared. They occur in three places, introducing the three chief component parts above pointed out, and again in the clause repealing the resolution of 1784. It has been urged that Dane's style was obscure and devoid of elegance. No one who has attempted to read and understand his writings will be apt to deny this, but the Ordinance is not a model of clearness or precision, outside of its parts that were adopted bodily from other sources. For example, the provision as to laws impairing contracts reads that such laws " ought " not to be passed; and as to slavery, the provisions are so enigmatical that no man, to this day, can say with assurance what is provided on that subject. It has been urged that Daniel Webster became satisfied that others had suggested some of the provisions of the Ordinance. Very probably he did; but on May 15, 1850, twenty years after the controversy began, he wrote to the citizens of Newburyport that the Ordinance "was drawn up by that great man of your own county, and a contemporary of your father's, Nathan Dane." [1]

The most interesting question in connection with the Ordinance is, what were the motives that caused the unanimous consent of Southern members to the apparent exclusion of slavery, and the consent of Northern mem-

[1] Webster's *Works*, vol. vi. p. 552.

bers to the division of the western territory ceded from
that unceded, and the reduction of the amount of population necessary for admission of a state. That the
proposal of the Ohio Company induced immediate action
is evident, but there is nothing to indicate that the company or Dr. Cutler undertook to dictate as to governmental features. If Cutler had made the slavery clause
a *sine qua non* of his purchase, as has been argued,[1]
it would have been presented in the printed report, and
Cutler would more probably have remained in New York
to urge its adoption, than have gone to Philadelphia on
a pleasure trip, as he did. The singular unanimity with
which the Ordinance passed shows that every one was
satisfied ; but why ? A statement of Colonel Grayson
gives a key to one side. Personally, Grayson had no
objection to the clause, for he was the most pronounced
anti-slavery Southern man in Congress. He had favored
King's resolution when it applied to the entire western
country, and on May 1, 1785, wrote to Madison concerning it : " I expect seven states may be found liberal
enough to adopt it." He was an active advocate of the
Ordinance. He wrote to Monroe on August 8, 1787,
urging him to use his influence to have it ratified by
Virginia. Nothing was done at that session of the Virginia legislature, and at the next Grayson stood for
membership, was elected, and was a member of the
committee which reported the bill confirming the Ordi-

---

[1] W. F. Poole in *N. Am. Rev.*, vol. cxxii. p. 229. This is by far
the most valuable study of the Ordinance yet published, with
possibly the exception of Mr. Force's publication in the *National
Intelligencer* of August 6, 1847, which is republished in *Western
Law Journal*, September, 1848, and *St. Clair Papers*, vol. ii.
p. 603.

nance.   Apparently, then, he was in a situation to know
why members voted as they did, and he said, in his letter
to Monroe of August 8 : "The clause respecting slavery
was agreed to by the Southern members for the purpose
of preventing tobacco and indigo from being made on
the northwest side of the Ohio, as well as for several
other political reasons."   These other reasons, so far as
he reveals them, he gives by setting forth the project
of the Ohio Company, concluding thus : "From the
great number of inhabitants in the Eastern States, and
in the Jerseys, I should not be surprised to see them in
a very few years extend themselves by additional purchases quite to the Mississippi, and thereby form a complete barrier for our state, at the same time greatly
validating the lands on the Virginia side of the Ohio." [1]

That the culture of indigo and tobacco should have
had anything to do with the Ordinance of 1787 may
strike the reader as verging on absurdity, but the connection is close and logical, and it is a *political* reason,
as Grayson said.   Indigo had been cultivated north of
the Ohio since the middle of the eighteenth century, and
profitably, too, though it produced only two cuttings a
year.[2]   The tobacco of the French settlements was considered, as we have seen, equal to the best product of
Virginia.   These crops, like all others whose preparation
for market requires attention during the entire year, gave
the most profitable employment to slave labor, and it was
supposed that free labor could not compete with slave
labor in their production.   In addition to this, the un-
healthfulness of indigo culture and preparation was considered sufficient to prevent free labor from engaging in

---

[1] Bancroft's *Hist. Const.*, vol. ii. p. 437.
[2] Hutchins's *Top. Desc.*, p. 43.

it at all. The Southern members reasoned that they
were gaining three advantages : 1. The monopoly of the
most profitable branches of agriculture for their western
territory, which was still unceded ; 2. Protection of their
western territory from the Indians subject to British influence, by the settlement of the country north of them ;
3. The speedy settlement of their western territory by
people of political sentiments similar to their own. This
last is a corollary of the other two. If their side of the
Ohio were best protected from Indians, it would be most
desirable to settlers. If slavery were excluded north of
the Ohio, all who desired to hold slaves must settle south
of it. If the most profitable branches of agriculture
could be followed only by slave labor, all shrewd agricul-
turists would desire to hold slaves. The northern territory, by express limitation, could not be made into more
than five states, and might be limited to three. The
southern territory had already two strong slave-holding
colonies in their northernmost part, which would have
been most subject to Northern influence, and the territory
below would make enough more to balance the Northern
element above the river.

Dane did not grasp their theory. He had no idea, as
he says, that the Southern States would consent to the
slavery clause, and must have been astonished when they
did so unanimously. He proceeded on the supposition
that he was gaining a political advantage to New England by the same measure, and that the concessions by
the North were such in form only. In his letter of
July 16th to King he said : " I think the number of free
inhabitants — 60,000 — which are requisite for the admission of a new state into the confederacy is too small ;
but, having divided the whole territory into three states,

this number appears to me to be less important. Each state, in the common course of things, must become important soon after it shall have that number of inhabitants. The eastern state of the three will probably be the first and more important than the rest, and will no doubt be settled chiefly by eastern people; and there is, I think, full an equal chance of its adopting eastern politics." From his stand, he was naturally surprised at the Southerners accepting the slavery clause. Both sides thought they had the advantage. In the slight discussion of the measure, each kept its actuating motives secret; and each had arrived at much the same conclusion as was reached, after open controversy, in the Missouri Compromise. The Southern States said : " Take the territory north of the Ohio and make free states of it ; but you must not make more than five states ; you must leave us untrammelled south of the Ohio ; you must give up our slaves when they escape to you." From that time for half a century the distinction of North and South on the question of slavery in new territories was maintained. Two years later North Carolina ceded her western lands, providing always, "That no regulations made or to be made by Congress shall tend to emancipate slaves." Congress accepted the cession, and in May, 1790, gave the territory south of the Ohio the same government as that north except as to slavery.[1] In 1798 Congress refused a petition for the suspension of the slavery clause in the Northwest Territory; but in the same year a proposition to exclude slavery from Mississippi Territory was rejected by a vote of 58 to 12 in the House of Representatives, the debate having turned on the diverse

[1] Poore's *Charters and Constitutions*, pp. 1006, 1007.

nature and conditions of the country north and south of the Ohio.[1]

In the Congress of 1787, of eighteen men, representing three Northern States and five Southern States, only one man, Abraham Yates, Jr., of New York, voted against the Ordinance, and he has commonly received only scorn and ridicule for his record. Dane, as has been mentioned, attributed his opposition to lack of sense; but Dane had evidently but a glimmering idea of what the effects of the Ordinance would be. He was not a broad man. Monroe counted him among the most " illiberal " men he had ever seen from Massachusetts.[2] The truth is that no one knows why Yates opposed the Ordinance, farther than that Nathan Dane afterwards said that it was not on account of objection to the slave clause.[8] He may have objected to the distinction between lands north and south of the Ohio; he may have objected to the property qualifications of electors and officers; he may have objected to limiting the future states of this section to five. Possibly it was narrowness and stupidity; possibly it was breadth and foresight; possibly some personal interest was interfered with.[4]

[1] Benton's *Abridgment*, vol. ii. pp. 221–224.

[2] Monroe to Jefferson, July 16, 1786. Dane's name has been confounded with Francis Dana's in some prints of this letter. Dana was not in Congress at the time. *Journals of Am. Cong.*, vol. iv. p. 606.

[3] Dane's *Abridgment*, vol. vii. p. 446. This does not appear to have been noticed by Governor Coles, who conjectured that Yates objected to the provision for fugitive slaves. *Hist. of Ord. of* 1787, p. 28.

[4] There was probably some bad blood in regard to Yates. He had been expelled from the office of Commissioner of the Continental Loan Office of New York, on May 1, 1786, for refusing to take the oath prescribed by Congress. On October 9, 1787, a

As to this last, it cannot be questioned that local and even individual interests affected legislation then as they have always done. Cutler found this to be true as he went on with his purchase. He found much difficulty in getting the terms he desired, which were, in chief, three shillings sixpence Continental money, or one twelfth of a dollar coin, per acre, for the tract, with sections 8, 11, and 26 of each township to be reserved by Congress for future sale, section 16 to be donated for school land, section 29 to be donated for religious purposes, and two entire townships to be donated for a university.[1] The proposal was vigorously opposed, and it is not clear that it should not have been, for the price was certainly very low. On July 19, Congress reached a conclusion as to what it was willing to do, but no allowance was made for a university or for religious purposes, and the price was fixed at a dollar an acre for the land, in specie, or Continental money on a specie basis, allowing, however, a discount of not over one third of a dollar for bad lands, expenses, etc. On the 20th Cutler refused absolutely to accept the terms, and said he was about to leave, as he could contract with some of the states on much better terms. Later in the day Colonel Duer came to him with a cool proposal "from a number of the principal characters in the city," that he should take in another company and buy lands as its agent, though apparently for his own company, all of which was to "be kept a profound secret." Having considered the "generous

motion to commit a report on his accounts, which his friends considered favorable, was defeated by the Virginia delegation and Arthur St. Clair, though a large majority of the house favored committing. *Journals Am. Cong.*, vol. iv. pp. 633, 792.

[1] Bancroft, *Hist. Const.*, vol. ii. p. 433.

conditions" offered him for his services, and being urged
by Colonel Duer and Winthrop Sargent, Cutler consented, and thenceforward Duer and Sargent took an
active interest, and the negotiation proceeded more
rapidly. On the 23d a new impetus was added. Cutler
had desired that General Parsons should be governor
of the new territory, but had come to the conclusion that
Arthur St. Clair, then President of Congress, desired
this position, as there was a strong interest in his behalf,
especially among Southern members. On the evening
of the 23d, Cutler announced to a company of his
Southern friends that he would be satisfied if Parsons
were made first judge and Sargent secretary of the territory; that he heartily wished St. Clair to be governor,
and would work for him with the Eastern members.

Whether or not this had any effect on St. Clair,[1] it is
certain that Cutler and others thought it did. On the
26th Cutler recorded: "General St. Clair assured me
he would make every possible exertion to prevail with
Congress to accept the terms contained in our letter.
He appeared much interested and very friendly, but
said we must expect opposition. I am fully convinced
that it was good policy to give up Parsons and openly
appear solicitous that St. Clair should be appointed governor. Several gentlemen have told me that our matters went on much better since St. Clair and his friends
had been informed that we had given up Parsons, and
that I had solicited the Eastern members in favor of
his appointment." The negotiation was now pushed by
every agency that could be commanded. Cutler pre-

---

[1] It has been broadly asserted that it did (*N. Am. Rev.*, vol.
cxxii. p. 229), and acrimoniously denied (*Mag. of West. Hist.*,
vol. i. p. 49).

tended that he was about to leave in disgust and abandon the purchase ; his friends in Congress worked
actively ; the Board of Treasury supported the measure ;
the " principal characters of the city " did their part ;
St. Clair and his friends did theirs.   On the evening of
the 26th only two members held out against the sale on
Cutler's terms, which he had amended as to price.
These were Mr. Few of Georgia, and Mr. Kearny of
Delaware, but these two were enough to defeat the measure, for there were only eight states present and only
two members from each of these states.   On the 27th
the bill passed, making the reservations for university
and religious purposes for which Cutler had stipulated.
That night he entered in his journal : " By this ordinance we obtained the grant of near five million of acres
of land, amounting to three million and a half of dollars ;
one million and a half of acres for the Ohio Company,
and the remainder for a private speculation, in which
many of the principal characters of America are concerned.   Without connecting this speculation, similar
terms and advantages could not have been obtained for
the Ohio Company."   This seems to be an apology to
conscience for his own part in the affair, but what a com-
mentary on all concerned !   To a prominent politician
of the present day is ascribed the maxim : " It is safer
to go a hundred miles to see a man than it is to write to
him."   This is indeed a dictation of wisdom ; but even
after taking that precaution, it were well to remember
that your friend may keep a diary.

CHAPTER VI.

WHILE historians have devoted much attention to the authorship of the Ordinance of 1787, and particularly of the slavery clause, they have neglected to consider a question of much more importance: What did the Ordinance provide in regard to slavery? At first blush this question seems uncalled for. The sixth article of compact provides plainly: "There shall be neither slavery nor involuntary servitude in the said territory, otherwise than in the punishment of crimes, whereof the party shall have been duly convicted: provided always, that any person escaping into the same, from whom labour or service is lawfully claimed in any one of the original states, such fugitive may be lawfully reclaimed, and conveyed to the person claiming his or her labour or service as aforesaid." On this clause alone is founded the common understanding that slavery was absolutely prohibited in the Territory Northwest of the Ohio; but unfortunately for the peace of mind of those who had the duty of construing the Ordinance, there were other provisions inconsistent with the apparent import of this clause. Suffrage was restricted to "free male inhabitants;" population was to be estimated of the "free inhabitants;" and, in the provisions for conveyance of property, there was saved "to the French and Canadian inhabitants, and other settlers of the Kaskaskies, St.

Vincents, and the neighbouring villages, who have heretofore professed themselves citizens of Virginia, their laws and customs now in force among them, relative to the descent and conveyance of property." Then there were other documents that affected the rights of the people who came under the Ordinance. The deed of cession by Virginia provided, "That the *French* and *Canadian* inhabitants, and other settlers of the Kaskaskies, St. Vincents, and the neighboring villages, who have professed themselves citizens of Virginia, shall have their possessions and titles confirmed to them, and be protected in the enjoyment of their rights and liberties." There had been no similar provision for these ancient inhabitants in the old French-English treaty; but there was one made in Jay's treaty of 1794, under which the British forces finally evacuated the West, which protected the rights of all those of the ancient inhabitants who had not claimed citizenship of Virginia.

In order to arrive at a proper understanding of the actions of the early settlers, it will be necessary to inquire what construction was given to these various provisions by those in authority. As we shall find these in conflict, we may well afford to keep in mind the great difficulty of stating a principle in language so that it will be explicit beyond question, and also the fact that those expressions which are ordinarily considered commendable for their conciseness and simplicity are not infrequently subject to the most variant interpretations. Of this the most common instances are seen in the laws of all communities, even those which are drawn with the utmost care; for no one can say certainly what they mean until the highest tribunal of the jurisdiction has announced the construction it will put upon them, and

sometimes not then. Aside from any spirit of factious
or interested controversy, there frequently occur expressions about whose meaning equally conscientious men
differ, and each may have so much in his favor that, in
the light of different surroundings, the same language
may properly be given a meaning at one place totally
distinct from what it properly bears at another place.
One of the most remarkable instances of this occurs in
the common American declaration of natural rights. In
Massachusetts the declaration of rights in the Constitution of 1780 opens with the article: "All men are born
free and equal, and have certain natural, essential, and
unalienable rights; among which may be reckoned the
right of enjoying and defending their lives and liberties;
that of acquiring, possessing, and protecting property;
in fine, that of seeking and obtaining their safety and
happiness."[1] It cannot be said with absolute accuracy
that slavery was abolished previous to this in Massachusetts, for at one time it certainly existed, and no law
had as yet prohibited it; still from 1770 juries had invariably given judgment to slaves who sued their masters for wages, finding each time that the plaintiff was
not a slave.[2] In 1836 the Supreme Court of Massachusetts held that, if slavery existed in Massachusetts in
1780, it was abolished by this clause of the declaration,
for "it would be difficult to select words more precisely
adapted to the abolition of slavery."[3] The same conclusion had been reached by the court in the first case
that came before it involving the question, after the

---

[1] Poore's *Charters and Constitutions*, p. 957.

[2] Walsh's *Appeal from the Judgments of Great Britain*, etc.
pt. i. p. 313.

[3] Commonwealth *v.* Aves, 18 Pickering, 193, at pp. 209, 210.

adoption of the Constitution, and again in 1796, and
again in 1808, even as to slaves born before the declaration of rights was made.[1]   In other words, this was
construed to be a declaration of emancipation to all persons held in slavery in Massachusetts.

The New Hampshire Constitution of 1784 opened
with the clauses : " All men are born equally free and
independent ; " " All men have certain natural, essential,
and inherent rights, among which are the enjoying and
defending of life and liberty ; " " Among the natural
rights, some are in their very nature unalienable, because
no equivalent can be given or received for them." [2] The
Supreme Court of that state held this to mean that all
persons born in New Hampshire after that date were
born free, while those held in slavery at that date still
remained slaves.[3]   The Virginia Bill of Rights of 1776,
which was reaffirmed in their Constitution of 1830,
opened with this article : " That all men are by nature
equally free and independent, and have certain inherent
rights, of which, when they enter into a state of society,
they cannot, by any compact, deprive or divest their
posterity ; namely, the enjoyment of life and liberty,
with the means of acquiring and possessing property,
and pursuing and obtaining happiness and safety." [4]
This provision is as capable of sustaining a construction
of emancipation as either of the others, but it was never
construed to affect slavery at all.   Under it, the posterity

[1] Inhabitants of Winchenden *v.* Inhabitants of Hatfield, 4 Mass.
p. 123, at pp. 128, 129 and note.

[2] Poore's *Charters and Constitutions*, p. 1280.

[3] Poole's *Anti-Slavery Opinions*, p. 58.   The case is unreported,
the New Hampshire reports extending back only to 1816.

[4] Poore's *Charters and Constitutions*, pp. 1908, 1913.

of many men were held to be deprived and divested of
their natural rights by action that occurred prior to their
birth, and no distinction was made between cases where
the slavery resulted from compact and those that arose
from force and violence. Indeed, it was notorious that
freemen sold their own mulatto children born in Virginia. The construction was simply that this article had
no reference to, and no effect upon, slaves. The provision in the national Declaration of Independence, to
the same effect, was of course only an abstract statement of natural right, as the representatives had no
power to interfere with slavery in any of the territory
they represented, though it was often contended afterwards that slavery was inconsistent with the provision
of the Declaration.

So far as is known, the question of the meaning of
the Ordinance in regard to slavery was raised in the
courts of Northwest Territory but once, and then no
decision was reached; and the circumstances were such
that a decision would have been of little weight, had it
been made. In the summer of 1794, Judge Turner,
who had gone to Vincennes to hold court, became involved in an extensive quarrel with Henry Vanderburgh,
who was then probate judge and justice of the peace for
Knox County, and Captain Abner Prior, of the United
States Army, who was supervising Indian affairs on the
Wabash. Several matters were in controversy, and bitter feeling was produced. In the midst of this, a negro
and his wife, held as slaves by Vanderburgh, applied to
Turner's court for emancipation by writ of *habeas corpus,* instigated possibly by Turner. That Turner would
have held that the Ordinance freed them is beyond question, for he expressly declared that they were "free by

the Constitution of the Territory," but before the cause
came on for trial the negroes were seized and carried
away by a party of men who, as Turner alleged, were
employed by Vanderburgh. Turner then had the kid-
napers arrested, though some of them resisted and one
threatened the sheriff with a knife.[1] Complaints from
all parties were made to St. Clair, who, though declining
to adjust the difficulty, took sides against Turner, and
proceeded to give him some information as to the meaning of the Ordinance, which will be noticed later. The
French settlers were greatly excited over this attempt
to release their slaves. The grand jury of the county
found a presentment against Turner,[2] and later on the
citizens preferred charges against him which were submitted to Congress as grounds for impeachment, but, on
the suggestion of the Attorney-General, the House of
Representatives recommended a trial in the courts as
preferable.[3]

The earliest known decisions of this question in any
of the country originally covered by the Ordinance were
in some *habeas corpus* cases that arose in Michigan Territory, about two years after its separation from Indiana.
The court there arrived at the conclusion that slavery
still existed, but that it existed only as preserved by
Jay's treaty with Great Britain to British subjects residing in Michigan in 1796, the year of final evacuation
by the British forces. It was held that the Ordinance
did not go into effect there until that year, and that it
left in slavery all who were then slaves, but it prevented
any importation of slaves thereafter. The Chief Justice

---

[1] *St. Clair Papers*, vol. ii. pp. 325, 326.

[2] *Ibid.*, vol. ii. p. 342.

[3] Am. State Papers: *Misc.*, vol. i. pp. 151, 157.

summed up the decision of the court in these words: " I am, therefore, bound to say and do say, that a right of property in the human species cannot exist in this territory except as to persons in the actual possession of British settlers in this territory on 16th June, 1796, and that every other man coming into this territory is by the law of the land a freeman, unless he be a fugitive from lawful labor and service in some other American state or territory, and then he must be restored." [1] It will be observed that this decision had no effect on " the French and Canadian inhabitants, and other settlers of the Kaskaskies, St. Vincents, and the neighboring villages, who have heretofore professed themselves citizens of Virginia;" but it did preserve the slaves of all the similar class of ancient inhabitants who were outside the limits of the Virginia conquest, and within the United States, and also of those who had settled in the parts held by the British between July 13, 1787, and June 16, 1796.

The same conclusion as to the rights of slaveholders under the British treaty was reached by the Supreme Court of Missouri in 1845, in a suit for freedom brought by Pierre, a negro, against Gabriel S. Chouteau, his master. The plaintiff showed that his mother, Rose, a negress, was born in Montreal about the year 1768; that about the year 1791 she was taken by John Stark to Michilimackinac, and afterwards to Prairie du Chien; and that she remained at these places some four years as a servant or slave in his family. About 1795 Rose was taken to St. Louis by Andrew Todd, and sold to Didier, a priest, who in August, 1798, sold her to Au-

---

[1] MS. belonging to Mich. Hist. Soc. See Cooley's *Michigan*, pp. 136, 137.

guste Chouteau, from whom she came to the defendant.
The plaintiff, who was born while his mother was in the
possession of Auguste Chouteau, claimed that his mother
was a free woman because she was born in the British
province of Canada ; and that, even if a slave there, she
became free by her residence at Prairie du Chien, which
was in the territory covered by the Ordinance of 1787.
On the questions of fact the presumptions were all thrown
against the negro. It was held that the burden of proof
was on him to show that Canada was a free province,
and that he had failed to do so. It was assumed that
during his mother's stay at Prairie du Chien the place
was under British control, being one of the posts outside
the limits of the Virginia conquest. On this assumption
the court held that "the possession of these posts by
British subjects, at the time of her detention at them,
prevented the operation of the Ordinance within their
limits." It held that, under the Jay treaty, all the
settlers and traders in the parts held by the British were
left in full possession of their property of all descriptions, with a period of one year to make election whether
they would become citizens of the United States, leave
the territory, or remain there, without becoming citizens
or taking any oath of allegiance, in possession of their
property as before. Besides this, it held that as Rose
had been removed to St. Louis prior to the British
evacuation, she "never could have acquired any rights
under the Ordinance of 1787." Of course Pierre remained a slave.[1] As to this class of slaves — those held
under Jay's treaty — there appears to have been no conflict of opinion in the courts, and therefore slavery to
that extent must be admitted to have existed lawfully
under the Ordinance.

[1] G. S. Chouteau *v.* Pierre (of color), 9 Mo. p. 3.

That a similar conclusion of law would have been reached by the Missouri court at an earlier date, if the question had been presented, is very probable, but this particular case would have almost certainly been decided otherwise on the questions of fact, for in the years prior to 1830 all doubts were resolved in favor of freedom. Several of these earlier cases involved the rights of other classes of slaves held in the territories above the Ohio. The earliest reported one, which was begun in 1822 and reached the Supreme Court in 1824, presented the question of the status of a negress who had been taken to the Illinois country from Carolina, about the year 1797, and there held in slavery for three or four years, after which she was removed to Missouri. The words of Justice Tompkins, in giving the decision of the court as to the effect of the Ordinance, are worthy of preservation as an expression of public sentiment in Missouri at that day. He said : " It was urged, thirdly, that the slaves of persons settling in that country do not thereby become free. The words of the Ordinance are, ' That there shall be neither slavery nor involuntary servitude in the said territory.' We did not suppose that any person could mistake the policy of Congress in making this provision. When the states assumed the right of self-government, they found their citizens claiming a right of property in a miserable portion of the human race. Sound national policy required that the evil should be restricted as much as possible. What they could, they did. They said, by their representatives, it shall not vest within these limits, and by their acts for nearly half a century they have approved and sanctioned this declaration. What, then, shall be the consequence? The common - law judges of England, without any positive declaration of the will of the legislative body, availed themselves of every indirect admission of the master or lord in favor of the liberty of his slave, or villein, and the lord, having once answered the villein by plea in the courts of common law, was never after permitted to claim the benefit of his services as a slave. The sovereign power of the United States has declared that 'neither slavery nor involuntary servitude shall exist there;' and this court thinks that the person who takes his slave into said territory, and by the length of his residence there indicates an intention of making that place his residence and that of his slave, and thereby induces a jury to believe that fact, does, by such residence, declare his slave to have become a free man." [1]

In a case decided at the May term of 1827, the Missouri court first reached the question of the effect of the Ordinance on the ancient French inhabitants. This was an action brought by John Merry, a negro, to try the question of his freedom, in the form of an action for assault and battery, that being the manner of pleading required by the Missouri statute. He showed that his mother was held as a slave in the Illinois country, both before and after the passage of the Ordinance, and that while so held, about the year 1791, she gave birth to the plaintiff, who was also held there as a slave until a few years before the commencement of the suit. The defendants desired the court to put a construction on the Ordinance, but this was refused, Chief Justice M'Girk saying: "We cannot undertake to give the words a construction; no words are to be contrived [construed], unless a doubt arises; here, there is no doubt. The

[1] Winny, a free woman held in slavery, *v.* Phebe Whitesides, *alias* Prewitt, 1 Mo. p. 472.

Ordinance is positive, that slavery cannot exist; and
shall we, or any other court, say otherwise?" To the
plea that by the cession act the rights of these settlers
were preserved, the court replied: "The express words
in the cession act of Virginia, that the inhabitants shall
be protected in the enjoyment of their rights and liberties, are completely satisfied by securing to them the enjoyment of such rights as they then had, and not that
the things or objects that might then happen to be property should be so throughout all future time. This man
was not then born, and when he was born into existence,
the law forbid slavery to exist; and at the time of making the cession act, this man, *John*, was not property;
and at the time of his birth he could not be property.
There is nothing in the cession act forbidding Congress
to fix and point out things which might afterwards be the
subject of property. According to this view of the subject, *John* is free." [1]

This decision is closely analogous to the New Hampshire theory above mentioned, as to the effect of the
declaration that "all men are born equally free and
independent," in that it indicates a distinction in the
minds of the judges between those born after the passage of the Ordinance and those born before. This
analogy was completed by a decision of the same court,
rendered in 1829, holding that those held in slavery in
the Northwest Territory at the time of the passage of the
Ordinance remained slaves. In this case the plaintiff
Theoteste, otherwise known as Catiche, showed that she
was born a slave in 1782, at Prairie du Rocher, and was
held as a slave in Illinois until 1809. In that year she
was taken to St. Louis and sold to Manuel Lisa, and

[1] John Merry v. Tiffin and Menard, 1 Mo. 725.

afterwards conveyed from him to Pierre Chouteau.
The court held her to be a slave, distinguishing this from
the preceding case as follows: "The person holding
John Merry in slavery lost no right which had been
secured to him by the State of Virginia. But here is a
different case. The defendant claims to hold the plaintiff in slavery through another, whose right was vested
as early as the year 1782. It appears that either the
general terms ' neither slavery nor involuntary servitude
shall exist in the territory ' must yield to the provision
in the act of cession, or that the provision of that act
must be violated. This it cannot be supposed Congress
intended to do." [1] In the earlier period, therefore,
while holding views on the subject of slavery which forbid any supposition that they desired to encourage it,
the court of this state construed the Ordinance to be a
gradual emancipatory act, leaving the slaves in Northwest Territory as they were, except that their children
born thereafter were free-born, and preventing any subsequent importation of slaves from any point.

A decision similar to that in the John Merry case was
afterwards made by the Missouri court in the case of
one of the French slaves named Aspasia. She was born,
after the passage of the Ordinance, at Kaskaskia, of a
mother who was a slave prior to the Ordinance. She
was held in slavery in Illinois until 1821, when she was
purchased by Pierre Menard and soon afterwards given
by him to his son-in-law, Francis Chouteau, who resided
at St. Louis. Chouteau kept her until 1827, and then,
on account of her claiming freedom, returned her to
Menard. She sued for her freedom and was held to be
free. Menard took the case to the Supreme Court of

---

[1] Theoteste, *alias* Catiche, *v.* Pierre Chouteau, 2 Mo. p. 144.

the United States by writ of error, and it was there presented by Mr. Wirt, with great ability and ingenuity. He took the position that the Missouri court, in declaring the slave free, had violated a provision of the Ordinance, because the slave was guaranteed by the Ordinance to the owner. The court declined to take this view, on the ground that, if the right to hold slaves was in fact guaranteed by the Ordinance, still the right was not originated by that instrument. At the farthest the Ordinance could only be said to preserve rights that already existed, so far as slave-holding was concerned. If Aspasia had been held a slave by the Missouri court, it might then, the court said, be claimed that the Ordinance had been violated, because if she had the right to freedom she acquired it by virtue of the Ordinance. As it was, the United States courts could not take jurisdiction without invading ground that belonged exclusively to the state courts. It has sometimes been stated that this decision was against the slavery maintained by the French inhabitants, but it is not. It does not touch the question at all. The writ was merely dismissed for want of jurisdiction.[1]

The Missouri court did not amend its construction of the Ordinance in later years, but there was a sorry change of sentiment among the judges who afterwards came to the bench. In 1847 the case of Pierre came back to the Supreme Court, in substance, through his sister Charlotte. She, also, sued for freedom, and improved the case by showing that there were neither post nor British troops within a hundred miles of Prairie du Chien at the time Rose was there. In this case, the court, by Justice Napton, replied to the plaintiff's request

[1] Menard *v.* Aspasia, 5 Peters, p. 503.

for instructions favoring freedom : " Whatever may be the policy of other governments, it has not been the policy of this state to favor the liberation of negroes from that condition in which the laws and usages have placed the mass of their species. On the contrary, our statute expressly throws the burden of establishing a right to freedom on the petitioner, and the provision is both wise and humane. Neither sound policy nor enlightened philanthropy should encourage, in a slave-holding state, the multiplication of a race whose condition could be neither that of freemen nor that of slaves, and whose existence and increase, in this anomalous character, without promoting their individual comforts or happiness, tend only to dissatisfy and corrupt those of their own race and color remaining in a state of servitude." [1] What a change had been wrought in the twenty years since the negress Winny was at the bar of this same court ! In this decision the effect of the residence at Prairie du Chien was ignored, and when the case came back in 1855, after a rehearing in the lower court, the question of the effect of the Ordinance does not even appear to have been raised. The only point considered at the last hearing was whether Rose, the plaintiff's mother, had been lawfully held in slavery in Canada.[2]

Prior to this last decision the Dred Scott cases had come up in Missouri, and in the next year one of them went to the Supreme Court of the United States, which

[1] Charlotte (of color) *v.* Chouteau, 11 Mo. p. 193.

[2] Charlotte *v.* Chouteau, 21 Mo. 590. This case came twice afterwards to the Supreme Court, — 25 Mo. 465, and 33 Mo. 194. Charlotte finally gained her freedom in 1862. " Thus it took the court a quarter of a century to do for one person what an hour's work in the Convention did for 114,000 slaves." *Hist. Mag.* (Dawson's), April, 1865, p. 124.

made the startling decision, so well known, that Congress had no power to exclude slavery from any of the territories of the United States.[1] What would have become of Northwest Territory if such a decision had been made in its day? Certainly Illinois, and very probably Indiana, would have become slave states. Yet there was more reason to apply this doctrine to the Ordinance of 1787 than to the Missouri Compromise Act. If the Congress of the Union had no power to extend the provisions of the Ordinance west of the Mississippi, how much less had the Congress of the Confederation — clothed with the mere semblance of authority, and tottering in the last stages of dissolution — the power to prohibit slavery northwest of the Ohio? Happily for the Northwest! — happily for the Union! — the battle had been fought and won, and that territory had passed under the constitutions of sovereign states before this wretched doctrine was adopted. The question of constitutionality was not broached until all the original territory was occupied by free states.

In two of the Southern States, the only ones besides Missouri where the question of the effect of the Ordinance on resident slaves appears to have been raised, the courts adopted the broad construction that the Ordinance was emancipatory. It is to be observed, however, that these decisions were made before slavery took on its darkest aspect. In 1818 the Supreme Court of Mississippi gave freedom to three negroes who had been taken from Virginia in 1784 by John Decker, their master, and carried to the neighborhood of Vincennes, where they were held in slavery until July, 1816, a few days after the adoption of the first Constitution of Indi-

[1] Scott *v.* Sandford, 19 Howard, p. 393.

ana, and then taken South. The defendants in the suit
relied on the doctrine of vested rights, but the court
said : "According to the construction of defendant's
counsel, those who were slaves at the passing of the Ordinance must continue in the same situation. Can this
construction be correct ? Would it not defeat the great
object of the general government? It is obvious it
would, and it is inadmissible upon every principle of
legal construction." [1] In Louisiana the question was
disposed of with very little ceremony in a case decided
in 1830. The court held that a negro born in Northwest Territory after the passage of the Ordinance of
1787 was free, but its curt words give an intimation that
it held a similar opinion as to slaves held before the passage of the Ordinance. It said : "This Ordinance fixed
forever the character of the population in the region
over which it extended, and takes away all foundation
from the claim set up in this instance by the defendant.
The act of cession by Virginia did not deprive Congress
of the power to make such a regulation." [2] There was
a strong line of decisions in this state that a master who
took his slave into free territory (in which was included
the country north of the Ohio) with the intention of residing there, thereby emancipated such slaves, and this
continued the law of Louisiana until it was changed by
statute in 1846.

In Kentucky the question of the rights of the ancient
inhabitants was never before the Supreme Court, but the
court appeared to be of opinion that no slavery of any
kind could exist under the Ordinance. This was mani-

---

[1] Harry and Others *v.* Decker and Hopkins, 1 Miss. (Walker),
p. 36.
[2] Merry *v.* Chexnaider, 20 Martin, 699 (vol. viii. N. S. p. 358).

fested by their words in the decision of cases of slaves
who had been carried into Northwest Territory after the
Ordinance went into effect. In one of these, decided in
1821, — a case of a negress carried from Kentucky to
Indiana by John Warrick in 1807, and sold by him in
1814 to persons who brought her back to Kentucky, —
the court said: " If a slave, then, could exist and reside
in the territory, and be there a slave, the Ordinance
could not be true ; for slavery existed, the Ordinance
notwithstanding. For we cannot recognize the logic
that will prove a man free and a slave at the same time."
It was held that the negress was emancipated by her
master's carrying her to Indiana for residence.[1] A
similar ruling was made in 1825 as to a slave carried
into Northwest Territory.[2]

The Supreme Court of Illinois never reached a harmonious conclusion as to the respective rights of masters
and slaves who were in Northwest Territory on July 13,
1787. The first reported case did not come up until
1845, but, in his opinion, Judge Scates said : " It [*i. e.*
the same question of law] has once been before this
court, and the decision of the Circuit Court against freedom was affirmed by an equal division of this court."
Neither the title nor the date of this earlier decision is
given, and no case answering the description appears in
the Illinois reports, but, of course, it must have been
decided after Illinois became a state.

The case in 1845 arose on this state of facts: The
plaintiff's grandmother, Angelique, was a slave of Joseph
Trotier at Cahokia prior to the passage of the Ordinance.
Trotier was a resident of Cahokia as early as 1769, and

---

[1] Rankin *v.* Lydia, a pauper, 2 Marshall (Ky.), p. 467.
[2] Bush's Reps. *v.* White *et ux.*, 3 T. B. Monroe (Ky.), p. 100.

held Angelique in slavery as early as 1783.   He sold
her to his son-in-law Lebrun, who in 1798 sold her and
her daughter Pelagie, who was then four years old, to
Nicholas Jarrot, of Cahokia.   By his will, dated February 6, 1818, Jarrot bequeathed Pelagie to his daughter
Julia Jarrot, the defendant.   The plaintiff, Joseph, a
son of Pelagie, was born after the death of Nicholas
Jarrot, and while his mother was held in slavery by the
defendant.   The date of his birth was not known with
sufficient exactness to say whether he was born before
or after August 26, 1818, the date of the adoption of
the Constitution of Illinois.   The only data for determining this were the date of Jarrot's will, and the fact that
Joseph was born after Jarrot's death.   The majority of
the court — opinion by Judge Scates — held that if necessary they would presume, in favor of freedom, that he
was born after the adoption of the Constitution ; but as
they considered the provisions of the Ordinance sufficient
to liberate the French slaves, no importance was attached
to this presumption by them.   Judge Young delivered a
separate concurring opinion, but laid stress on the points
that defendant had failed to establish plaintiff's slavery,
and that plaintiff was free under the Constitution if not
under the Ordinance.   Chief Justice Wilson concurred
in the decision on the ground that the evidence showed
the plaintiff to have been born after the adoption of the
Constitution, but said he could not agree that he would
have been free if born before the adoption of the Constitution.   Justices Shield, Treat, and Thomas dissented,
but did not file opinions or state their reasons.[1]   The
question presented in this case, and it was so understood

[1] Joseph Jarrot, *alias* Pete, *alias* Joseph, a colored man, *v.* Julia
Jarrot, 2 Gilman (7 Ill.), p. 1.

and expressly stated by the judges to be, was whether the descendants of slaves held at the time of the passage of the Ordinance were or were not free. In the words of the decision, however, no distinction is made between the slaves and their descendants, though this may possibly have been due to the fact that at this time, fifty-eight years after the passage of the Ordinance, the question of the status of those held in slavery at the time of the passage was considered of no importance.

In Indiana the effect of the ordinance on slaves here prior to 1787 was never, so far as is known, expressly decided by the courts. During the territorial period, although questions arising from slavery were often before the courts, slavery of this class was always treated as an existing institution and its legality went unchallenged. In this period, however, there were decisions upholding the indenture laws, which were, under any theory of construction, more in violation of the Ordinance than the continuation of the preëxistent slavery ; for these laws provided for the importation of slaves, for holding them in unqualified slavery for sixty days, and for holding them thereafter in limited slavery, *i. e.*, for a term of years or for life, and their children for terms of years. There were also some most remarkable decisions in a series of cases for the emancipation of a negro and negress who had been brought into Indiana from Virginia by the Kuykendall family, and held here without compliance with the formalities of the indenture laws. Certain influential persons aided these negroes in maintaining *habeas corpus* proceedings by which they were released on a technical insufficiency of evidence for their claimants, but the court (Judges Davis, Vanderburgh, and Griffin — a full bench) expressed the opinion " that the persons mentioned in said writ are not fugitives from slavery." [1]   After this decision the claimants seized on the negroes, and were about to carry them out of the state when a new proceeding for their emancipation was begun.   This came on at the September term of 1805, but Judge Vanderburgh, who was sitting alone, caused the following entry to be made : " When a cause comes before me in which the freedom or slavery of a human being is involved I feel such diffidence to determine the important question, that in the case of *habeas corpus* continued to this term I determined to postpone it until the next, when I hope to have the assistance of either or both of my brethren."

At the April term, 1806, Judges Davis and Vanderburgh heard the case of the negress, decided that she was neither a fugitive from justice nor from slavery, and released her ; but to their decision they appended this extraordinary proviso : " But this order is not to impair the right that Vannorsdell [the defendant] or any other person shall have to the said negro girl Peggy, provided he, Vannorsdell, or any other person, can prove said negro Peggy to be a slave.   Nor shall this order impair the right of said Peggy to her freedom, provided the said Peggy shall establish her right to the same." In other words, although the case had twice been heard, and the girl had twice been set free, the judges were so uncertain as to the propriety of their decision that they deliberately attempted to prevent it from being final.   It is difficult to conceive why there should have been any uncertainty as to the effect of the Ordinance on imported slaves ; but if they were in doubt on that question, it is beyond comprehension that they could have doubted the

[1] Ter. Court Docket, Sept. term, 1804, p. 150.

right of the ancient settlers to hold their slaves which
were in the territory previous to 1787. There are at
least seven cases on the docket of the Territorial Court
of Indiana in which the question of the legal existence
of slavery might have been raised, including *habeas cor-*
pus proceedings, suit for wages by one held as a slave,
criminal prosecution for kidnaping negroes, and civil
action for the possession of negroes as property ; but if
the validity of the French slavery was ever questioned,
no indication of it appears on the records.

The only possible explanation of this is, that there
was always a universal agreement of the bar in the opinion that such slavery was legal, unless we suppose that
the question had been decided by the court in some
manner that did not show of record. In either case the
recognized intent of the law became the same. I have
before me an opinion of John Johnson, one of the ablest
lawyers of the territory, and one of the first judges of
the Supreme Court of the state, as to the status of Polly,
a negress belonging to Hyacinthe Lasselle, who was
afterwards declared free by the Supreme Court of the
state. It was given in the winter of 1815–16, preceding the adoption of the Constitution. The case is
stated thus : " In 1779 or 80 a negro woman was taken
prisoner by the Indians, of the age of 15. She was sold
to Isaac Williams of Detroit and sold by said Williams
to Antoine Lasselle. While the said woman was in the
possession of Lasselle, she had three children, two of
whom I. B. Laplant purchased. Question, are those
children slaves ? " On these facts, Johnson held that
the woman was doubly a slave : first, by conquest, because taken in war while in a state of slavery ; and
second, by the law of Virginia, which provided that " ne-

groes reduced to possession are considered as slaves."
He then proceeds: "By the articles of cession, and by
the Ordinance for the Government of this Territory, the
rights and privileges and also the property of the inhabitants are guaranteed to them.   Hence the said negro
woman being taken and considered as a species of property prior to the adoption of the Ordinance for the
Government of the said Territory, the 6th article thereof,
which prohibits involuntary servitude, cannot affect her
condition or the rights of her master.   Thirdly, the
children follow the condition of the mother and not of
the father.   This point is as well defined by law as any
other whatever, and the reason of it is this.   The slave
being considered as the absolute property of the master
for life, he has a right to all the undivided emoluments
arising from such slave, and the increase of such female
slave being part of the benefits arising from such kind
of property, as much so as her labor.   From the foregoing premises I am decidedly of opinion that the children
of the negro woman alluded to are slaves."   So far as
is known, the territorial bench was of the same opinion
as the bar.   In a political way, Judge Vanderburgh was
more nearly connected with the anti-slavery party than
any other of the judges, and yet, as we have just seen,
he resisted the emancipation of his slaves by Judge
Turner, and no record remains to us of any subsequent
change of his opinion on this subject.   In fact, he held
negroes while he lived, and his administrators sold them
as part of his estate.[1]

   In 1820, after Indiana had become a state, the matter
of the rights of the ancient inhabitants was presented to
the Supreme Court, in the *habeas corpus* case of the State

[1] *Western Sun*, February 8, 1817.

v. Lasselle.[1] This action was brought to test the right to freedom of the negress Polly, as to whom the above opinion of Judge Johnson had been given in the terri-torial period. The question of the effect of the Ordi-nance was fully discussed in the presentation of the case, but the court passed that point in their decision, and held that the girl was freed by the Constitution, saying: "Whether the state of Virginia intended, by consenting to the Ordinance of 1787, to emancipate the slaves on this side the *Ohio* River, or whether by the reservation alluded to [in the deed of cession], she intended to con-tinue the privilege of holding slaves, to the settlers then in the country, is unimportant in the present case." It has been stated by some writers that this was a decision that slavery could not exist under the Ordinance. The error is the more remarkable because the court plainly indicates its opinion that this slavery was legal until the Constitution brought it to an end. After stating the emancipatory effect of the Constitution, the court pro-ceeds: "We are told that the Constitution recognizes preëxisting rights, which are to continue as if no change had taken place in the government. But it must be recollected that a special reservation cannot be so en-larged by construction as to defeat a general provision. If this reservation were allowed to apply in this case, it would contradict, and totally destroy, the design and effect of this part of the Constitution. And it cannot be presumed that the Constitution, which is the collected voice of the citizens of *Indiana,* declaring their united will, would guaranty to one part of the community such privileges as would totally defeat and destroy privileges and rights guarantied to another." In other words, the

[1] 1 Blackford, 60.

preëxisting rights of the slaveholder must give way to
the general provisions which guaranteed freedom and
free-soil to all men ; the reservation of the deed of cession, protected by the Ordinance, was abrogated by the
Constitution.   In 1855, in a dissenting opinion, Judge
Gookins said, "The abolition of slavery in the Territory Northwest of the Ohio River, by the Ordinance of
1787 and the Constitution of 1816, is one ; " but this was
merely a statement of his opinion, the question not being
before the court in any sense.[1]

Whatever opinion one may have as to the proper construction of the Ordinance, it is evident that these decisions do not support the broad statements that have been
made concerning them, or the reflections that have been
made on the characters of those who claimed to hold slaves
lawfully north of the Ohio.   For example, Governor
Coles says : "The long and extraordinary acquiescence
in the continuance of the bondage of the French slaves
(as they were called) encouraged those who can always
find reasons for doing what will promote their own immediate interest, or what they like to do, to set up a
right to the French negroes' services ; some contending
for it under the treaty of 1763, and some under the
terms of cession from Virginia.   But it is useless to
expose or dwell longer on the errors of these prejudiced
and interested partisans.   It is enough to confute and
silence them, to recite the facts that the highest judicial
tribunals of individual states and of the Federal Government have decided and put the question at rest, that
slaves cannot be lawfully held in the country northwest
of the Ohio River.   At an early period, it was so decided by the Supreme Court of Indiana; afterwards, a

[1] Beebe *v.* The State, 6 Ind. p. 501, at p. 547.

similar decision was made by the Supreme Courts of Missouri and Illinois; and in 1831 these decisions were concurred in and confirmed by the highest judicial authority of the United States. A doubt can no longer exist that such a decision would have been made at any, even the earliest, period after the adoption of the Ordinance, if the question had been brought before the judiciary."[1] In fact, as appears above, the question was never decided by the Supreme Court of Indiana. In fact, the Supreme Court of Missouri had decided that those held in slavery at the passage of the Ordinance remained slaves, and only those born afterwards were free. In fact, there is no mention in the Illinois reports of any decision of this question which could have been made prior to 1831, except the one which Judge Scates said was against freedom. In fact, the decision of the Supreme Court of the United States, in 1831, put in its broadest anti-slavery bearing, was that the freeing of a negro, born in Northwest Territory after the passage of the Ordinance, by the Supreme Court of one of the states, was not an infraction of rights created by the Ordinance.

Moreover, while there was a conflict of opinion on this subject among the judges, after the Ordinance had become a thing of the past, there was never any such conflict in the executive and legislative constructions of the Ordinance while it was in force. These were invariably against the freedom of the French slaves, and usually that the Ordinance permitted laws for the introduction of slavery in a modified form. There was from the first a difference of opinion as to the effect of the Ordinance which necessitated official construction of its meaning.

---

[1] *History of the Ordinance of* 1787, p. 18.

The slaveholders of the Wabash and Illinois settlements feared the effects of the Ordinance. Their slaves had been guaranteed to them by the French and British treaties, by the proclamations of General Gage and General Clark, by the laws of Virginia and the Virginia cession act; but, in the Ordinance, the guaranty, if it were a guaranty, was in a vague and uncertain form, applying on its face to the "descent and conveyance of property," and only by implication to the preservation of the property itself. On June 30, 1789, Bartholomew Tardiveau[1] addressed Governor St. Clair on this subject, urging him to procure a declaration by Congress of the exact meaning of the Ordinance in regard to slavery. He stated that while recently at the national capital he had called the attention of Congress and of the President to the matter, and to the apprehensions of settlers concerning it, and members had assured him "that it would be brought up in Congress, and that there would not be the least difficulty; . . . that the intention of the obnoxious resolution had been solely to prevent the future importation of slaves into the Federal country; that it was not meant to affect the rights of the ancient inhabitants; and promised to have a clause inserted in it explanatory of its real meaning, sufficient to ease the apprehensions of the people, but it was not done." He stated further that the report had been circulated in the Illinois settlements that as soon as St. Clair arrived their slaves would all be set free, and in consequence many of the wealthier inhabitants had crossed to

---

[1] Tardiveau was thoroughly acquainted with the condition of the French settlers, and devoted much time to advancing their welfare. General Harmar placed great confidence in him. *St. Clair Papers*, vol. ii. p. 27.

Louisiana with their slaves, selling their estates for a trifle, while others, suspecting some trickery in the report, still held their estates till the intentions of Congress should be assured.[1] On receipt of this letter, instead of seeking a construction from Congress, St. Clair made an official declaration of the meaning of the Ordinance, saying that it was not the intention of Congress to free slaves already held in Northwest Territory, but only to prevent any future importation of slaves. The slavery clause, he said, was " a declaration of a principle which was to govern the legislature in all acts respecting that matter, and the courts of justice in their decisions in cases arising after the date of the Ordinance." He held that retroactive laws were repugnant to free government, and that Congress would have made compensation to the owners if it had contemplated emancipation ; but he recognized that "they had the right to determine that property of that kind afterwards acquired should not be protected in the future, and that slaves imported into the Territory after that declaration might reclaim their freedom." [2]

The more St. Clair considered the matter, the more firmly did he adhere to this theory. On October 11, 1793, he said in a letter to Luke Decker, of Vincennes : " I have again been considering the subject of slavery as it stands with us according to the Ordinance of Congress for the government of the Territory, and I am more and more confirmed in the opinion which I expressed to you, viz. : That the declaration that there shall be neither slavery nor involuntary servitude in the said Territory otherwise than in the punishment of

---

[1] *St. Clair Papers*, vol. ii. pp. 117-119.

[2] *Ibid.*, vol. i. pp. 120, 206 ; vol. ii. p. 119, n.

crimes whereof the parties shall have been convicted, was no more than the declaration of a principle which was to govern the legislature in all acts respecting that matter, and the courts of justice in their decisions upon cases arising after the date of the Ordinance, which is the 13th day of July, 1787, but could have no retroactive operation whatever; and the grounds upon which that opinion is founded are — that, in the first place, retroactive laws being generally unjust in their nature have ever been discountenanced in the United States, and in most of them are positively forbidden; and that slaves being a species of property countenanced and protected in several of the states, and in that part of the Territory which you inhabit, by the ancient laws, and had been acquired under those laws, Congress would not divest any person of that property without making him a compensation, though they doubtless had a right to determine that property of that kind afterwards acquired should not be protected in future, and that slaves imported into the Territory after that declaration might reclaim their freedom. And this I take to be the true meaning and import of the clause of the Ordinance, and when I was in the Illinois country I gave the people there my sentiments on this subject in the same manner, which made them easy." [1]

Again, on December 14, 1794, after receiving information concerning the trouble which had arisen from the attempt to release Vanderburgh's slaves, he wrote to Judge Turner: "Permit me, sir, to offer you my opinion upon the subject, which is shortly this: that the declaration in our Constitution, that there shall be no slavery nor involuntary servitude in the Territory, ap-

[1] *St. Clair Papers*, vol. ii. p. 318.

plies to, and can be taken advantage of only by, those slaves who may have been imported since the establishment of that Constitution. . . . So far as it respects the past, it can have no operation, and must be construed to intend that, from and after the publication of the said Constitution, slaves imported into that Territory should immediately become free; and by this construction no injury is done to any person, because it is a matter of public notoriety, and any person removing into that Colony and bringing with him persons who were slaves in another country, does it at the known risk of their claiming their freedom ; whereas, on the other hand, had the Constitution the effect to liberate those persons who were slaves by the former laws, as no compensation is provided to their owners, it would be an act of the government arbitrarily depriving a part of the people of a part of their property — an attempt that has not been made and would not be submitted to, and is not to be drawn from the mere construction of words. I have troubled you with my thoughts upon this subject, because I have heard that there is great agitation among the people respecting it; and they should be set at rest, because it was formerly brought before me by some of these people, to whom I gave my opinion nearly as I have stated it to you." [1]

This construction is one entitled to great weight. It is not merely the opinion of the governor of Northwest Territory. It is also the declaration of the man who was President of the Congress that passed the Ordinance. It is the declaration of a delegate to that Congress from a Northern state. It is the opinion of a resident of the Northwest Territory who at all times

[1] *St. Clair Papers*, vol. ii. p. 331.

opposed the importation of slaves north of the Ohio. Nor is it strange that he held such views. When one reflects on the surroundings at the passage of the Ordinance he can scarcely question that the intention of Congress was as stated in Tardiveau's letter and in these declarations of St. Clair, no matter what may be his opinion as to the legal intendment of the words of the Ordinance. It is not credible that a Congress, a majority of the members of which were from slave states, would unanimously vote to emancipate the slaves of a portion of their countrymen, without either compensating them or giving them an opportunity to remove to slave territory. Such a proceeding from any expectation of public benefit was contrary to the spirit of the Ordinance itself, for it provided that, "Should the public exigencies make it necessary, for the common preservation, to take any person's property, or demand his particular services, full compensation shall be made for the same." That a majority of this Congress, as of every other, were largely actuated by local interest, is probably true, but to say that Southern members designed, by an arbitrary exercise of power, to take away from professed and acknowledged citizens of Virginia something that they themselves held to be lawful property, would be to ascribe to them a lack of regard for the property rights of others such as they never manifested at any other time.

It is questionable whether any member of Congress had any such thing in contemplation. When Mr. Wirt argued the question of Aspasia's status to the Supreme Court, as above mentioned, he maintained that it could not have been the intention of Congress to deprive the ancient settlers of their slaves by the Ordinance, for six reasons : " 1. Because it would have violated one of the conditions on which Congress had accepted the cession from Virginia. 2. Because the existence and continuance of slavery to some extent is acknowledged by unavoidable implication in those parts of the Ordinance which refer to the number of free males. 3. Because the French settlers are excepted from the action of the Ordinance. 4. The contemporaneous construction by those who drafted the Ordinance. 5. The recognition of slavery, as existing at the date of the Ordinance. 6. The admission of Illinois into the Union, and the approval of her Constitution, which was admitted by Congress to have expounded this Ordinance correctly." [1] The last argument refers to the form of the 6th article of the Constitution of Illinois, which makes its provisions as to slavery and involuntary servitude expressly of future effect; but this has no legitimate force to show the meaning of the Ordinance farther than showing the opinion of the Congress of 1818, for it is clear beyond peradventure that the right of the people to form a constitution was nowise limited, abridged, or controlled by the Ordinance. This statement may occasion surprise, for it is contrary to the views of many of the greatest American statesmen and lawyers. Daniel Webster, as we have seen, contended that the articles of compact were "not only deeper than all local law, but deeper also than all local constitutions." Nathan Dane maintained that no state formed out of the Northwest Territory had power to adopt in its Constitution any provision inconsistent with the Ordinance.[2] Thomas Jefferson

---

[1] Menard *v.* Aspasia, 5 Peters, p. 505.

[2] Dane's *Abridgment and Digest of American Law* (Boston, 1824), vol. vii. pp. 442–450.

had the same idea in view, as is shown by the words of
his ordinance. Nevertheless, the theory that any lawmaking power can establish an unalterable rule, binding
on its successors of equal power, has long since been
exploded. That one could make a law binding on a
superior power, such as the Ordinance would have been
under this theory, is *a fortiori* impossible. As to the
Ordinance itself, this theory has universally been repudiated by the courts.[1] It is well settled by the decisions
that the Ordinance was abrogated in each state by the
adoption of a constitution, and that thereafter it did not
exist, even as a law, unless reënacted by the state.

One curious phase of this question, which arose about
the year 1845, is worthy of mention. It was an ingenious attempt to evade the fugitive slave law as to slaves
escaping from other than the original states. Two cases
presenting the question were heard in 1845. The first
was that of a negro who escaped from a steamboat while
being carried from Arkansas to Virginia, the boat at the
time being tied within low-water mark at Cincinnati.
He was recaptured, but by writ of *habeas corpus* he was
at once taken before Judge Read of the Supreme Court
of Ohio, and the question of his freedom was raised.
The second case was that of a negro named Sam, his
wife Moriah, and their child. These had been taken
into Illinois from Kentucky in 1835, by Tipton their
master. He kept them there some six months, and
then, on account of talk in the neighborhood that they
were free, he ran them off to Missouri and sold them,
but they afterwards escaped. In 1844, Vaughan, their

----

[1] Permoli *v.* 1st Municipality, 3 Howard, p. 589, at p. 610;
Strader *et al. v.* Graham, 10 Howard, p. 82; State *v.* Lasselle,
1 Blackford, 60; Joseph *v.* Jarrot, 2 Gilman (7 Ill.), p. 1.

owner, heard they were in Hamilton County, Indiana, and came to claim them. He took them by force, but they were released by the neighbors (who soon gathered in large numbers) and were not afterwards heard of. Vaughan then sued one of these neighbors for damages in the U. S. Circuit Court for Indiana, where the cause was heard by Judge McLean. In both these cases the point was made that the negroes were free because they were not fugitives from any of the original states, with which alone the articles of compact in the Ordinance were made. It was contended that the Ordinance was superior to any constitution, and that neither by the Constitution of the United States, nor any law of Congress, could the privilege of reclaiming fugitive slaves be extended beyond the original states, parties to the compact. The theory was repudiated by both judges, though in the first case the negro was returned to his master, and in the second the negroes were found to be free.[1]

The remainder of Mr. Wirt's arguments are valid, and the facts on which they are based are already before the reader, except as to the fourth — " contemporaneous construction by those who drafted the Ordinance." Curiously enough, the authority referred to under this head was Nathan Dane. In the pages referred to by Mr. Wirt [2] Mr. Dane says : " It is clear the people of the said northwestern territory accepted the said Ordinance *in toto*, and invariably practiced on it as to slavery while in a territorial condition, and since they have become States. . . . The exclusion of negro-slavery from

---

[1] State *v.* Hoppess, 2 *Western Law Journal*, vol. ii. p. 279; Vaughan *v.* Williams, *Ibid.*, vol. iii. p. 65. See also discussion of the question, *Ibid.*, vol. iii. p. 529.

[2] Dane's *Abridgment*, vol. vii. pp. 412–50.

said territory, by law and in practice, has been as notorious as the settlement of it, — near forty years. It has
been a fact universally known in the United States, that
slavery has never been admitted in the said territory or
States therein." It would certainly be difficult to state
more broadly than this, that the law and practice in all
Northwest Territory had been in strict conformity to the
Ordinance, and yet it was true that the slaves held there
at the time of the passage of the Ordinance, and their
progeny, had been continuously held in slavery since.
This, too, was as notorious as it could well be made. It
was recognized by the government ; it was provided for
in the laws ; its extent was specifically pointed out in the
national censuses ; it was a matter of observation to all
who came into the territory. If it may be supposed that
Mr. Dane used this language understandingly, Mr. Wirt
was right in claiming that the man who drafted the Ordinance did not understand it to emancipate the slaves
of the French settlers. Still, it must be admitted that
Dane used language elsewhere that indicates an opinion
that the Ordinance abolished the French slavery at once
and forever.[1]

Whatever Mr. Dane may have thought in regard to
this, we have adduced enough evidence to show that
there was a difference of opinion as to the meaning of
the Ordinance among men who should fairly be considered unbiased. Further than this, there were two classes
of slavery which were officially recognized as lawful in
Indiana and Northwest Territory generally, during the
territorial period : the first, that among the British subjects, under Jay's treaty, as acknowledged by the courts ;
the second, that of the French settlers who professed

[1] Dane's *Abridgment*, vol. ix. Appendix " A."

themselves citizens of Virginia, as recognized by the executive and legislative departments. As to all the ancient inhabitants of Northwest Territory, therefore, it must fairly be conceded that slavery was lawfully permitted to exist until abrogated by the state constitutions.

This French slavery was derived from two distinct sources, and by a curious coincidence the slavery of each origin was preserved in general by a method different from the other. That which originated in Canada existed in Michigan, Wisconsin, Northern Illinois, and Northern Indiana, and was preserved by Jay's treaty. That which originated in Louisiana existed in Kaskaskia, Cahokia, Vincennes, and the neighboring villages, with the surrounding country; and was preserved by the executive and legislative construction placed on the Ordinance of 1787. That slavery did in fact exist in both the French colonies is unquestioned, but whether or not it existed lawfully in Canada has been much disputed. It was fought over for more than a quarter of a century in the case of Charlotte v. Chouteau, mentioned above, the juries sometimes finding that it did so exist, but finally that it did not. The ablest lawyers differed on the question, the line of argument of those who doubted its lawful existence being that no authorization of it from the French government could be found. The authorization for which they sought in vain was given, however, in 1688. In November of that year M. de Lagny reported officially as follows: " Working people and servants are very scarce, and so extraordinarily dear in Canada that they ruin all those who undertake anything. The introduction of Negro Slaves is supposed to be the best means of remedying the difficulty. The Attorney General of the Council, at present in Paris, assures that if his Majesty approve this proposal, some of the principal inhabitants will cause some to be purchased in the Islands on the arrival of the vessels from Guinea, and he, himself, is resolved to do so." On this communication De Seignelay, the minister, made the following minute : " His Majesty approves the importation by the inhabitants of Canada, of Negroes for agricultural purposes, but it is well to remark to them, that it is to be feared that those Negroes coming from a climate so different, may perish in Canada, and this project would then be useless." [1] Of course the declaration of royal approval was all that was necessary to legalize anything in the French colonies at that time, and on this little thread hung all the slavery of Canada.

The colonial authorities continuously recognized that slavery had a lawful existence thereafter. In 1709 the Intendant of Canada, by ordinance, authorized the inhabitants " to purchase negroes and panis [2] from the Indians," because they would be useful in the cultivation of the soil. In 1736 Intendant Hoegnart proclaimed that it would be " useful to the colony to hold negroes and Indians of a distant nation, called panis, as slaves, and therefore the negroes and panis who had been or might be bought, should be held by their purchasers as slaves ; " and thereupon he ordained all emancipations of slaves should be void except such as were made by " written documents passed before public notaries." [3] In 1746–47 four negroes and a pani, who had been cap-

[1] *N. Y. Col. Docs.*, vol. ix. p. 398.

[2] A pani was an Indian held as a slave. The name was taken from the Pawnees, or Panis, who were located beyond the Indians with whom the French were on amicable terms, but it was applied without reference to the slave's nationality.

[3] 25 Mo. pp. 476, 477.

tured from the English, escaped from Montreal, and on
being recaptured were sent to the French Islands by the
authorities and sold.[1]   In 1750, a controversy having
arisen as to whether captured slaves should be treated as
prisoners, Governor La Jonquiere declared that " every
negro is a slave wherever he be," and consequently he
refused to surrender captive slaves as prisoners, because
they were property only.[2]   This action was subsequently
confirmed by the entire council.[3]   At the surrender of
Montreal, in September, 1760, the 47th article of capitulation made between Lord Amherst, the British commander, and the Marquis de Vaudreuil, Governor and
Lieutenant-General of Canada, provided : " The negroes
and panis of both sexes shall remain in their quality of
slaves in the possession of the French and Canadians to
whom they belong ; they shall be at liberty to keep them
in their service in the colony or to sell them." [4]   The
definitive treaty of February 10, 1763, made no provision that can be construed to apply to slavery.   The only
things guaranteed to French subjects were the right to
retain the Catholic religion, and to remove with their
effects, if they so desired, within eighteen months after
the execution of the treaty.[5]

On October 7, 1763, George Third issued a proclamation for the regulation of the territory ceded by France,
but this also is silent as to slavery in Canada, except so
far as it may be considered referred to by the provisions
giving the colonial executives power to make laws, and

[1] *N. Y. Col. Docs.*, vol. x. pp. 131, 138.
[2] *Ibid.*, vol. x. p. 210.
[3] *Ibid.*, p. 213.
[4] 25 Mo. p. 467 ; *N. Y. Col. Docs.*, vol. x. pp. 1107–1120.
[5] Cobbett's *Parliamentary Hist.*, vol. xv. pp. 1294, 1295.

to establish courts of justice for the determination of all causes "according to law and equity, and, as near as may be, agreeable to the laws of England." It has been argued that the common law was extended over Canada by this proclamation, and that slavery was abolished because it could not exist under the common law. The legal aphorism that slavery could not exist at common law was always more poetical than exact, but, however true it may have been in England, it had no application in the British colonies. Many of the colonies had the common law, but all of them had slavery, and had it lawfully. England fostered the slave trade from the middle of the sixteenth century to the opening of the nineteenth. It was regulated and aided by her laws, and so far as possible her ships were given a monopoly of it. It is estimated by some authorities that she sent more than 100,000 slaves annually to her American colonies. It is notorious that she would not let the colonies prohibit the trade, and that her action in this matter was one of the grievances complained of in the original draft of the Declaration of Independence.[1] It is not probable that by this proclamation it was intended that the common law should take the place of the former laws except as to proceedings in the courts of justice.

As the spirit of independence grew strong in the original English colonies, Great Britain undertook to strengthen herself by placating the people of the acquired colonies. The effect of this was the series of laws enlarging the rights of Catholics passed in 1774, and of these the most important to us was the one that restored the ancient customs and usages to Canada.[2]

---

[1] Walsh's *Appeal from the Judgments of Great Britain*, etc., part i. pp. 325–330.

[2] 14 Geo. III. c. 83.

The practice of slavery continued under all these changes without any interference from the authorities. The slave trade under British laws continued to supply Canada, as other colonies, with slaves. By act of parliament in 1790, extending to all the American colonies, a duty of forty shillings was laid on each negro imported.[1] In sum, there was never any action by the British government indicating any intention to abolish slavery in Canada. That was left to the Canadians, and they were not late in acting. The rigors of the climate made negro slavery unprofitable; there had been but few negroes imported; public sentiment was moving towards universal freedom. On July 9, 1793, the parliament of Upper Canada prohibited the importation of slaves, and provided for gradual emancipation by enacting that every child thereafter born of a negress slave should be free at the age of twenty-five years.[2] On these facts, then, it would seem plain that slavery existed lawfully in Canada from 1688 until it died out under the law of 1793.

As to Louisiana, the legal authorization was explicit. When the grant was made to Crozat in 1712, he was given not only permission to import negroes, but also the monopoly of their importation. He was restricted from taking them to any other country.[3] In 1717, after the death of Louis XIV., Crozat surrendered his grant, and in August of the same year Louisiana was given to the Western Company, more commonly called the Mississippi Company, on the same terms. Under this name, and as reconstructed in 1719 under the title of the Company

---

[1] 37 *Brit. Stat. at Large*, p. 24.
[2] *Rev. Stats. of Up. Can.*, ch. viii. p. 18.
[3] Joutel's *Journal*, pp. 204, 205.

of the Indies, this corporation held Louisiana until April 10, 1732. Negroes were brought to Louisiana during the existence of these companies and scattered through the Mississippi valley ; they were brought chiefly by the companies, and were sold on a credit of three years to settlers engaged in agriculture. There was no importation of them of note as far north as the Illinois country until 1720, when the Company of St. Phillips, a corporation which acted under the Company of the Indies, began its operations in the Mississippi valley. The special purpose of this company was the discovery and working of mines. It was represented in America by Philip Francis Renault, who came to the Illinois country in 1720 with 200 miners and other laborers, and 500 negro slaves. He established the village of St. Phillips, a few miles above Kaskaskia, and worked several of the lead mines of Illinois and Missouri. He continued work after the Company of the Indies surrendered its charter, but left the country in 1744, after selling his slaves to the colonists.[1] In 1722 a number of families ascended the Mississippi from New Orleans, in company with the troops under " Captain Renaud," and settled in the Illinois country ; and to these " M. de Bienville accorded negroes to cultivate their lands." [2] In 1723 a colony of German families was sent over by the company to form a settlement on the Upper Mississippi, and these also were furnished with negroes.[3] The importations of 1720 and 1722 were the principal sources of the negro slaves of the Illinois. A few of them also were brought to the Wabash settlements, but the greater part of those held at these settlements were brought from the English col-

[1] *Annals of the West*, pp. 672–674, 788.
[2] Margry, vol. v. p. 579.   [3] *Ibid.*, p. 583.

onies, where they had been captured by the Indians and
sold to the French traders. In the almost continuous
wars of three quarters of the eighteenth century, to
which the Indians of the Mississippi valley were incited
by the European nations who colonized there, negroes
were frequently captured by the Indians and sold to the
whites with whom at the time they happened to be allied.
They learned the market value of these captives at a
very early date. A white prisoner they would kill on
very slight provocation, or on manifestation of inability
to keep up with them on their marches, but a negro
was never killed if it could be avoided, because they
preferred a considerable annoyance to the loss of his
value in goods.

The number of slaves held in the District of Illinois
is not definitely ascertained, and the estimates are not
harmonious. In 1750 the priest Vivier accounted the
population of the Illinois villages at 1,100 whites, 300
negroes, and 60 Indian slaves. There was some increase after this time, and from all indications the population of all kinds in the District was greatest just at the
close of the French occupation. For this period has
been estimated 700 white men, 500 white women, 850
children, and 900 negroes of both sexes; and it is
thought that one third of the whites, with a greater proportion of the blacks, left the country with De Villiers,
Laclede, and St. Ange.[1] Lieutenant Fraser reported
in 1766, that "the greatest part of those who inhabited
our side of the River abandoned it on our getting possession of the Colony." The most satisfactory data for
the English period are furnished by Hutchins, who
gives Kaskaskia 500 white and 400 to 500 negro inhab-

[1] Davidson & Stuvé's *Illinois*, p. 163.

itants; Prairie du Rocher, 100 whites and 80 negroes;
Cahokia, 300 whites and 80 negroes. It is to be presumed that the panis were counted as negroes in these
estimates. In 1771 the men capable of bearing arms
in the Illinois country were estimated at 530, of whom
230 were negroes.[1] Another estimate for the same
period places the negroes in the Illinois at 300.[2] Vincennes was usually estimated to have 60 families at this
time, and there were probably as many negroes as families, if not more. It should be remembered that, after
the adoption of the Ordinance of 1787, the only places
from which actual slaves could be brought into Indiana
proper were the Michigan and Illinois settlements. A
number of them were brought from the latter after
1800, when Vincennes was the capital of Indiana Territory, and therefore drew office-holders and wealthy citizens to it.

[1] Hutchins's *Top. Desc.*, pp. 36–40.
[2] Bouquet's *Expedition*, p. 147.

CHAPTER VII.

On July 21, 1787, eight days after the passage of the Ordinance, Congress adopted a resolution directing that either the Superintendent of Indian Affairs or Colonel Josiah Harmar [1] should proceed to Vincennes and hold a treaty-council with the Shawnees and the Wabash Indians. Harmar had arrived at Vincennes two days before the adoption of this resolution, in obedience to orders previously given him to take possession of the place from Clark. He remained there until the latter part of October, excepting a trip of three weeks to Kaskaskia, endeavoring to arrive at some amicable arrangement with the Indians, but without success. Soon after his arrival he appointed Major John F. Hamtramck commandant of the post. A better selection could not have been made. He was an able officer, a severe disciplinarian, and a man of clear judgment; all of which were valuable qualities in one who was required not only to command a military post, but also to exercise arbitrary civil power over a frontier settlement; for the government of Northwest Territory was not organized until 1788, and was not in fact extended over the French settlements until the summer of 1790. The old court, which had been

---

[1] He was brevetted brigadier-general by Congress ten days later.

acting under its original authorization by Virginia,
though entirely out of its proper powers, was peremp-
torily abolished by General Harmar; and as no new civil
authorities were established, Major Hamtramck remained
for three years the autocrat of the Wabash, — the sole
legislative, executive, and judicial authority. He had
the good sense to assume all the power that he considered
best for the public welfare, and to assert it with firmness.
One of his first official acts was a proclamation, issued
October 3, 1787, prohibiting the sale of intoxicating
liquors to Indians. This was the first known liquor law
of Indiana. In May, 1789, in consequence of a petition
to him representing an improper appropriation of parts
of the village common by some of the inhabitants, he
prohibited all persons, "under the penalty of a fine for
the first trespass and imprisonment for the second, from
cultivating any lot or piece of ground on the commons,
or occupying any part thereof, without regular permission." The most arbitrary of his ordinances was one of
March 24, 1790, in these words: "Many persons having sold their goods and lands, to the prejudice of their
creditors, the inhabitants and others of the district of
Post Vincennes are expressly prohibited, henceforth,
from selling, or exchanging, or mortgaging any part of
their goods, lands, or slaves, under any pretext, without
express permission from the officer commanding this
place. This ordinance to remain in force until the arrival of his excellency, the governor." These regulations cut off much of the freedom of the settlers, but
their effects were seen to be beneficial, and Major
Hamtramck's adjustments of personal controversies were
so satisfactory that the inhabitants very justly considered
him a benefactor. When the acting governor arrived,

in the summer of 1790, the citizens presented him an
address in which the services of Major Hamtramck were
commended in terms of warmest gratitude.[1]

The permanent settlement of Ohio by families dates
April 7, 1788, when the pioneers of the Ohio Company
led by General Rufus Putnam arrived at the mouth of
the Muskingum and founded Marietta. In July, Arthur
St. Clair, who had been elected governor of the territory by Congress on October 5 preceding, arrived and
began the organization of the government. The judges
appointed who qualified were Samuel Holden Parsons,
James Mitchell Varnum, and John Cleves Symmes, who
with the governor proceeded at once to the work of
legislation assigned to them by the Ordinance. From
August to December, laws were made for the regulation
of the militia, organization and procedure of courts, oaths
of office, and appointment of coroners ; punishments were
prescribed for murder, arson, burglary, robbery, perjury,
larceny, and forgery, ranging from death for the first
three, to fine, disfranchisement, and the pillory for the
last ; drunkenness was made finable to the extent of fifty
cents for the first offense and one dollar thereafter ; pro-
fanity was not made punishable, but all persons were ad-
monished to abstain from it, and discourage it in others,
to " prevent the necessity of adopting and publishing laws
upon this head ; " marriage was required to be preceded
by publication of the banns for three Sundays at worship, or posting notice under the hand and seal of a
judge in some public place, or special license from the
governor. On July 27, St. Clair issued a proclamation organizing Washington County, which was made to
embrace all of Ohio east of the Scioto, or about one half

[1] Dillon, ed. of 1859, pp. 204, 236, 407.

of the present state.   No other counties were organized
until 1790 ; so that there were no means for enforcing
the laws made prior to that time, nor was any attempt
made to enforce them outside of this one county.

The delay in the practical organization of the territory was due to Indian hostilities, the chief cause of
which was the objection of the great majority of the Indians to the advance of the Americans above the Ohio.
The bad feeling was increased by the ill-will and perpetual conflicts between the Indians and the Kentuckians,
who were almost as ready for war as the savages.[1]   The
British, in addition to retaining their posts on our side of
the Canada line, made every effort to have the Indians
insist on independence, both as to government and sovereignty of territory, of all the lands north of the Ohio ;
and furnished supplies and provisions to the hostiles all
through the troubles.   Their object was to have the Indians remain an independent power, and a permanent
barrier between the United States and the British provinces, as they formally demanded in 1814 at the opening negotiations of the treaty of Ghent.[2]   The United
States government was obliged to have these lands to
relieve itself of debt and support its existence ; and it
held that its conquest of the country, when the resident
tribes were allied with Great Britain to maintain her
supremacy, left the Indians entitled only to such terms
as the conqueror would concede.[3]   St. Clair was instructed by Congress to use a pacificatory policy with

[1] *Western Annals*, p. 342; *State Papers*, vol. v. pp. 84, 88;
Dillon, p. 218; *St. Clair Papers*, vol. ii. p. 198.

[2] Am. State Papers: *Indian Affairs*, vol. i. pp. 93, 148, 158,
164, 190, 196, 243, 323, 337, 487, 489, 547; Ramsay's *U. S.*, vol.
iii. pp. 361, 362.

[3] *Journals of Congress*, vol. iv. pp. 294, 295.

the Indians, but " to neglect no opportunity that might
offer of extinguishing the Indian rights to lands westward as far as the River Mississippi, and northward as
far as the completion of the forty-first degree of north
latitude." A small portion of the Indians consented to
a considerable cession, but the Wabash tribes would not
join in any treaty of cession, and the majority of other
tribes united in this course. The treaty of Fort Harmar, on January 9, 1789, was little more than a farce,
and hastened rather than retarded war. The Indians
claimed that the few who joined in the treaty were not
chiefs, had no authority, and were intimidated by the
whites. The war opened in the following summer and
raged for five years, the Indians having rather the better of their enemies until they were overwhelmed by
Wayne at the Rapids of the Maumee in August, 1794.
In September Wayne's army moved to Kekionga, and
there established a fort which was garrisoned by a strong
force of infantry and artillery under Colonel Hamtramck,
the former commandant of Fort Knox.[1] The new post
was named Fort Wayne, and the place has been so called
ever since.

In the spring of 1794, John Jay went to London to
negotiate a treaty with England ; he concluded his work
on November 19. By this treaty it was provided, among
other things, that the king should withdraw all his troops
from posts within the boundaries of the United States
on or before the first day of June, 1796. On learning
of this, the Indians realized that their hope of support
from England was gone, and in August, 1795, reluctantly
made such cessions as Wayne demanded. These com-

---

[1] The fort built at Vincennes in 1788 was named Fort Knox, at
the request of General Harmar. *St. Clair Papers*, vol. ii. p. 92.

prised all of Ohio east of the Cuyahoga River and south
of a line drawn slightly north of east from Loramie's
store, near the head of the Big Miami; military reservations at fourteen of the most important points in the
Indian country, — those in Indiana being Fort Wayne,
the Little River portage, and the old Wea towns near
Lafayette; a tract six miles deep along the Detroit, including the French settlements; Clark's grant of 150,000
acres at the Falls of the Ohio; Fort Massac, Michilimackinac, Vincennes, "and all other places in possession
of the French people and other white settlers among
them, of which the Indian title has been extinguished;"
and the southeastern corner of Indiana, lying east of a
line drawn from Fort Recovery to the mouth of the
Kentucky River.

These cessions covered all the lands for which the
United States had any desire, and founded a peace that
lasted for sixteen years. Population at once began
pouring rapidly into the new lands, its movements being
largely controlled by the great land companies which
were operating there. The majority of the settlers were
from New England and the Middle States, though the
South was well represented in the lands of the Miami
Company, and in large majority in the Virginia Military
Lands. The Scioto Company, organized by Duer and
his associates, — "principal characters of America," who
sold their influence to Cutler, — became bankrupt after
securing the foundation of Gallipolis by a colony of
Parisians, whose sufferings are so directly connected
with American thrift that they are humiliating to contemplate.[1] The increase of population in Indiana was

[1] Volney's *View*, p. 355; Am. State Papers: *Pub. Lands*, vol.
i. p. 24; Dillon, p. 200; *Western Annals*, pp. 487–491; *St. Clair
Papers*, vol. ii. p. 154, note.

very small as compared with the growth of Ohio. Settlements were made in the southeastern corner of the state, and in Clark's Grant, soon after the close of the Indian war, but they were unimportant in extent, and had no material effect on the government of Northwest Territory. The additions to the old French settlements by American immigration were of greater consequence.

When General Harmar came to Vincennes, in 1787, he described it as containing " near four hundred houses — log and bark — out-houses, barns, etc.; the number of inhabitants, about nine hundred souls, French, and about four hundred souls, Americans." [1] A striking view of the post at this time is furnished by the journal of Joseph Buell, an orderly-sergeant in Harmar's regiment. He was a man of excellent character, and withal a typical New-Englander of the period in his religious and political notions. His description, therefore, will serve for a statement of the general estimation in which the French settlers were held by the Yankee emigrants who were soon to begin crossing the mountains and peopling the wilderness : — " Post Vincent is a beautiful place, was it settled with respectable people ; but they are a mixture of all nations. The principal inhabitants are French, intermarried with Indians, and pay but little regard to religion or law. They are under guidance of an old Roman Catholic friar, who keeps them in ignorance as much as he can, and fills them full of superstition. The people give themselves up to all kinds of vice, and are as indolent and idle a community as ever composed one town. They might live in affluence if they were industrious. The town has been settled longer than Philadelphia, and one half of their dwelling houses

[1] *St. Clair Papers*, vol. ii. p. 27.

are yet covered with bark like Indian wigwams. The inhabitants are quite numerous, and people from all parts of the United States are emigrating to this place."[1] The scheming friar to whom this Puritan soldier refers is none other than our good friend Father Gibault, and the superstition with which he filled his parishioners does not appear to have been anything worse than Catholicism.

The French settlers were at this time in great destitution, but their condition cannot justly be attributed to indolence. In 1790 they besought Governor St. Clair to interpose and save them from the expense of government surveys of their lands,[2] and he reported on this subject as follows: "A part only of the surveys have been returned, because the people objected to paying the surveyor, and it is too true that they are ill able to pay. The Illinois country, as well as that upon the Wabash, has been involved in great distress ever since it fell under the American dominion. With great cheerfulness the people furnished the troops under General Clark, and the Illinois regiment, with everything they could spare, and often with much more than they could spare with any convenience to themselves. Most of the certificates for these supplies are still in their hands, unliquidated and unpaid ; and in many instances, where application for payment has been made to the State of Virginia, under whose authority the certificates were granted, it has been refused. The Illinois regiment being disbanded, a set of men pretending the authority of Virginia embodied themselves, and a scene of general depredation and plunder ensued. To this succeeded

---

[1] Hildreth's *Pion. Hist. Ohio Valley*, p. 155.
[2] Dillon, ed. of 1859, p. 224.

three successive and extraordinary inundations from the Mississippi, which either swept away their crops or prevented their being planted. The loss of the greatest part of their trade with the Indians, which was a great resource, came upon them at this juncture, as well as the hostile incursions of some of the tribes which had ever before been in friendship with them ; and to these was added the loss of their whole last crop of corn by an untimely frost. Extreme misery could not fail to be the consequence of such accumulated misfortunes." [1] In fact there was actual famine at Vincennes in the early part of 1790. On January 23, St. Clair wrote tendering supplies from the government storehouse at the Falls of the Ohio, if they were needed ; and on March 19 Major Hamtramck wrote in reply : " I have this day sent a boat to the Falls for 800 bushels of corn, which I shall deliver to the people of the village, who are in a starving condition ; so much so that on the 16th instant a woman, a boy of about thirteen, and a girl of about seven years were driven to the woods by hunger, and poisoned themselves by eating some wild roots, and have died of it." [2]

The American immigrants to the French settlements did not amalgamate readily with their new neighbors. The two races differed widely in their habits and their ideas of government. There was little but a common dislike of the English to unite them. The French were vivacious, noisy, and spendthrift; the Americans serious, taciturn, and thrifty. The past misfortunes of the French begot new ones. Their trade was gone, and they could not compete with the Americans in agriculture.

---

[1] *St. Clair Papers*, vol. ii. p. 168.

[2] *Ibid.*, vol. ii. pp. 131, 132, note.

The recent Indian war had impeded their farming, and
occasioned the loss of most of their cattle. They had
not the patience to clear away forests. They were so
social in their dispositions that the solitary life necessary
to those engaged in opening new land was intolerable
to them. The Americans relied on agriculture. They
came into the wilderness to open farms, and they pursued their purpose patiently and systematically. Men,
women, and children drudged and saved, while their
French neighbors gossiped and danced. Congress did
not recognize the extensive claims which the French
settlers based on purchases from the Indians, but it gave
them the lands for which they could establish governmental grants from France or England ; it gave them
their common fields ; and it gave donations of 400 acres
to the heads of families who resided in the country in
1783. Before the last-named were allotted, many of the
French were in the depths of poverty. If they had
been in condition to hold their lands, and had possessed
the patience to improve them, they might still have attained comparative wealth, but as it was they preferred
to sell. Americans were standing ready to buy, and the
price paid was often as low as fifty cents the acre, and
this not infrequently paid in goods at fancy prices.
When the time for issuing patents came, the French
claims were largely in American hands. There were of
course exceptions to this among the wealthier class of
French settlers.

In a political way the Americans regarded the French
as an inferior race. There was nothing in their composition of the wild French republicanism of 1793. Their
fathers had settled in America with an easy-going faith
that royalty and nobility were very proper and good in-

stitutions, and their descendants had grown up in the
same unambitious views. They had no conception of
the modern ideas of civil liberty and political rights.
They regarded self-government as an imposition on the
people. They did not wish to make any laws. Heaven
forbid ! Why should they trouble themselves with such
stuff ? An honest commandant and the customs of the
country were sufficient for their wants.[1] In the eyes of
the American settlers, people with such ideas were fitted
only to be serfs; and yet self-government was nothing
more than a matter of sentiment during the existence of
Northwest Territory. There was only one election of
law-makers in all that time, — the legislature of 1799, —
and no election of executive officers at all. The privileges of citizenship consisted chiefly in obeying or dis-
obeying the laws which the Governor and Judges saw
fit to make. As a natural result of the race differences,
however, the Americans soon gained the ascendency in
public affairs. When Volney visited Vincennes in 1796,
he found that the Americans already controlled the place,
and that the French considered themselves down-trodden
and oppressed. They attributed their unhappy lot to
some mysterious kind of injustice, while the Americans
coolly informed them that it was due solely to their own
indolence and prodigality.[2]

Near the close of 1789 St. Clair started to the Western
settlements. On January 2, 1790, at Losantiville (Cin-

[1] The customs which obtained in the French settlements are
commonly referred to as the *coutume de Paris*. The laws and
customs of Paris were established as the law of the greater part
of the Mississippi valley by the grant to Crozat; but they had
become so modified in the lapse of years that *coutume du pays*
would be more appropriate.

[2] *View of U. S.*, pp. 367–393.

ciunati), he created Hamilton County out of the lands lying between the Big and Little Miamis. On April 27, at Kaskaskia, he established St. Clair County, including all of Illinois south of the Illinois River and west of a line drawn from Fort Massac to the mouth of Mackinaw Creek. On June 11 he returned, on account of alarming reports of Indian hostilities, but deputed Secretary Sargent to act in his stead. Sargent proceeded to Vincennes, and, on June 20, organized Knox County, which was made to include all the country between Hamilton and St. Clair counties from the Ohio to the great lakes. These, with Washington County, were the only counties organized before 1795, and during this period the northern parts of Knox County were in possession of the British. From 1790 the laws of Northwest Territory were enforced in the Western settlements, and were the source of much discontent among the French inhabitants, who did not understand them and believed them prejudicial to their interests. While at Vincennes, Sargent, with Judges Turner and Symmes who accompanied him, passed three stringent laws against the sale of liquor to Indians and soldiers, and against gaming. These were considered oppressive by the French, who had always maintained that "God-given liberty of living" which is supposed to entitle a man to get drunk, or furnish materials for intoxication to others, when he likes. The law against the sale of liquor to Indians was repealed in 1795, and Vincennes soon became the scene of the savage dissipation described by Volney.

None of the laws passed prior to 1795 were valid, because they were not "laws of the original states," which alone the Governor and Judges were authorized to enact. The Judges, from the first, favored framing original laws, because no state had laws suited to the needs of a half-dozen frontier posts scattered over a wilderness hundreds of miles in extent. St. Clair opposed such an assumption of power, but finally assented to it.[1] On May 24, 1794, the national House of Representatives adopted a resolution disapproving the territorial laws for this reason, and afterwards a joint resolution declaring them void was read twice and committed, but no further action was taken.[2] Governor St. Clair stated that it passed the House, but was rejected by the Senate, because, "as they considered them all *ipso facto* void, they thought it improper to declare any of them so by an act of the legislature."[3] On May 29, 1795, the Governor and Judges convened at Cincinnati, and adopted quite an elaborate code of laws from divers states. These were printed by Mr. Maxwell of Cincinnati, and have since been known as the Maxwell Code. The former laws were treated as being still in existence, though their validity was questioned, until 1799, when they were reënacted by the legislature on recommendation of the governor.[4] In 1795 Randolph County was created of the southern part of St. Clair County. In 1796 Wayne County was created, including all of Michigan and portions of Ohio, Indiana, Illinois, and Wisconsin. In 1797 the counties of Adams, Ross, and Jefferson were organized, — all within Ohio. No other counties were established while Indiana remained a part of

[1] *St. Clair Papers*, vol. ii. p. 334.
[2] Am. State Papers: *Misc.*, vol. i. p. 82; *Annals 3d Congress*, pp. 1214, 1223.
[3] *St. Clair Papers*, vol. ii. p. 356.
[4] *Laws N. W. Ter.*, pp. 93 note, 211.

Northwest Territory, but in 1798 Hamilton County was extended westward to the Indian boundary line, from Fort Recovery to the mouth of the Kentucky River.

In 1798, it having been ascertained that the territory contained "five thousand free male inhabitants of full age" (there were, indeed, more than twice that number), an election for delegates to a general assembly was called. Of the twenty-two representatives elected, sixteen were from Ohio, three from Michigan, two from Illinois, and one from Indiana. Of the five members of the council selected by President Adams from ten persons nominated by the representatives, the only one from outside of Ohio was Henry Vanderburgh, of Vincennes, who was made president of the council. He was a man of much native ability, who rose to the position of captain in the Fifth New York Regiment, Continental Line, during the Revolution, and soon after its close settled at Vincennes and married into the family of Racines, one of the oldest and most prominent there. The Knox County representative, Colonel John Small, was also a man of prominence at Vincennes, where he settled in 1785 with the first influx of American families. He was a universal mechanic, — gunsmith, millwright, blacksmith, surveyor, etc., — and was for many years the most prominent miller in that region. He served as Adjutant-General of Indiana Territory under Governor Harrison, to whom he was always a warm friend.[1]

---

[1] Somewhat extended biographical notices of the prominent men of early Indiana, which originally formed part of this work, have been omitted in revising. The ground will be fully covered in an exhaustive collection of biographies entitled "The Legislators of Indiana," which is being prepared by Hon. W. H. English of Indianapolis, and is expected to appear in a few months.

It is stated by Judge Burnet that politics scarcely
entered into the question in the election of representatives,[1] and this might naturally be expected of the first
election in a new country ; but politics certainly did influence the action of the legislators, who were nearly
evenly divided between the two great parties of the day.
Closely connected with national politics, but not wholly
identified with it, was the question of division of the
Territory. It was certain that a state must soon be
formed from the eastern portion, but on the boundaries
of this state depended the determination of its politics.
If it extended no farther west than the Little Miami, it
gave promise of being Federalist, and with strong New
England sympathies. If it extended to a line drawn
north from the mouth of the Big Miami to the national
boundary, as provided by the Ordinance, it would be
close politically, but probably Republican. If it extended
to this line, but was cut off on the north so as to exclude
the Michigan settlements, it would be Republican, for
Wayne County was a Federalist stronghold.[2] Governor
St. Clair was an ardent Federalist. He had published
a pamphlet in support of Mr. Adams's administration,
and had made a defense of the alien and sedition laws,
which was printed in the newspapers and subsequently
in pamphlet.[3] He considered it best for his party so to
divide the territory that both parts would be held in
territorial government as long as possible, and thus give
the executive opportunity to gain the good-will of the
people through official patronage and other favors. In
December, 1799, he wrote a long letter to Senator Ross,

[1] Burnet's *Notes*, p. 289.
[2] *St. Clair Papers*, vol. ii. p. 580, note.
[3] *Ibid.*, vol. ii. p. 442.

of Pennsylvania, urging that from party policy Hamilton and Wayne counties should be placed in the Western division,[1] which would leave each division with too little population for advance to state government. He refrained from circulating his views in the territory, and wisely, for a large majority of the people in the eastern division desired state government. At the same time the people of the Illinois and Wabash countries were opposed to a union with Hamilton and Wayne counties, because the western division would then have sufficient population for the second or representative stage of territorial government, and those two counties would have dominated in that government. The people of Knox County petitioned Congress this same winter for an immediate return to the first stage, assigning as their reason that the second stage subjected them to heavier taxation, and was of no advantage whatever to them.[2]

There was much personal feeling connected with the public affairs of the territory. St. Clair was charged with nepotism and overriding the judiciary, and he had given cause for both complaints. The judiciary was not popular. Judge Turner, whose arbitrary conduct had called forth severe rebukes from the governor and almost caused his impeachment in Congress,[3] had resigned, and Return Jonathan Meigs had succeeded him in 1798; but Meigs, like Symmes and Putnam, was distrusted on account of his connection with the great land companies, and naturally so, because nearly all of the litigation of

[1] *St. Clair Papers*, vol. ii. p. 482.

[2] *Ibid.*, vol. ii. p. 489.

[3] *Ibid.*, vol. ii. pp. 330, 342, 345, 348, 372; Am. State Papers: *Misc.*, vol. i. pp. 151, 157.

the territory grew out of transactions with one or the other of these companies. Judge Symmes was considered a peculiarly dangerous heretic by the French settlers, because, in a charge to a grand jury in Wayne County, he had tried to persuade these Catholics that their payment of tithes and devotion of so much time to worship were neither enjoined by the Scriptures nor conducive to temporal welfare. This indiscreet show of bigotry caused so great excitement that the judge was glad to make conciliatory explanation from the bench.[1] St. Clair's popularity was also impaired by his continuous friendship for Winthrop Sargent, the Secretary of the Territory, of whom it was said that "his pride, his insolence, and his tyranical disposition had rendered his name odious to the Western country."[2] Sargent resigned in 1798, and was succeeded by William Henry Harrison, who was a much more acceptable man to the people, but who had little sympathy with St. Clair's ideas. He was a pro-state man and a Republican in politics, though he maintained a judicious reserve on this subject, as did many other Republicans, so long as the Federalist party was in power. He afterwards explained that his appointment by President Adams was due to the influence of General Wayne and President Washington, and that politics had nothing to do with it.[3] He had served in the recent Indian war as aid-de-camp to Wayne, and had left the army shortly after his marriage to the daughter of Judge Symmes.

The territorial House organized on September 23, 1799, and on October 3 proceeded to the election of a

---

[1] Burnet's *Notes*, p. 282, note.

[2] *Natl. Intelligencer*, December 24, 1800.

[3] Harrison to Lyons, June 1, 1840.

delegate to Congress. Judge Burnet states that he was talked of as a candidate, but the only candidates named before the House were Arthur St. Clair, Jr., son of the governor, and William Henry Harrison. Harrison was elected, receiving eleven of the twenty-one votes. There are a few straws which indicate the political current in the House. Edward Tiffin, afterwards Republican governor of the state, was elected speaker; the contested election of Dunlavy *v.* Martin, from Hamilton County, was decided in favor of the latter by a vote of nine to eight, — a close analogy to the vote for delegate; and, just before the close of the session, an address to President Adams, indorsing his administration, was voted against by five members of the House, though others, who were afterwards leading Republicans, supported it.[1] With these facts in view, we may accept with large credence Mr. Harrison's account of the election, which is as follows: "In 1799 I was selected by the *Republican party* of the Territorial Legislature to be their candidate for the appointment of delegate to Congress. Between Mr. Arthur St. Clair, Jr. (the son of Governor St. Clair), the Federal candidate, and myself, the votes were divided precisely as the two parties stood in the Legislature, with the exception of one Republican, who was induced by his regard for the Governor to vote for his son. The vote was 11 to 10, — not one of the nine Federalists voting for me." [2]

[1] *St. Clair Papers*, vol. i. p. 213; vol. ii. pp. 447–452, note.

[2] Harrison to Lyons, June 1, 1840, in Richmond *Whig*, June 15, 1840, and *Natl. Intelligencer*, June 18, 1840. This letter is not to be considered authoritative historically except as corroborated. It is a political document, carefully worded with reference to the issues of the campaign of 1840. It was probably written, or revised, by what the general called his "conscience-keeping com-

Harrison was but twenty-six years of age when he went to Philadelphia charged with the delicate task of getting a Republican scheme of division through a Federalist Congress. He exerted a strong influence in the House, though he had no vote; and he was ably seconded in the lobby by Colonel Thomas Worthington, who, in addition to laboring in a general way for the Republican plan, was representing the Chillicothe interest in an attempt to have that town made the capital of the eastern division of the territory. St. Clair put the Federalists on their guard as to Worthington in his letter to Senator Ross, above mentioned, but he apparently regarded Harrison as an unsophisticated youth who might be beguiled into supporting his own plan. On February 17, 1800, he wrote to Harrison, urging the division of the territory into three parts, one east of the Scioto, one west of the Big Miami, and the third the intermediate country. In this letter there is not the slightest allusion to party policy; the argument is based entirely on population, convenience, and other matters of a general nature.[1] Unfortunately for St. Clair's political welfare, he had in the preceding December written a letter to Timothy Pickering, then Secretary of State, in which he disclosed his real motives substantially as in the letter to Senator Ross; and Pickering showed this letter to Harrison, who on the same day confided its contents to Worthington.[2] In this manner St. Clair's political enemies were put in full knowledge of his actual designs when he was on paper before them professing entirely different ones. To the party hatred engendered by this

mittee,'' — three gentlemen sent to North Bend by the Whig leaders to look after the campaign correspondence.

[1] *St. Clair Papers*, vol. ii. p. 489.   [2] *Ibid.*, vol. ii. p. 570.

and subsequent political plotting and counter-plotting must largely be attributed the harsh policy under which St. Clair was permitted to pass his old age in destitution and humiliation, — a result which will ever be a blot on the fair fame of his adopted land.[1]

Mr. Harrison's course in this Congress was such that it led many persons, including both friends and foes in politics, to believe him a Federalist; and in his future career nothing gave him more trouble than this charge of Federalism. He denied it repeatedly, and the circumstantial evidence supported his denial, but his opponents never abandoned their ground. In 1805 it was openly charged that he had turned Republican when Jefferson became President, in order to hold his office of Governor of Indiana.[2] On March 20, 1826, in the Senate, John Randolph, who had been with him in the Congress of 1800, declared him to have been at that time " an open, zealous, frank supporter of the sedition law and black-cockade Administration."[3] In 1840 the charge was renewed with unflagging persistence; and it was declared that he returned from Congress wearing the black cockade, and introduced " the odious badge of Toryism" at Cincinnati.[4] On the other hand, Judge Burnet in 1840 solemnly averred, of his own knowledge, that Harrison in 1800 was "a firm, consistent, unyielding Republican of the Jefferson school;" and

---

[1] Burnet's *Notes*, pp. 381–383; *St. Clair Papers*, vol. i. pp. 248–256.

[2] *Letters of Decius*, p. 25.

[3] *Debates 1st Sess. 19th Cong.*, vol. ii. pt. 1, p. 359.

[4] *Indiana Democrat*, June 27, 1840. The Federalists wore the black cockade as an offset to the tri-colored cockade of France, which was worn by Republicans to indicate their friendship for France during Mr. Adams's administration.

General Solomon Van Rensselaer confirmed him.[1] To Randolph's attack Mr. Harrison replied, on the same day, that he had approved Mr. Adams's administration " as to the course pursued by it in relation to the Government of France," and that he considered Mr. Adams " an honest man and a pure patriot." He continued: " But, sir, my opposition to the alien and sedition laws was so well known in the Territory, that a promise was extorted from me by my friends in the Legislature, by which I was elected, that I would express no opinions in Philadelphia which were in the least calculated to defeat the important objects with which I was charged. As I had no vote, I was not called on to express my sentiments in the House. The Republican party were all in favor of the measures I wished to have adopted. But the Federalists were the majority. Prudence, therefore, and my duty to my constituents, rendered it proper that I should refrain from expressing sentiments which would injuriously affect their interests, and which, if expressed, could have not the least influence upon the decisions of Congress." [2] It is most probable that Harrison's line of action caused Pickering to consider him a Federalist, and therefore to show him St. Clair's letter; for though Pickering had regarded Mr. Adams's conduct with " indignation and disgust " for two years past,[3] and though he was summarily removed from office on March 12, 1800, he had no love for Republicanism. His troubles with the President were due to his preferring Hamilton

---

[1] *Natl. Intelligencer*, February 6, June 6, July 16, 1840.

[2] *Debates 1st Sess. 19th Cong.*, vol. ii. pt. 1, pp. 364, 365. A similar but more guarded statement is made in the letter to Lyons above quoted.

[3] *New England Federalism*, p. 331.

to Adams as a leader. Harrison's revelation of the contents of the letter to Worthington, on the same day, however, must be accepted as conclusive proof of his Republicanism at that time.

Harrison secured substantially what he wanted. The matter of division was referred to a committee composed of Messrs. Craik, Harrison, and Bird. On March 3, 1800, they reported a resolution that the territory be "divided into two distinct and separate governments, by a line beginning at the mouth of the Great Miami River, and running through a north course, until it intersects the boundary line between the United States and Canada." [1] They gave their opinion that this would at once give the second stage of government to the western division, as it was "supposed to contain at the present time fifteen thousand inhabitants." A bill to this effect was brought in and passed, but it was amended by the Senate. The House refused at first to concur in the amendment, but a committee of conference was appointed, and the House receded from its position; so the bill as passed made the boundary the old Greenville treaty line, from the mouth of the Kentucky to Fort Recovery, until it intersected a line drawn north from the mouth of the Big Miami, and thence north on the latter line to the national boundary. It was provided, however, that when a state should be formed from the eastern division, all the land west of the north line from the mouth of the Miami should be thrown into Indiana Territory. The western division was given a government as provided in the Ordinance, except that it was to pass to the second stage, or representative government, whenever a majority of the freeholders so desired, no

[1] *Annals 6th Cong.*, pp. 583, 1320.

matter what the population might be; but in such case the number of representatives was to be not less than seven nor more than nine. The Chillicothe people also secured their object, for that town was made the capital of the eastern division. Vincennes was made the capital of the western division.[1]

At this Congress, also, Mr. Harrison secured the passage of an act which was an unfailing source of popularity to him while he lived, and which forms his strongest claim to statesmanship with the historian. Up to this time the western lands, by law, were not sold in tracts of less than 4,000 acres. This was doubtless made the law through the influence of the land companies, and on the theory that more rapid settlement and a better class of settlers could be obtained through the companies. The result of it was that the small purchaser had to buy his lands of the companies. It is questionable if the system were ever a wise one, but even if so originally, it was no longer beneficial to any one, and was a serious impediment to the growth of the country; and one of the principal objects with which Harrison had been charged when he came to Congress was a radical change of this system. He brought his plans before the House, and the matter was referred to a committee of which he was made chairman, — a signal honor, by the way, for this was the first time in the history of the House that a territorial delegate was made chairman of a committee. He reported a bill authorizing the sale of land by half and quarter sections.[2] The House passed the bill, but the Senate made objectionable amendments. A com-

[1] *Annals 6th Cong.*, p. 1498.
[2] The report is in the *Duane Collection of Pamphlets*, vol. xcviii. Library of Congress.

mittee of conference was appointed, of which Harrison
was a member, and the matter was compromised by
authorizing sale in sections and half sections. Purchasers were given the easy terms of one fourth down
and balance in two, three, and four years, with six per
cent. interest, and a discount of eight per cent. if paid
before due. For public convenience, land offices were
established at Cincinnati, Chillicothe, Marietta, and
Steubenville, at each of which there were to be public
sales, at fixed times, for three weeks, and private sales
thereafter.[1] Thus the most injurious effect of the great
land companies was swept away just as Indiana Territory was ushered into existence.

During the time that Indiana was a part of Northwest Territory, three attempts were made to secure a
repeal or modification of the sixth article of compact, or
slavery clause, of the Ordinance. The first was a petition to Congress from the Illinois country, dated at Kaskaskia, January 12, 1796. This petition declared the
belief of the signers that the sixth article was " contrary
to the promises and assurances made them, on behalf of
the State of Virginia," by General George Rogers Clark,
when he took possession of the country ; and also contrary to a fundamental principle of natural justice, in
that it retroactively dissolved vested rights. It continued : " Your petitioners then were, and now are, possessed of a number of slaves, which the article above recited seems to deprive them of (perhaps inadvertently)
without their consent or concurrence. It may be said,
as it is the better opinion, that all such as were slaves at
the date of that ordinance are to continue so during their
lives ; but then it is also said that the issue of such slaves

---

[1] *Annals 6th Cong.*, p. 1515.

born after that period are absolutely free. Your petitioners, however, humbly contend that such after-born
issue are as much slaves as those born before, because
the owners of their parents have, and, as your petitioners
humbly conceive, always had, as fixed and incontrovertible a right to, and interest in, the future issue and increase of such slaves as they have to the slaves themselves. That, notwithstanding the articles in the said
Ordinance are said to be 'articles of compact between
the original States and the people and States of the said
Territory,' it is, however, a truth that they were made
ex parte by the original States only; for sure your petitioners are that, if the people then in the Territory had
been called upon to make such compact, they never
would have consented to enter into one that would deprive them of their most valuable property.

"Your petitioners humbly hope they will not be
thought presumptuous in venturing to disapprove of the
article concerning slavery *in toto*, as contrary not only to
the interest, but almost to the existence of the country
they inhabit, where laborers cannot be procured to assist
in cultivating the ground under one dollar per day, exclusive of washing, lodging, and boarding; and where
every kind of tradesmen are paid from a dollar and a
half to two dollars per day; neither is there, at these
exorbitant prices, a sufficiency of hands to be got for the
exigencies of the inhabitants, who, attached to their native
soil, have rather chosen to encounter these and many
other difficulties than, by avoiding them, remove to the
Spanish dominions, where slavery is permitted, and consequently the price of labor much lower." For these
reasons the petitioners asked a repeal of the slavery
clause, with a provision that slaves could be imported

only from the states of the Union; but, apparently being
doubtful of obtaining so great a concession, they also
asked that, if the clause were not repealed, Congress
might pass a law declaring that the Ordinance, as it
stood, meant that when slaves were brought into the
territory they became free, but were still bound to serve
their owners for life; that they were apprentices, dif-
fering from ordinary apprentices only in the extent of
their terms of service. If this course were preferred,
they asked Congress to provide " how far, and for what
period of time, the masters of servants are to be entitled
to the service of the children of parents, born during
such servitude, as an indemnity for the expense of bringing them up in their infancy."

This petition was forwarded to Congress by Governor
St. Clair,[1] and was probably called forth by the action
of Judge Turner, a few months earlier, in attempting to
release Vanderburgh's slaves; for the petitioners state
that they ask the act declaring the meaning of the Ordinance because " a diversity may happen in the opinions
of different judges." It was referred to a committee of
which Joshua Coit, of Connecticut, was chairman, and
on May 12, 1796, he reported adversely. The committee say: " The petitioners being only four in number,
and producing no power by which they claim to petition,
even in behalf of the inhabitants of the said counties;
and no evidence appearing of the wishes of the rest of
the inhabitants of the said counties; and your committee
having information that an alteration of the Ordinance,
in the manner prayed for by the petitioners, would be
disagreeable to many of the inhabitants of the said Territory; they have conceived it needless to enter into any

[1] *Annals 4th Cong. 1st Sess.*, p. 1171.

consideration of the policy of the measure, being persuaded that, if it could be admissible under any circumstances, a partial application, like the present, could not be listened to." [1] The justice of this decision could scarcely be questioned, even by the petitioners. It was certain that the New England settlers of the eastern part of the Territory, who were a majority of its population, were opposed to the introduction of slavery. It was evident that the petition of four men could not possibly be considered a consent of the people of the Territory to the amendment of the Ordinance.

The four signers were John Edgar, William Morrison, William St. Clair, and John Du Moulin. Whether the petition was of their own motion, or was their request as representatives in some way chosen by the people, is not known. They professed to sign it " for and on behalf of the inhabitants " of Randolph and St. Clair counties, and there is not, so far as has been ascertained, any further evidence on the subject now in existence. It is unquestionable that what they asked was generally desired by the people of those counties, and that they were the most influential men of those counties. John Edgar was a refugee Irish naval officer, of liberal education and agreeable manners, noted for his intelligence and benevolence. He amassed a large fortune at Kaskaskia by milling and dealing in land, and held numerous offices, both elective and appointive. William Morrison, since coming to Kaskaskia in 1790, had by native talent and energy become the foremost merchant of the Upper Mississippi valley. St. Clair and Du Moulin were almost as influential in St. Clair County as the others were

---

[1] For petition and report see Am. State Papers : *Pub. Lands,* vol. i. pp. 60, 61.

in Randolph. William St. Clair, youngest son of the then Earl of Roslin, and a cousin of Governor St. Clair, was then serving as clerk of the St. Clair County court. John Du Moulin was a highly educated Swiss, who acquired a considerable fortune by land speculations, and was very popular as a militia commander. He was at this time chief justice of the court of common pleas in St. Clair County. It is certain that these four men could have secured the signatures of a majority of the people of the two western counties to their petition if they had desired to present it again; but they realized that the other objection — the adverse wishes of the Ohio people — would be fatal to their project so long as the Territory was undivided. They accordingly dropped the matter, but revived it as soon as Indiana became a separate territory.

The second attempt to introduce slavery into Northwest Territory was directed to the legislature of 1799. It was a petition from several officers of the late Virginia Line, " praying for toleration to bring their slaves into this Territory, on the military lands between the Little Miami and Scioto rivers." This was presented at the beginning of the session and promptly disposed of. On September 27, the fourth day of the session, William Goforth, of Hamilton County, reported for the committee to which it was referred, " that the prayer of the petitioners was incompatible with the articles of compact contained in the Ordinance of Congress made for the government of this Territory, and, therefore, could not be granted." On the reading of this report, it was " Resolved unanimously, That this House doth agree to the same." [1] It is evident that the prohibition of the

[1] *St. Clair Papers*, vol. ii. p. 447, note.

introduction of slaves was a hardship to these Virginia soldiers. They were entitled to their bounty lands north of the Ohio, and many of them were desirous of settling there, but this provision barred their way. True, they might have disposed of their slaves before coming, but Virginia sentiment at that time was against such action. There was a notable attachment to family servitors, and a common aversion to masters who disposed of such slaves from mere monetary considerations. In addition to this, living without slaves necessitated a complete change in their habits of life, which these people were unwilling to make. The action of the legislature on the first memorial was not encouraging, but they determined to make one more attempt ; and this time they carefully put their request in the most restricted and least objectionable form that would serve their purpose. On November 19, " A memorial of Thomas Posey, on behalf of himself and several officers and soldiers of the Virginia line, on the continental establishment of the late army of the United States, was presented to the House and read, praying that an act may be passed authorizing persons holding slaves under the laws of the State in which they acquire that species of property, and removing into this Territory, to bring their slaves with them, under certain restrictions." [1] No action appears to have been taken on this petition. In consequence of its failure, many of the Virginians gave up their intentions of coming north of the Ohio, and settled in the southern territories. General Posey was among the number.

It is not surprising that these petitions were not granted, for a majority of the members of the legisla-

---

[1] *St. Clair Papers*, vol. ii. p. 451, note.

ture were Eastern men, and both they and their constituents were heartily opposed to having slavery fastened on the government of their new homes; but it appears remarkable that the vote on the first petition should have been unanimous. Judge Burnet says of this: "The public feeling, on the subject of admitting slavery into the Territory, was such that the request would have been denied, by a unanimous vote, if the Legislature had possessed the power of granting it. They were not only opposed to slavery on the ground of its being a moral evil, in violation of personal right, but were of opinion that, whatever might be its immediate advantages, it would ultimately retard the settlement and check the prosperity of the Territory, by making labor less reputable, and creating feelings and habits unfriendly to the simplicity and industry they desired to encourage and perpetuate." [1] This flattering estimate of the representatives is clearly erroneous. John Edgar, who represented Randolph County in this legislature, had petitioned Congress to admit slavery three years earlier, as we have just seen; and he labored ardently to secure the same end afterward. Shadrach Bond, who represented St. Clair County, joined in a petition for the admission of slaves in 1800, and in another in 1805. John Small, who represented Knox County, was always identified with the pro-slavery party in Indiana Territory, and was himself a slaveholder, even after Indiana became a state. [2] In their pro-slavery senti-

---

[1] Burnet's *Notes*, p. 306.

[2] He died in the summer of 1821; and by his will, which is dated April 19, 1817, and probated July 5, 1821, he devised his negro women "Judah" and "Nancy," his boy "George," and his girl "Queen Ann" to his widow and children. (*Knox County probate record.*)

ments these three men represented their constituents, for at this time a large majority of the people in the country west of the Miami favored the introduction of slaves.

There was a special cause for this feeling on the part of the French people which did not affect other inhabitants of the Territory. It was set forth in a communication to President Washington by Governor St. Clair, on June 11, 1790, as follows: "St. Louis is the most flourishing village of the Spaniards in the upper part of the Mississippi, and it has been greatly advanced by the people who abandoned the American side. To that they were induced partly by the oppression they suffered, and partly by the fear of losing their slaves, which they had been taught to believe would all be set free on the establishment of the American Government. Much pains had indeed been taken to inculcate that belief (particularly by a Mr. Morgan, of New Jersey), and a general desertion of the country had like to have been the consequence. The construction that was given to that part of the Ordinance which declares there shall be neither slavery nor involuntary servitude was, that it did not go to the emancipation of the slaves they were in possession of and had obtained under the laws by which they had formerly been governed, but was intended simply to prevent the importation of others. In this construction, I hope the intentions of Congress have not been misunderstood, and the apprehensions of the people were quieted by it. But the circumstance that slaves cannot be introduced will prevent many people from returning who earnestly wish to return, both from a dislike to the Spanish Government and that the country itself is much less desirable than on the American side.

Could they be allowed to bring them back with them, all those who retired from that cause would return, to a man." [1] The desire for the return of these exiles, which was so often manifested by the Illinois people, was not wholly due to the mercenary expectation of an increased value of property from increased population. They longed for the companionship of their old neighbors. Their feeling was one that few Americans can fully comprehend, but of its existence there can be no question. The old French settlers never removed from one locality to another if they could avoid it ; and, when they did, they considered the necessity of a separation from their friends a most grievous calamity. [2]

The desire for the introduction of slavery was not limited wholly to the people west of the Miami, though pro-slavery men were rare to the east of that stream. Even in 1802, if we may believe the declaration of Governor St. Clair, made in a public speech at Cincinnati, there were " a few people who wish to introduce negro slavery amongst us, and these chiefly residing in the county of Ross." [3] But more than this, a majority of the legislature of 1799 were apparently brought to a point of hesitancy by the consideration of the circumstances of the would-be settlers from Virginia ; for on November 15 the House appointed Elias Langham of Ross and John Smith of Hamilton a committee to bring in a bill on the subject of fugitive slaves, "and declaring the admission of persons of color by indenture." Although no action resulted in this line, the appoint-

[1] St. Clair Papers, vol. ii. p. 175.

[2] Reynolds's Pioneer Hist. of Ill., p. 192 ; Volney's View of the U. S., p. 389.

[3] St. Clair Papers, vol. ii. p. 588.

ment of the committee indicates a willingness on the part of the legislators to permit the introduction of negroes in a servile condition until some other consideration intervened. This may have been a belief that they had no power to authorize the action, or a desire to leave the Ordinance unchanged and unimpaired. A striking instance of their respect for that instrument is seen in the fact that they discontinued the preparation of a memorial which had been begun, requesting Congress to give their representative the right of voting as well as of debating, for the reason that the proposed request was contrary to the provisions of the Ordinance; and yet they must have known that the Ordinance could be changed by Congress with their consent. From these facts we must consider Judge Burnet's recollection of the event obscured by that golden haze which so often comes upon the human memory as men advance to new surroundings and lose the bitterness of old antagonisms. The unanimity of the vote cannot be attributed wholly to the sentiments of the legislators as to the desirability of the introduction of slaves.

CHAPTER VIII.

"St. Vincennes, July 4, 1800. This day the Government of the Indiana Territory commenced, William Henry Harrison having been appointed Governor, John Gibson Secretary, William Clarke, Henry Vanderburgh & John Griffin Judges in and over said Territory." So opens the executive journal of the Territory, though Secretary Gibson was the only official who acted for some six months. Governor Harrison did not arrive until January 10, 1801; and the territorial court did not convene until March 3 of the same year. The Governor at once called a meeting of the Governor and Judges, which began January 12 and lasted for two weeks. Six laws and three resolutions were passed, most of them concerning the establishment of courts and the practice therein, five of which were amendatory of, supplemental to, or in repeal of, laws of Northwest Territory. No attempt was made to reënact the laws of Northwest Territory in Indiana Territory at any time, though the laws of the former, passed prior to the division, were always treated as in force in the latter. The theory adopted was that the division of the old Territory was merely for administrative purposes; that the laws were as much in force in one division as in the other; and that there was no need of reënacting them in either. This is perhaps the only instance of such a construction

in any country where the common law obtained.' It was
carried much farther by the territorial court in 1803,
in a curious question concerning the law regulating prison
bounds; for it was then held that a law passed in
Northwest Territory after 1800 was still in force in
Wayne County, which was added to Indiana Territory in
1802, notwithstanding the fact that an entirely different
law was in force in the remainder of Indiana.[1] This
construction was of vital importance to the infant Territory, for, having dropped back to the first stage, under
the Ordinance, it could adopt only laws of the original
states, which, as had been demonstrated in Northwest
Territory, were inadequate to the needs of the people;
whereas the laws of Northwest Territory as revised and
extended by the late legislature, were very satisfactory.

In 1800, Indiana's civilized population of 5,641 souls
were grouped about little villages which were nearly all
situated on the boundary lines of the Territory, and as
far apart as they could possibly be placed. At Mackinaw, the extreme northern settlement, were 251 citizens.
The fur-traders scattered about the lakes were estimated
at 300. In the settlement at Green Bay were 50 people.
At Prairie du Chien, on the Upper Mississippi, were 65.
Farther down the Mississippi the settlements were more
extensive. In and about Cahokia were 719 people.
Just below, in Belle Fontaine township, were 286. In
L'Aigle, the southernmost township of St. Clair County,
were 250. At and about Kaskaskia were 467. At and
about Prairie du Rocher were 212. In Mitchel township were 334. Around on the Ohio were 90 souls at

---

[1] Docket of Ter. Court, September Term, 1803, p. 103. This
docket is preserved in the office of the Clerk of the Supreme
Court at Indianapolis.

Fort Massac. Farther up, in Clark's Grant, were 929.
In the interior was nothing that could be called a settlement except Vincennes, which had 714 inhabitants,
while in its immediate vicinity were 819 more. There
were, however, 55 fur-traders scattered along the Wabash, and about 100 at "Opee." [1] In what is now Indiana the population was about 2,500; the exact number cannot be given, because a part of those reported as
in the neighborhood of Vincennes were west of the Wabash. In what is now Illinois were a little more than
2,500, nearly all of them in the region about Kaskaskia
and Cahokia, which was commonly called the Illinois
country. Of the total population, 163 were reported free
negroes and 135 slaves. But this is erroneous, as 42
negroes and no slaves were reported from Cahokia,
where there were certainly a number of slaves. The
number reported from that place in 1810 was 40, and
there must have been near that number ten years earlier;
hence we may estimate the slaves in Indiana Territory
in 1800 at 175, and the free negroes at 123. Of the
slaves reported, 28 were about Vincennes and on the
Wabash, and the remainder were in Randolph County.[2]

The only purely American settlement was in Clark's
Grant, though there were Americans scattered all
through the French settlements and a large number of
them at Vincennes. The French were largely in the
majority in the Territory, and most of the American
politicians conformed to their ideas for evident reasons.
These people were nearly all Federalistic in their sym-

[1] Peoria, *i. e., au Piorias.* This is an example of that com-
pound of French abbreviation with American orthography from
which such results as Okas for Kaskaskia, Cahos, Cos, or Okos
for Cahokia, and Opost for Post Vincennes were obtained.

[2] Census of 1800.

pathies. Monarchical institutions had no terrors for
them, and political denunciations of a tendency of the
government towards such institutions fell lightly on their
ears. Their leaders had been favored by the Federal
executives, both national and territorial, to such an extent that they held nearly all the offices; and the mere
holding of an office added much to the dignity and influence of a man among the French settlers. But American politics had little weight with them as compared
with their local welfare, and the one thing which they
considered essential to their welfare was the introduction
of slaves. Their views were natural. Emigrants who
objected to slavery usually stopped in Ohio; those who
wanted slavery went to Kentucky, or the Spanish possessions beyond the Mississippi. Their neighbors who had
hastily crossed the river for fear of losing their slaves
could not return, and all on account of this absurd
American law. The French settlers and their American allies wanted this law changed, and, inasmuch as a
majority of the inhabitants of the Territory were of that
mind, they had hopes that Congress would relent. Before the organization of the Territory was completed the
Illinois people prepared a memorial to Congress, making
known their wants and supplicating relief. The ingenuity of that portion of it which refers to the question of
slavery will best be seen in the following extract: "The
mode your Petitioners wish and pray you to adopt is to
permit of the Introduction into the Territory of any of
those who are slaves in any of the United States, who
when admitted shall continue in a state of Servitude during their natural lives, but that all their children born in
the Territory shall serve, the males until thirty-one and
the females until twenty-eight, at which time they are to

be absolutely free. To the adoption of such a modification of Slavery your Petitioners cannot conceive any well-founded objections will be made. It cannot but meet with the support of those who are friends to a gradual abolition of Slavery, and your Petitioners cannot entertain the Idea that any will be found to oppose a measure which in the course of a very few years will in all human probability rescue from the vilest state of Bondage a number, and without doubt a considerable number, of Souls yet unborn. Your Petitioners do not wish to increase the number of Slaves in the United States by the introduction of any from foreign Dominions; their wishes on the contrary tend considerably to diminish the number by emancipating those who, whether born in the States where their parents reside, or removed into the Spanish Dominions, would otherwise be born slaves."

In addition to this modification of the sixth article of compact, the petitioners asked the extinction of the Indian title to the greater part of Southern Illinois, which was held by the little remnant of the Kaskaskia tribe; the granting of tracts of land to persons who would open roads through the unsettled parts of the country and maintain taverns along the same; and the establishment of one or two garrisons of troops, — all these being in anticipation of rapid settlement of the country when the slavery restriction should be removed. This petition had 270 signatures, chiefly French. Among the more prominent English and American signers were John Edgar, John Rice Jones, William Morrison, Robert Morrison, and Shadrach Bond. It does not appear to have been circulated for signature at Vincennes. It was forwarded to Congress, but did not there receive the consideration which its philanthropic professions

might seem to demand. It was not presented to the
House, though addressed to both House and Senate;
at least there is no mention of it in the House records,
and no copy of it on the House files. It was presented
to the Senate on January 23, 1801, and at once laid on
the table, whence it was not removed.[1]

The Illinois people soon learned that their petition
would avail nothing, but they were not at all disheartened. The first result of the failure was a determination to have a representative in Congress to urge their
wishes. This they could not have without advancing to
the second grade of territorial government; but as the
law establishing the Territory had fixed no minimum of
population for this advance, there was no reason why it
could not be made at once, if Governor Harrison were
willing. On April 11, 1801, John Edgar wrote to Governor St. Clair: "During a few weeks past we have
put into circulation petitions addressed to Governor
Harrison, for a General Assembly, and we have had the
satisfaction to find that about nine-tenths of the inhabitants of the counties of St. Clair and Randolph approve
of the measure, a great proportion of whom have already
put their signatures to the petition. I have written to
Judge Clark, of Clark County, to Mr. Buntin and Mr.
Small, of Post Vincennes, urging them to be active in
the business. I have no doubt but that the undertaking
will meet with early success so as to admit of the House
of Representatives meeting in the fall."[2]

It is possible that Mr. Edgar's confidence was based
on a belief that the governor was, like himself, a Fed-

[1] *Annals 6th Cong.*, p. 735. Most of the above particulars are
taken from the original on the Senate files.

[2] *St. Clair Papers*, vol. ii. p. 533.

eralist, for Mr. Harrison had made no parade of his
Republicanism since coming to Indiana.   He afterwards
declared that his appointment as governor by Mr.
Adams was not a favor from a political friend; that
"it was necessary to get me out of the way" in Ohio to
secure a Federal state there; and that he refused the
appointment until convinced by his friends that "there
was no doubt of Mr. Jefferson's election in the ensuing
November, and that I would be continued Governor of
Indiana, and some Republican would succeed Governor
St. Clair in the Northwest Territory."[1]   In the same
letter, however, he says: "I therefore accepted the appointment with a determination, as Indiana had no voice
in the choice of the President, that I would take no part
in the contest."   The closeness of his adherence to this
resolve produced in 1805 the charge: "No sooner was
Mr. Jefferson elected to the presidency than you began
to apprehend danger. . . . From the firmest Federalist
you wheeled about like the cock on a steeple, and declared yourself a Republican."[2]   On the other hand,
while Edgar may have counted on Harrison's Federalism, it is possible that he counted on the governor's not
daring to put himself in opposition to the known wishes
of the people, or even that he supposed the governor to
have no discretion in the matter, for the division act
provided that the second grade "shall be in force and
operate in the Indiana Territory, whenever satisfactory
evidence shall be given to the governor thereof that such
is the wish of a majority of the freeholders."

Whatever may have been their theories, Edgar, Morrison, and their friends secured and submitted the

[1] Harrison to Lyons, June 1, 1840.
[2] *Letters of Decius*, p. 25.

requisite petitions, and left the governor confronted by
a serious political problem. A Republican himself, and
anticipating a continued ascendency of his party in the
nation, he still knew that the people of Indiana were
mostly Federalists; and he had before him the task of
winning their favor and political friendship. If a legislature were established, the members would exercise an
influence which would weaken his own; would pass acts
for political purposes; would probably be enabled to
maintain their political ascendency in the Territory.
True, he would still have an absolute veto, but he knew
from St. Clair's experience that a resort to the veto
would speedily make him an object of popular odium.
His only safe course was to prevent the advance to the
second grade; but to do this without sacrificing his hopes
of popularity, he must satisfy the people that it was to
their interest to remain in the first grade. He accordingly prepared a "letter to a friend" which at once
found its way into print. Its effect is thus stated by one
of his bitterest enemies: "Previous to this famous letter
of the governor against the second grade of government,
the people, whether right or wrong, had generally petitioned the governor to adopt the measure. A declaration of his own opinion, accompanied with an exag-
gerated calculation of the expenses incident to this form
of government, alarmed the people, by a representation
of heavy taxes; and they immediately changed their
opinions, for no other reason than those stated by the
governor." [1]

This dangerous point being safely rounded, Harrison
proceeded judiciously to secure the good-will of the
people and the support of the influential men, by his

[1] *Letters of Decius*, p. 7.

appointments, by his efforts to secure various land
claimants their rights, and by his endeavors to promote
the sale and settlement of government lands. For the
last-named purpose a session of the Governor and Judges
was called in January, 1802, at which two laws were
passed, providing for county surveyors in each of the
counties and regulating their duties and fees. No other
laws were passed at this session, and there is nothing
noteworthy in these except a provision that slaves might
be levied on to secure surveyors' fees. On July 20,
1802, Harrison delighted the orderly element of Vincennes, and conferred a lasting benefit on the place, by
issuing a proclamation forbidding the sale or gift of
liquor to Indians within a mile of the town, and also
calling upon the citizens to aid in arresting and " to inform against all those who violate the Sabath by selling
or Bartering Spiritous Liquors or who pursue any other
unlawfull business on the day set apart for the service
of God." [1]

Meanwhile the pro-slavery sentiment had not abated.
In the fall of 1802 Harrison went to the Illinois country
to attend to official business, and while there the desirability of the admission of slavery was strongly urged
upon him. The Ordinance had provided no mode for
ascertaining the consent of the people to an alteration of
the articles of compact, but Governor Harrison expressed
his willingness to call a convention to consider the expediency of the admission of slavery into the Territory,
and other subjects mentioned in the memorial of 1801,
if petitioned so to do.[2]   Petitions were at once put in

---

[1] *Executive Journal,* July 20, 1802.

[2] *Letters of Decius,* p. 27. In many respects these letters are
unjust to Harrison, but as to the slavery question, from the view

circulation, but before many of them were sent in Harrison returned to Vincennes, where, on November 22, he issued his proclamation for the convention. It directed that elections should be held at the court-houses of the various counties on Tuesday, December 11, for delegates to a general convention; the sheriffs were to hold the elections, unless they were candidates, in which case the coroners were to serve; the apportionment of delegates was four to Knox County, three each to Randolph and St. Clair, and two to Clark.[1] Two days later a supplemental proclamation was issued directing the delegates elected to assemble at Vincennes on Monday, December 20.

The delegates to this convention ranked among the most intelligent and public-spirited men of the Territory. From Knox County were returned Governor Harrison and Colonel Francis Vigo, together with William Prince, a lawyer of considerable ability who was repeatedly elected to office by his fellow-citizens, and Luke Decker, a substantial farmer who came to the Wabash from Virginia early in the nineties, bringing his slaves with him.[2] The most diligent inquiry at every point where there

of the present day, they are not. Public sentiment in the Territory, when they were published, favored the admission of slavery, and the writer avoided giving Harrison credit for his efforts in that direction as far as possible.

[1] Clark County had been organized from the eastern part of Knox, on February 3, 1801. It included all of the Territory east of Blue River (the present dividing line between Harrison and Crawford counties) and south of the east fork of White River. On the same day Randolph and St. Clair counties were extended east to a line drawn north from the "Great Cave," *i. e.* Cave-in-rock. No other changes were made in the counties until 1803.

[2] The names of these delegates were obtained from the original poll-book.

seemed a possibility of obtaining information has failed
to reveal the names of the two delegates from Clark
County, though an old resident hazards the conjecture
that they were Davis Floyd and one of the Beggs
brothers, of whom mention will be made hereafter. The
only certainty as to these two delegates, whoever they
may have been, is that they opposed the introduction of
slavery.[1]   The Randolph County delegates were Pierre
Menard, Robert Reynolds, and Robert Morrison.[2]   Menard was the celebrated fur-trader who served as the
first lieutenant-governor of Illinois.   Reynolds was an
Irish Protestant of broad, strong mind; he was the
father of Governor Reynolds.   Robert Morrison, a
brother of William Morrison, was a Pennsylvanian who
was eminent in official and social life in the Illinois
country; his wife was a pioneer in Western literature,
distinguished by a versification of the Psalms, by numerous contributions to scientific and literary period-
icals, and by the composition of many of the petitions
and memorials that went to Washington from the Illinois country in territorial times.   From St. Clair County
the delegates were Jean François Perrey, Shadrach
Bond, and Major John Moredock.[3]   Perrey was a
Lyonnais, of noble lineage on his mother's side, the
son of a prominent French judge, and himself educated
in the civil law.   He was an *emigré* of 1792.   He did
not practice law in Illinois, but held judicial office, and
was noted for his learning, his honesty, and his benevolence.   Shadrach Bond, a nephew of the member of the
legislature of 1799 of the same name, was from Mary-

[1] Am. State Papers: *Misc.*, vol. i. p. 485.
[2] Reynolds's *Pion. Hist. of Ill.* pp. 133, 242, 249.
[3] *Ibid.*, pp. 117, 240, 271.

land. Reynolds quaintly says of him: "The whole creation should be a man's school-house, and nature his teacher. Bond studied in this college, and Providence gave him a diploma." In later years he represented Illinois in Congress, and was the first governor of the state. John Moredock was a bright, indolent, good-natured, uneducated young fellow, who inherited a large fortune, and was deeply skilled in all the accomplishments and vices of the frontier.

At the organization of the convention on December 20, 1802, Governor Harrison was made president, and John Rice Jones secretary. Jones was a prominent character in early times. He was a Welshman by birth, an accomplished lawyer, and noted for his energy and his powers of vindictive oratory. The delegates passed a week in consultation, and on December 28 they agreed on their memorial to Congress. This document, after reciting the authority by which the convention met, proceeds at once to the slavery question as follows: "The Sixth Article of Compact between the United States and the people of the Territory, which declares there shall be neither slavery nor involuntary servitude in it, has prevented the Country from populating, and been the Reason of driving many valuable Citizens possessing Slaves to the Spanish side of the Mississippi, most of whom but for the prohibition contained in the Ordinance would have settled in this Territory, and the consequences of keeping that prohibition in force will be that of obliging the numerous Class of Citizens disposed to emigrate, to seek an Asylum in that country where they can be permitted to enjoy their property. Your memorialists however and the people they represent do not wish for a repeal of the article entirely, but that it may be suspended for the Term of Ten Years and then to be again in force, but that the slaves brought into the Territory during the Continuance of this Suspension, and their progeny, may be considered and continued in the same state of Servitude, as if they had remained in those parts of the United States where Slavery is permitted and from whence they may have been removed." It will be observed that the project of gradual emancipation, proposed in the former petitions, is here dropped, and the slavery asked for is absolute and unending.

In addition to this request, the convention also asked for action by Congress as follows : The extinction of the Indian title to the southern portion of the Territory ; the right of preëmption to actual settlers on public lands ; special grants of lands for the support of "Schools and Seminaries of learning" for "the two settlements in the Illinois, the settlement of Vincennes, and that of Clark's Grant;" the granting of four hundred acres of land to persons who would "open good waggon roads and Establish houses of Entertainment thereon for Five Years," on the routes between the principal settlements ; the grant of the saline spring below the mouth of the Wabash to Indiana Territory ; permission to the ancient inhabitants of the Illinois to locate their donation grants outside of the surveys originally made for them ; an extension of the right of suffrage by dispensing with the qualification of a freehold of fifty acres ; and the payment of a salary to the Attorney-General of the Territory. The memorial concluded with an expression of hope that, although their requests were numerous, "their neglected and orphan-like Situation" might cause them to receive consideration.[1]

[1] These particulars are taken from the original, on the House files.

This petition was sent to Washington by a special agent appointed by the convention, and this agent also carried two other papers which are worthy of mention. The first was a letter of Governor Harrison enclosing the formal resolution of consent to the suspension of the sixth article, which had been adopted by the convention on December 25. The governor's letter is purely formal. The resolution consents to the suspension of the sixth article "for the space of ten years from the day that a law may be passed by Congress for suspending the said article : Provided, however, that should no law be passed by Congress for suspending the said article before the 4th day of March, 1805, then the consent of the people of this Territory, hereby given, shall be void and of no effect." [1] The second document was a recommendation to the President, by the convention, that Governor Harrison be reappointed to his then office, — an indorsement which was occasionally alluded to in the political controversies of the Territory as having been obtained by the undue influence of Harrison over the convention.[2] The convention also recommended John Rice Jones for appointment as chief justice of the territorial court, from which, together with the recommendation of a salary for the Attorney-General, — the office then held by Jones, — it is apparent that he had no little influence with the convention. He was at this time a firm personal and political friend of Governor Harrison, but a few years later became one of his bitterest enemies.

[1] Governor Harrison's letter is not on the files. The only printed copy in existence, so far as has been discovered, is in the collection of the *Executive Documents 7th Cong. 2d Sess.*, in the Boston Public Library.

[2] *Letters of Decius*, pp. 8, 28. The governor's term was three years, and expired in 1803.

The letter, resolution, and petition were laid before the House of Representatives on February 8, 1803, and referred to a committee composed of John Randolph of Virginia, Mr. Griswold of Connecticut, Robert Williams of North Carolina, Lewis R. Morris of Vermont, and Mr. Hoge of Pennsylvania. On March 2 the committee reported adversely on all the requests excepting the grant of the right of preëmption to actual settlers and the payment of a salary to the Attorney-General. The portion of the report which refers to slavery appears to have been designed, by the great commoner of Roanoke who presented it, not only to influence the House, but also to appeal to the sober judgment of the people of Indiana. It is in these words : "The rapidly increasing population of the State of Ohio sufficiently evinces, in the opinion of your committee, that the labor of slaves is not necessary to promote the growth and settlement of colonies in that region ; that this labor, demonstrably the dearest of any, can only be employed to advantage in the cultivation of products more valuable than any known to that quarter of the United States ; that the committee deem it highly dangerous and inexpedient to impair a provision wisely calculated to promote the happiness and prosperity of the Northwestern country, and to give strength and security to that extensive frontier. In the salutary operation of this sagacious and benevolent restraint, it is believed that the inhabitants of Indiana will, at no very distant day, find ample remuneration for a temporary privation of labor and emigration." [1] This report was referred to a committee of the whole for the next day, but the next day was the last day of the session, and nothing more was heard of the petition

[1] Am. State Papers : *Pub. Lands*, vol. i. p. 146.

for the time. At the beginning of the next session, however, on December 15, 1803, the petition and the report
of Mr. Randolph's committee were recommitted to a new
committee, composed of Mr. Rodney of Delaware, Mr.
Boyle of Kentucky, and Mr. Rhea of Tennessee. On
February 17, 1804, this committee reported favorably
to a suspension of the sixth article of compact for ten
years, permitting the introduction of slaves "born within
the United States, from any of the individual states:
Provided, That such individual state does not permit
the introduction of slaves from foreign countries: *And
prov'ded further*, That the descendants of all such slaves
shall, if males, be free at the age of twenty-five years,
and, if females, at the age of twenty-one years." In other
respects the report was as the former one, except that it
recommended the repeal of the freehold qualification for
electors.[1] This report was referred to a committee of
the whole for the following Monday, but it was not then
called up. There was action on the petition subsequently, but not until after the period of consent fixed
by the Vincennes convention; it was in connection with
other matters to be considered hereafter.

Governor Harrison's connection with this convention
had much influence over his future political career, and
usually a favorable influence. Temporarily, it gained
him the confidence and approval of a large majority of
the people of the Territory. In the campaign of 1840
the Whigs paraded Harrison's connection with the convention as conclusive evidence of his friendship to the
slaveholders; the Democrats made as little mention of
it as possible, one of their chief arguments against him
being that he was in sympathy with the abolition move-

---

[1] Am. State Papers: *Misc.*, vol. i. p. 387.

ment; the Abolitionists were divided. One faction, which had its chief strength in New York, found the record of General Harrison on the slavery question quite as unsatisfactory as that of Mr. Van Buren, and denounced both nominations as surrenders to the slave power. In January, 1840, the New York Anti-Slavery Society resolved to issue a call for a national convention to consider the nomination of a presidential candidate, to be held at Albany on April 1. This was a new departure, and was opposed by the great majority of Abolitionists, who did not wish to "drag the question into politics." The national executive committee took no action on the subject, but "The Emancipator," their organ, advocated holding the convention. The state societies of Rhode Island, Connecticut, and Massachusetts unanimously condemned the movement, and that of the last-named state issued an address sharply criticising all parties concerned in it, and begging Abolitionists, "for the honor and purity of our enterprise," to frown upon it. The convention met, but only six states were represented, and of the 121 delegates 104 were from New York. The "Liberty Party" was organized, and James G. Birney and Thomas Earle were nominated for President and Vice-President.[1] The nominees declined, but they received 7,059 votes out of about two and one half millions that were cast.

It is unquestionable that Harrison believed in the theory of a constitutional right of the Southern people to carry slavery into the territories, not only from his action in Indiana and from repeated public declarations, but

[1] Birney and Francis J. Lemoyne had been named for the same offices by a convention of the society of Western New York, at Warsaw, in the preceding November.

also from his votes, in February, 1819, against the prohibition, restriction, and gradual abolition of slavery in
Missouri and Arkansas.[1] His Ohio constituents did not
approve of these votes, and defeated him at the congressional election of 1822, " on account of his adherence to that principle of the Constitution which secures
to the people of the South their preëxisting rights." [2]
In that campaign, to the charge of being a pro-slavery
man he replied : " I am accused of being friendly to
slavery. From my earliest youth to the present moment I have been the ardent friend of human liberty.
At the age of eighteen I became a member of an Abolition Society established at Richmond, Virginia ; the
object of which was to ameliorate the condition of slaves
and procure their freedom by every legal means. My
venerable friend Judge Gatch, of Clermont County, was
also a member of this society, and has lately given me a
certificate that I was one. The obligations which I then
came under I have faithfully performed. I have been
the means of liberating many slaves, but never placed
one in bondage."

In the campaign of 1840 a very different state of
affairs existed, there being far more danger politically
from the charge of abolitionism, then preferred against
him, than from any pro-slavery taint ; and his campaign
biographers succeeded in breaking completely the force
of his broad statement of eighteen years earlier. One
of them followed a quotation of it, as above given, with
these words : " It is proper to remark that this society,
established by the Quakers, but not confined to them,

---

[1] *Annals 15th Cong. 2d Sess.*, vol. i. pp. 1214, 1215 ; vol. ii. pp.
1237, 1238.

[2] *Natl. Intelligencer*, October 20, 1822.

was, according to the statement of Judge Gatch, a
'Humane Society;' and it seems to have been of a character to which no exceptions were taken in Virginia.
A number of the citizens of Richmond were members,
and its principles were not understood to be at all in
conflict with the rights guarantied to the owners of
slaves by the Constitution and the laws of the land.
Within a few months after his first connection with this
society, General Harrison, then but eighteen years of
age, removed from Virginia, since which time he has
never attended one of its meetings, nor been either
directly or indirectly connected with any society touching the question of slavery." [1]   Thus was punctured the
bubble of his performance of the " obligations " imposed
upon him as a member of this abolition society; and
the remainder of his statement is chiefly oratorical froth.
For example, from the condition of negroes in the
United States, it is not evident how he could have
" placed one in bondage " if he had desired to, unless he
had engaged in kidnaping free negroes.   It is presum-
able that he did not here refer to slavery by indenture,
for he had placed negroes in bondage by that method.
That he was "the means of liberating many slaves "
may possibly have been true, but I have failed to discover the evidences of it; though in one case, shortly
after the Vincennes convention, he did interfere in behalf of negroes.

The circumstances were these: In the spring of 1804,
Simon Vannorsdell, acting as agent for the heirs of John
and Elizabeth Kuykendall, arrested two negroes named
George and Peggy, at Vincennes, and was about to
carry them out of the Territory.   Harrison issued a

[1] *Tippecanoe Text Book*, pp. 69, 70.

proclamation forbidding this, based on information that
Vannorsdell was " about to transport from the Territory
certain indented servants, without their consent first
had and obtained, with a design as is supposed of selling them for slaves." [1] Vannorsdell was indicted, and
habeas corpus proceedings were instituted to free the
negroes.   At the September term of court, Vannorsdell
was discharged, no one appearing to prosecute him; but
the court released the negroes from his custody.   Vannorsdell, assisted by John Huling, at once rearrested the
negroes, but a new *habeas corpus* proceeding was instituted for their release.   This was continued to the next
term, Harrison, General W. Johnston, and John Johnson
becoming bail for the negroes.[2] At the June term,
1805, the negroes were produced, but pending the proceedings George had indented himself to Harrison for a
term of eleven years, and the case as to him was dropped.
Peggy was released by the court in April, 1806, as has
been mentioned,[3] and afterwards sued Vannorsdell for
wages during her detention, but the trial resulted in a
finding for the defendant.[4]

Harrison's enemies attacked him for his " officious
and interested interference " in this case with the following ingenious dilemma : " In this case the governor has
done an enormous injury either to the poor unhappy
negroes or to the heirs of John and Elizabeth Kuykendall.   And the truth of this assertion rests on this simple
argument: The negroes were free, or they were not
free; if they were free, what greater injury could the

---

[1] *Executive Journal*, April 6, 1804.
[2] Ter. Court Docket, September Term, 1804.
[3] *Ante*, ch. vi.
[4] Ter. Court Docket. September Term, 1808, p. 337.

governor do a man than to deprive him of his liberty
for eleven years ? — And in what terms should the
character of such an executive be spoken of ? — If the
negroes were not free, why should the governor by an
illicit interference prevent the heirs from a free disposition of their property ? — The case is so plain against
the governor that it does not require a comment." [1]
Neither conclusion is just, because circumstances existed
which modified the premises stated.   That Vannorsdell
had no right to remove the two negroes is assured by the
two decisions, and by the fact that he was indicted for
kidnaping another negro in 1806.[2]   On the other hand,
it is very certain that the negroes would have been
carried South and sold if some one had not interfered in
their behalf.   It was perhaps light consolation to George
that he came out of the difficulty a slave for eleven
years while Peggy went free, and yet it is probable that
Harrison did as much in behalf of these two unfortu-
nates as any one then in the western part of the Territory would have done, even though he did not make the
record as a philanthropist that he might have made.   At
least, he and his friends did something, while his political
enemies, who were so shocked at his doings, failed to extend a helping hand to the negro over whose fate they
lamented on paper for political purposes.

The action of Congress on the petition of the Vincennes convention created great dissatisfaction in the
Territory outside of Clark County, and set the people
to thinking of other methods of escaping the obnoxious
provision of the Ordinance.   Two noteworthy results
followed.   The first was " A Law Concerning Ser-

---

[1] *Letters of Decius*, p. 39.
[2] Ter. Court Docket, September Term, 1806, pp. 246, 248.

vants," which was passed at the next session of the
Governor and Judges. It provided that a person coming into the Territory "under contract to serve another
in any trade or occupation shall be compelled to perform such contract specifically during the term thereof."
The contract of service was assignable to any citizen of
the Territory, if the servant consented. The provisions
for maintaining the respective rights of master and servant were as just as such things can reasonably be made,
with perhaps the exception of a provision that any one
who bartered with a servant for " any coin or commodity
whatsoever," without permission from the owner, was
subject to receive thirty-nine lashes at the public whip-
ping-post. This act applied to " negroes and mulattoes
and other persons not being citizens of the United
States." The only distinction made between white servants and others was a provision that " No negro,
mulatto or Indian shall at any time purchase any servant, other than of their complexion ; and if any of the
persons aforesaid shall nevertheless presume to purchase
a white servant, such servant shall immediately become
free." [1]

The obvious intention of this law was to produce a
legal relation of master and slave which had formerly
existed in England under the common law, and which
is thus stated by Blackstone : " A slave or negro, the
instant he lands in England, becomes a freeman ; that
is, the law will protect him in the enjoyment of his person and his property. Yet, with regard to any right
which the master may have lawfully acquired to the per-

---

[1] *Laws, 3d Sess. Governor and Judges,* p. 26. The law is dated
September 22, 1803, and was passed by Harrison, Vanderburgh,
and Davis.

petual service of John or Thomas, this will remain exactly in the same state as before; for this is no more than the same state of subjection for life, which every apprentice submits to for the space of seven years, or sometimes for a longer term." [1]   As to its objectionable feature of "selling white men," this law did not differ from the " Act concerning Servants " adopted in 1807. In subsequent political controversies, however, the earlier law was overlooked, probably because the printed copies of those laws were very rare, and yet it was the more formidable of the two as an argument against Harrison. In the other case he merely approved a law passed by the legislature, and justified himself on the ground that he never would obstruct the wishes of the people, as expressed by the lawmaking power, by interposing the veto. [2]   In this case he was one third of the legislative power as well as sole executive.

The second manifestation of the desire of the people to escape from the Ordinance was a petition from the Illinois counties to be added to the Territory of Louisiana, as soon as it should be organized.   The controversy over the navigation of the Mississippi had been complicated by the secret retrocession of Louisiana to France by Spain in 1800, and our diplomats had since been vainly endeavoring to purchase the eastern bank to its mouth, from the new owner.   In the spring of 1803 they made an unexpected settlement of the matter by entering into an unauthorized treaty for the purchase of all Louisiana.   Information of this reached Indiana in the

[1] *Commentaries*, book i. p. 424.   Of course this could not be considered English law after Lord Mansfield's decision of the Sommersett case in 1772.   Loft's *Rep.* p. 1 ; 11 *St. Tr.* p. 340.

[2] *Nat'l Intelligencer*, September 29, 1840.

summer of the same year, and it was assumed that the
treaty would certainly be ratified by Congress at the
special session in October, which had been called by
President Jefferson, although grave doubts existed as to
the constitutionality of the purchase. The Edgar and
Morrison party at once put petitions in circulation, and
had little trouble in obtaining signers, for annexation to
Louisiana appeared to offer relief from all the vexations
of which the Illinois people had been complaining.
Slavery and speedy population would be theirs. By this
move, also, the Edgar and Morrison party would get rid
of Harrison, under whose administration they were getting a very small share of the offices. In fact the Harrison party charged that this was their only motive, and
claimed that they had formed a plan for Edgar to be
governor, and Robert Morrison secretary, of the new
territory.[1]

The petition was presented to Congress, considered in
committee, and reported upon ;[2] but Congress adopted
other plans. So much of the new purchase as lay south
of 33° north latitude (the southern line of Arkansas)
was organized as the Territory of Orleans ; the northern
part was named the District of Louisiana. For purposes
of government the latter was joined to Indiana Territory, but it was not made a part of Indiana ; nor was
it made a dependency of Indiana ; nor was the Ordinance made its fundamental law. The provision was
that the governor, judges, and secretary of Indiana
should perform the duties of their respective offices for

[1] Woollen's *Biog. and Hist. Sketches of Early Ind.*, p. 5.
[2] *Annals 8th Cong. 1st Sess.*, pp. 489, 555, 623. There were
several other schemes before Congress and numerous candidates
for the offices. *Edwards Papers*, p. 30.

Louisiana also.[1]   Indiana Territory and the District of
Louisiana, therefore, were two distinct and independent
governments, but with the same officers.   In this way,
at least, the law was construed and carried into operation.
The Governor and Judges assembled in the fall, and on
October 1 passed six laws for the District of Louisiana ;
but, although they were passed at Vincennes, these laws
did not affect Indiana ; nor was any law of Indiana, in
form, extended over Louisiana.   The law that received
most attention at this legislative meeting was a long and
minutely detailed code for the regulation of slavery.   Its
provisions were fairly humane, and it was so satisfactory
that it remained unmodified for years ; indeed, many of
its provisions were in force so long as slavery existed in
Missouri.[2]

The extent of the District of Louisiana was enormous,
but its civilized population did not exceed 10,000, and
these were nearly all within thirty miles of St. Louis.
The increase of official labor was found very burdensome, especially by the judges and the secretary ;[3] and
the people of Louisiana were in a furor of indignation
over the form of government provided for them.   They
held a convention at St. Louis in September, 1804, and
remonstrated vigorously ; their principal grounds being
the inconvenience of having their officials so distant from
them, and a fear that Congress had joined them to a
territory in which the Ordinance was in effect as a pre-

[1] *Annals 8th Cong. 1st Sess.*, p. 1293.   The act was approved
March 26, 1804.

[2] For these laws see Rev. Laws of La. Terr. 1808.   The existing laws of the District were retained in force by the act of Congress " until altered, modified, or repealed by the Governor and
Judges of Indiana Territory."

[3] *Annals 1st Sess 8th Cong.*, p. 453.

liminary to the abolition of slavery.[1] Their objections
were heard, and on March 4, 1805, the District of
Louisiana was erected into a separate territory, with the
Mississippi for its eastern boundary.[2]

During the year of Louisiana's government by Indiana
officials, Indiana Territory advanced to the second grade ;
and the manner in which this change was made formed
a fruitful theme for political controversy in the Territory. The condition of Indiana was not what it had
been when the advance to the second grade was asked
in 1801. When Ohio became a state, a large amount
of territory had been added to Indiana, and from this
two new counties had been organized. On January 24,
1803, Wayne County was created of the lands east of a
north and south line through the western extreme of
Lake Michigan, and north of an east and west line
through the southern extreme of the same. On the same
day the lands east of the Greenville treaty line were
added to Clark County, and so remained until March of
the same year, when they were made an independent
county under the name of Dearborn. A vast addition
to the lands available for settlement had been made by
treaties with the Indians. By the first of these, on June
7, 1803, there was no real acquisition of territory, but the
bounds of the ancient " Vincennes tract " were definitely
fixed, so that its survey and sale might be completed.
On August 13, 1803, the Kaskaskias had surrendered all
of Illinois south of the Kaskaskia River except two small
reservations. On August 18, 1804, the Delawares had
ceded all of southwestern Indiana, below the Vincennes
tract and the old road from Clarksville to Vincennes,

[1] Am. State Papers : *Misc.*, vol. i. p. 400.
[2] *Annals 8th Cong. 2d Sess.*, p. 1684.

and on the 27th of the same month the cession was ratified by the Piankeshaws, the only tribe recognized as
holding a conflicting title. In March, 1804, Congress
had passed a law for the survey and sale of the two
cessions first mentioned, and to establish land offices at
Kaskaskia and Vincennes.

There had been some increase of population by immigration, and there was every prospect of a more rapid
increase ; and yet the population was still so scanty that
an advance to the second grade would be a burdensome
expense to the people. It would have been much more
so if the expense had been as great as Harrison had
pictured it three years earlier. Besides this, the people
of Wayne County were clamoring for separation from
Indiana Territory ; and they had come near securing it
at the last Congress. In brief, the change of position
since 1801 was so slight, and the inconsistency of a
change of opinion on the subject so manifest, that Harrison did not advocate the measure openly, though he
voted for it and his friends worked for it; and the opposition took the ground that there had been no material
increase of population in the Territory.[1] It is not credible that the change of population was the cause of the
desire for the advance, though it was the principal assigned reason. The key to the movement will be found
in some additional reasons afterwards given by one of
its most active advocates, as follows : " That the people
[on entering the second grade] would be entitled to a
partial representative government; that they would have
absolute control over one branch of the legislature ;
that it would give them a representative in Congress,
and although he would not be entitled to vote, yet from

[1] *Letters of Decius*, p. 7.

his situation he would acquire respect and attention, and would give a faithful representation of our situation; and that some sacrifices ought to be made to obtain even the partial exercise of the rights considered so dear and of such universal importance to the several states." [1]

On their face these reasons would appear to have been as cogent in 1801 as in 1804, but there were changed circumstances in 1804 which gave them a much greater weight politically. The great desire of a majority of the people was to obtain an authorization of the introduction of slavery, but during four years of the first grade their efforts to secure it had been fruitless. Three times their prayers had been presented to Congress, and three times Congress had turned a deaf ear to them. If they had a representative in the body, one who would make it his business to urge their needs and desires, a more respectful attention might be hoped. The legislative authorities of the Territory had done all they could to legalize the introduction of slavery by indenture, but the result was not satisfactory. The Vannorsdell cases had called the attention of legal men to the nature of the statutory provisions, and their inadequacy to the end in view was very manifest. The courts might rightfully be given authority to enforce contracts made outside the Territory if valid where made, but no authority could be given to enforce a contract that was void where made. Slavery was clearly duress; a contract made under duress was null at common law; the common law obtained in all the nation except the newly acquired French territory. The Governor and Judges could not remedy the defect because there was no law of any of the original states that would better the situa-

[1] Woollen's *Sketches*, p. 6.

tion; but a legislature would not thus be restricted in the adoption of measures, and could probably devise some satisfactory remedy.

It was plain that the road to slavery led through the second grade; and for political reasons, independent of personal inclinations, the Harrison party were desirous of securing the introduction of slavery. The prospects of a rapid increase of population warned them that the second grade must soon be reached; and a political party must be in the good graces of the people when it was reached, if it were to remain in existence. A majority of the people in the Territory desired the introduction of slavery, but that majority was constantly dwindling away, because the immigration was restricted to non-slaveholders, who were almost unanimously opposed to the introduction of slavery; and unless some means of inducing an immigration of pro-slavery men were found, there was almost a certainty of an anti-slavery majority at no distant time. This would mean a suspension of power, if not a lasting quietus, to the Harrison party, for they were already firmly committed to the pro-slavery movement. They were obliged to fight through on the position they had taken; and, as Harrison could not consistently refute his own arguments, the leadership devolved on Benjamin Parke, a young gentleman from New Jersey who had been practicing law in Vincennes since 1801, and whose talents, learning, and elevated moral character had given him high standing in the Territory. Other prominent men of Knox County, who favored the advance, were Colonel Vigo, John Rice Jones, Henry Hurst (clerk of the territorial court), John Johnson, and General W. Johnston.[1]

[1] Woollen's *Sketches*, p. 7.

Inconsistent as was Harrison's position, his enemies were in a worse one. Edgar and Morrison, who had championed the advance to the second grade in 1801, were now violently opposed to it, and for no conceivable reason except that their political foes favored it. In 1801 they claimed that the increase of taxation would be small, and of slight importance as compared with the great benefits to be derived from the change. In 1804, notwithstanding the increase of population and taxable property, and the bright prospect of rapid settlement in the newly purchased lands, they could see nothing but ruin for the people from the impending increase of taxation. For months they had been bemoaning the great extent of the governor's official power, and denouncing him for a tyrannical exercise of it; yet now they could see only danger to the liberties of the people from a measure which largely diminished that power. Their cause was weak, and even in Randolph County they met with active opposition under the leadership of Pierre Menard and Dr. George Fisher — the sheriff of the county. In Knox County the principal opposition to the advance came from Henry Vanderburgh and William McIntosh. McIntosh was a Scotchman who had lived in Vincennes since the Revolutionary war. He had formerly been very friendly with Harrison, having received from him in February, 1801, appointments of Major of Militia and Treasurer of the Territory, but had recently fallen out with his patron. His opposition to the measure resulted in a bitter newspaper controversy, and that in a challenge from Parke, which was not accepted.

On August 4, 1804, proclamation was made directing an election to be held in the several counties on September 11, to ascertain the will of the people as to the second grade. This left a very brief time for consideration of the question; in fact the proclamation was not received in Wayne County in time to admit of holding an election.[1] The vote shows conclusively that the election was not fully advertised, for the number of votes in the various counties varied inversely with their distance from Vincennes. In the entire Territory only 400 votes were cast, and of these 175 were in Knox County. In Dearborn only 26 votes were cast, and they were all against the advance. In Clark 48 votes were cast, and a majority of 22 favored the advance. In Randolph there were 61 votes, with a majority of 19 for the advance. In St. Clair there were 81 votes, and a majority of 37 against the advance. In Knox County the majority for advance was 151, but the majorities in the other counties cut this down to a total of 138 majority in the whole Territory. That this election was legal, as the Harrison party afterwards maintained, is doubtless true; but that it furnished any "satisfactory evidence" to the governor of "the wish of a majority of the freeholders" is credible only on the theory that the governor was disposed to be easily satisfied. On December 5, 1804, he issued a proclamation announcing the result of the election, and declaring that "Indiana Territory is and from henceforth shall be deemed to have passed into the second or representative grade of Government, and that the Good people of the Territory, from the date thereof, are entitled to the rights and priviledges belonging to that situation."

[1] *Executive Journal*, December 5, 1804.

CHAPTER IX.

THE proclamation declaring the advance to the second grade called for an election, on January 3, 1805, of nine representatives, the maximum allowed by the division act. The apportionment was three for Wayne County, two for Knox, and one each for Dearborn, Clark, Randolph, and St. Clair. The members-elect convened at Vincennes on February 1, and on proceeding to consider the qualifications of members of their house, declared the election in St. Clair County null and void because the polling had been forcibly stopped by a mob of opponents to the second grade.[1] The only additional business of the House was to make the nominations for the Council, which were as follows: John Rice Jones and Jacob Kuykendall of Knox, Samuel Gwathmey and Marston G. Clark of Clark, Benjamin Chambers of Dearborn, John Hay and Jean François Perrey of St. Clair, Pierre Menard of Randolph, James May and James Henry of Wayne.[2] On receiving these names, President Jefferson returned them to Governor Harrison, and delegated to him the right of selection,[3] but

[1] *Laws 2d Sess. 2d Gen. Ass.*, p. 13.

[2] Congress had detached Michigan (Wayne County) from Indiana Territory by act of January 11, but information of the change had not yet reached Vincennes.

[3] Dawson's *Harrison*, p. 71.

this was not made public until long afterwards. As those rejected could hardly have failed to consider the selection a personal slight, the appointments were announced as being made by the President.[1]   Wayne County having been detached, the governor appointed one councilor from each of the five counties remaining, as follows : Benjamin Chambers of Dearborn, Samuel Gwathmey of Clark, John Rice Jones of Knox, Pierre Menard of Randolph, and John Hay of St. Clair.

Of these men, Menard and Jones are already known to the reader. Benjamin Chambers was a Pennsylvanian, a son of the Revolutionary general, and was one of the first surveyors of southeastern Indiana.   He became proprietor of Lawrenceburgh after the failure of Vance, the original owner.   In 1803 Harrison had appointed him a judge of the Common Pleas, and lieutenant-colonel of the Dearborn militia.   Samuel Gwathmey was a Virginian whom Harrison had appointed clerk of the courts of Clark County in 1801, and treasurer of the county in the following year.   He was also one of the first trustees of the town of Jeffersonville.   He held slaves in the territorial period.[2]   John Hay, a son of Governor Hay of Canada, received a collegiate education at Three Rivers, but entered the fur-trade on the death of his father in 1785.   In 1793 he settled at Cahokia, where he was universally loved for his most estimable qualities, and where he was kept continuously in offices of trust by St. Clair, Harrison, and the authorities of the general government.   He was a personal as well as political friend of Harrison, and headed the cavalcade of Illinois people who escorted the governor to St. Louis

[1] *Liberty Hall and Cincinnati Mercury*, July 2, 1805.
[2] *Western Sun*, April 30, 1814.

in 1804, when he took possession of Upper Louisiana for the United States.

The detachment of Michigan left the House with only five members, but, there being a vacancy for St. Clair County, the governor, on April 18, 1805, directed a special election to be held in that county on May 20 for two representatives, thus increasing the membership of the House to the minimum under the division act. The legislature convened on July 29, in response to a call of June 7. The representatives were Jesse B. Thomas of Dearborn, Davis Floyd of Clark, Benjamin Parke and John Johnson of Knox, Shadrach Bond and William Biggs of St. Clair, and Dr. George Fisher of Randolph. Of these we have met Parke, Bond, and Fisher. Jesse B. Thomas was a native of Maryland, who came to Kentucky in 1799, and, after reading law with his brother, settled at Lawrenceburgh in 1803. He soon drifted into politics, and never drifted out. He was regarded as "tricky" by his contemporaries, and owed much of his political success to practicing upon his favorite maxim, "You cannot talk a man down, but you can whisper him to death." Davis Floyd was a Virginian who had served under George Rogers Clark. He settled in Clark's Grant, where he kept a tavern and operated a ferry across the Ohio. He was appointed recorder of Clark County in 1801, and sheriff in 1802, by Harrison. His political career was tempararily suspended a little later by a conviction of implication in Aaron Burr's conspiracy, for which, however, he received a sentence of three hours' imprisonment only.[1] John Johnson also was a Virginian. He

[1] *Western Sun*, November 25 to December 16, 1807. This episode constituted the chief effect of Burr's project in Indiana,

settled at Vincennes at the organization of Indiana
Territory, and soon took rank as one of the ablest lawyers in the Territory, although he was not a fluent
speaker. He took an active part in local politics, always
as a consistent pro-slavery man. William Biggs, a
Marylander, was a noted character in St. Clair County.
He served under Clark in the famous Illinois campaign,
and located among the French settlers soon afterwards.
In 1788 he was captured by a party of Kickapoos and
carried to the Wabash towns, whence he was soon ran-
somed by Bazadone, the Spanish merchant whose goods
had been impressed by Clark two years earlier.

As soon as the composition of the legislature was
known, it was announced that Benjamin Parke would be
a candidate for representative in Congress. The "Letters of Decius" then began to appear in opposition to
him, urging that he was a tool of Harrison, who wanted
him in Washington to secure his reappointment as governor in the following year. They dwelt at length on
the extensive powers of the executive, his facilities for
influencing the legislature, and the injurious effects of
such influence on the interests of the people. Their
intense bitterness, the skill with which they are composed, and their subsequent appearance in pamphlet
form, point to William McIntosh as their author, for he
had both wealth and talent, and was unflagging in his
hatred of the governor. They recommended Judge
Thomas T. Davis as the best man for the office. They
must have had some effect, for Parke received but three
majority;[1] and yet it is evident that Davis did not

---

and it was not lasting, for Floyd soon regained his standing and
afterwards became one of the leading men of the state.

[1] *Liberty Hall*, September 17, 1805.

actively oppose Parke and the governor, for on March 1
following he was appointed Chancellor of the Territory
in place of John Badollet, resigned. To the effect produced by these letters may also be attributed the friendly
warning against the use of the veto power which appears
in the reply of the assembly to Harrison's message at
this session.[1] As to Benjamin Parke, it will be conceded without hesitation that the " Letters of Decius "
fell short of their mark most deservedly, for he was one
of the purest and most useful men that ever entered
public life in Indiana. His pro-slavery views are the
only known taint on his character, and this may be considered blotted out by years of honest, faithful service in
Congress and on the bench, by bravery which won him
promotion at Tippecanoe, by constant friendship to
public education, by labors for the success of the Vincennes Library and Vincennes University, by founding
the State Law Library (now Library of the Supreme
Court), and by organizing the Indiana Historical Society,
of which he was the first president. We may with reason be thankful that his public career was not checked
at the outset by Decius, for we have had no such men
to spare.

The next business of the legislature that is of present
interest was a provision for the introduction of slavery
by indenture, for which purpose " An Act concerning
the introduction of Negroes and Mulattoes into this
Territory " was passed. It provided that any slaveholder of any of the states or territories of the Union
might bring a slave over fifteen years of age into Indiana ; and within thirty days might enter into an agreement

[1] Ind. Hist. Soc. Pamph. No. 1, p. 22; Dawson's *Harrison*, p.
71.

with such slave, before the clerk of a court of common pleas, as to the number of years such slave would serve his then owner. If the slave would make no agreement, the master might within sixty days thereafter remove him from the Territory. The clerk was required to make a record of the agreement; and no indentured servant could be removed from the Territory except on his own consent given before a judge of the common pleas. Slaves under fifteen years might be brought in and held, the males until thirty-five years of age and the females until thirty-two, without any formalities excepting a registry of the name and age of the negro with the clerk. The children born of slaves under indenture were to serve the master of the mother, males until thirty years of age and females until twenty-eight. Masters were required to give bond in $500 that the slave should not become a public charge if he became free at the age of forty years or upwards. The act did not apply to white apprentices, but certain provisions of an act passed at the same session concerning white apprentices were made applicable to indented slaves, by which provisions, in case of ill usage, an apprentice (and by the latter act a slave) might make complaint before a justice of the peace, and the justice might cancel his indenture.[1]

This act at the time was satisfactory to a majority of the people of Indiana, but it was "much to the dissatisfaction of the minority;"[2] and this minority was one that grew daily in numbers and in determination to abolish the system of slavery thus thrust upon them. Outside of the Territory, the reception of the law was

[1] *Acts 1st Sess. 1st Ass.*, pp. 5–25.
[2] Espy's *Tour in the Ohio*, p. 23.

not flattering to the legislature which adopted it. The " Liberty Hall " of Cincinnati published an abstract of the law, surrounded by those heavy turned rules through which editors are accustomed to mourn, and introduced by these words : " If it were possible, with tears of blood we are constrained to publish the following sketch of the law of the Indiana Territory respecting Negroes." [1] When a man's grief makes him so incoherent as that, we must at least give him credit for sincerity. The " National Intelligencer " emerged from the non-opinionative editorial style of those days, and roundly denounced the law and its makers. It declared that it was a violation of the Ordinance and a menace to the entire Union ; that other territories might do the same thing if Indiana were sustained in this action ; that the slave trade would be stimulated to an activity during the remaining months of its protected existence that was not anticipated by the framers of the Constitution ; that the Governor and Council ought to be removed if they supported the law ; and that Congress ought to refuse every application of Indiana to become a state until she retraced her steps.

This editorial was reprinted in the Cincinnati paper,[2] and attracted general attention. An ingenious Indianian, who wrote over the name " Eumenes," replied in defense of the law. He maintained that it was an advantage to Indiana, because its effect would be to open and clear 700,000 acres of rich land. It was an advantage to the South, for it would relieve the over-crowded plantations of surplus negroes. It was no less than a blessing to the slaves, for they would be removed from

---

[1] *Liberty Hall*, September 17, 1805.
[2] *Ibid.*, March 31, 1806.

the Southern States, " where they are driven in famished
droves — where farms are overstocked with them —
where they are hired out for want of employ to every
mercenary wretch, whose only study is how he may
strain the most labor with the least sustenance — where
they are fed on cotton seeds, stinking fish, and the very
off-scouring of the soil — where they are lashed, slashed,
fettered, and trodden down — where the least glimmering of hope never comes, but slavery without end. From
this soul-sinking situation, worse than non-existence, they
are brought into the Indiana Territory, where they are
bound to serve for seven years [1] to an industrious farmer,
who works in the same field with them : here they are
decently clad and well fed with good, wholesome food :
here they may learn industry, frugality, and in short
how to gain a comfortable living ; cheered and delighted
with the sure and certain prospect of future freedom to
themselves and their children." [2]

Eumenes could hardly have been less judicious in his
selection of arguments. In response to him, " Benevo-
lensus," of Hamilton County, Ohio, quoted the words
just given, and followed them thus : " Good God, what a
wretched, but yet what a just picture of human misery,
the review of which makes the blood thrill in my veins :
yet these are the tyrants who are to grace and populate
the Indiana Territory ; for, according to Eumenes,
those are the slaves to be brought thither to have their
condition ameliorated !   Will this writer prove that the

---

[1] This error apparently arose from a supposition that the law
provided for an apprenticeship similar to that existing for white
children, which was not the case.   There was no limit to the
time of service either in the law or the practice under it.

[2] *Liberty Hall*, June 2, 1806.

tyrant will lose his mercenary and vicious disposition
when he enters the Territory? Or will it be possible
that the crossing, or even all the waters of the Ohio will
regenerate him? . . . How much happier their condition will be when they have the honor of working in the
same field with their masters!! I suppose the master
will not exact less labor when the extent of their services
is circumscribed than if they were to serve him during
life. From such kind of compassion Good Lord deliver
us. . . . I have been making some enquiries respecting
the growing population of Indiana Territory, but cannot
find any comparison in the numbers to those who come
to this state. — The bait has not taken. — The cunning
slave-holder feels too flimsy a security to bring his horde
to a country where the term of holding them is so precarious. — And those who are opposed to that hellish
traffic are afraid to risk themselves in a country where
there is a prospect of its introduction." [1]

Our Indiana champion did not escape with this drub-
bing. In the same issue came "Corpus Collosom," of
Clermont County, with these arguments: "I cannot see
how the master's working with the slave will lessen his
misfortunes, or mitigate his toil ; as the master that has
seven years interest in the slave will feel the same operate on him that a master in the South who has hired a
slave, with this exception ; the master in the Territory
will work with the slave, and I think this will make the
case worse. If they will live better, as you indicate, in
your Territory, they will work much harder ; at chopping
down trees, rolling logs, splitting rails, and all the most
hard and servile labour of opening lands in a heavy
timbered country. . . . You get seven years out of the

[1] *Liberty Hall*, July 14, 1806.

most useful part of their lives, and then they are set
free ; many of them with enfeebled and broken constitutions will be abandoned to get their living by hiring
out by the day, month, or year.   I think, sir, that if all
your pompous arguments are stript of their sophistry
they expose these simple facts, that you want ten thousand men to serve you for seven years, without paying
them that do the labour any valuable consideration for
their labour and toil ; and when you can hold them no
longer you will let them go free, and have ten thousand
more under indenture in the same way."   This double
attack left Eumenes in a wiser but less pugnacious frame
of mind.   He roused himself for one more effort, but in
this he abandoned all his former grounds except the
proposition that the slave would be happier with future
freedom in prospect, and his opponents were content to
let him hobble off on this feeble crutch.[1]

As to the legality of this law there is no room for
question, although it was not overthrown by the territorial courts of either Indiana or Illinois.   Slaves were
held here under it long after Indiana became a state,
and yet no case arising from it came before the Supreme
Court of the state.[2]   In Illinois, under the state government, a very peculiar condition arose from the recognition of this law in the Constitution.   In December, 1828,
the Supreme Court of the state held that registered or
indented servants were chattels, subject to attachment

---

[1] *Liberty Hall*, August 11, 1806.

[2] The case of Mary, a woman of color, 1 Blackford, 122,
which is sometimes cited as putting an end to indentures under
this law, has no reference to them. It arose on an indenture
made October 24, 1816, after the adoption of the Constitution.
For Kentucky decisions against the validity of this law, see *ante*,
p. 281.

and levy for debt.[1] At the same time they held that indentures under the territorial law of 1807, which is the same as that of 1805, were void because repugnant to the Ordinance; but that nevertheless the indented negroes were bound to perform their service, because the third section of the sixth article of the Constitution provided: " Each and every person who has been bound to service by contract or indenture, in virtue of the laws of the Illinois territory heretofore existing, and in conformity to the provisions of the same, without fraud or collusion, shall be held to a specific performance of their contracts or indentures, and such negroes and mulattoes as have been registered, in conformity with the aforesaid laws, shall serve out the time appointed by such laws." [2] This construction was followed in 1836, with special stress laid upon the point that the indenture must have been in conformity with the territorial law.[3] It was also proceeded under as existing law in 1844.[4] At this time there must have been very few indented servants with unexpired terms, especially as the court had already held that the children of indented servants were absolutely free, notwithstanding the provision of the Constitution, " That the children hereafter born of such persons, negroes or mulattoes, shall become free; the males at the age of twenty-one years, and the females at the age of eighteen years." [5] This was the limit of the advance of the Illinois court towards freedom on this line, but in 1845 it made the decision abolishing the French slavery

---

[1] Nance *v.* Howard, Beecher's Breese, p. 242.

[2] Phœbe *v.* Jay, Beecher's Breese, p. 208.

[3] Choisser *v.* Hargrave, 1 Scam. 317.

[4] Williams *v.* Jarrot, 1 Gilm. 120.

[5] Boon *v.* Juliet, 1 Scam. p. 258.

as to negroes born after the passage of the Ordinance;[1]
and the remnant of the indenture slavery died out, with
the last relics of the ancient system, under the Constitution of 1848, which dropped the clause as to indented
negroes.[2]

A case involving the validity of the indenture law
came before the Supreme Court of Missouri in 1834, and
that court arrived at a conclusion which was doubtless
satisfactory to the judges, though it was reached by a
very unique piece of legal construction.   They held the
territorial law of 1807 to be void, as repugnant to the
Ordinance; and also that the provision of the Illinois
Constitution could not bring any of the indented slaves
under legal obligation of service to their masters, notwithstanding they conceded the people of Illinois to have
had the right of introducing absolute slavery by their
Constitution if they so desired.   The ground of the decision was that the constitutional provision applied only
to cases of indenture made " without fraud or collusion,"
and that any indenture made during the territorial
period was necessarily "in fraud and violation of the
Ordinance."[3]   This was of course equivalent to a decision that the constitutional provision was nugatory, for
on this theory it could apply to no indenture whatever.

There was another matter before this legislature of
1805 which claims our attention.   It was a petition for
the introduction of slavery, addressed to Congress, and
professedly made from motives of the purest philanthropy.   It has no mention of benefits to be derived
from the change by the people of Indiana.   It disclaims

[1] Jarrot *v.* Jarrot, 2 Gilm. 1.
[2] Poore's *Charters and Const.*, pt. i. p. 449.
[3] Hay *v.* Dunky, 3 Mo. 588.

any "sordid motive, or one that springs merely from a view to the present circumstances and situation of this country." It considers only the relief of the South from its surplus of slaves, and the great blessings which will result to the slaves from a removal to Indiana Territory, following, as to these, the line of argument which was afterwards used by Eumenes. The territorial House refused to adopt this petition, but their action was not due to the anti-slavery sentiments of the members, for the only one of them who was not a pro-slavery man was Davis Floyd of Clark. A majority of the constituency of Jesse B. Thomas of Dearborn were anti-slavery at this time, but the line had not been sharply drawn on this question at the late election there. He had no firmly fixed principles on the subject, and on this occasion had no vote, being speaker of the House. The rejection, therefore, was due to some other feature of the petition. It contained a request for the extension of suffrage, but no one objected to that. It asked a cession to the Territory of the saline springs within its boundaries, but no one objected to that. It asked a change of location of the land donations to the ancient inhabitants of the Illinois, but no one objected to that. It also contained a protest against a projected division of the Territory, and this was the rock upon which the pro-slavery members split. After reciting that application for a division of the Territory would be made at the next session of Congress, and stating an opinion that the division would be very detrimental to the interests of the people, the petition gives the grounds for this opinion, as follows: "The seat of Government is established at Vincennes, situate as near the centre between the western and eastern extremes of the Territory as conven-

ience and propriety will admit. It has been said that
the distance from the exterior parts of the Territory
to Vincennes operates a serious inconvenience to the
inhabitants thereof. Your Petitioners believe there is
no reason neither just nor plausible in support of the
Opinion. The administration of Justice, and of the
Government generally, is arranged in such a manner
that a Journey to Vincennes is in very few instances
necessary. The General Court holds one annual session
in each county for the trial of issues of fact belonging
thereto and made up in the General Court. It is true
that were there a greater number of Judges of the General Court, some delay in the trial of causes might be
saved, as there could be two instead of one annual session in each County. But the Territory has recently
adopted the second grade of Government by which
a considerable expence must necessarily be incurred.
Taxes will be as heavy as the people can support for
several years. Land is almost the only source of Territorial revenue. If the contemplated division takes
place one section of the Territory will necessarily have
to support the expence that is now collected from the
whole."

To this extent the protest was reasonable enough, but
it went farther, and in so doing it revealed a project
which had been formed in the interest of Knox County.
The petitioners say: "They wish that the United States
may be relieved from the expences and inconveniences
of the Territorial Government, and for this purpose that
the citizens of the Territory should be permitted to form
a State Government as soon as their population would
authorize the measure. At present the Ordinance con-
templates a division of the Territory into two States.

But many years must elapse before the two sections will arrive at a degree of population by which this desirable object can be effected. With submission they would therefore propose to connect the two divisions in one State Government, until they severally obtain a population that will authorise a division into two States. They conceive that no disadvantage could result to the United States from this arrangement, and they are confident that it would be productive of essential benefits to the country. The consideration of self Government alone is sufficient to render it desirable. The Indian Title, except a part of the Piankashaw claim, has been extinguished from the Miami to the Mississippi; and from the measures recently taken by the General Government for the Surveying and disposal of Public Lands, a short time will connect all the settlements from one extreme of the Territory to the other. It is less than three hundred miles from the Miami to the Mississippi; from the upper settlements, opposite the Missouri, it is less than two hundred miles to the Ohio; and from Vincennes on the Wabash to the Ohio it is about fifty miles. *This tract of country lies in a convenient form for a State.* The character, customs, and manners of the people are nearly the same; their respective interests are the same; as also the climate, soil, and productions. And the country at any future period can be divided into two States if an accumulated population renders it expedient or necessary." [1]

This petition brought an issue on a new question in Indiana politics. The anti-Harrison faction in the Illinois country had begun agitating the question of separation from Indiana in 1804. just after the failure of their

[1] Original paper, House files.

project to be added to Louisiana,[1] and this movement
constantly gained strength as Knox County grew in importance through the advance to the second grade, and
through favors by the executive to Knox County men.
At this time a petition for the continuance of the territorial government, as it then stood, might have passed
the House; but a proposal to advance to a state government, especially when coupled with an intimation that
in the subsequent division of this original state it would
be desirable to make one state of the lands to which the
Indian title had then been extinguished, was a very
different matter. That would ultimately result in the
formation of two states like Kentucky and Tennessee,
having their greatest extension east and west, which was
not only contrary to the provision of the Ordinance, but
also to the interests of the Illinois people, for it would
necessarily continue them perpetually in a secondary
condition. In a state extending from the Miami to the
Mississippi and from the Ohio to the neighborhood of
39° 30', the capital would naturally remain at Vincennes; at least it could never go to the Mississippi settlements. But under a division in accordance with the
Ordinance, the capital of the Western territory was certain to go to Kaskaskia or Cahokia for a time, and probably for a long time. The representative and the councilor from Randolph were strong enough Harrison men
to support the petition, but the St. Clair County men
were unanimously against it, and with the anti-slavery
representatives of the eastern counties were able to defeat it. After this action by the legislature, the petition
was forwarded to Congress as "The petition of the sub-
scribers, members of the Legislative Council and House

[1] Woollen's *Sketches,* p. 5.

of Representatives of the Indiana Territory, and constituting a majority of the two Houses respectively." It bore the signatures of Benjamin Chambers, John Rice Jones, and Pierre Menard, of the Council, and Jesse B. Thomas, John Johnson, George Fisher, and Benjamin Parke, of the House; but Chambers afterwards denied that he signed it.[1]

The Illinois petition, which this petition was designed to counteract, was also presented to Congress at the next session. It was quite a formidable document, directed towards two ends, a separation from Indiana and the introduction of slavery to the Illinois country, but particularly to the former. The petitioners, after reviewing their disappointment at not being joined to Louisiana, and their continuing desire for the introduction of slavery, proceeded to a detail of the disadvantages which accrued to them from their connection with the country east of the Wabash. They portrayed the road to Vincennes as "one hundred and eighty miles through a dreary and inhospitable wilderness, uninhabited, and which, during one part of the year, can scarcely afford water sufficient to sustain nature, and that of the most indifferent quality, besides presenting other hardships equally severe, while in another it is in part under water, and in places to the extent of some miles, by which the road is rendered almost impassable, and the traveller is not only subjected to the greatest difficulties, but his life placed in the most imminent danger." But

---

[1] Am. State Papers: *Misc.*, vol. i. p. 485. The charge made by the anti-slavery people, in 1807, that this petition "by some legislative legerdemain" found its way to Congress as "the legislative act of the Territory," is unfounded. No such authority was claimed for it.

the mere difficulty of getting across those terrible prairies of Illinois was not their worst feature. "From the obstacles already but very partially described, and from the peculiar nature of the face of the country lying between these settlements and the Wabash, a communication between them and the settlements east of that river cannot, in the common course of things, for centuries yet to come, be supported with the least benefit, or be of the least moment to either of them. This tract of country consists chiefly of extensive prairies, which scarcely afford wood or water, which utterly precludes the possibility of settlement to any extent worthy of notice. From the existence of this serious fact, a bar to the interchange of mutual good offices, and of private interests and concerns, is raised upon a foundation too firm to be shaken or surmounted."

From these premises the petitioners argued that there could never be any harmony of political interests between the two sections ; that nothing could be expected but discord and hatred. which would eventually destroy the peace and prosperity of the entire Territory. Nay, more : "Already have the seeds of discord been sown ; already have they presented a prospect of rapid growth ; but your petitioners offer up their earnest and sincere prayers to Heaven to avert, through the guardians and protectors of their liberties and property, the sad and much dreaded effects of the threatened commotions." From the consideration of these evils the petitioners passed to the unwarrantable manner in which they had been "precipitated into the second grade." They declared that the governor had called for the vote of the people on petitions from Knox County alone ; that a majority of the Illinois people, who voted at all, voted against the change; that the votes of Clark and Dearborn taken together had been against it; that Wayne had cast no vote; and on these facts they sneered in italics at the governor's being "*satisfied* that there was a *majority of the freeholders in the territory* in favor of entering into the second grade of government." This petition was the strongest as to number and respectability of signatures that had gone up from the Indiana Territory. Among its three hundred and fifty signers were John Hay and William Biggs of the legislature, but Shadrach Bond's name does not appear. He was not ready to take so radical a stand against the Knox County party, although he refused to follow it to the other extreme of advance to state government without separation.

In proper chronological order the account of this petition should have preceded that of the members of the legislature, for it was prepared and circulated during the summer of 1805. After they had learned that the counter-petition by the members of the legislature was forwarded, the Illinois people concluded that further action ought to be taken by them, and accordingly a committee of citizens from the several townships was appointed to take the matter in charge. This committee met on November 5, 1805, and decided to submit an additional memorial on their grievances and their wrongs. The subjects to be considered in this memorial were decided by resolution in the committee meeting, and one of them is worthy of preservation as illustrating the animus of the pro-slavery anti-Harrison faction, for it shows clearly their unhappy situation between a desire to criticise the legislature and their fear of giving offense to the people by any apparent opposition to the introduction of slaves. They say: "And whereas the Ordinance of

1787. for the Government of this Territory, is *Respected*
by the people as the Constitution of *their* Country, this
Committee entertain a hope that the General Government, after Guaranteeing to the people the privileges in
that ordinance Contained, will not pass unnoticed the
Violation thereof By the late act of the Legislature of
this Territory Authorizing the importation of Slaves,
and involuntary servitude for a term of years. And
altho' this committee entertain no doubt but that the Act
in Question will render service, by adding a Spring to
the Growth of this Country, They express the disapprobation of a people, who never will Consent to a Violation of that ordinance, for *this* privilege of slavery.
When Congress shall deem a Change of the Ordinance
expedient, they will Cheerfully agree to the measure."
When the memorial came to be drawn, however, it
dawned on the committee that this ground would best
be left unoccupied, for, after all, the masses were much
less interested in the inviolable preservation of the Ordinance than they were in the introduction of slavery.
Hence they omitted this feature entirely, and substituted
for it a fervent appeal for either a conditional or an
absolute revocation of the sixth article of compact.
They sated their longing for criticism of the Harrison
faction by a protest against the petition for a state government, charging that its object was " to continue the
seat of government at Vincennes, where some of our
principal characters have ample possessions," and by
lamenting the increase of executive power through the
creation of a court of chancery for the Territory, of which
there was a single judge appointed by the governor.[1]
This memorial, together with the minutes of the meet-

[1] *Laws 1st Sess. 1st Ass.*, pp. 11–13.

ing of the committee that prepared it, was presented to the House of Representatives on January 17, 1806.[1]

There was still another petition that went from Indiana to this Congress, and we must not overlook it, for it was the first expression of the anti-slavery people, although on its face it has no reference whatever to slavery ; probably because they supposed they had sufficient grounds for their request outside of that subject. The Dearborn County people were becoming quite as weary as their Illinois brethren of the increasing greatness of Knox County and the domineering spirit of the faction in power. They derived no appreciable advantage from the advance to the second grade, against which they had voted, and yet they were subjected to increased taxation on account of it. They were opposed to the introduction of slavery, either with or without the consent of Congress, and yet it was to be forced upon them by the indenture law. They prepared a memorial setting forth that they were separated from the seat of government by nearly two hundred miles of " a Wilderness occupy'd only by Indians and likely for many years to Remain Unoccupied by any Other persons ; " that the intervening country was " in General Very Broken and therefore Very unlikely to afford a communication to the seat of Government ; " and that they were situated near to, and in easy communication with, the State of Ohio. For these reasons they asked that they might be reannexed to that state. This memorial had one hundred and five signers, nearly all of them residents of the Whitewater Valley, and among them were a number of the old Quaker settlers who afterwards took an active part in the slavery controversy ; though at this time the settlers

---

[1] See original papers, House files.

of this sect had just begun their great emigration to southeastern Indiana.[1]

All of these petitions, together with the previous petitions and reports thereon, were referred by the House of Representatives to a select committee of seven, as follows: Mr. Garnett of Virginia, Mr. Morrow of Ohio, Mr. Parke of Indiana, Mr. Hamilton of Pennsylvania, Mr. Smith of South Carolina, Mr. Walton of Kentucky, and Mr. Van Cortlandt of New York — three Northern States, three Southern States, and Indiana Territory. The petition of the Vincennes convention of 1802 was also referred to this committee, although by its own terms it had become void on March 4, 1805. Mr. Parke was apparently of influence on the committee, for their report, as presented by Mr. Garnett on February 14, 1806, favored everything that the Harrison party wished except the advance to a state government prior to division. As to that point the committee said: "A Territory, when once erected into a State, cannot be divided or dismembered without its own consent; the formation, therefore, of two States out of this Territory, originally intended by the Ordinance of 1787, could not constitutionally be effected, if the two sections were once permitted to form one State, without the consent of that State, however necessary the extent and population of that Territory might render such division." They also said that a division of the Territory so soon after entering the second grade would be impolitic and unjust, but that it should be made as soon as either section had sufficient population to enable it to form a state government. As to slavery, the committee swallowed the philanthropic

[1] Original, House files. This petition is in the writing of George Holman, one of the most influential of the signers.

view bodily, and reported that as " our Western brethren are not only willing but desirous to aid us " in relieving the South of its surplus negroes, it would be expedient to suspend the operation of the sixth article for ten years, so as to permit the introduction of slaves born within the United States. They also reported in favor of removing the property qualifications of voters, and against the proposals for division from Dearborn, Randolph, and St. Clair counties.[1] The report was referred to a committee of the whole house for February 20, but was not taken up. Later in the session, on March 26, John Randolph presented two additional petitions, from Randolph and St. Clair counties, for the division of the Territory and the introduction' of slavery to the western part. These were accompanied by a census estimate, prepared by Robert Morrison, who had taken the last national census in that region, in which the population of these two counties was said to be 4,311 souls. These documents were referred to the same committee, but no further action was taken.[2]

This action of Congress threw the questions back to the Territory, but with a material modification. The question of advance to a state government by the entire Territory was no longer of any importance, for it had been ascertained that Congress would never authorize it. The only remaining branch of the separation question was whether a division could be obtained before one of the sections was ready to form a state government. The Harrison party was opposed to this ; but it was not a serious matter, for division was now only a question of time, and Congress had intimated its intention of

[1] Am. State Papers: *Misc.*, vol. i. p. 450.

[2] *Annals 1st Sess. 9th Cong.*, pp. 466, 848.

putting that time at the greatest possible distance. Under these circumstances the General Assembly convened again on November 3, 1806, and the two factions of the pro-slavery party readily reached the conclusion, that, by fighting each other when there was no occasion for it, they were wasting the strength they would need to secure the object which both wanted. They accordingly came to an amicable agreement to unite in the effort for the introduction of slavery, and let the people fight out the question of division, free from legislative interference. On this understanding the legislators proceeded harmoniously with their pro-slavery work. They adopted a series of resolutions declaring that the suspension of the sixth article would be highly advantageous to the Territory, to the South, and to the negroes; that nine tenths of the people of the Territory desired it; that slaves were held in the Territory when the Ordinance was adopted; that the Ordinance was adopted without the "knowledge and approbation" of the people of the Territory; and on these grounds they directed their representative in Congress to use his best endeavors to secure a suspension of the article. These resolutions were declared to have been passed by a unanimous vote, and were certified by Jesse B. Thomas, Speaker of the House, and Pierre Menard, President *pro tem.* of the Council.[1]

The pro-slavery work of this legislature was not limited to this petition. On account of doubts which had arisen as to the legal nature of the indenture contracts, it was enacted that the time of service of indented negroes and mulattoes might be levied upon and sold as personal property. The negro was required to

---

[1] Am. State Papers: *Misc.*, vol. i. p. 467.

serve the purchaser for the remainder of his term, and the purchaser was required to perform whatever contract had been made by the original master. If no contract of compensation had been made, the purchaser was made liable for "freedom dues;" that is to say, at the close of the term of service he must furnish the negro with "one new and complete suit of cloathing, suited to the season of the year, towit: a coat, waistcoat, pair of breeches and shoes, two pairs of stockings, two shirts, a hat and a blanket." [1] There was also enacted a stringent law for the police of slaves. If a slave or servant was found ten miles or more from the home of his master, without a pass, any one might take him before a justice of the peace, who could order him punished by not more than twenty-five lashes. If a slave went upon the plantation of a person other than his master, without leave from his master, such person might punish the offender with ten lashes. A slave who participated in a riot or unlawful assembly, or made seditious speeches, was punishable with thirty-nine stripes, on conviction before a justice. Any person who harbored a slave or servant was made subject to a fine of one hundred dollars, while aiding one to escape was finable in five hundred dollars.[2]

Notwithstanding the harmony at Vincennes, the fight between the two factions of the pro-slavery party went merrily on in the Illinois country. The separationists got together their committee which had been elected the year previous, and made a renewal of their plea for an independent government. With the exception of a claim to a population of 5,000 souls, they made but one

---

[1] Laws 2d Sess. 1st Genl. Ass., p. 13; 4 Gov. and Judges, p. 26.
[2] Ibid., p. 21.

new argument, which was a statement that, in view of
the complications which might arise from the European
peace, then in prospect, " they cannot but shudder at
the horrors which may arise from a *disaffection in the
West:* — and can it be much, to the American people
to grant to their brethren in this distant region a government to which, in an evil hour, they can speedily fly for
direction and support." [1] Elijah Backus was sent to
Washington as agent to urge the claims of the petitioners upon Congress. The Harrison faction in Randolph County rallied and produced a counter-petition, in
which they denounced the committee of the opposition
party as a sham and a fraud, which "turns the name
convention into contempt and ridicule." They declared
that no election whatever for members of this committee
had been held in two of the townships ; that in Kaskaskia no notice of an election was given ; and that the
members elected from that place constituted one half of
the meeting by which they were elected. They denied
that any advantage could be gained by division, and expressed fear that it would make their situation worse.
The signatures show that the Harrison party was losing
ground in Randolph. Nearly all of the one hundred
and two signers were French, and forty-two of them
could not write their names. Of the few names that
would be familiar to an Illinois historian of to-day, those
of George Fisher, Hippolyte Menard, and François Menard were the most prominent [2]

The resolutions of the legislature, asking the suspension of the sixth article, were presented to the House of
Representatives on January 20, 1807, and referred to a
select committee, of the approved North and South

---

[1] Original, House files.   [2] Original, House files.

representation, as follows : Parke of Indiana, Varnum of Massachusetts, Alston of North Carolina, Kelly of Pennsylvania, Sandford of Kentucky, Jere. Morrow of Pennsylvania, and P. R. Thompson of Virginia. They reported, on February 12, that it would be expedient to suspend the 6th article of compact for ten years, "from and after the 1st day of January, 1808." This qualification was made out of deference to the feeling concerning the slave-trade, which was now almost unanimously against that villainous traffic. The subject had been almost constantly agitated since the formation of the Constitution, and it was certain that with the last day of 1807, to which the Constitution protected it, the slave-trade would exist no longer, so far as the United States was concerned, except as a forbidden and criminal occupation. In addition to that, the sentiment had grown so strong that no proposition met with favor if it in any way stimulated or increased the slave-trade during the few remaining months of its necessary existence. The increase of slave territory within the United States would naturally have this effect, and in consequence the time of the act's taking effect was deferred. How much farther the slave-trade question affected the introduction of slavery into Indiana is a query for whose solution I have found no exact evidence, but it is my belief that but for the constitutional continuance of the slave-trade to 1808, and the indignation and bitterness that resulted from it, the sixth article would have been suspended and slavery would have been admitted north of the Ohio.

At the opening of this session of 1806-7, Mr. Jefferson said in his message : " I congratulate you, fellow-citizens, on the approach of the period at which you

may interpose your authority, constitutionally, to withdraw the citizens of the United States from all further
participation in those violations of human rights which
have been so long continued on the unoffending inhabitants of Africa, and which the morality, the reputation,
and the best interests of our country have long been
eager to proscribe. Although no law you may pass can
take prohibitory effect till the first day of the year one
thousand eight hundred and eight, yet the intervening
period is not too long to prevent, by timely notice, expeditions which cannot be completed before that day." [1]
The subject engrossed much of the attention of Congress
during the session, although there was practical unanimity as to the general purpose of the proposed law ; in
fact, the slave-trade had already been prohibited in all of
the states except South Carolina. The prohibitory law
passed the Senate without division, both in its original
form and as amended. In the House there was much
debate, but it was confined almost wholly to matters of
detail, the chief point of controversy being the disposition of such slaves as might be imported contrary to law
after the importation was prohibited. It was conceded
that these must be taken from their holders, if the prohibition were made effectual, for the forfeiture of vessels
engaged in the trade, and fine and imprisonment of the
owners and crews, had already been tried with little
effect : the ship-owners, particularly those of Rhode
Island, had invented systems of collusion in the purchase of libelled vessels which made the loss trifling in
comparison with the enormous profits of the trade. But
if the slaves were taken from their holders, what was to
be done with them ? Evidently it would not do to set

[1] *Annals 2d Sess. 9th Cong.*, p. 14.

them free, ignorant of our language and with no means of support, on the shores where they happened to be landed; and to take them back and set them free on the coast of Africa would generally have been equally inhumane. It was proposed that they should be forfeited to the United States for such disposition as should be thereafter provided, but this was objected to because it recognized a right of property in the negroes. It was proposed that they should be bound to service for a term of years, but this met a similar objection. The dilemma was finally solved by divesting the holder, or any of his assignees, of all title, and leaving the negro imported contrary to law to be dealt with as the state to which he was brought might see fit.[1]

The bill passed the House by a vote of 63 to 49, but this was no test of the feeling of the members as to the importation of slaves. The large negative vote here was called out by a compromise amendment for the prevention of the transportation of slaves coastwise for the purpose of sale, and this the dissenting members declared had nothing to do with importation. The original bill had passed by a vote of 113 to 5, and a part of these few negatives were due to a feeling that the bill did not prevent importation through Florida.[2] The majority in the House which would have voted against the suspension of the sixth article was at least as great as that on the final passage of the prohibitory act, and it probably would have been considerably greater. John Randolph led the opposition to the law, on account of the provision as to the coastwise trade, and yet, as we have seen, he favored the maintenance of the Ordinance as it stood.

---

[1] *Annals 9th Cong. 2d Sess.*, p. 1266.

[2] *Ibid.*, pp. 486, 626.

The report of the committee was referred to a committee of the whole for February 16, but it was not called up, and then the slavery matter dropped for that session. The matter of division advanced but one step farther. The petitions from the Illinois people, for and against division, were presented on February 20, and referred to the same committee as the slavery resolutions. On the 26th Parke reported favorably to division, and a resolution was adopted "That it is expedient to divide the Indiana Territory,"[1] but no other action was taken.

Thus again both questions were thrown back to Indiana to form the leading issues of a new campaign. The failure of Congress to act resulted in renewed local disputation that served to push forward the crystallization of those party organizations which were still in an immature state. A decision either way would have altered the character of immigration; would have prevented the local occurrences of the next two years; would have changed the color of Indiana politics for years to come. These questions that are difficult of settlement — these questions that will not down — are the ones whose heat melts public feeling for the mold, and when once molded a generation may pass before its outlines can be altered.

[1] *Annals 9th Cong. 2d Sess.*, p. 624.

CHAPTER X.

THE terms of the representatives to the first General Assembly expired on June 30, 1807 ; and in anticipation of this a law had been passed at the last session providing for an election on the first Monday in February of that year.[1]   At this election there was an increased show of strength by the anti-slavery people in the eastern counties, and by the anti-Harrison faction in the Illinois country, but not enough to affect materially the representation.   The greatest change was in Dearborn, but, by assuring every one that he was heartily in favor of whatever they wanted, Jesse B. Thomas was again elected there.   Shadrach Bond and William Biggs were returned from St. Clair, and George Fisher from Randolph, as before.   Davis Floyd of Clark had his hands full with his trial for complicity with Burr, and James Beggs was elected in his place.   The delegates from Knox County were General W. Johnston and Luke Decker, but this was not a political change, for their party affiliations were the same as those of their predecessors, Benjamin Parke and John Johnson.   The councilors, of course, held over.

Of the three new members we have already met Decker as a member of the Vincennes convention of 1802.   General Washington Johnston was a native of

[1] *Laws 2d Sess. 1st Genl. Ass.*, p. 5.

Culpepper County, Virginia. He came to Vincennes in
1793, and was the first attorney at the bar of that county
of whom there is any record. He was very active in
the work of the Masonic order; usually delivered the
customary oration on the day of St. John the Evange-
list, the patron saint of the Vincennes lodge; and was
one of the organizers of the grand lodge of Indiana in
1817–1818. He held many offices, in some of which
we shall find him hereafter. James Beggs might have
made more claim to greatness than any other member
of this legislature. He was one of three brothers who
came west in the latter part of the last century, settled
for a short time in Kentucky, and then came north of
the Ohio because it was free soil, or at least more nearly
so than Kentucky. They were all Virginians of Irish
descent, the sons of Thomas Beggs, a commissary in
the Revolutionary army. Being fairly well-to-do, each
bought a five hundred acre tract in Clark's Grant and
settled down to farming. James was a graduate of
William and Mary's; the other two had good common-
school educations. They were religious pioneers. John,
the oldest, was a Baptist — later a follower of Alexander Campbell, and the others were stanch Methodists.
They had enough Virginia in them to be very fond of
reading and not at all covetous of hard work. John was
for some years a judge of the Clark County courts.
Charles was a captain of militia, and served with credit
at Tippecanoe. James was several times in the legislature. Beyond this they were not known in public life,
but in the Falls country they were men of distinction,
men of great strength, of great heart, of great brain.
Their qualities made them factors of great importance
in local politics, and during the territorial period they

were the head and front of the anti-slavery party in Clark.

The Assembly convened for its first session on August 17, 1807, at Vincennes.[1] Benjamin Parke was announced as a candidate for reëlection as soon as the session was called, and no organized opposition was made to him. Several articles appeared criticising his failure to secure the legislation that the people desired, but none of any importance except some that emanated from Elijah Backus, Receiver of the Land Office at Kaskaskia, who had acted as agent of the Illinois people at the preceding Congress. He accused Parke of preventing him from being heard before the committee, and of hindering action on the proposed division; but Parke denied this squarely, and in turn charged that Backus had been purely ornamental as an emissary to Washington, not even being of service in securing the favorable committee report; all of which he supported by his affidavit.[2] This vindication, together with assurances which Parke gave of his intention to work for slavery and division, gave him his election in the week following, by a vote of eight out of the eleven members present; the three anti-slavery men scattered.

The pro-slavery party continued in harmony during this session, as in the preceding one. They adopted a memorial to Congress asking the suspension of the sixth article, but it added nothing to what had already been put before Congress except a formal resolution of consent to the suspension. It was adopted both in the

[1] *The Western Sun*, July 25, 1807. The laws for this year make the beginning on August 16, but as that was Sunday, the *Sun* is evidently correct.

[2] *Western Sun*, September 5, 1807.

House and in the Council by two-thirds majorities, but President Chambers of the Council refused to sign it. Finally he was persuaded to leave the chair, and Gwathmey, whom he had appointed President *pro tem.*, signed the memorial.[1] This legislature also adopted the revision of the laws of the Territory which had been made by John Johnson and John Rice Jones, in pursuance of an act of the last session. The revision is in fact very little more than a compilation of the laws; but in it the extensive titles of the originals are dropped, and no guides are substituted to show the source from which any enactment was taken. In consequence of this, and because the revision soon entirely displaced the separate collections of acts, many laws were subsequently referred to as passed in 1807, though in fact they had been in effect for years. The indenture law and the act concerning servants were among these, there being no change made in the provisions already in force as to slaves or servants. The legislature was prorogued on August 26, having taken no other action that is of present interest.

The anti-slavery people were now thoroughly roused to the danger of the situation, and determined to make a vigorous resistance in Congress. In Clark County a mass meeting was called for October 10, at Springville, then county seat, to take action on the legislative resolution. There was a large attendance and a general harmony of sentiment. John Beggs was elected chairman and Davis Floyd secretary. On motion, Abraham Little, John Owens, Charles Beggs, Robert Robertson, and James Beggs were appointed a committee to draw a memorial against the legislature's resolutions. It is probable that James Beggs prepared the memorial. He

[1] Am. State Papers: *Misc.*, vol. i. p. 485.

was best fitted of the committee-men to do so, and its
occasional verging on Scripture style, together with its
statement that "a great number of citizens, in various
parts of the United States, are preparing, and many
have actually emigrated to this Territory, to get free
from a Government which does tolerate slavery," indicate him the author. This memorial is peculiarly
memorable because it promulgated a theory which was
new to Indiana and to the nation — the doctrine of
"Squatter Sovereignty." It antedates by forty years
the letter of General Cass in which this doctrine is commonly supposed to have been first enunciated. After
reviewing briefly the history of the slavery controversy
in Indiana, the memorial proceeds: "And although it
is contended by some, that, at this day, there is a great
majority in favor of slavery, whilst the opposite opinion
is held by others, the fact is certainly doubtful. But
when we take into consideration the vast emigration into
this Territory, and of citizens, too, decidedly opposed to
the measure, we feel satisfied that, at all events, Congress
will suspend any legislative act on this subject until we
shall, by the constitution, be admitted into the Union,
and have a right to adopt such a constitution, in this respect, as may comport with the wishes of a majority of
the citizens. . . . The toleration of slavery is either
right or wrong; and if Congress should think, with us,
that it is wrong, that it is inconsistent with the principles
upon which our future constitution is to be formed, your
memorialists will rest satisfied that, at least, this subject
will not be by them taken up until the constitutional
number of the citizens of this Territory shall assume
that right." Beyond this the petitioners asked nothing.[1]

[1] Am. State Papers: *Misc.*, vol. i. p. 485.

In Dearborn County the people were of similar sentiment, but they were especially indignant over the reënactment of the obnoxious indenture law of 1805. Their situation too differed from that of Clark in that they were distant from the other settlements of Indiana, from which also they were separated by lands that were still in possession of the Indians. They were adjoining Ohio and in close political sympathy with its people. Cincinnati was even more their metropolis than it is to-day. Instead of proposing to remain and fight the question out, as the Clark County people had done, they asked the same remedy that they had proposed two years earlier. They prepared a memorial to Congress " stating that a law for regulating slaves in that territory had been unconstitutionally passed, and praying a revisal of that act, or that the said county may be annexed to the State of Ohio." [1] This memorial was presented to the House by Jeremiah Morrow of Ohio, on January 7, 1808. The alternative proposed by it, of a revisal of the indenture law by Congress. was an apparently simple remedy, though there might be some question as to its legality. The Ordinance reserved to Congress the right of rejecting the laws of the Governor and Judges, but it made no such provision as to the laws after advance to the second grade. It gave the legislature only authority to make laws not repugnant to the Ordinance, and that was all that was said on the subject. As a matter of fact, however, Congress treated the Ordinance much the same as any other law, and had it felt disposed to alter it, or to annul any of the territorial laws, ample author-

[1] *Natl. Intelligencer,* January 8, 1808; *Annals 1st Sess.* 10*th Cong.,* p. 1331. The original is not on the files; it was probably among the papers destroyed by the British vandals in 1814.

ity would have been found for so doing. However invalid any of those laws may have been, Congress gave a tacit approval to them by failing to abrogate them.

While these movements were progressing in the eastern counties, an event of almost equal importance occurred in Knox. This was the falling-out of Harrison and John Rice Jones. What was their difference has never been stated by any one who could well have known, but the most probable cause in view was the failure of Jones to receive an appointment on the territorial bench. On November 15, 1807, Judge Thomas T. Davis, who was then chancellor of the Territory, died at Jeffersonville. On November 24, Waller Taylor was appointed chancellor in his place by Harrison. Davis had also been one of the judges of the Territorial Court, and the vacancy there was evidently saved for Benjamin Parke until spring, when he was appointed by the President. On receiving this appointment Parke resigned the office of Attorney General, which he had held while a congressman, and on June 2, 1808, Thomas Randolph was appointed to that place by the governor. Taylor and Randolph were Virginians who had lately come to Indiana. Both were men of culture, and both served as aids to Harrison at Tippecanoe. They and Parke formed the innermost circle of Harrison's friends in subsequent times, and Jones probably realized that one or the other of them would be certain to get any desirable office that was vacant in the future. Taylor went down politically with his party under the Territory, but after the organization of the State was twice elected to the national Senate. He died August 26, 1826, in Virginia. Randolph at the time of his appointment was thirty-seven years of age. He was a graduate of William and Mary's, a lawyer by profession, and had served one term in the Virginia legislature. He was rated very high by his friends, and was without doubt a man of good parts, but he appears to have been put a trifle out of balance by his pride of ancientry and his broad appreciation of his own merits. He was of the Pocahontas blood.

John Rice Jones was no small loss to the Harrison party. He was at that time a councilor, with more than two years to serve; he had full knowledge of the inside workings of past political movements; he had the ability to use his knowledge to the best advantage; and he was absolutely tireless in his political work. Soon after his defection he formed an alliance with William McIntosh and Elijah Backus for newspaper work against the opposition, and their bitter articles goaded their enemies almost to madness. That their attacks were largely the product of pure malevolence is evident, but for all that they had considerable effect with the people, as we shall shortly see. For the present we must turn again to Congress.

The petition of the legislature and the memorial of the Springville meeting were presented to the Senate on November 7, 1807, and were referred to Messrs. Franklin of North Carolina, Kitchel of New Jersey, and Tiffin of Ohio. They reported on the 13th that it was inexpedient to suspend the sixth article, and a resolution to that effect was adopted on the 17th.[1] The House had received these same communications on the 6th and referred them, but no action upon them was taken after the report in the Senate. The Dearborn County petition did not reach the House until January 7. It was

[1] *Annals 1st Sess.* 10th *Cong.*, pp. 22, 23, 31.

then referred, but no action was taken. From this line of treatment of the petitions, and from Mr. Parke's subsequent declaration that Congress would not permit the introduction of slavery if a majority of the people asked for it,[1] it would seem apparent that a majority of the members had settled down on the squatter-sovereignty principle as the proper solution of the question. If their want of action had been due to a disapproval of slavery they would probably have put a stop to the indenture system. It certainly was not due to mere neglect, for they gave prompt attention to other Indiana matters. At this same session Mr. Parke secured the passage of an act reducing the freehold qualification of voters to fifty acres of land, or a town lot of the value of one hundred dollars.[2]

During the session of Congress the anti-Harrison people were making a move for division that involved a new feature. At the last session of the legislature Davis Floyd had been elected Clerk of the House, notwithstanding he was then under indictment for treason for complicity in the Burr expedition, and had just been convicted of misdemeanor for his action in the same matter. The full proceedings of Burr's trial at Richmond, extending from May 22 to October 20, 1807, had been communicated to Congress by the President on November 23, 1807. It was very generally understood that Jefferson wanted Burr convicted, and the conclusion naturally followed that anything hostile to Burr, or to any person involved with Burr, would be soothing to the President. The anti-Harrison faction of the pro-

[1] *The Western Sun*, February 25, 1809.
[2] *Annals 1st Sess. 10th Cong.*, p. 2834, — approved February 26, 1808.

slavery party seized on the opportunity to make fair
weather at Washington.   On January 4, a public meeting was held at the court-house in Vincennes, at which
resolutions were passed denouncing the legislature for
its action, and declaring that Indiana had no sympathy
with Burr; which resolutions were duly forwarded to
Jefferson.[1] A similar meeting was held at Kaskaskia
on February 18, John Edgar presiding, at which resolutions were adopted disapproving Floyd's election, declaring that the Randolph County members were not
present when he was elected, stating that the union of
the Illinois country with the eastern part of the Territory was "a grievance of the greatest magnitude," and
demanding a division of the Territory.[2] A copy of
these resolutions was directed to be sent to Jefferson.
The opposition faction did not pay any attention to the
Floyd matter until July 6, 1808, when the governor
revoked Floyd's commissions as major of the Clark
County militia and pilot of the Falls.   This was probably done at the suggestion of the President, for on this
same day the governor announced several appointments
that came from Washington.[3]

The Illinois people also prepared two memorials to
Congress, reciting their reasons for desiring a separate
government as in former petitions, and specially urging
that inasmuch as the region east of the Wabash had
three fifths of the representation, and all of the appointive officers, "they who live in the country which is to
constitute the Western State are oppressed with taxes,
the avails whereof are expended in the country which is
to form the Eastern State, and at the discretion of those

[1] *Western Sun*, January 6, 1808.   [2] *Ibid.*, March 23, 1808.
[3] *Executive Journal*, July 6, 1808.

over whom they can have no control." These were presented to the House on April 6, by Matthew Lyon of Kentucky, and were referred to a committee of which Lyon was chairman and Parke a member. On the 11th the committee made a report setting forth the bases of the petitions, but giving their opinion that on account of the press of business before Congress, and the inability of the treasury to meet the expense of an additional territory, it was for the time being inexpedient to make a division.[1] This closed the action of Congress for the session so far as Indiana was concerned.

And now came a revolution. Pierre Menard and John Hay had withdrawn from the Legislative Council, and on the recommendation of the governor the President had appointed George Fisher of Randolph and Shadrach Bond of St. Clair to their places, thus taking two of Harrison's strongest friends from the House. On July 6 the governor called for an election, to be held on July 25, to fill these vacancies. The time was short, but the campaign was one of the most bitter ever known in Indiana Territory. The Illinois people were in a state of disappointment and indignation. For three years the governor's right-hand man had been in Congress seeking to secure the introduction of slavery, and now they seemed farther from it than ever. He had professed, too, not to stand in the way of division, but Backus was accusing him of doing so, and division had been withheld for apparently trivial causes; besides which the Knox County interest were openly working against division. Meanwhile the governor and his friends absorbed all the territorial offices; Knox County

[1] *Annals 1st Sess. 10th Cong.*, p. 1976; Am. State Papers: *Misc.*, vol. i. p. 922.

was being built up out of all proportion to the remainder
of the Territory ; and the country east of the Wabash
controlled legislation unless the Illinois delegation combined with one or the other of the eastern factions.
These points were urged with vigor, and at the same
time the peculiar circumstances attending the advance
to the second grade were resurrected and held up as
incontrovertible proof of the governor's tyranny.

It is not surprising that with such arguments in their
favor the anti-Harrison faction triumphed.   In Randolph, Rice Jones, eldest son of John Rice Jones, was
elected.   He was a young man of twenty-seven years,
of great native talent and unusually broad education.
He had graduated in letters at Transylvania University,
in medicine at Philadelphia, and in law at Litchfield,
Connecticut; and had established himself in the practice of the latter at Kaskaskia in 1806.[1]   From St. Clair
County was elected John Messinger, one of the most
useful men in the Illinois country.   He was a son-in-law
of Matthew Lyon, that impetuous Irishman who succeeded in martyring himself to the alien and sedition
laws in Vermont, and afterwards found a balm for his
wounded feelings in elections to Congress from Vermont,
Kentucky, and Arkansas.[2]   Messinger was a Massachusetts boy, reared on a farm, and qualified as a carpenter,
a millwright, and a surveyor, by his own efforts.   He
was thoroughly versed in all branches of mathematical
science, particularly so in surveying and astronomy.   He
was the author of a surveyor's handbook, and was for
some years professor of mathematics at the Rock Spring
Seminary, one of the earliest Illinois educational insti-

---

[1] Reynolds's *Illinois*, pp. 140, 141.
[2] *The Edwards Papers*, p. 20, note.

tutions. He also devoted many of his odd hours to the
instruction of his own and his neighbors' children ; and,
although not a church-member, was an active agent in
the circulation of the Bible through the settlements of
St. Clair County.[1] He was, in short, a type of the
hard-headed, practical Yankees, who came west in early
times and built their lives into the foundations of our
commonwealths, while others were doing the ornamental
work.

On September 26, the legislature of 1808 met at
Vincennes pursuant to a call of the governor issued on
August 17. The situation was one that made a political combination a necessity. Councilors Chambers and
Gwathmey did not attend. Councilor Jones and Representatives Jones, Biggs, and Messinger were in favor
of division and the introduction of slavery, but were opposed to Harrison. Representatives Thomas and Beggs
were opposed to the introduction of slavery, but had no
objection to division. Councilors Bond and Fisher and
Representative Decker were in favor of the introduction
of slavery, but were opposed to division, and were supporters of Harrison.[2] Representative Johnston belonged
with the last-named party, but was desirous of going to
Congress, and was willing to be guided by his legislative
constituents to some extent, even against the policy of
his party. The combination that naturally resulted was
between the anti-slavery and anti-Harrison pro-slavery
factions. The former had no serious objections to the
introduction of slavery into Illinois, provided Indiana
became free-soil ; they had no objection to division, because it would soon throw their capital east from Knox

[1] Reynolds's *Illinois*, pp. 227, 277–280.
[2] *Western Sun*, November 19, 1808.

County, which would be acceptable to the great mass of their constituents. The latter party, if they could secure division, had no objection to the prohibition of slavery in the Indiana part of the Territory — in fact they were pleased with that prospect of revenge on the Harrison party. The only difficulty in the way of this combination was the selection of a delegate to Congress to fill the vacancy caused by Parke's resignation. The Illinois people favored John Rice Jones, but the anti-slavery people would not support him because he had long been identified with the Harrison party and was a pronounced pro-slavery man. Jesse B. Thomas was a candidate, but the Illinois people were afraid to trust him because it was said, and commonly believed, that he had made pledges to the Harrison party both before and since his election, as well as to themselves. Across these walls of doubt the combination did not pass for many days. Meanwhile the Harrison party adhered to Michael Jones, Register of the Land Office at Kaskaskia, as their candidate for Congress, hoping eventually to catch the Illinois vote. General W. Johnston caucused by himself, and was evidently aiming to induce a union of the delegates east of the Wabash on him.

Early in the session it was demonstrated that the people had a lively interest in the slavery question. Petitions poured in from all sides. On October 1 came the petition of John Griffin and others against slavery. On the 4th came the petitions of "sundry inhabitants" of Dearborn and Clark against, and "sundry inhabitants" of Knox in favor of, slavery. On the 5th came the petition of John Johnson and others of Knox for, and of William Nixon and others against, slavery. On the same day all the slavery petitions were referred to a select committee composed of Johnston, Messinger, and Decker — an eminently judicious selection for Mr. Thomas, the Speaker, as it would necessarily put Johnston, his most dangerous opponent, on record on the slavery question; and this record, whatever it might be, was certain to cut off some support beyond all hope of recovery.[1] On the 7th of October four more petitions were presented, all against slavery: from Christopher Wyant and others; from John Alton and others of Knox; from E. Mc-Namee and others; and from John Allen and others of Knox.

On the 11th the Illinois members put the Congressional candidates to the test, by taking up resolutions to make the delegates in Congress thereafter elective by the people, and for a division of the Territory. This disposed of Johnston. A vote against the proposed change in electing the Congressional delegate would be acceptable only to the Harrison faction, for it was believed that the executive could exercise much more control over the legislature in their choice, by means of appointments and other favors, than he could over the people at large. With him a vote for division was suicidal not only for the present but for the future also, for he lived in Knox County, and the overwhelming majority there was against division. He voted against the resolutions, but he also tried to force Thomas to a record on the same questions by proposing that the standing rules be suspended and the Speaker be given an opportunity to vote. To this proposition Thomas replied that he believed a majority of his constituents were favorable to a division, and as the House already stood in favor of it there was no occasion for a vote from him.[2]

[1] *Western Sun*, November 19, 1808.
[2] *Ibid.*, November 19, December 6, 1808; March 4, 1809.

The petitions still continued to come in. On the 13th three anti-slavery petitions were presented : from Charles Beggs and others ; from Robert Robinson and others ; and from George Leach and others. On the next day came a petition from John Badollet and others against slavery, and a petition of William McClure and others for slavery. On the same day was presented a petition of William Achison and others of St. Clair, praying that all anti-slavery petitions before the House "may be thrown under the table." This facetious proposition came very nearly dooming the petition to the ignominious fate it had suggested for the others, for a motion to that effect was defeated by a majority of only one vote. It was very evident that there must be no trifling on the slavery question, so far at least as the country east of the Wabash was concerned. Here were fifteen petitions on the subject of slavery, eleven of them against any legislative action for its admission, and of the signers a majority of over 600 were against it, much the greater part of whom were from Dearborn and Clark.[1] The pro-slavery people had never suspected the strength of the opposition until now.

Whether Johnston still had hopes of an election to Congress, or merely looked forward in a general way to a political future in Indiana, is difficult to say, but that he faced about on the slavery question is certain. He had acted openly and avowedly with the pro-slavery party at the preceding session of the legislature, though he afterwards declared that he was always morally opposed to the introduction of slavery, and had favored its introduction as a representative only because a majority of his constituents were so minded.[2] On the morning of

[1] *Western Sun*, November 12, 1808.

[2] *Ibid.*, February 4, 11, 18, 1809.

October 19 he presented to the House the report of the
select committee of which he was chairman — a report
which appears to be wholly his own work, and one which
is entitled to rank among the ablest, if not as the ablest,
of state papers ever produced in Indiana. By way of
exordium it sketches the feeling in the United States at
the close of the Revolution on the subject of slavery, the
abolition of the slave-trade by the majority of the states,
the passage of emancipation laws by part of them, and
the effort of Congress in the formation of the Ordinance
of 1787, "to prevent the propagation of an evil which
they could not totally eradicate." The committee shows
the existing indenture law to be "contrary both to the
spirit and letter of the Ordinance," and then, leaving
questions of construction, it declares "that the most flagitious abuse is made of that law; that negroes brought
here are commonly forced to bind themselves for a number of years reaching or extending the natural term of
their lives, so that the condition of those unfortunate
persons is not only involuntary servitude but downright
slavery."

Although the committee would not concede that a
moral wrong like slavery could be justified by any theory
of expediency, they maintained that policy alone should
prevent the admission of slaves to the Territory. It was
desirable to obtain population, but the non-slaveholding
states were far more thickly populated than those where
slavery was tolerated, and consequently the greatest emigration must be expected from them, unless it were prevented by the admission of slavery. It was desirable
that the population should be enterprising and industrious, but it had been demonstrated that "the hand of
freedom can best lay the foundation to raise the fabric

of public prosperity." The experience of the country was before them. "The old states north of Maryland, without one single precious commodity, exporting nothing but bulky articles, present everywhere the spectacle of industry and animation. The style of their agriculture is superior; their mills, bridges, roads, canals, their manufactories, are in point of number without a parallel in the Southern States, and they, besides other parts of the world, export to those states manufactured commodities to a large amount annually." The State of Ohio was an instance directly in point both as to the number and the character of the settlers. "Our eyes witness growing into importance, where but a little while before Indian hordes and savage beasts roamed without control, farms, villages, towns, multiplying with a rapidity unprecedented in the history of new settlements; the same cause will produce the same effects. . . . The industrious will flock where industry is honorable and honored."

As to the pernicious effects of slavery on the manners and morals of the whites, the committee carried Mr. Jefferson's argument [1] to its full development, in a series of pictures of those horrors of slavery which, when constantly seen, must necessarily blunt the moral perceptions and crush the finer instincts of humanity; but carried beyond their purpose by the force of the argument they ask: "At the very moment that the progress of reason and general benevolence is consigning slavery to its merited destination; that England, sordid England, is blushing at the practice; that all good men of the Southern States repeat in one common response ' *I tremble for my country when I reflect that God is just;* '

---

[1] *Notes on Virginia*, Query 18.

must the Territory of Indiana take a retrograde step
into barbarism and assimilate itself with Algiers and
Morocco?" As to the political effects on the people,
the committee argued that the power and influence of
the wealthy slaveholder would increase until he dominated his humble neighbor who held no slaves, and
thereby the true principles of republican government
must give place to the relation which we know was produced between the planters and the "poor white trash"
of the South. "The lord of three or four hundred
negroes will not easily forgive; and the mechanic and
laboring man will seldom venture a vote contrary to the
will of such an influential being."

Passing from local considerations, the committee urged
that the permission of slavery by Congress would be an
act of injustice to the Northern States which neither
reason nor policy could justify. "The negro-holders
can emigrate with their slaves into the extensive Mississippi Territory, the Territory of Orleans, and the more
extensive Louisiana. By opening to them the Territory
of Indiana, a kind of monopoly of the United States
land is granted to them, and the Middle and Eastern
States as well as enemies of slavery from the South are
effectually precluded from forming settlements in any of
the territories of the United States. . . . The national
legislature cannot with justice make such an unequal
distribution (if they may be allowed the expression) of
the lands with the disposal of which they are entrusted
for the benefit of ll, but especially of those states whose
overflowing population renders emigration necessary."
Rising still higher, the committee recognized the national
necessity of keeping free soil and free institutions at
least on an equal footing of strength with slavery. It

was not altogether a new thought. The controversy on the details of abolition of the slave-trade had already gone far towards developing the North and South animosities; and John Randolph had predicted in the final debate on that subject that if ever the Union were disrupted, it would break on the line between freedom and slavery. Slavery extends, say our committee, "from the line of Pennsylvania and the Ohio River to the Floridas, and from the Atlantic to the Mississippi. By the purchase of Louisiana, where it was found existing, it may spread to our indefinite extent North and West, so that it may be said to have received a most alarming extension, and is calculated to excite the most serious fears. By admitting it to Indiana, that is to say opening to it the vast tract of country lying between the State of Ohio, the river of that name, the Lakes, and the Mississippi, the comparative importance of the Middle and Eastern States, the real strength of the Union, is greatly reduced, and the dangers threatening the internal tranquillity of the United States proportionably increased."

For the reasons which they had thus placed before the House, the committee said they were "of opinion that slavery cannot and ought not to be admitted into this Territory; that it is inexpedient to petition Congress for a modification of that part of the Ordinance relative to slavery; and that the act of the legislature of Indiana for the introduction of negroes and mulattoes into the said Territory ought to be repealed, or which purpose they have herewith reported a bill." They also proposed that a copy of their report, together with a copy of one of the petitions upon which it was founded, be forwarded to the Speaker of the national House of Representatives, with a request that he lay it before Congress.[1]

The report carried that little legislative body beyond the power of debate or objection. It was at once resolved, without division, that the House concur in the report. The bill which the committee had reported for the repeal of the indenture law was then taken up, hurried through three readings, passed, signed, and sent to the Council, all before the House adjourned for the morning. This is a most extraordinary record; for this bill would have abolished the indenture system both in Illinois and in Indiana, and yet it passed without dissent a house which on all previous declarations of opinion had stood five to one for slavery. Moreover, it is certain that the political life of a majority of the members would have ended if this bill had become a law. Three of them were from Illinois, with pro-slavery constituents; two were from Knox, with pro-slavery constituents, and one of these was himself a slaveholder. And yet it was not surprising that the report should have had a great temporary effect. Coming from a man who, as they all knew, had theretofore advocated the introduction of slavery; deftly introducing the well-known quotation from Mr. Jefferson, who was then the autocrat of public opinion as well as of political movements; and placing before the hearers in clear, strong terms those arguments, and those only, which could not be answered or evaded; it swept away every foundation of the pro-slavery party except the selfish motive of personal interest. On that unsightly but firm base the pro-slavery men reconstructed their shattered fabric as soon as they regained their senses. Five days later the same bill

[1] *Western Sun*, December 17, 1808.

was defeated in the council without division. Jones,
Bond, and Fisher, the only members present, although
they had disagreed on every proposition of a political
nature thus far presented to them, had too much regard
for their political future in Illinois to repeal the indenture law; and so it was saved as a rich legacy to our
sister state by these three men.[1] The Representatives
also regained their political discretion in a few days, and
passed an additional law for the police of slaves, by
which any one who permitted slaves or servants of color
to assemble on his premises, " for the purpose of dancing
or revelling," was finable in twenty dollars, while the
revelers were made subject to thirty-nine stripes on the
bare back.[2]

   After the 19th of October there was nothing to hinder
the combination on Thomas, for delegate to Congress, by
the eastern counties and the Illinois country. He had
declared openly for division, and had given the strongest
private assurances that he would labor for division in
Congress. It was openly charged at the time that he
had said to the Illinois representatives that " if they
would not take his word he would give his bond," and
that John Rice Jones had actually required him to give
a written guaranty to secure the division.[3] It is not
strange that Jones, himself a candidate for the office,
should have put him to this test, and it is recorded as a
fact by Illinois historians that a bond was required and
given.[4] On the 26th the legislature proceeded to the
election of the congressional representative. Thomas
received six votes, Michael Jones three, and Shadrach

[1] *Western Sun*, December 17, 1808; February 4, 1809.
[2] Laws of 1808, p. 21.   [3] *Western Sun*, November 5, 1808.
[4] Ford's *Illinois*, p. 30; Davidson and Stuvé's *Illinois*, p. 242.

Bond one. The vote for Bond, who was not a candidate, was probably cast by Johnston, as aside from it there was a strict party vote.[1] Thomas at once resigned as Speaker of the House, and was succeeded by Johnston, who served till the 26th, when the Assembly was prorogued.

The Harrison party felt their first defeat very deeply, and threw the greater part of the blame upon Thomas, who, it was claimed, had made most solemn pledges prior to his election that he would not in any way support a division of the Territory.[2] So exasperated were they that they held an indignation meeting at Vincennes and burned him in effigy. At Kaskaskia appeared a more serious outgrowth of the bitter political feeling — the murder of Rice Jones by Dr. Dunlap. It was asserted by the anti-Harrison faction that this was due to the machinations of the opposers of division,[3] but it was evidently a personal matter. In the late campaign Jones had spoken slightingly of Shadrach Bond, for which Bond challenged him. They met, but before firing a reconciliation was effected by William Morrison, who was acting as second to Jones. After Jones had gone to Vincennes, Dr. Dunlap, who was Bond's second, made public reflections on his courage, and a bitter newspaper controversy ensued. On December 7, Dunlap shot and killed Jones on the street at Kaskaskia. His friends pretended that he acted in self-defense, but he fled from justice, and witnesses declared it a cold-blooded murder.[4]

[1] *Western Sun*, October 29, December 24, 1808.

[2] *Ibid.*, May 13, 1809.

[3] Edwards's *Illinois*, p. 29.

[4] *Western Sun*, August 27, September 10, 1808, April 29, 1809; *Executive Journal*, December 12, 1808.

We must now turn again to Congress, whither John
Rice Jones, as President of the Council, had forwarded
the report of Johnston, the resolution of the House adopting the same, and one of the anti-slavery petitions on
which it was based. He also forwarded certain resolutions which had been adopted by the Council on the last
day of the session, asking that the councilors and the
delegate to Congress be made elective by the people,
and that the term of office of the former be reduced to
four years. These were presented to the House on
November 18.[1] On December 2, a petition from the
grand jury of St. Clair County for the division of the
Territory was presented ; and on the 13th all of these
were referred to a committee composed of Thomas of
Indiana, Kenan of North Carolina, Bassett of Virginia,
Taggart of Massachusetts, and Smilie of Pennsylvania.
On the 15th were received statistics and depositions as
to the number of inhabitants of the Illinois country, and
on the 16th a petition from Knox County against division. These were referred to the same committee.
The pro-slavery people, divided in factions, stunned by
the action of the legislature, and certain that, if the
consent of Congress to the introduction of slavery could
not be obtained by Parke it would not be obtained
by Thomas, sent in no petition.

Thomas had little opposition to contend against, and
he remained true to his latest pledges. On December
31 he reported for the committee in favor of the division of the Territory. He dwelt on the inconveniences
arising to the people, and the enervation produced in
the government, by the scattered locations of the settlements. He said that a large majority of the people of

---

[1] *Annals 2d Sess. 10th Cong.*, p. 501.

the Territory favored division, and that the only objection urged against it was the increased expense which would result to the national government from the establishment of a separate government. As to this he claimed that the increased value of public lands on account of the establishment would far exceed its cost. From the evidence before them, the committee estimated the number of inhabitants of the Illinois country at 11,000, and those east of the Wabash at 17,000. From comparison with the census of 1810 it is apparent that both of these estimates were very nearly correct.[1] An act for the division of the Territory was passed through both houses without difficulty, and approved on February 3, 1809.

Thomas also secured the passage of an act in conformity with the resolutions of the Council, making the councilors and the delegate to Congress elective by the people, and reducing the terms of the former to four years. The qualifications for electors for these offices were made the same as those of electors for territorial representatives. This act also put the power of apportionment of representatives in the hands of the Assembly, with a proviso that until there should be six thousand free, white, male adults in the Territory the maximum number of representatives should be twelve and the minimum nine.[2] For himself Thomas secured an appointment as one of the judges of the territorial court of Illinois, and after the close of the session of Congress he removed to the new territory, where he afterwards became prominent in politics, and was one of the first

---

[1] *Annals 2d Sess. 10th Cong.*, p. 971; Am. State Papers: *Misc.*, vol. i. p. 945.

[2] Act of February 27, 1809; *Annals 2d Sess. 10th Cong.*, p. 1821.

senators from the state. John Rice Jones also left us at this time. He went first to Illinois, and thence, in 1810, to Missouri, where he took his usual active part in politics. He was a member of the constitutional convention of that state in 1819, and was elected by the first state legislature one of the judges of the state supreme court, which position he held with credit to himself during the remainder of his life.

The division act reduced Indiana Territory to the present dimensions of the State, with the exception that our boundaries were carried ten miles to the north by the enabling act of April 19, 1816, and with the further exception that it seems to have been the intention of Congress in 1809 to have the north and south line between Indiana and Illinois extend from Lake Michigan to Vincennes, instead of stopping at the Wabash as afterwards provided. We gained territory by both changes. It should be borne in mind, however, that the practical extent of the Territory was less than one third of the State, the remainder being still in possession of the Indians. Two large additional extinctions of Indian title were made on September 30, 1809, by the treaty of Fort Wayne, with the Miamis, Eel Rivers, Delawares, and Pottawattamies, which was negotiated by General Harrison. The greater tract adjoined the Vincennes cession, and was bounded on the north by a line drawn from the mouth of Big Raccoon Creek, on the Wabash, to a point on the East Fork of White River about ten miles above Brownstown. This was commonly called "the ten o'clock line." because the direction was explained to the Indians as towards the point where the sun was at ten o'clock. The common tale about this indefinite description being given for the purpose of cheating the

Indians is fictitious. The treaty provided that the line should be so run that the tract would be thirty miles wide at its narrowest point, and this formed the basis for its survey. The other tract was twelve miles in width, lying west of and parallel to the Greenville treaty line. It was commonly known as "the twelve mile purchase." By a treaty of December 9, with the Kickapoos, the Indian title to the strip of Indiana west of the Wabash and below the Vermillion was extinguished. The territory opened by these purchases was about 3,000,000 acres. There was no further purchase of lands within our boundaries from the Indians until after the organization of the state.

These purchases of 1809 were the ones which brought on the troubles with Tecumthe. His position was that no tribe of the Northwestern Confederacy could sell any land without the consent of all the tribes. With him the question was as with us would be the query, Can a state sell any portion of its territory to a foreign power without the consent of the United States? In abstract justice the question could be answered only by an examination of the compact between the tribes; but for practical purposes it was only necessary for the national executive to decide on what theory we should proceed. When Tecumthe was informed by General Harrison that the President must decide the question, and that he probably would not adopt his view, he replied: "As the great chief is to determine the matter, I hope the Great Spirit will put sense enough into his head to induce him to direct you to give up this land. It is true he is so far off he will not be injured by the war. He may sit still in his town, and drink his wine, while you and I will have to fight it out." The President, however, adhered to the theory that the title was in the separate

tribes, and that their relinquishments could not be revoked by all or any part of the confederacy. For the
Indians was left submission or war, and that the latter
resulted was a natural consequence.

At the time of the division agriculture was the chief
vocation of the people of Indiana, but manufacturing
was quite well developed in its rudimentary forms. In
1810, when the population had increased about forty per
cent., and the business of the Territory proportionately,
Indiana had 33 grist-mills, 14 saw-mills, 3 horse-mills, 18
tanneries, 28 distilleries, 3 powder-mills, 1,256 looms,
and 1,356 spinning-wheels. The value of the manufac-
tures for that year was about $200,000, more than three
fourths of which was in home-made fabrics of wool, cotton, hemp, and flax, produced by the busy fingers of the
pioneer women. New Orleans was the only market for
goods exported from the Ohio Valley, the shipments
down the river being made in barges and flatboats.
Steamboats were as yet unknown on the western waters.
A boat was built on the Upper Ohio in the winter of
1804–5, by Captain McKeever, and sent down the
river to obtain her machinery, but she did not return.[1]
The first steamboat on the Ohio was built at Pittsburgh
in 1811, by Nicholas J. Roosevelt, who ran her to New
Orleans in October of that year, making the trip in
fourteen days.[2]   During the next five years two or three
small boats were in use on the Ohio, but steam navigation did not become of practical importance until after
1817. No steamboat ascended the Wabash until the
summer of 1823.[3]

In a political way the separation from Illinois had an

[1] *Liberty Hall*, June 25, 1805.
[2] Preble's *Hist. Steam Nav.*, pp. 66–71.
[3] *Western Sun*, May 10, 1823.

effect far more important than the mere reduction of territorial extent. It took out of our politics altogether the anti-Harrison faction of the pro-slavery party ; and also greatly weakened the Harrison faction, which had been very strong in Randolph — in fact had controlled that county until the last special election. This left the anti-slavery party on a footing of numerical equality with the opposition, if not in the majority ; and at the same time the suffrage act made the governmental condition of the Territory far more favorable to a successful contest by that party than ever before. From a form of government in which the governor was everything and the people nothing, the Territory had in eight years advanced to a form of government more nearly republican than anything contemplated by the Ordinance for the territorial period. Suffrage had been liberally extended ; the power of apportionment for legislators had been given to the General Assembly ; and the danger of control of the legislature by the executive had been reduced to its lowest possibilities by making the council and the delegate to Congress elective by the people. The governor still held an absolute veto, the right of prorogation, and the appointment of officers ; but the use of these was closely watched, and the appearance of arbitrary action was at once resented. The only veto ventured by Governor Harrison that was considered objectionable was that of a bill for the removal of the capital from Knox County, in 1811, and this was complained of at the next session of Congress as an act of tyranny.[1] On the whole it may be said that from 1808 the Territory of Indiana was governed by the people ; and to judge of the wisdom of their action we must proceed with the narrative of events.

[1] *Annals 12th Congress,* p. 846.

CHAPTER XI.

THE division of the Territory necessarily changed the features of political strife in both sections, though the heat of party feeling, the animosities and attachments of partisan organizations, remained for a time. In Illinois the opposing factions were almost ready to fly at each other's throats, and it was not due to any lack of hatred and prejudice that they failed to carry their old quarrels into the new government. The anti-Harrison faction had secured division, but they had failed to reap the fruits that they had expected, for Ninian Edwards of Kentucky was appointed governor, and he was an entirely new factor in their local politics. Attempts were made to involve him in the factional fight, but he firmly declined to have any connection with it, and remonstrated with both parties on their unpatriotic partisanship. He afterwards said: " I determined to risk the whole combined opposition of both parties rather than yield myself up to the control or enlist under the banners of either." [1] Under his influence the old controversies soon fell out of sight, and party lines were drawn on new questions. One of the marked results of the new alignment was the election of Shadrach Bond as the first representative in Congress when Illinois passed to the second grade, in 1812, although he had clung to the Knox County party

[1] Edwards's *Illinois*, pp. 29-33.

to the last, without regard to the wishes of the great majority of the people of Illinois.

The fact of division, however, was not immediately known; and east of the Wabash, at least, was not anticipated, for political affairs went on there for two months after the approval of the division act just as if no division had been made. By the election law of 1807, an election for representatives to the General Assembly was to occur on the first Monday in April, 1809,[1] in accordance with which candidates appeared and made their campaigns during the months of February and March, and the election was actually held on April 3.[2] Although this election was of no effect whatever, we have occasion to note its features in Knox County, where there occurred a visible change of front on the slavery question. The petitions presented to the last legislature had revealed an anti-slavery strength that Knox County people had not dreamed of, and the politicians of discernment recognized them as a warning to stand from under. Moreover, the leaders of the Harrison party in Knox were satisfied that the only possibility of preventing division was through a combination of the Knox County representatives with the anti-slavery representatives of Dearborn and Clark, against the Illinois delegation; and therefore they were not desirous of stirring up any additional strife as to slavery.

There were five candidates in Knox, of whom two were to be elected. Of these John Johnson and Dennis Sullivan made no special exposition of their views, nor

---

[1] Laws of 1807, p. 232.

[2] Previous to this time the polls were kept open for three days, but by act of September 16, 1807, the time of voting was limited to one day. Laws of 1807, p. 490.

was there occasion that they should, for they were well-known Harrison men, favoring the introduction of slavery and opposed to division. The difference between them was that Johnson had respectable qualifications for the office and Sullivan had not. General W. Johnston was a candidate for reëlection. He declared that his own feelings had always been against the introduction of slavery; that he had formerly favored it from deference to the wishes of his constituents; and that he had changed his positions because he was satisfied that a majority of the people no longer desired the importation of slaves. He was opposed to division, and showed that he had lost his election to Congress by the last legislature for that cause.[1] Thomas Randolph, the Attorney General, appeared as a candidate, apparently with a view to the race for Congress before the legislature. He sought to divert the minds of the people from local affairs to those of the nation, which had scarcely been considered in Indiana politics since the organization of the Territory. He urged as the matter of primary importance our complications with the European powers, particularly England, which had already brought us to the verge of war; and insisted that everything else should be subordinated to national considerations. As to slavery, he said in response to a published letter addressed to him: "Your former delegate will inform you that Congress would not give its sanction to the introduction of slaves was there a majority of the citizens of the Territory in favor of it. You say, and I believe it probable, a majority is opposed to it. I differ with them in opinion; my voice would be in favor of the introduction. Let us not, however, agitate this question when

[1] *The Western Sun*, February 4, 11, 18, March 4, 1809.

more important subjects loudly demand our attention." [1]
In this same letter he explains at length his opinion that
it is the imperative duty of a representative to be controlled by the wishes of his constituents.

The situation was not satisfactory to the pro-slavery
voters. John Johnson was an acceptable candidate, but
Dennis Sullivan lacked ability, and Randolph, in addition
to a want of interest in local matters, was evidently
trimming on the slavery question. It might, of course,
be desirable to have a delegate in Congress from the
Territory who could adjust our differences with European
powers, but it was not apparent that a person of such
qualifications was needed in the territorial assembly;
besides which if he should be elected to Congress from
the assembly a temporary vacancy would be caused,
and this might prove disastrous to Knox County interests. It was on account of this dissatisfaction that John
Haddon appeared as a candidate in the latter part of
March. He declared himself in favor of the introduction of slavery, but said he would be governed by the
wishes of his constituents on this as on other questions. [2]
If he had offered a week earlier he could scarcely have
failed of election. As it was, the poll resulted: John
Johnson 203, G. W. Johnston 140, Haddon 120, Randolph 110, Sullivan 66. No one but Johnson received
a majority of the votes cast, and G. W. Johnston owed
his plurality to his personal popularity and the division
of the pro-slavery vote among the other candidates.

It is probable that Harrison had received intelligence
of the approval of the division act previous to the election, and let it go on for the purpose of feeling the pub-

[1] *Western Sun*, February 25, 1809.
[2] *Ibid.*, March 25, 1809.

lic pulse, for news had been published three weeks earlier
at Vincennes that the bill awaited only the approval of
the President, and that in all probability this would not
be withheld.[1]   On April 4, the day after the election,
the governor issued a proclamation announcing the division, redistricting Indiana, and calling an election for
May 22. He apportioned three representatives to Knox,
two each to Dearborn and Clark, and one to Harrison,[2]
making in all eight representatives.   It is evident that
the suffrage act of February 27, 1809, had not yet
reached him, for it gave him no authority to district the
Territory, and made the minimum number of representatives nine; besides this, the law gave him authority to
apportion the councilors, but he did not do so until April
10, when he assigned one each to Dearborn, Clark, and
Harrison, and two to Knox.   By the new law the delegate to Congress was to be elected at the same time as
the members of the legislature.   Thomas Randolph and
John Johnson at once announced themselves candidates
for this office.   Randolph comprehended the situation.
He realized that the vote of Indiana must now be in opposition to slavery, and, at the outset, he undertook to
cut away from his former position altogether, while at
the same time he conciliated the pro-slavery voters by
reiterating his personal preference for the introduction
of slaves.   In his address to the people he said : " It is
my belief that a great majority of the people of the Territory are opposed to me in opinion.   I therefore yield

----

[1] *Western Sun*, March 11, 1809.

[2] By act of October 11, 1808, the legislature had organized the
county of Harrison from parts of Knox and Clark.   It extended
six ranges, or thirty-six miles, east from the second principal
meridian, and from the Ohio to the Indian boundary.   The county
seat was established at Corydon.

the point. I think this question ought now to sleep. I think the interests of the Territory demand it; and should I be honored with your suffrages I will not make an attempt to introduce negroes into the Territory, unless a decided majority of my constituents should particularly instruct me to do so." [1] Johnson adopted the policy of keeping quiet on the slavery question, and making his race on general grounds. [2]

But now appeared a new champion in the field, — a young Hercules, stripped for the fray, and wielding the mighty bludgeon of " No slavery in Indiana." This was Jonathan Jennings, then only twenty-five years of age. He was a native of New Jersey, but soon after his birth his parents moved to Fayette County, Pennsylvania, and there the child grew to manhood, receiving his education at the Presbyterian school at Cannonsburg, in the adjoining county of Washington. His father was a Presbyterian minister, and both his father and his mother had taken degrees in medicine. In 1806 he emigrated to Indiana; stopped for a short time at the rising village of Jeffersonville; and then pushed on to Vincennes, where he completed his legal studies, and at the April term, 1807, was duly examined and admitted to the bar. [3] While here, he was employed as a clerk by Nathaniel Ewing, then receiver of the land-office. He also added to his earnings by those odd jobs that fall to young lawyers, among which was an employment for six days, as assistant to the clerk of the House of Representatives, in copying a portion of the revised laws of 1807. [4] But

[1] *Western Sun*, April 15, 1809.
[2] *Ibid.*, April 22, 1809.
[3] Territorial Court Docket, pp. 274, 284.
[4] Rev. Laws 1807, p. 537.

Jennings was not satisfied with Vincennes. He was ambitious of entering public life, and there was little opportunity for him in Knox County. He had been reared with anti-slavery ideas, and meant to hold to them, but tenets of that kind were obnoxious in Knox. The governor, too, was very influential there, and he had a host of personal friends whom he desired to advance, among whom Jennings was not included. Over in Clark County was growing up the village of Charlestown, which had been laid out in 1807 by Charles Beggs, and there, Jennings knew, were people who agreed with him in sentiment; there, too, was an open field for his ambition; there, too, was a Miss Anna Hay, who was said by those who knew her to be the very prettiest woman in all Indiana, and who some months later became Mrs. Jennings.

Several days after the election proclamation, Jennings was preparing to mount his horse for the journey to this place, when Ewing, who had come out for a farewell chat, said to him, "Look us up a good candidate for Congress." Jennings turned to him with the question, "Why would n't I do?" The thought struck Ewing favorably, and after a few minutes' conversation they concluded that Jennings would have a fair prospect of success in the race, if the people of the eastern counties would accept him as a candidate.[1] With a determination to make a trial, the young aspirant mounted his horse and traveled on to Charlestown, where he found the Beggs brothers and their numerous friends. He talked the matter over with them; a meeting was called; and it was decided that Jonathan Jennings should be the candidate of the anti-slavery people in Clark. Up rose

---

[1] The incident comes to me through the family of the late Judge Isaac Naylor, of Crawfordsville, to whom Ewing related it.

Jennings and posted away over the Indian trails to Lawrenceburg, but there matters were not so smooth.   In
the lower part of Dearborn, which it will be remembered
then included all Indiana east of the Greenville treaty
line, the Harrison party had considerable strength.   The
local leaders were General James Dill and Captain Samuel Vance.   Dill was an Irish barrister, whose neat queue,
white flannel summer suit, and perpetual boutonnière
are remembered by old people as the accompaniments of
a very smooth tongue and the most agreeable of manners.   He had married Mrs. Eliza Lawrence, the oldest
daughter of General St. Clair.   Vance was the husband
of one of the daughters of Mrs. Lawrence.   Both were
personal friends of Harrison, and had been kept in office
by him since the organization of the county, Dill as recorder and Vance as clerk of the courts.   In addition to
their official position, their influence was extended by
the common understanding that they controlled the official patronage of the county.   Randolph was at this
time on terms of intimate friendship with the family,
and a year later was married to Catharine Lawrence.

As a matter of course Jennings received no encouragement in that quarter, but in the northern part of the
county there was a fairer prospect.   For several years
there had been pouring into the upper Whitewater valley a veritable tide of emigration from North and South
Carolina.   These settlers were nearly all Quakers, many
of them of Huguenot descent, who had left the South on
account of their dislike of slavery.   There were also a
number of settlers from New Jersey and Pennsylvania,
and a few from other states, but they hated the institution of slavery almost to a man, as did their descendants
after them.   It was this feeling that made the White-

water valley a line of the Underground Railway in later
years. It is the memory of generations of opposition to
slavery that has made the region unalterably Republican
since that party was in existence, and probably will make
it so until some political earthquake shakes the American
people from their present party ruts. This section at
this time was very closely connected with Clark's Grant
in sentiment, and quite largely so by personal acquaintance, for several of Clark's old soldiers had located on
the Whitewater. Of these, two of the most influential
were George Holman and Richard Rue, whose captivity
among the Indians forms an interesting chapter in the
history of the border wars.

As soon as intelligence had been received in this portion of the county of the call for an election for Congressman, and of the announcement of the Knox County
candidates, preparations were made for a public meeting
to decide upon a candidate. Notice was given at the
log-rollings and other gatherings of the vicinity, and the
entire masculine portion of the community assembled at
the designated place, which was near Elkhorn Creek,
about a mile above its mouth. A number of logs that
had been cut for a building served for seats, and for this
reason the assemblage has since been known as "the
Log Convention." It required but a few minutes for
the convention to decide that opposition to the introduction of slavery into the Territory was the platform on
which they wished to stand. All of them were opposed
to the existing indenture law, as well as to any change
in the Ordinance, and as a corollary they wanted nothing of Thomas Randolph, or John Johnson, or any other
person who had been identified with the pro-slavery
movement, as a candidate for Congressman. They

agreed unanimously that their candidate should be George Hunt, a member of one of those wonderfully multiplicative North Carolina families which have so extended their roots and branches through the White-water country that thereabouts every one seems related to everybody. He had lived in the neighborhood for two years, and was a man of some capacity. He was a competent surveyor, and afterwards served as clerk of the Wayne County courts, being the first occupant of that office. His nomination, however, was made with a proviso that if Clark County had selected a suitable candidate, who was in harmony with their ideas, Hunt would be withdrawn.

For the purpose of obtaining definite information on this point, Joseph Holman, a son of George Holman, then lacking a few months of his majority, was delegated to confer with the people of Clark. He proceeded thither on horseback, over the old trail to the Falls, and on arrival at Charlestown learned of the meeting there and the nomination of Jennings. He passed a few days in consultation with the people; found that their ideas were in harmony with those of his neighbors; and started on his return. In the mean time Jennings had arrived in the upper Whitewater country, but his youthful appearance had well-nigh ruined his prospects. Some called him "a beardless boy," and intimated that he would not be able to find his way to Washington if he were elected; while others were so irreverent as to denominate him "a cold potato." To make the matter worse, Dill and Vance came up from Lawrenceburg and circulated charges against Jennings, in the interest of Randolph. They soon discovered that Randolph would not be acceptable to the people here, and therefore, in

order to prevent the vote from going to an opposition
candidate, they proposed Vance as a candidate on whom
Dearborn County could harmonize, and induced Hunt
to withdraw in his favor. Possibly his subsequent appointment to the clerkship was in consideration of this
complaisance.

At this stage of the proceedings young Holman returned from Charlestown and found his neighbors gathered at one of their log cabins. As he entered, Jennings,
who was unknown to him, asked, "What news from
Clark's Grant?" Not deeming it prudent to announce
the result of his mission in the presence of a stranger,
Holman withdrew with one of his friends to the outside,
where an exchange of information was made. When
they came in they whispered the information brought by
Holman to those present, except Jennings, and every
one arose and walked away without a word to the youthful candidate. This was somewhat discouraging, but
as he was walking slowly away, behind the others, the
Holmans came up to him and entered into conversation.
Young Holman showed him the handbills that had been
put in circulation, including the charges against him
which had been largely instrumental in producing the
coolness of the settlers; and then the skies began to
brighten. The most serious of these charges, and the
one that had been injuring him most, was that while
in the land-office he had bid up land against actual settlers and forfeited his bids in the interest of speculators,
who afterwards bought it in at a reduced price. The
occurrence on which this charge was founded was the
bidding-in of a piece of land known as the McFadden
tract, which had been forfeited on account of complications in the title. It was explained by Jennings's friends

that this tract was finally sold to Governor Harrison, who bought off the rival bidders, John Johnson, Parmenas Beckes, Jonathan Jennings, General W. Johnston, and Elias McNamee, by paying them $150. The opposition party made no denial of this statement, but explained that Harrison had bought it in to protect some poor men who claimed title.[1]   Jennings refuted the charges to the satisfaction of the Holmans in a very few minutes, and won them so completely to his support that for several days Joseph Holman accompanied him about the neighborhood, during which the two succeeded both in breaking down all the prejudice that had arisen and in securing the support of the settlers for Jennings.[2]

The campaign was now well under way. Jennings put in his remaining time in Dearborn, Clark, and Harrison. Knox he had little to hope from, and all that could be obtained there, Ewing, McNamee, and McIntosh were working for. Randolph had Knox County well under control, and Dill and Vance were making a vigorous fight for him in Dearborn; but the anti-slavery people of Dearborn and Clark were working actively against him. In personal approach to the voters, Jennings was far superior to his opponent. He knew how to bend far enough to conciliate and yet retain respect. I have the honor to number among my friends a venerable gentleman who saw the two in this campaign and noted the differences of their methods.[3]   It was at a

[1] *Western Sun*, April 29, May 6, May 27, 1809.

[2] Young's *History of Wayne Co.*, pp. 94–96. I am also indebted for some particulars to Hon. W. H. English, who was a neighbor and intimate friend of the Holmans, and had often heard from them the story of the Log Convention.

[3] Mr. Samuel Morrison, of Indianapolis. He died March 1, 1888, since the above was written.

log-rolling on the farm of David Reese, in Dearborn County. Randolph came up on horseback and was received by Reese with the common salutation of " Light you down." Randolph dismounted, and having chatted for a few minutes was asked by Reese, "Shall I see you to the house?" Randolph accepted the invitation, and, after remaining there for a short time, rode away. On the next day came Jennings, who had a similar reception, but to the invitation to repair to the house he replied, "Send a boy up with my horse and I'll help roll." And help roll he did until the work was finished; and then he threw the maul and pitched quoits with the men, taking care to let them outdo him though he was very strong and well skilled in the sports and work of the frontier farmers. So he went from house to house; and long after he had gained rank among the great men of the commonwealth the people treasured up their anecdotes of his doings in his campaigns: how he used to take an axe and "carry up a corner" of a log-house; how he took a scythe in the field and kept ahead of half a dozen mowers; and other agricultural deeds which proved him a man of merit.[1]

There was no making headway against such a man in those days. General Dill followed Jennings about in his canvass, but he found only bad news to report to Randolph. In one letter he says, " Wherever Jennings goes he draws all men to him;" and in another, dated at Brookville, he declares that the only man there who

---

[1] The custom in mowing was for one man to lead off, and after he had gone far enough to give scythe-room, another began, and so on. The best mowers were started first, so that those following would not be held back. In no branch of farm-work was there more rivalry than in this.

favors Randolph is Enoch McCarty, and even he says
that Jennings will be elected.[1]   As the reports came in
Randolph realized the danger to him of Johnson's candidacy, and made every effort to have him withdraw,
but in vain.   At length he issued a handbill warning the
people that Johnson's candidacy was a scheme to defeat
him and elect Jennings, but he conceded that Johnson
was not knowingly playing this part, and expressed his
"high respect for this gentleman."   Some of Johnson's
supporters were brought to regard his case as hopeless,
but the more rabid pro-slavery men were disgusted with
Randolph's concession on the slavery question and esteemed it little choice between Randolph and Jennings;
so they stood by Johnson.   In the mean time the little
anti-Harrison clique in Knox had been insisting that the
anti-slavery people should not be lulled to sleep by Randolph's professions, and urging as a notorious fact that
he was "under the particular patronage of the executive."[2]   Randolph repeatedly denied that he had any
connection with Harrison except personal friendship, but
the charge could not be shaken off; and worse than that,
by dint of reiteration the entire Harrison interest became known as the Virginia Aristocrats, while the opposition coolly appropriated the title of the People.   These
names continued all through the territorial times, and
until national politics became superior to local politics in
the state.   Protestations and explanations were useless.
Any candidate identified with the Harrison party was a
Virginia Aristocrat, or a tool of the Virginia Aristocrats,
for campaign purposes, and he might as well resign himself to it at the outset.   In fact the Harrisons, Ran-

---

[1] Woollen's *Sketches*, p. 30.
[2] *Western Sun*, April 22, 1809.

dolphs, Taylors, Dills, and Vances were aristocrats, if we ever had any in Indiana, but no one could discover that their aristocracy was particularly detrimental to the general welfare, and but for their prominence in politics they might have been as aristocratic as they liked without rousing any objection.

The eventful 22d of May arrived and the votes were given. When they were counted it was found that Dearborn had given Jennings 143 votes and Randolph 72. In the northern or first district every vote had been for Jennings except that of George Hunt, the original nominee of the Log Convention. Clark had given 219 for Jennings and 16 for Randolph. Harrison had given 22 for Jennings and 83 for Randolph. Knox had given 44 for Jennings, 231 for Randolph, and 81 for Johnson. Hence the total stood: Jennings, 428; Randolph, 402; Johnson, 81.[1] It would be difficult to imagine a political disaster that would make an association of people sorer than were the Harrison partisans over this defeat. Waller Taylor desired to drown his disgust in blood, and for that purpose sought to pick a quarrel with Jennings. On June 3 he wrote to Randolph from Jeffersonville concerning his successful rival : " I expected the fellow would have been so much elated with his success that he would have been insolent and overbearing, but he says very little on the subject, and is silently preparing to go on to the city. Our meeting was not cordial on my part ; I refused to speak to him until he threw himself in my way and made the first overtures, and then I would not shake hands with

[1] *Western Sun,* July 8, 1809. The figures given in Randolph's memorial to Congress are, Jennings, 421 ; Randolph, 381. *Liberty Hall,* January 31, 1810.

him. He has heard, I am told, of everything I said
against him, which, by the by, was rather on the abusive
order, but he revenges himself on me by saying that he
never did anything to injure me, and professes esteem.
He is a pitiful coward, and certainly not of consequence
enough to excite resentment, nor any other sentiment
than contempt. He may rest in peace for me. I will no
longer continue to bother myself about him. I expect
before you have received this you will have passed
through the list of your enemies in asking them over the
Wabash to partake of your company and the amusement
you wish to afford them. I make no doubt they will decline your invitation, although it may be couched in the
most polite and ceremonious style; if they do, you will
have acquitted yourself agreeably to the rules of modern
etiquette, and can then be at liberty to act afterward to
them in whatever way may best suit your humor." [1]

Randolph was already moving in the line suggested.
In those days nearly everything political that appeared
in the newspapers was contributed over fictitious signatures, the editor reserving the right to furnish the names
to the parties attacked. Little distinction was made as
to party, if the article were reasonably decent, in its admission to print. Elihu Stout, the editor of the "Sun,"
had supported Randolph, but had published almost as
much matter against him as for him. When Randolph
demanded the name of the author of the articles against
him, he was informed that Dr. McNamee was the man.
He forthwith challenged McNamee, who was a Quaker
and consequently noncombatant, whereupon that gentleman repaired to Judge Vanderburgh and had Randolph
put under bonds to keep the peace. Randolph then

[1] Woollen's *Sketches*, p. 394.

posted the doctor as " a base slanderer, an infamous liar, and a contemptible coward," and so the peace was kept.[1]

But far beyond any little circle of personal friends were the Harrison party exasperated by the election of Jennings, and they let no opportunity pass without expressing their sentiments. On the fourth of July, at a public celebration near Vincennes, where Governor Harrison presided, the following toast was proposed and drank : " Jonathan Jennings — the semblance of a delegate — his want of abilities the only safety of the people — three groans." On the same day, at a meeting in Harrison township, in the same county, Dennis Sullivan proposed : " Jonathan Jennings — may his want of talents be the sure means to defeat the anti-republican schemes of his party." [2] It is astonishing how this hatred of Jennings lasted in Knox County ; and it can easily be followed through the accounts of the national birthday celebrations, for that was one of the few days in the year on which the primeval newspaper appeared to have a local editor. In none of these, for more than a decade, was there a respectful allusion to Jennings, and very seldom a toast to him of any kind ; yet political differences were then more largely thrown aside on the fourth of July than on other occasions, and the number of persons toasted was limited only by the amount of fluid on hand and the capacity of the celebrators.

The legislature which was chosen at this same election convened on October 16, 1809, in compliance with the governor's proclamation of August 8. Its constitution is immaterial to us, because it was decided by Congress to

---

[1] *Western Sun*, June 10, June 24, July 1, 1809.
[2] *Ibid.*, July 8, 1809.

be a body unauthorized by law.[1] The suffrage act passed by Congress had provided for the redistricting of the Territory by the legislature, but there was no legislature to redistrict it, and could be none until it was redistricted. The terms of the old legislature extended to June 30, 1809, but the division act took effect on March 1, and its passage was not heard of in Indiana until after it was in effect. Possibly the old legislature might have been called, as a quorum remained in Indiana; but on learning of the passage of the division act, while still in ignorance of the suffrage act, the governor had redistricted the Territory himself, and had called for only eight representatives, which was one less than the minimum prescribed by the law. Still, Governor Harrison and a majority of the legislature maintained that the organization was valid; but the minority disputed it, and after wrestling with the problem for five days they agreed to suspend. They adopted a memorial to Congress, reciting the situation, and asking an act to restore order from the existing chaos. It is noteworthy also that this assembly, although it had an anti-slavery majority, passed resolutions asking the reappointment of Governor Harrison, — the House unanimously and the Council three to one.[2] His term expired that summer, but President Madison had not yet reappointed him.

The memorial was sent to Congress; thither went Jennings; thither also went Randolph to contest the election. On December 4, Randolph presented his memorial, which included the memorial of the assembly, setting forth the circumstances of the apportionment and the election; and this was referred to the committee on

---

[1] The names of the members are in Dillon, p. 438.
[2] *Western Sun*, November 4, 1809.

elections, composed of Messrs. Findley, Clay, Sturges, Troup, Taylor, Van Rensselaer, and Garnett. On the 22d this committee reported that the election was illegal and void on account of the facts set forth in the memorial of the assembly. They stated, however, that both Randolph and Jennings advocated the legality of the election before them ; that Randolph " argued in support of the governor's authority to order the election ; " that he based his case on the irregularity of part of the returns from Dearborn, where Jennings had a majority, and on the failure to hold any election in two precincts of Dearborn ; that Jennings claimed he had never had any notice of the irregularities alleged ; that he said he could show them not to exist if he had opportunity ; and also that he claimed that the election in Knox County was not conducted in accordance with the provisions of the law. The report was hardly just, for, whatever Randolph may have argued before the committee in person, he certainly did argue the total invalidity of the election in his memorial. In that, after setting forth the irregularities mentioned by the committee, he said : " In addition to these reasons for giving to the people the privilege of having another election, the memorial of the legislature of the Territory strongly evinces the propriety. When it is considered that it must be the object of Congress to preserve the republican system in its purest state, your memorialist cannot believe it will sanction an election illegally conducted, and an election in which a respectable portion of the people have been deprived of their right of suffrage ; he therefore prays that the seat of the said Jennings be vacated, that another election may be had," etc.[1]

[1] *Liberty Hall*, January 31, 1810.

On January 8, the House, in committee of the whole, agreed to this report and so rose, but while the House was considering their report an adjournment was made. Attempts to proceed to final action were made on the 9th, 10th, 11th, and 12th. On the last two days when the case was up, there were protracted debates on the construction of the suffrage act and the act for division, of the last session ; and in these the friends of Jennings gained ground rapidly, for when the yeas and nays were taken, at three o'clock on the afternoon of the 12th, the House stood 83 to 30 against the adoption of the report. A motion was then made to recommit, but it was negatived without division.[1] During the contest Jennings managed to let it be generally understood that he was in opposition to Governor Harrison, and Randolph in friendship with him, and this had some weight in the determination of the case. One of the members, who considered the election invalid, said in explanation of his vote : " I shall vote against the sitting delegate, because I am clearly of opinion that the election was illegal ; but I am sorry for it, for I understand that the sitting delegate is the people's man, and the other is the Governor's man, his Secretary of State, or Attorney General, or something or other." [2]

As to the legislature, the House arrived at an opposite conclusion. The memorial, which had been presented on November 28, was referred to Messrs. Poindexter, Cochran, Breckenridge, Witherspoon, and Jennings. The committee held that the election of the legislators was wholly unauthorized by law. On December 5, Mr. Poindexter reported a bill giving the governor power to

[1] *Annals 11th Congress,* pp. 1173–1199.
[2] Jennings's handbill of October 10, 1810.

apportion and call an election for the next assembly, and also power to call special elections in case of the death, resignation, or removal of a councilor or a delegate to Congress. The bill became a law, and under this settlement of the difficulty the territorial government was resumed.

On February 21, 1810, the governor issued his proclamation calling for an election on April 2. He made no change in the apportionment for councilors, but redistricted the Territory for representatives with provision for nine members, three each from Knox and Dearborn, two from Clark, and one from Harrison. The councilors chosen at this election were Solomon Manwaring of Dearborn, James Beggs of Clark, John Harbison of Harrison, William Jones and Walter Wilson of Knox. The representatives were Ephraim Overman, Richard Rue, and John Templeton of Dearborn ; John Paul and Thomas Downs of Clark ; Dennis Pennington of Harrison ; Peter Jones, John Caldwell, and General W. Johnston of Knox. The delegates and councilors from Knox were pro-slavery men, with the exception of Johnston ; the remainder of the members were all anti-slavery men. This legislature — the Third General Assembly of Indiana — convened at Vincennes on November 12, 1810, and passed a number of laws, among which were a few that we have occasion to notice. Early in the session they created the new counties of Jefferson, Franklin, and Wayne, from portions of Clark and Dearborn. By the apportionment act, passed later on, one representative was given to each county except Knox, which still retained three. This act also provided that the delegate to the 12th Congress should be elected on the first Monday in April, 1811, the delegate to the 13th Congress on

the first Monday in August, 1812, and that thereafter
delegates to Congress should be elected biennially on the
first Mondays in August. The great work of this assembly, and the one to which we turn with special interest, was the repeal of the indenture law.

There were three distinct features of the repeal act.
The first was the immediate and unconditional repeal
of the indenture law of 1807. The second was a provision to prevent the kidnaping and unlawful removal of
negroes from the Territory. It enacted that any one
who attempted to remove, or aided in removing, any
negro, without first proving his right to do so under the
laws of the United States and the Territory, before a
judge or justice of the peace, and receiving a certificate
thereof which should be filed in the county clerk's
office, should be fined $1,000, disqualified from holding
any office of trust or profit, and be subject in damages
to the party aggrieved. The third was the repeal of so
much of the act concerning servants as allowed the importation of negroes indented in other territories or
states, and provided for the enforcement of these foreign
indentures.[1] This law passed the House without difficulty. In the Council the Knox County men opposed it,
and the Dearborn and Harrison County men favored it.
This made a tie, and James Beggs, the president, voted
for its passage. The governor was very willing to take
action which might get the slavery question out of politics, for his party was evidently doomed to defeat, in
everything outside of Knox County, so long as it remained. He approved the repeal act on December 14,
1810, and this blot of the past five years was removed
from our statute books.

[1] Laws of 1810, p. 54.

The deciding vote of James Beggs on this occasion has always been a matter of just pride to his family. In a recent letter his venerable daughter, Mrs. Susan Armstrong, of Laporte, says : " My Father being President of the Council gave the casting vote which made Indiana a free state ; for which I say God bless James Beggs." To her pious benediction we may all fervently add, So may it be ; for these acts, in the few years they had been in force, had spread their pernicious influence far enough to demonstrate their dangerous character. Under them the number of slaves in Indiana proper had increased from 28 to 237. In the Illinois division they appear by the census reports to have increased only from about 140 to 168 ; but it is evident that the indented negroes of Illinois were not counted as slaves in the census of 1810, for 613 free negroes were reported in that year, while in 1820 the report from Illinois was 917 slaves and only 506 free negroes. After Illinois became a state, and the operation of the indenture law as to new importations was stopped, the number decreased naturally to 747 slaves in 1830, and to 331 in 1840 ; and thereafter the institution died out under the decisions of the courts and the Constitution of 1848, as has been recited. What might have resulted in Indiana had the law continued in force, no one can say ; but on any line of conjecture, we have cause to be thankful to our Indiana men of that early day who thus, from pure principle, uprooted and exterminated this iniquitous and unconstitutional system.

After the session of the legislature came on the second campaign of Jennings and Randolph, though in one sense it had commenced before the legislature convened. After the congressional committee on elections had

agreed on their report, Randolph, supposing that the
report would be adopted and a new election would
occur, had written a letter announcing himself a candidate, and this duly appeared in print. Jennings followed close on his heels with a handbill setting forth
Randolph's memorial and the congressional proceedings
thereon, but without comment. Randolph replied, denouncing this handbill as an attempt to show that he
had asked the election to be held illegal on account of
the governor's not having authority to call for it. This
line of defense was injudicious, to say the least ; for by
putting this construction on the publication of the bare
record, he admitted the very thing he wished to deny.
Besides that, he certainly had put before the committee
all the papers on which they found the election illegal,
and he had asked that Jennings's seat be vacated, and a
new election held. True, the committee said he argued
in favor of the legality of the election, but the grounds
which both they and he said he did urge were only
irregularities in Dearborn County, and these could not
have vitiated the entire election. Their utmost result
would have been to displace Jennings and seat himself ;
but he did not ask for the seat ; he wanted another
election. Jennings answered Randolph in another and
very ingenious broadside that left him in worse position
than ever, for, in addition to being confronted with a
charge of attempting to deprive the Territory of a representative in Congress, he now had before him the explanation of what seemed a very plain case of misrepre-
sentation. The most satisfactory thing he could do was
to call Jennings a liar, and this he did with great fer-
vor.[1] All this occurred in 1810.[2] The writs for the

[1] Woollen's *Sketches*, p. 308.
[2] Jennings's last-mentioned circular was dated Oct.

election were not issued by the governor until February 2, 1811.[1]

Jennings was obliged to leave the Territory to attend the session of Congress, in the winter of 1810, but his campaign did not cease. It is said that he sent copies of his handbills to every voter in Indiana. He also trusted much to letters. In those days, when window-glass was a rarity, and greased paper served the purpose in the frontier cabins, old residents say that the well-known writing of Jonathan Jennings (he was an unusually good penman) could be seen in the sashes of every schoolhouse in the Territory. Meanwhile his opponent had a clear field, and he and his friends let none of it lie fallow. Randolph canvassed the entire Territory, and he had stanch friends in all parts looking after his interests, — Harrison and a host of smaller fry in Knox, Waller Taylor in Clark, and Dill and Vance in Dearborn. But Jennings also had many active and influential friends ; and he was aided by two moves which were blamed to the opposition. One of these was the appointment of Solomon Manwaring, who was temporarily unpopular, judge of the common pleas for Dearborn, in place of Benjamin Chambers, resigned.[2] The other was the enforcement of the militia law, which was obnoxious to the Quaker settlers of the Whitewater. The act of September 17, 1807, had made the militia to consist of " every free, able-bodied, white, male citizen of the Territory " between the ages of eighteen and forty-five, excepting only the judges and clerk of the

1810. The record first published by him began to appear in the *Liberty Hall* on January 31, 1810.

[1] *Executive Journal.*

[2] *Ibid.*, December 14, 1810.

Supreme Court, the Attorney General, ministers of the gospel licensed to preach, jail-keepers, and such persons as were exempt by the laws of the United States. Any one who refused to perform militia duty was subject to fine in the courts.[1] This did not excite material objection until 1810, when the anticipation of war with England, and consequent hostilities by the Indians, had called for its strict enforcement. On August 25, 1810, at the monthly meeting of the Society of Friends held in Richmond, a memorial was adopted, addressed to the governor and legislature, asking an amendment of this law, and Benjamin Harris and Andrew Hoover were appointed delegates to present it to the governor. On December 19, 1810, the legislature amended the law so that Friends were exempted absolutely in time of peace, and made subject in time of actual war " to such additional tax or contribution in lieu of military services as the legislature may think proper to impose." [2] Although Harrison approved this amendatory act, it was passed by an anti-Harrison legislature, and there was enough opposition to it from the minority to make it almost a party question. In fact, after war had come, a majority of the legislature considered the discrimination uncalled for ; and by the elaborate militia law of January 3, 1814, exemption in time of peace was granted only on payment of a special tax of five dollars annually.[3]

The slavery question was also kept in the campaign by Jennings, who was too adroit a politician to let an issue like that die away. Randolph was very anxious to be rid of it, and insisted that the repeal of the inden-

---

[1] Rev. Laws, 1807, ch. xlii.

[2] Laws, 1810, p. 104 ; Minutes Richmond Monthly Meeting.

[3] Laws, 2d Sess. 4th Genl. Ass., p. 25.

ture law had entirely settled it. On December 15, the day after the governor approved the repeal act, he issued a letter to the people in which he said : " Nor will I from party views cant upon a subject now finally put to rest. An act concerning the introduction of negroes and mulattoes into this Territory is repealed." [1] But Jennings would not let him off so easily, nor would the people, for with them, as with the generality of mankind, the antagonisms of yesterday had more weight in politics than the problems of to-day. It is wonderful how many more of the political campaigns of this child-world of ours are fought out on the memories of the past than on the questions of the present.

To the astonishment and mortification of Randolph and his friends, Jennings was again victorious. Dearborn, where they had expected a majority, divided almost evenly ; Clark and the new counties rolled up majorities that overcame Knox and Harrison ; and the thing was done. Here ended Randolph's political career. When the army was organized that summer for the Wabash campaign, Harrison would have given him an appointment, but, there being no vacancies, he volunteered as a private and acted as aid-de-camp to Harrison. At Tippecanoe he fell by an Indian bullet, mortally hurt. General Harrison bent over him and asked if there was aught he could do to help him. Randolph replied no, — that he was spent, — but to watch over his child. And so he died as a gallant gentleman in the service of his country, and they buried him on the field by the side of his friend, the Kentucky hero, Jo. Daviess.

Harrison's connection with territorial politics lasted but little longer, and with no permanent effect. The

[1] *Western Sun*, December 15, 1810.

partisan action of the legislature in extending special
thanks to Boyd's regiment to the exclusion of the remainder of the army, the controversy over the comparative merits of the militia and the regulars, and the stupid
performances of Boyd, turned popular sympathy largely
in Harrison's favor, but did little for his party.   Public
approval should have gone to him much more than it
did for his actual service in the Tippecanoe campaign,
but party feeling was strong, and by partisans very little
credit was conceded to him.   Jennings shrewdly kept
out of the wrangle, and exerted himself in securing pay
and pensions for the soldiers, as a result of which he
made friends all around.   He entered the lists as a
candidate for reëlection to Congress the next year, the
election for the 13th Congress being held on the first
Monday in August, 1812.   Waller Taylor took the field
against him.   He, also, endeavored to avoid any issue on
the slavery question.   In his handbill of June 17, 1812,
he says: "With respect to Territorial politics, and to
that question, the discussion of which has caused so much
sensibility in the Territory, I mean the introduction of
negroes, I must observe that I never have been an advocate for their admission.   If I have expressed an
opinion upon the subject, it has been that it would be a
present benefit and a future evil.   Being well assured
also that an immense majority of the people are opposed
to the measure, I here pledge myself to you not only to
refrain from taking any measure myself to favor their
introduction, but to oppose it should it be brought forward by others."   It was a vain attempt.   The men
who had been fighting against slavery since the foundation of the Territory, and those who had been coming to
the Territory because it was free and because they hated

slavery, could not forget and would not forgive so readily. The majority went against him, and Jennings was
shown to be invincible before the people.

This was the last territorial election in which Harrison was a factor of any importance. Already his
time had been much occupied with the military preparations of the frontier for the war which was just beginning, and by his appointment to the command of the
Army of the Northwest, on September 24, his civil service in Indiana was brought to an end. The affairs of
the Territory were conducted by Secretary (acting Governor) Gibson until May 25, 1813, when General Thomas
Posey was installed as governor. Here, therefore, we take
leave of Governor Harrison. Of his influence on the development of Indiana, outside of the performance of his
official duties, our knowledge is unhappily meagre. His
biographers who might have told us most were aiming
at political results, and confined their treatises chiefly
to a review of his acts in connection with the negotiation
of Indian treaties and other public business, which for
historical purposes might be gathered as well, if not
better, from the public records. The great mass of his
papers and letters were destroyed at the burning of the
old homestead at North Bend some thirty years ago.
There are probably many of his private letters scattered
over the country, but no one has taken the trouble to
collect them. Enough is available, however, to show
that his influence, aside from this matter of slavery, was
for the good of the commonwealth. We know that public education had no more earnest champion than William Henry Harrison. He labored for it much, and he
often urged others to labor for it. Nor was his endeavor
merely to secure the limited result of a rudimentary edu-

cation to the masses, which some modern lights would
have us consider sufficient. He was broad enough to
know that the public welfare called for some citizens of
the highest culture, — that it required a Jefferson to
draw the Declaration of Independence, a Hamilton to
devise a sound financial policy, a Marshall to declare
the import of the Constitution, — and therefore he labored for the university maintained by the state as he
did for the log schoolhouse. In this regard he was a
blessing to the Territory.

We know that his administration of Indian affairs
was one that did credit to his humanity, his integrity,
and his judgment. Not only did he seek to be just to
this unfortunately situated race in his dealings with
them, but also to protect them as far as possible from
the evils of their contact with civilized life, particularly
from the frightful effects of the use of liquor. In this
respect he ranked with Washington and Jefferson of the
earlier statesmen, and with all intelligent, fully civilized
Americans of the present who are informed in the Indian question. It is true that in the territorial times he
was accused of defrauding the Indians, but he offered a
reward of $100 for the name of the author of the charge ;
and when he learned that William McIntosh was responsible for it, he at once sued him for slander. The jury
gave him a verdict for $4,000, but he did not desire
more than vindication ; he remitted two thirds of the
judgment to McIntosh, and gave the other third to some
of the orphans of men who had fallen in the war of 1812.[1]
Afterwards, in Congress, this charge was repeated, by
insinuation, by Jonathan Jennings, who demanded a

[1] *Western Sun*, February 15, 1812; Woollen's *Sketches*, p. 305;
Dawson's *Harrison*, p. 176; Ter. Court Docket, April Term, 1811.

committee of investigation; but the most important result of it was a sharp attack on Jennings by the editor of the Vincennes "Sun," who said that "Governor Harrison will live in the grateful recollection of the people of this Territory when his puny and contemptible slanderers will be thought of only to be scorned." [1]

As against these charges, better evidence than verdicts or reports of committees is found in the universal confidence which the Indians had in him. Situated, as he was, among French settlers who had long been on terms of intimate friendship with the Indians, and watched by enemies who were ready to magnify his least inadvertence into a crime, it was impossible that he should have defrauded the red men and still been trusted by them. In this connection it may be added that no man in public life ever had so many serious charges preferred against his honesty, and came forth from his trials so fully vindicated by his judges and by the people, as did William Henry Harrison. His private life had its blots, but his public record was remarkably clean. That he was not a great man his political friends conceded, but that he was an honest man was never seriously questioned by his political enemies after he had been heard in his own defense.

There was one peculiarity of Harrison's character that might almost class him as a monomaniac. It was his reverence for the republics of Greece and Rome. He thought about them, talked about them, and wrote about them continually, and if he dreamed at all he must have dreamed of them. In the first days of our republic, the attention of statesmen was naturally directed to these republics in the search for experience by which to guide

[1] *Western Sun,* April 20, 1816; *Annals* 14*th Cong.,* p. 1273.

our steps; and although our government was in fact modeled after that of England, the hostility of the people to that nation caused it to be based professedly on the lines of the old republics. On this account, and because the style of polite writing then in vogue naturally followed that of the British writers of preceding years in its wealth of classic allusion, the early literature of all kinds in America had a very strong flavor of the antique; but Harrison surpassed all of his contemporaries in this idiosyncrasy. In his state papers, if Leonidas, Epaminondas, and Lycurgus escaped, Cincinnatus, Scipio, or the Gracchi were sure to be taken in the net. As a rule, this craze was only an amusing personal characteristic. It was of no special moment that Daniel Webster should have found it necessary to kill " seventeen Roman proconsuls as dead as smelts " in Harrison's inaugural address,[1] or that the Whig managers should have been put to some trouble to find a suitable horse to carry the venerable President-elect to his inaugural, in imitation of the Roman consuls.[2] But his admiration of the ancients carried him farther, and while governor he exerted himself to graft portions of the old republican systems on Indiana Territory. In his celebrated letter on the militia system, addressed to Governor Scott of Kentucky, he declares that " professorships of tactics should be established in all our seminaries, and even the amusements of the children should resemble those of the ancient gymnasia, that they may grow up in the practice of those exercises which will enable them to bear with ease the duty of the camp and the labours of the field." [3]

[1] Harvey's *Reminiscences of Webster*, pp. 160–163.
[2] I had this from the late Maj. Ben. Perley Poore, the accredited custodian of Washington anecdote.
[3] Dawson's *Harrison*, p. 123.

In his message of November, 1810, to the legislature, he proposed that military instruction be made a prominent feature in the public schools. He said : " Let the masters of the inferior schools be obliged to qualify themselves, and instruct their pupils in the military evolutions, whilst the university, in addition to those exercises, may have attached to it a professorship of tactics, in which all the sciences connected with the art of war may be taught." [1]

That such a system might be advantageous to a nation that was often involved in war is possibly true ; certainly it were much to be preferred to the maintenance of standing armies. For this reason the project seemed not out of place in a frontier territory where war might come at any time ; but with us that period was of necessity limited, and when the exigence of self-defense is removed a universal military education has no harmony with our theories of government. The government of the United States was not formed for purposes of conquest, but to secure the blessings of peace to its people, and a universal preparation for war cannot be included among these. No people has realized as we have that the glory and profit of war go to the few, its hardships and sufferings to the many, and yet we have not been found lacking in military ardor when war was inevitable. When we have felt it necessary to draw the sword, we have made its arbitrament final. We have not sheathed it until the dispute which brought it forth had been settled forever. Thus, in time of war we have prepared for peace — for lasting peace.

[1] Dawson's *Harrison*, p. 171.

CHAPTER XII.

THE EMANCIPATION.

GOVERNOR POSEY, like Harrison, was a Virginian and a soldier. He was born on July 9, 1750; served as a private in Dunmore's war; entered the Revolutionary army as a captain, and earned his way to a colonelcy by the close of the war; and capped his early military career by creditable service, under Wayne, against the Indians in Georgia and at the Maumee. He desired to settle in Northwest Territory, but, after the legislature of 1799 had refused permission to bring slaves into the Virginia bounty lands, he located in Kentucky, where he was elected to the state senate and chosen speaker of that body — *ex-officio* lieutenant-governor. When troops were called for in 1809, in anticipation of hostilities with France and England, Posey was commissioned major-general of the Kentucky levies, but war did not come, and the forces were disbanded. Soon afterwards he removed to Louisiana, where, in 1812, Governor Claiborne appointed him to the United States Senate to fill a vacancy caused by the resignation of John N. Destrihan. At the next meeting of the Louisiana legislature another senator was elected, and, before his successor reached Washington, Posey was appointed to the governorship of Indiana by President Madison. At this time Posey was almost sixty-three years of age, and was somewhat broken in health.

With his Virginia training, his military life, his political experience, and his social culture, it was only natural that the personal friends of General Harrison became Posey's personal friends; and in equally natural sequence he fell heir to Harrison's political estate as well as to his office, though he was not much of a politician. The political parties of Indiana remained as they had been since the separation from Illinois, with no material issues beyond those that grew from local interests and party strife, except the decision of the slavery controversy, which, by the proposal of the Springville meeting and the tacit acquiescence of Congress, would occur on the adoption of a constitution for state government. Jennings held his forces in line on this basis with but little trouble, and the opposition were able to bring forward no man who could defeat him. For the congressional election of 1814 they supported Judge Elijah Sparks of Dearborn, a native of Virginia, who had been a Methodist preacher until thirty years of age and then entered upon the practice of law. He was a good citizen and a man of reputable attainments, but it was child's play for Jennings to beat him, for the immigration to the Territory was constantly adding strength to his party.

The anti-slavery party also continued to control the legislature, and through it, as well as through their congressional influence, they prepared for the final struggle. It may be that they gave more attention to the slavery question than there was need for; it is quite possible that they may have given it some of its prominence for political effect; but at any rate they maintained that eternal vigilance which is the price of liberty, and left no preparation unmade which might secure a free soil

to themselves and to their posterity. At the session of
1815 a petition was adopted asking Congress for an
enabling act. It was accompanied by an official census
which showed the thirteen counties of the Territory to
have a free, white, male population of 63,897. Embodied in the memorial was this clause : " And whereas
the inhabitants of this Territory are principally composed
of emigrants from every part of the Union, and as various in their customs and sentiments as in their persons,
we think it prudent, at this time, to express to the
general government our attachment to the fundamental
principles of legislation prescribed by Congress in their
Ordinance for the government of this Territory, particularly as respects personal freedom and involuntary servitude, and hope they may be continued as the basis of
the constitution." [1] This memorial was presented to
Congress on December 28, 1815, by Mr. Jennings, and
was referred to a committee of which he was made
chairman. He reported a bill in accordance with the
prayer of the petition, which, after some amendment, was
passed and became a law on April 19, 1816. The act
provided for the election on May 13, 1816, of forty-
three delegates, as apportioned in the memorial of the
legislature, who were to meet in convention and decide
whether it were expedient to form a state government ;
if so, they were empowered to form a constitution themselves, or to provide for an election of representatives
who should form a constitution. There was not to be
any submission of their work to the people for approval ;
it was to stand as they had left it, " *Provided,* That the
same, whenever formed, shall be republican, and not repugnant to those articles of the ordinance of the thir-

[1] Dillon, p. 555.

teenth of July, one thousand seven hundred and eighty seven, which are declared to be irrevocable between the original states and the people and states of the territory northwest of the river Ohio."

This law reached Indiana only in time for notice of the election to be given on May 2, eleven days before it occurred, but the preliminary discussions had been going on for some time, in anticipation of the passage of the bill. There was more warmth than usual in the canvass, principally over the slavery question, which was forced as an issue by the anti-slavery people. The opposition politicians tried to turn the contest to other grounds. They attacked Jennings for voting for the donation of lands to Canadian refugees; giving our "choicest lands" to these people, while our own "virtuous citizens" (*i. e.* squatters) had been ordered off the national property by Madison, and Jennings had not even protested. Still worse, he had attended a caucus at Washington for the nomination of a President of the United States, "thus influencing improperly the free and unbiased voice of the people on that important subject."[1] That sounds oddly in these days of slavery to party, when staying out of a caucus is a political felony; but the fault is ours, not theirs. Our ancestors were wiser than we in some things, and this was one of them. Nothing has done so much to repress that independence of thought and adherence to principle that once made men Americans as the degraded partyism of modern times. Already have we reached a point where thousands of men, their moral vision blurred by party feeling, condone actual crimes committed in the supposed service of party. How more pitiful, how very pitiful, to see men, who otherwise are

[1] *Western Sun*, April 20, 1816.

honest, crouch beneath the party whip and prostitute their talents to the advocacy of measures which they believe to be wrong, or to opposing measures which they believe to be right!

The charges against Jennings fell on dull ears, for party lines had become strong in the Territory. The people were interested in a great question, and would hear of nothing else. Early in February, Moses Wiley had sounded the alarm by an article in our Vincennes newspaper, in which he said: "If slaves are admitted, the pernicious tendency is too obvious to dwell on ; partial admission is but little better. I have no doubt but you, my fellow-citizens, are all on your watch; if not, rise and look out! Now is the time! I am for not admitting the principle on no grounds whatever." [1] With almost equal disregard for the health of our language, "A Citizen of Gibson" labored on the other side, maintaining that the betterment of the condition of the negroes was the only point entitled to consideration, and on that ground favoring their introduction. Said he: "Let the people maturely consider this question abstractedly, and let them say and instruct their conventionalists to say, whether the corn of Indiana would or would not be more nourishing and palatable to the poor negro than the cotton-seed of South Carolina or Georgia." [2] In reply to this, "Another Citizen of Gibson" took the position that the only question was, "Would it be good policy to admit slavery into the new intended state or would it not? Would it make us more wealthy and happy as a state, or would it not?" [3] On this sound basis he built

---

[1] *Western Sun*, February 3, 1816.

[2] *Ibid.*, March 2, 1816.

[3] *Ibid.*, March 30, 1816.

an able argument for its exclusion, to which no answer was attempted in the "Sun," and yet it had little convincing power with the pro-slavery men of the western counties, for both Knox and Gibson elected pro-slavery delegates.

The controversy was more heated in the eastern counties, where the free-soil men seemed in continual fear that their adversaries would take some turn by which slavery would be fastened on the state. The settlers there had no newspapers, but they were all able to talk; and they argued the question in all its phases. Mr. Timothy Flint, who traveled through this section of the Territory just at this time, says: "The population was very far from being in a state of mind, of sentiment, and affectionate mutual confidence, favourable to commencing their lonely condition in the woods in harmonious intercourse. They were forming a state government. The question in all its magnitude, whether it should be a slave-holding state or not, was just now agitating. I was often compelled to hear the question debated by those in opposite interests, with no small degree of asperity. Many fierce spirits talked, as the clamorous and passionate are accustomed to talk in such cases, about opposition and 'resistance unto blood.' But the preponderance of more sober and reflecting views, those habits of order and quietness, that aversion to shedding blood, which so generally and so honorably appertain to the American character and institutions, operated in these wildernesses, among these inflamed and bitter spirits, with all their positiveness, ignorance, and clashing feeling, and with all their destitution of courts and the regular course of settled laws, to keep them from open violence. The question was not long after finally settled in peace." [1]

The election of May 13 passed off quietly, but its result was awaited with anxiety. From the first, the returns indicated an anti-slavery victory, and these indications were received joyfully in the eastern counties, as also in western Ohio, whose settlers were closely united in sympathy with those along our eastern line. The next issue of the " Western Spy " said : " A gentleman of respectability from Indiana informs us that from the sentiments of the members elected to the convention, as far as they are known, he has no doubt that a constitution will be formed which will exclude involuntary slavery from that rising state. We sincerely hope this expectation will be realized." [2] The pro-slavery people felt that they were defeated, but were not disposed to concede it while there was any chance of escape, and there was one such chance that they thought worth trying. On June 1, the " Sun " issued an extra, urging that a state government should not be formed, on the grounds that there would be a greatly increased expense of government and a great loss of taxes, the latter on account of a provision in the enabling act that lands sold by the national government should not be taxable for five years after sale. It was too late in the day for a proposition of that kind. They could not even hold their own party to it.

On June 10 the convention assembled at Corydon, in Harrison County, whither the seat of government had been removed under an act of March 11, 1813. It could hardly be said that the convention was composed of great

[1] *Recollections of the Last Ten Years*, p. 57.
[2] Quoted in *Liberty Hall*, May 27, 1816.

men, though there were some master minds gathered
there; nor was it necessary that it should be. In 1816,
the paths of the Constitution-making were well defined
and plainly marked; and with any set of delegates
there would have been a selection of the same general
outline of government, with some slight differences of
detail, except as to slavery and a few points of local
concern. The majority of the members were frontier
farmers, who had a general idea of what they wanted,
and had sense enough to let their more erudite colleagues put it in shape. Wayne County was represented
by Joseph Holman, of Log Convention fame; Hugh Cull,
the pioneer Methodist preacher; Jeremiah Cox and Patrick Baird. The most able member from Franklin was
James Noble, who was senator from Indiana from 1816
to 1831, dying in the middle of his third term. With
him were Robert Hanna, who filled a part of Noble's
unexpired term as senator in 1831–1832, Enoch Mc-
Carty, James Brownlee, and William H. Eads. From
Dearborn came our old acquaintances James Dill and
Solomon Manwaring, and with them was Dr. Ezra Fer-
ris, a sturdy Baptist elder, who spent his life fighting
disease and Democracy through the week and Campbell-
ism and the Devil on Sundays. Switzerland County was
represented by William Cotton; Jefferson, by David H.
Maxwell, Samuel Smock, and Nathaniel Hunt. Jonathan Jennings headed the Clark County delegation; the
other members were James Scott, one of the first judges
of the supreme court, Thomas Carr, John K. Graham,
and James Lemon. The leading member from Harrison
County was Dennis Pennington, a man of little culture
but of strong mind, who was for many years the most
influential politician of that county, and represented it

for several terms in the state and territorial legislatures. Davis Floyd was a delegate from the same county; also Daniel C. Lane, John Boone, and Patrick Shields. At the head of the Washington County delegation was John De Pauw, an attorney, a son of the Charles De Pauw who came over with Lafayette to aid us in the Revolution. His colleagues were Samuel Milroy, Robert McIntire, William Lowe, and William Graham. The Knox County delegation was the strongest of all in ability, and though it was in a hopeless minority on the party questions that divided the convention, it did a large part of the convention work and was entitled to much of the credit for the result. It was composed of John Johnson, John Badollet, William Polke, Benjamin Parke, and John Benefield. The more important men from Gibson were David Robb and Alexander Devin. With them were James Smith and Frederick (Reichart) Rapp, an adopted son of George Rapp, the founder of the Society of Harmonists. The remaining members were Daniel Grass of Warrick, Charles Polke of Perry, and Dann Lynn of Posey.

The convention organized by electing Jonathan Jennings president, and William Hendricks secretary. The latter was a Pennsylvanian who had settled in Madison two years earlier.[1] The next business of the convention, under the enabling act, was to decide whether a constitution should be formed; and if so, whether they should form it or provide for another convention. A resolution

---

[1] He was the first representative of the State in the lower house of Congress, serving for three terms in that capacity. In 1822, at the close of his third term, he was elected governor of the State, receiving all the votes cast, 18,340 in number. From this office he was elected to the national senate in 1825, and served there for two terms.

to proceed to the formation of a Constitution was offered
on the first day, but on motion of John Johnson its consideration was postponed to the next day, when a vote
was taken and only eight members were found opposed
to proceeding.   Committees were then appointed to prepare the various parts of the Constitution, and the first
week was consumed in their work.   During this time,
on the 13th, a petition was received from citizens of
Wayne, asking that "constitutional provisions may be
made effectually to prohibit the introduction of slavery
and involuntary servitude into the state about to be
formed; also, that the Society of Friends, commonly
called Quakers, may in times of peace be exempted
from bearing arms."   It was referred to the appropriate
committees.

On the 20th the convention first came to a vote involving the slavery question, in considering the mode of
amending the Constitution, the article for which happened to be taken up before much of the instrument
had been formed.   This article provided that at intervals of twelve years the Constitution might be revised if
a majority of the people voted for a revising convention,
and the succeeding legislature, by a majority of both
houses, provided for it by law; "But, as the holding
any part of the human creation in slavery, or involuntary servitude, can only originate in usurpation and
tyranny, no alteration of this constitution shall ever take
place so as to introduce slavery or involuntary servitude
in this state, otherwise than for the punishment of
crimes, whereof the party shall have been duly convicted."   John Johnson moved to amend this by substituting for the words "no alteration of this Constitution
shall ever take place," the words, "it is the opinion of

this convention that no alteration of this Constitution ought ever to take place." No more excellent position could have been found for a stand by the pro-slavery party, for the article as reported was in fact only an expression of opinion, and could not bind a future constitutional convention. Nevertheless the anti-slavery men were determined to put the appearance of an eternal quietus on the slavery question by as strong an expression of their opinion as possible. The yeas and nays were called for by Mr. Dill. All the members from Gibson, all from Knox except Benefield, Dill of Dearborn, Scott and Lemon of Clark, Lane of Harrison, and Lynn of Posey, a total of only thirteen, voted for the amendment; and, small as this vote was, the yeas of the Clark County members at least must be credited to an objection to a futile attempt to bind subsequent conventions, and not to any pro-slavery sentiment. Johnson then moved to strike out the words " involuntary servitude " where they occurred in the article, thus making a distinction between ordinary slavery and that of the indenture system, but the negative was so decisive that no division was taken. No further amendment being attempted, the article went into the Constitution as reported from the committee.[1]

The subject of slavery in general was within the province of the Committee on General Provisions, which was composed of Messrs. Maxwell, De Pauw, Scott, Robb, and Baird. On the 21st, Mr. Maxwell, of this committee, reported their work, which included the following: " Sec. 7. There shall be neither slavery, nor involuntary servitude, in this state, otherwise than for the punishment of crimes, whereof the party shall have

[1] Const. of 1816, Art. 8; *Conv. Journal*, pp. 38, 39.

been duly convicted ; [nor shall any male person, arrived at the age of twenty-one years, nor female person, arrived at the age of eighteen years, be held to serve any person as a servant under pretence of indenture or otherwise, unless such person shall enter into such indenture while in a state of perfect freedom, and on condition of a *bonâ fide* consideration received, or to be received, for his or her service, except as before excepted :] Nor shall any indenture of any negro, or mulatto, hereafter made and executed out of the bounds of this state, be of any validity with the state ; [neither shall any indenture of any negro or mulatto, hereafter made within the state, be of the least validity except in the case of apprenticeships.] " [1]   On the 24th the convention went into committee of the whole on this report, and here they were confronted by a question of consistency.   The portion of the section preceding the first bracket put slavery and involuntary servitude on the same basis in the State that they had in the Territory, except that there was in the Constitution no reservation of rights to the ancient inhabitants which could be construed to preserve their slaves to them, as there had been in the Ordinance. Under the provision as it stood in the Ordinance, the anti-slavery men had always contended that the indenture law was unconstitutional, and therefore if they now added to it a special clause prohibiting indentures they would be conceding that the slavery article of the Ordinance did not of itself have the effect which they had continuously claimed for it.   Moreover, by excepting apprenticeship and other service under voluntary contract from this additional provision, they made the inconsistency greater, for these were clearly neither slav-

----

[1] *Conv. Journal*, p. 41. The brackets are mine.

ery nor involuntary servitude ; and excepting them was a virtual admission that the slave indentures partook of their nature, whereas the position of the anti-slavery men had been that there was not, and could not be, anything of the essence of legal contract in the formalities of the indenture system.

After due consideration, the committee decided to stand by the words of the Ordinance and strike out the portions included above in brackets, and so they reported to the convention.[1] This report was concurred in, and the section went into the Constitution in these words : "There shall be neither slavery nor involuntary servitude in this state, otherwise than for the punishment of crimes, whereof the party shall have been duly convicted. Nor shall any indenture of any negro or mulatto hereafter made and executed out of the bounds of this state be of any validity within the state." [2] The latter clause of the section was intended to prevent the introduction of any servitude similar to slavery which might exist or be created in a slave state. For example, if Kentucky had enacted a manumission law by which, when a master gave a slave freedom, the slave, in consideration of the grant of freedom, or some other consideration provided by the law, might enter into a voluntary contract of service for life or for a term of years, an Indiana legislature could have provided for the enforcement of such agreement within this state, if not prohibited by the Constitution. Obviously the only certain way to prevent any collusion, pretense, or misconception in the matter, either by the legislature or the courts, was to bar the enforcement of any foreign con-

---

[1] *Conv. Journal*, p. 53.
[2] Const. of 1816, Art. 11, Sec. 7.

tract of indenture of negroes ; and the convention made
assurance doubly sure by doing so. In addition to these
provisions, two clauses that affected the status of slavery
were inserted without any opposition in the bill of rights,
or first article of the Constitution. The first was the
opening section : " That the general, great and essential
principles of liberty and free government may be recognized and unalterably established, WE DECLARE, That all
men are born equally free and independent, and have
certain natural, inherent and unalienable rights ; among
which are the enjoying and defending life and liberty,
and of acquiring, possessing, and protecting property,
and pursuing and obtaining happiness and safety." The
other was the 24th section : " To guard against any encroachments on the rights herein retained, we declare
that everything in this article is excepted out of the general powers of government, and shall forever remain
inviolable." The convention concluded its work and
adjourned on June 29, 1816, and the Constitution accordingly bears that date. The State was admitted
into the Union by resolution of December 11, 1816; and
the State government was actually commenced on November 7, 1816.[1]

Naturally the interest of the people was absorbed in
the convention. It was the great event of the period.
But more than all else they were anxious to know just
what would be done in regard to slavery. An estimable
lady of Lawrenceburgh, who preserves her faculties unimpaired at the advanced age of eighty-five years, informs
me that she remembers clearly the day when the news
of the final action reached that place, and that the message which passed from mouth to mouth was, " She has

[1] *Annals 14th Cong. 2d Sess.*, p. 1348; *Ex. Journal.*

come in free! She has come in free!" Other matters
were not of so much importance, and there was a quiet
faith that they had been properly cared for. And yet
after all this controversy, and all the care of the convention, the slavery question was not yet definitely settled.
As to the effect of the Constitution on future importations there was no question, but as to its effect on pre-
existent slavery and servitude there remained a wide
divergence of opinion. In the eastern counties it was
generally considered that slaves and servants were emancipated, and masters acted on that theory, though still
feeling themselves charged with the care of keeping their
old servitors from want. One master told his negro
man and woman that they were free, and might do whatever they liked. If they desired it, he would give them
a cabin and bit of land and they might take care of
themselves ; or, if they preferred, they might continue
to live with him, and he would give them a wage allowance and care for them. After a protracted consideration
of the subject they concluded to remain. Another master made a similar proposal to his negro woman, but she
replied, "No, damn you ! I 'll go to Cincinnati and soon
be as rich as any of you." And sure enough she did
locate at Cincinnati, opened a little eating-house, and acquired a competence. This difference of sentiment was
due only to the spirit of the negroes, for they were all
treated kindly.

In the western counties a few masters removed their
slaves from the State, and some of these were afterwards
released by the courts of Southern States, as we have
seen. The great majority, however, simply continued to
hold their slaves in Indiana. The idea which commonly
obtained was that the Constitution could have no effect

on preëxisting slavery ; that the property in slaves was
a vested right, secured by the Ordinance, and could not
be impaired.   Even the courts in that section proceeded
on this theory.   The first case in which the question
was involved came to trial on October 5, 1816, before
David Raymond, president judge of the first circuit.[1]   It
was a replevin suit brought against Thomas Jones by
Mason Pecongar *alias* The Owl, an Indian who had
adopted civilized life and settled near Vincennes, for the
recovery of a colored girl and a cross-cut saw.   The jury
found for the plaintiff as to the girl, but a new trial was
granted and the case was continued.   It was settled out
of court, for no further mention of it occurs in the records.[2]   In 1817, Bob and Anthony, held as slaves by
Luke Decker, Jr., brought suit for their freedom in
Orange County.   They were sons of Dinah, a female
slave brought by Luke Decker, Sr., from Virginia, prior
to 1787.   They gained their freedom, but not until the
case had been fought for five years in various courts, and
after the question involved had been decided by the Supreme Court in another case, which we will examine
presently.

The masters of indented negroes in this section also
held to their servants, probably from an enlargement of
that quality of the mind which gives one a vague sense

---

[1] This was the old circuit court, organized under the law of
1814.   Under the Constitution of 1816 there were three circuit
courts, each composed of a president and two associate judges,
the former elected by the legislature and the latter by the people.
The president judge could hold court alone, and the two associates
could sit in the absence of the president.   The Supreme Court
was composed of three judges appointed by the governor with
the advice and consent of the Senate.

[2] *Knox County Records ; Hist. Knox Co.*, p. 186.

of ownership in anything he has once owned. In fact many of them were not sufficiently versed in the intricacies of the law to perceive any distinction between their cases and those of the ancient inhabitants. If this point of vested rights was of any importance, they had their slaves before the adoption of the Constitution as well as the older settlers. Of course there was understood to be a reservation of rights to the ancient inhabitants by the Ordinance, but what did that amount to? The property of a freeborn American less sacred than that of a Frenchman? Perish the thought! This was the line of argument of the statesman from "Egypt" with the *lucus a non lucendo* name, Mr. John Grammar, who said in the Illinois legislature, on a proposition to emancipate indented slaves : "I will show that are proposition is unconstitutionable, inlegal, and fornenst the compact. Don't every one know, or leastwise had ought to know, that the Congress that sot at Post Vinsan garnisheed to the old French inhabitants the right to hold their niggers, and haint I got as much rights as any Frenchman in this state? Answer me that, sir." [1]

It must be confessed, too, that no very strict regard was paid to the rights of indented negroes. An illustrative instance is recorded by Sol Smith, the great theatrical pioneer of the Mississippi valley, who was even more famous and popular in his day than his namesake Sol Smith Russell is now. In 1819 he served for a time as an apprentice at Vincennes, and in describing his experience there he thus refers to his master's wife : "This lady had been 'raised' in Kentucky, and having been in the habit of commanding slaves, and the laws of Indiana not permitting her to own any of those convenient

[1] Washburne's *Sketch of Edward Coles*, p. 71.

appendages to a household, she made use of her husband's apprentices in place of them. She had one negro — his name was Thompson — who had been brought from Kentucky under indentures. He was to be free at the age of twenty-one, and he was now at least thirty-five ! Mrs. —— made him believe he was but fourteen, and that he had yet seven years to serve. Thompson used to ask us boys in the office if we didn't think he was fifteen years of age. Of course we could not encourage him in such abolitional ideas. So he served on in blessed ignorance, and whether he has yet arrived at the desired age of twenty-one I am not informed." [1]   There may be some slight exaggeration in this, for Sol Smith was not a man to let a story be spoiled for lack of a little color ; but in its general tenor it would have applied to many cases in Indiana. The negroes were ignorant, and there were few persons who were willing to incur the enmity of their neighbors by interfering in their behalf. Hence there arose, as G. W. Johnston had reported in 1808, "the most flagitious abuse " of the indenture system.

It should be borne in mind that there was nothing secret or clandestine about slaveholding in the western counties. It was the common opinion that the Constitution had no effect on preëxistent slavery. Indented negroes and other slaves were advertised and sold publicly,[2] and it is hardly necessary to say that this would not have occurred, for lack of purchasers, if there had been any serious question as to the titles to them. The custom continued with so little interruption that in the census of 1820 there were still reported one hundred

---

[1] *Theatrical Management in the West and South*, etc., p. 20.

[2] *Western Sun*, October 12, 1816 ; February 8, 1817 ; September 6, 1817 ; June 27, 1819 ; October 16, 1819.

and ninety slaves in Indiana, — only forty-seven less than there were in 1810. One hundred and eighteen of these were held in Knox County, thirty in Gibson, eleven in Posey, ten in Vanderburgh, and the remainder scattered in Owen, Perry, Pike, Scott, Sullivan, Spencer, and Warrick. In the other twenty-four counties no slaves were reported.

But now there was gathered at Vincennes a little group of men who did not adhere to the Knox County idea, and were not influenced by local bias. The most active of these was John W. Osborn, a son of Captain Samuel Osborn of the British navy, born in 1794. He was a native of New Brunswick, but came to the United States and joined the American army in the war of 1812, because he was convinced of the justice of the American cause. He came to Vincennes in 1819, edited the "Western Sun" for about a year, and remained there for some time afterward, settling up his business. In later years he was widely known as one of the most influential men in every work of progress in Indiana. He established the first newspaper at Terre Haute in 1823, and edited it until 1829, when he began farming on account of bad health. In 1834, he left the farm, went to Greencastle, and founded "The Ploughboy," one of the most popular newspapers of its day. He sent out with it, gratis, an eight-page sheet in pamphlet form called "The Temperance Advocate," which was the first temperance paper published in the West. He was the prime mover in the establishment of Asbury (now De Pauw) University, and was one of its first trustees. In 1838 he began publishing the "Indiana Farmer" at Indianapolis. At the breaking out of the civil war he went to Sullivan, and established "The Stars and

Stripes," an aggressive war paper. He died in 1866, after a long life of usefulness, devoted chiefly to temperance, education, and opposition to slavery. Among his associates was Amory Kinney, afterwards a distinguished lawyer, who then resided at Washington but practiced at Vincennes. He was born in Vermont in 1791. He studied law in western New York with Samuel Nelson, afterwards a judge of the Supreme Court of the United States, and was admitted to practice at Vincennes in 1819. Another *confrère* was Moses Tabbs, a Marylander, and a son-in-law of that distinguished signer of the Declaration of Independence, Charles Carroll of Carrollton. He came to Vincennes, and was admitted to the bar in 1818. A fourth member of the group was Colonel George McDonald, the preceptor and father-in-law of Judge Blackford. He was a New Jersey lawyer, well advanced in years, who had entered the practice at Vincennes in December, 1819. These gentlemen were desirous of testing the constitutionality of slavery in Indiana, and they soon found an opportunity.

At this time the principal inn of Vincennes was kept by Colonel Hyacinthe Lasselle. It was a famous old tavern, situated on the corner of Second and Perry streets, a large two-story frame building with great porches extending along the street sides. It was here that Governor Posey lived while at Vincennes, and here that all the great banquets of early times were held. Lasselle was a member of a family which is inseparably connected with the history of the Wabash from a very early day. He was born at Kekionga in 1777. His father, Colonel James Lasselle, was a trader and Indian agent there until the attack of La Balme in 1780–1781. In the confusion of the fight he and his family fled from the trading-house, which stood on the bank of the St. Joseph's, and made their way across the point to the Maumee, where they found a canoe, and all safely escaped down the river, except Marie Anne, a child of seven years, who fell overboard and was drowned. They went first to Detroit, thence to Montreal, and thence to Pointe Claire, where they remained under rather adverse circumstances, Colonel Lasselle having become so dissipated that the care of the family fell on his wife. She, however, was a woman of character and energy,[1] and succeeded in giving her children creditable training. Thrown on his own resources at an early age, Hyacinthe went in 1793 to Detroit, where his older brothers, Francis and James, were engaged in trade. He remained with them until Fort Wayne was built, when he went into business for himself at that point. In 1797 he moved over to the Wabash, and for seven years traded among the Indians there, at Godfroy's village, near the Missisinewa, at the mixed village of Chepaille,[2] and at the Piankeshaw village at the mouth of the Little Vermillion. In 1804 he arrived at Vincennes, and a year later was married there to Julie Frances Busseron, a daughter of the Major Francis Busseron who rendered good service to Clark in the great campaign that gave the Northwest to the United States.

In the course of his wanderings Lasselle had gathered quite a number of slaves, the greater part of whom had been captured by the Indians from the Americans and purchased by the French traders. Several of them came to him from his uncle Antoine Lasselle, the French trader who was captured just after Wayne's battle at

---

[1] Her maiden name was Therese Berthelet.

[2] Often written Chepoy. It stood on the site of Williamsport.

the Maumee and tried as a spy.[1] Among these was a
bright mulatto girl, the daughter of a negress that had
been taken by the Indians in 1779, who was named
Polly. She was neat, polite, and intelligent, and having
been reared as a house-servant was regarded rather as a
member of the family than as a slave. By the traditional account, this was the indirect cause of her being
selected for the test case. It is said Lasselle told all
his slaves that they might consider themselves free, after
the adoption of the Constitution, and that all except
Polly availed themselves of the opportunity, though most
of them tired of eking out a precarious existence by
doing odd jobs in the neighborhood, and came back to
the flesh-pots and comfortable quarters of the hotel.
They certainly clung to him long after the slavery question was finally determined, for in 1833, when he removed to Logansport, three families of them followed
him there. It is also said that the proceedings to determine Polly's status were brought with Lasselle's consent,

---

[1] I have never seen the true cause of his acquittal in print.
His prospects were not flattering until, during the trial, he gave
the Masonic signal of distress. Major Hamtramck, the presiding
judge, who was a member of the fraternity, then threw his influence in Lasselle's favor, and he was acquitted on the ground
that he was taken under arms. The acquittal was just, though
the ground on which it was based verged on the ridiculous. Lasselle had no thought of acting as a spy. He had gone into the
action with the Indians in Indian dress. He was too corpulent to
keep up with his dusky comrades when they scampered through
the fallen timber before Wayne's bayonets, and therefore crawled
under a log to wait until night gave him a chance to escape. Un-
luckily for him, the American camp was pitched close to his
hiding-place and he was discovered by some soldiers who were
carrying water. His being "under arms" consisted in the fact
that he had kept his rifle with him.

and that all the expenses of the defense were borne by several slaveholders who did not wish to have a precedent established by default. It is a singular fact that there is no mention of the case whatever in the Vincennes paper, either during its pendency or after the decision of the Supreme Court; and this shows that there was no warmth of feeling on the subject, and goes to confirm the tradition that the case was the result of a quiet, friendly agreement.

At any rate, *habeas corpus* proceedings were instituted by the gentlemen mentioned, the three attorneys, Kinney, Tabbs, and McDonald, giving their services without charge. McDonald died before the case was decided by the Supreme Court. Jacob Call, a Kentuckian, who was for some time judge of the Knox Circuit Court, and once a representative in Congress, was employed for the defense. Lasselle answered that Polly was his slave by purchase, the issue of a woman bought of the Indians prior to the treaty of Greenville. The lower court decided that she was his slave. An appeal was taken to the Supreme Court, and the question was presented there with an elaborate discussion of the law and history relating to it. On one side it was contended that slavery was excluded from the Territory by the Ordinance, and from the State by the Constitution. On the other it was maintained that the Ordinance not only did not prohibit the slavery that existed at the time of its adoption, but that also it expressly preserved it, and that the slave property guaranteed by it could not be divested by the Constitution. The court (Judges James Scott, Jesse L. Holman, and Isaac Blackford) took a middle ground. They held that the Virginia deed of cession and the Ordinance were immaterial; that the question must be

decided by the provisions of the Constitution. Said
they : "That legislative authority, uncontrolled by any
constitutional provision, could emancipate slaves, wil!
hardly be denied. This has been done in several of the
states, and no doubt has been entertained either of the
power of the legislature to enact such a statute, or of
the binding force and efficacy of the law when enacted.
By the power of a statute, an estate may be made to
cease in the same manner as if the party possessing it
were dead. A man may, by statute, be made an heir,
who could not otherwise be one. . . . It must be admitted that a convention, chosen for the express purpose,
and vested with full power to form a Constitution, which
is to define, limit, and control the powers of the legislature, as well as the other branches of the government,
must possess powers at least equal, if not paramount, to
those of any ordinary legislative body. From these positions it clearly follows that it was within the legitimate
powers of the convention, in forming our Constitution,
to prohibit the existence of slavery in the State of Indiana." They then review the provisions of the Constitution above set forth, and add : "It is evident that, by
these provisions, the framers of our Constitution intended
a total and entire prohibition of slavery in this state ;
and we can conceive of no form of words in which that
intention could have been more clearly expressed." [1]

It was accordingly held that Polly was free.

The decision was not satisfactory to the persons interested in the defense. They determined to appeal the
case to the Supreme Court of the United States, and the
papers for the appeal were prepared. They lie before
me now. The bond bears the prim sign-manual of Las-

---

[1] State *v.* Lasselle, 1 Blackf. 60.

selle, the wild scrawl of Francis Vigo, the schoolboy
flourish of Robert Buntin, and the bold signature of
Christian Graeter. The blanks are prepared for signature by Judge Scott, but the papers were not presented
to him. It is said that Lasselle, after considering the
matter, refused to let the case go farther. At any rate
he took possession of the incomplete appeal papers and
filed them with his private papers, where they were found
after his death. In accordance with the wishes of Polly,
he furnished her with clothing and money and sent her
to St. Louis, where she had relatives. There was no ill-
feeling between them. Polly prospered in her new
home, and afterwards returned to visit her old master's
family.

This decision of course brought the slavery question
to an absolute end, so far as any basis of legal right was
concerned. There was no longer any excuse whatever
for holding a negro in involuntary servitude in Indiana
except pure ignorance. It is a fact, however, that negroes were actually held as slaves for many years afterwards. A local census of Vincennes, taken by order of
the Board of Trustees in 1830, shows thirty-two slaves
then held at that point, twelve males and twenty females,
four more than there were in all Indiana in 1800![1] The
national census of the same year makes no mention of
these, but lists three slaves in Indiana, a girl in Orange
County, a girl in Decatur, and a woman in Warrick.
The national census of 1840 also credits Indiana with
three slaves, a girl in Putnam County, and a man and a
girl in Rush. This is the last record of this extraordinary continuance of actual slavery in a state where slavery
could not exist. These cases were simply violations of

[1] Cauthorn's *Vincennes*, p. 23.

a plain law, and, aside from being reflections on the characters of the communities that tolerated them, are of no historical importance.

And now we have come to our journey's end. We have traced the slavery of Indiana through its origin, its development, and its extermination. If the writer has done his work properly, the reader now realizes that the slavery of Indiana, small as was its actual extent, was the chief agency in the moulding of our infant growth. It made political parties that otherwise would never have existed. It put men in office who but for it might have lived in obscurity. It excluded men from office who but for it would have been on our lists of public men. It put laws on our statute books, and erased them. It put articles in our first Constitution. It was the tap-root of our political growth, — the great central matter of controversy to which all other questions were subordinate. It drew broad party lines here when national party lines were practically blotted out ; and when those lines were drawn, leaders of the dominant party were excused for offenses that would otherwise have ended their political careers, while leaders of the opposition suffered for the merest trifles. In short, it made a quarter of a century of our political history, and, at the end of that time, left the people of Indiana more strongly opposed to the institution of slavery than they ever could have been without it. It had some effect, too, in the councils of the nation, long after it had been disposed of ; for when in the debate on the California bill, in June, 1850, the question arose as to slavery in the territory acquired from Mexico, the refusals of Congress to admit slavery to Indiana served as precedents against it.[1]

[1] *Cong. Globe*, 1st *Sess*. 31st *Cong.*, *App.*, pt. i. p. 681.

More than this, if our work is well done, justice has been given to an almost forgotten generation of Indiana men. It has at various times been loosely stated that this man from the North, or that man from the South, saved Indiana from slavery. Not so. The men of Indiana did that. We honor Randolph, and Grayson, and Jefferson for their sentiments, as we do also Coit, and Dane, and King, but these men did not exclude slavery from Indiana, and, if we may believe the testimony that has been cited, they did not intend to do so. That we owe a debt of gratitude to the Congress that made the Ordinance, and to those that persisted in maintaining it as it was framed, is evident; but our gratitude cannot flow to either side of the line between North and South. If we consider the benefits derived from the Ordinance, we see benefactors from Virginia and Massachusetts standing side by side. If we look to the congressional action on petitions, we see that every Congress, regardless of politics, declined to amend the Ordinance. If we look to the composition of the congressional committees that acted on the petitions, we find them divided as evenly as possible between the North and the South, usually with an Indiana man in the balance; and of their six reports, three favoring the admission of slavery and three opposing it, we find two favoring and one opposing by chairmen from the North, and one favoring and two opposing by chairmen from the South; in no instance do we find a minority report. If we look to the sentiment of the nation at the climax of the struggle in Indiana in 1807, we find Congress almost a unit for the abolition of the slave-trade, and yet we find no effort in Congress, from any section, to nullify the indenture law, as the anti-slavery men of Indiana had asked them.

If we look to the influence of literature, we find nothing from the North that had more effect in Indiana than Jefferson's "Notes on Virginia." At this day, when it seems fashionable to belittle Mr. Jefferson at all opportunities, we commend to the people of Indiana the consideration of how much of the great anti-slavery report of General W. Johnston, and the revolution of sentiment connected with it, may be justly attributed to the influence of the words of Thomas Jefferson. Nor is this suggestion thrown out for the purpose of bringing him into prominence to the disadvantage of his contemporaries from the North. It is merely to restore, for our own purposes, the historical balance which the reaction of recent years has falsified. Nothing can now detract from the influence he had in determining our early controversies, and nothing should obscure his just credit in our remembrance of it. We do not go beyond the bounds of our State to give praise for the final solution of our local slavery question, for Congress put the solution upon the men of Indiana and they worked it out on Indiana soil. For the privilege of solving it, under the Ordinance, without the interference of Congress, our thanks go abroad, but to no section. As to this we write, as was inscribed on our contribution to the great monument to the greatest of Americans: INDIANA KNOWS NO NORTH, NO SOUTH, NOTHING BUT THE UNION.

INDEX.

ghan's description of, 115 ; abandonment of, 116, note ; slavery at, 126 ; under Virginia, 151 ; Indian council at, 162.

Post Vincennes, *see* Vincennes.

Pourré, Capt. Eugenio, expedition of, 160.

QUAKER settlers, support Jennings for Congress, 381, 392, 395, 398 ; object to militia laws, 408, 409 ; ask for constitutional provision against slavery, 426.

RACINE, Jean Baptiste, *see* Ste. Marie.

Randolph, John, opposes introduction of slavery to Indiana, 308 ; sentiments as to slave-trade, 353 ; prediction of, as to slavery, 374.

Randolph, Thomas, sketch of, 361, 362 ; candidate for representative, 386 ; candidate for Congressman, 388 ; campaign of, 391, 395-397 ; defeated, 398 ; challenges McNamee, 399 ; contests Jennings's seat, 401-403 ; second campaign against Jennings, 406-410 ; death of, 410.

Renault, Philip Francis, brings negroes to Illinois, 258.

SAM (a slave), case of, 250, 251.

Sargent, Winthrop, secretary of Northwest Territory, statement of, as to French land titles, 95, 96, 98 ; general dislike of, 277.

St. Ange, Jean, commands at Fort Chartres, 53, note ; petitions for appointment for his son, 60.

St. Ange, Louis, appointed commandant of Vincennes, 60 ; character of, 62 ; prepares to fight Indians, 66 ; leaves Vincennes, 72 ; at Fort Chartres, 73 ; meets Pontiac, 74 ; surrenders Fort Chartres, 76 ; testifies to land titles at Vincennes, 79 ; at St. Louis, 82 ; will of, 83 ; death of, 84 ; grants land to Piankeshaws, 98 ; deeds from, 101.

St. Ange, Pierre Grosson, at Vincennes, 55 ; death of, 60.

St. Clair, Gen. Arthur, connection of, with Ohio Company's purchase, 217, 218 ; declarations of, as to meaning of slavery proviso, 245-248, 291 ; sympathy of, for French settlers, 268, 269 ; visits Illinois country, 271, 272 ; political movements of, 275-281 ; statement of, as to proslavery feeling in Northwest Territory, 292.

St. Clair, William, petitions for slavery, 287.

St. Jerome, French name of Wabash River, 16.

Ste. Marie, concessions of land by, 78-80 ; commands at Vincennes, 82.

Scott, Judge James, in constitutional convention, 424 ; vote of, as to slavery, 427 ; on Committee on General Provisions, 427 ; on supreme bench, 439.

Shawnees (Showonees, Chaouanons), early location of, in Ohio valley, 22 ; join La Salle, 27-31 ; location in La Salle's confederacy, 32 ; migrations of, 63 ; driven to hostility, 132 ; oppose advance of Americans, 196.

Slavery, origin of, among Indians, 25 ; on the Wabash, 126 ; regulation of, 127 ; condition of slaves, 128, 129 ; phases of, in American politics, 190 ; proposals to exclude, in Northwest, 191-193, 197 ; influence of, on passage of Ordinance of 1787, 212-215 ; meaning of Ordinance as to, 219-252 ; origin and nature of, in Indiana, 253-258 ; extent of, in Indiana, 259, 260 ; efforts to introduce, in Northwest Territory, 284-289 ; feeling as to, in Northwest Territory, 290-293 ; number of slaves in Indiana in 1800, 296 ; petition of 1801 for, 297, 298 ; Vincennes convention to secure admission of, 302, 308 ; General Harrison's views of, 309-314 ; Indiana laws of 1803 as to, 315, 316 ; laws of 1805 as to, 329-336 ; amendments of 1806, 348, 349 ; national sentiment as to, in 1806, 1807, 351-354 ; petitions of 1808 for and against, 368-370 ; report against, 370-374 ; effect of same, 375, 376 ; change of sentiment in Indiana, 385, 387, 388 ; Jennings opposes, 389-398 ; indenture law repealed, 405 ; growth of, in Indiana, under indenture system, 406 ; question kept in territorial campaigns, 410, 411, 418, 419 ; in electing constitutional convention, 421-423 ; prohibited in Constitution, 426-430 ; dies out in eastern counties, 431 ; continued in western counties, 432, 433 ; treatment of slaves, 434 ; extent of, in Indiana in 1820, 435 ; test case, 437-440 ; slavery ends, 441 ; summary of question, 442-444.

Slavery proviso (in Ordinance of 1787), origin of, 191-193, 197 ; introduced in Ordinance, 204, 206 ; political causes for adoption of, 211-215 ; question as to meaning of, 219-222 ; decisions of the courts as to mean-

www.ingramcontent.com/pod-product-compliance
Lightning Source LLC
Chambersburg PA
CBHW031822270326
41932CB00008B/514